MICHAEL FRY is a historian and writer
who lives and has worked in Edinburgh since 1970.
Since 1988 he has published seven books on Scottish history,
each of which has overthrown some cherished myth.

MICHAEL FRY

EDINBURGH

A History of the City

PAN BOOKS

First published 2009 by Macmillan

This edition published 2010 by Pan Books
an imprint of Pan Macmillan, a division of Macmillan Publishers Limited
Pan Macmillan, 20 New Wharf Road, London N1 9RR
Basingstoke and Oxford
Associated companies throughout the world
www.panmacmillan.com

ISBN 978-0-330-45579-4

1 3 5 7 9 8 6 4 2

A CIP catalogue record for this book is available from
the British Library.

Typeset by SetSystems Ltd, Saffron Walden, Essex
Printed in the UK by CPI Mackays, Chatham ME5 8TD

CONTENTS

Introduction vii

Linguistic Note x

ONE: 'CITY OF FIRE ON NIGHT' *1*

TWO: 'PRECIPITOUS CITY' *53*

THREE: 'PERILOUS CITY' *107*

FOUR: 'CITY OF PALACES, OR OF TOMBS' *162*

FIVE: 'CITY OF EVERYWHERE' *216*

SIX: 'CITY OF REFUGE' *271*

SEVEN: 'A VERY OLD-FASHIONED CITY' *325*

ENVOI *382*

NOTES 389

INDEX 407

Picture Acknowledgements

Capital Collections: 4,6, 7, 9, 10, 11, 15,18, 20, 35

Courtauld Gallery: 32

Edinburgh Library: 12

Getty: 36 (AFP/Getty) 19 (Tim Graham)

National Galleries of Scotland: 1, 5, 13, 14, 22, 23, 26, 29, 30, 31

National Library of Scotland: 21, 27

National Portrait Gallery: 16, 17, 28

City of Edinburgh National Museums of Scotland: 2, 3

Royal Commission on the Ancient Historical Monument of Scotland: 33

Royal Scottish Geographical Society: 24

Scotland's Images: 8, 25 (National Trust for Scotland)

Scottishviewpoint.com: 34

Introduction

One of the excellences of Edinburgh is the number and richness of its archives. Research for this book has been carried out at the National Library of Scotland, the Edinburgh City Archive, the Edinburgh Room of the Central Library, Edinburgh University Library and the library of New College. I wish to thank the staffs of all of these for the unstinting courtesy and efficiency of their service. Sometimes, in the depths of the northern winter, the chill within their hallowed halls seemed to exceed the chill without of 'the foulest climate under heaven' (Robert Louis Stevenson). But the warmth of the welcome more than compensated.

I am especially grateful to a number of individuals who helped me to find my way through public collections and otherwise offered information, rare books or sundry other aids to research. At the National Museum of Scotland I received invaluable advice and assistance from David Forsyth and Andrew Heald. John Cairns, professor of legal history at the University of Edinburgh, supplied me with offprints of learned articles and supplementary comment. Willis Pickard kept me right on education in Edinburgh. Although I could have asked Robin Angus about many matters, his help with religious history proved the most useful. Stuart Kelly furnished me with several literary references. Brian Monteith was my consultant on popular culture. Henry Cowper and the late Angus Calder gave me their reminiscences, the latter also his illuminating thoughts on the relationship between Mary Queen of Scots and John Knox. Ross Leckie construed some Latin that was foxing me. Two patriotic sons of Midlothian, Peter Smaill and Andrew Wauchope of Niddrie, briefed me on the rustic hinterland of Edinburgh and were perhaps a little disappointed that I still wanted to write about the city itself. In the county, Mrs Althea Dundas-Bekker of Arniston kindly answered an enquiry and let me read a manuscript that will bear fruit not in the present work, as I had hoped, but elsewhere.

The student of Edinburgh is fortunate that so many primary sources for its past and present have found their way into print. The earliest serious study of the Scottish capital was published in 1779, and is still of value. Before long, Sir Walter Scott raised this history into a scholarly and popular obsession. He was born in the city, dwelt in the city, loved the city and made it come to life in everything he wrote about it. Yet even he, despite stupendous energy and diligent interrogation of the literary remains, could not exhaust all there was to say. In the same meticulous spirit others sought to complete his telling of a great story. It went about as far as it could in the three weighty volumes of James Grant's *Old and New Edinburgh* (1880), published by the house of John Cassell. This set out street by street, sometimes house by house, every picturesque detail, together with much more, that had ever been recorded. The modern historian seldom has reason to retrace the ground Grant covered.

The essentially antiquarian approach to Edinburgh's past was far from exhausted, all the same. The rebuilding of the ancient core of the city proceeded in the nineteenth century, in contrast to the twentieth century, in a spirit of respect for its historic character; few visitors today will be aware that most of the urban fabric is Victorian. But some living at the time viewed the losses with dismay. One result was the foundation of the Old Edinburgh Club in 1908, which brought out an annual *Book of the Old Edinburgh Club*, putting into print the papers read to it. This soon became a valuable supplement to and extension of the older labours. Like much else in the city, it had trouble keeping going through the mid-twentieth century, and in fact ceased publication for a number of years. Thanks to the efforts of Dr Iain Brown it has now revived. The old and the new series continue to be valuable sources for the history of Edinburgh.

A different sort of historiography became possible from 1869 with publication of the first volume of *Extracts from the Records of the Burgh of Edinburgh*, one of many public-spirited undertakings patronized by the greatest lord provost of the nineteenth century, William Chambers. The editor was James Marwick, the town clerk, who completed three more volumes by 1882. The project lapsed until taken up again in 1926 by Marguerite Wood and then by Helen Armet, whose devotion produced a further nine volumes, taking the series down to 1718, the last of these published in 1967. The editorial work was exemplary, faithful in all textual particulars to the manuscript originals and with marginal notes to guide the modern enquirer through a daunting mass of detail. Nothing more has so far followed, and it is perhaps high time for the town council to consider continuing the series down to, say, the municipal reform of 1833.

In a different category, one work on a scholarly par with the public records is the wonderful volume on Edinburgh in the series *The Buildings of Scotland* (1984 and subsequent editions) by John Gifford, the late Colin McWilliam and David Walker. I have used it as a primary source, indeed as a Bible. I have seldom found in it anything with which I might venture to disagree – the only notable exception being my view of what the High Street looked like, or could have come to look like, in the seventeenth century.

Given the amplitude of the available materials, it is surprising that since those pioneering works of the nineteenth century no history of Edinburgh from beginning to end, from the eruption of the volcano to the recall of the Scottish Parliament, has been attempted. In recent times some excellent books have appeared on portions of that history – on the Reformation, on the Civil Wars, above all on the Enlightenment. But there has been no general work on Edinburgh matching those on other cities from the hands of, say, Jan Morris or Alistair Horne, Peter Ackroyd or A. N. Wilson. They and others have transformed urban history into something much more than a dry academic specialism. Edinburgh, the first of modern cities, rebuilt in the eighteenth century as a machine for rational living, deserves no less.

I have made that era the focal point of what I have to say, starting each chapter with an enlightened episode. This is the coign of vantage from which the reader can then view the city in the light of history and take the measure of its future development. It does not turn out quite as one might expect.

Edinburgh,
September 2008

Linguistic Note

Over the thirty centuries of its history, Edinburgh has used several languages. Only in the last two centuries has Standard English become the most important, and even then in writing rather than in speech.

When the term Scots is employed in the text below, it should be taken to mean, in particular, the spoken vernacular of Edinburgh and the written expression of it. This is similar to, but in pronunciation and vocabulary not identical with, the dialects spoken immediately to the north, west and south. If Scotland had remained an independent country the Scots of Edinburgh would doubtless have become her standard language, but that was not to be. The speaker of Standard English will find its relationship to the Scots of Edinburgh varies: sometimes they are close and mutually comprehensible, sometimes less so, or hardly at all.

Quotations in Scots I have left alone if it seems to me that a speaker of Standard English will readily understand them. If there is just a word or two that might not be understood, I have given an equivalent in square brackets. But in all cases where it appears to me that understanding might be seriously disturbed for any reader not familiar with Scots, I have provided a full translation. The same is, of course, true for those languages used at one time or another in Edinburgh which now have to count as alien to the city: Brythonic or Old Welsh, Old Northumbrian, Gaelic, Latin and French.

CHAPTER ONE

'CITY OF FIRE ON NIGHT'

(Alexander Smith)

ON CLEMENT DAYS during the summers of the 1770s, two men and a dog might have been seen climbing the slope in front of Salisbury Crags, which overlook Edinburgh from the east. They would scramble up to a level where the hard basaltic bedrock stood exposed. For the people of the city to take walks over the surrounding hills was, of course, nothing unusual – in these peaceful and civilized times, as a love of nature grew modish, it had become a regular pastime for anyone with enough leisure or energy. But the two solid citizens, recognizable as such by their rather formal frock-coats, their three cornered hats and the big silver buckles on their shoes, were bent on more serious business. Unusually for gentlemen, this involved a degree of manual labour. They would hammer with a mallet at the rock and carry specimens away with them.

We know about this from the pictorial record left by one of the pair, John Clerk of Eldin, a scion of the local landed gentry. At Penicuik, the Clerks' estate six miles south of Edinburgh, the family made money from coal-mines, which had triggered his own interest in all that lay underground. But their pursuits were as much intellectual and political as economic. Their family tree contained an architect of the Treaty of Union between Scotland and England in 1707, while a much younger generation would bring forth James Clerk Maxwell, the greatest physicist of the Victorian era. Their versatile genes also carried artistic talent, in connoisseurship and in modest abilities of their own. Clerk's geological drawings, together with more lightsome sketches of him and his companion on their outings, show just where they went and what they discovered.

The companion was James Hutton, a wealthy industrial chemist, better known to us today as the 'father of geology'. Born in Edinburgh in 1726, he died there in 1797 and rests in the graveyard of Greyfriars. He went to the city's High School, then at the age of fourteen to its university. While his family were merchants, with some land in Berwickshire, they set him first to learn the law. But as he spent his entire time on chemical experiments, he was allowed to switch to medicine. He completed his education at Paris and Leiden, like many well-to-do young Scotsmen in those days. Once home again, he set up a factory to manufacture sal ammoniac, or smelling salts, for which he also devised a commercial application as a flux in the refinement of metals. All the sal ammoniac then used in Britain was imported from Egypt. Hutton synthesized it by a process he invented, using soot for his raw material. There was no shortage of that in Auld Reekie, blackened by the smoke of Midlothian's coal; he would buy it from the bemused tronmen, the local chimney-sweeps. He made a lot of money. While yet middle-aged, he found the independence to do as he really wanted and follow his fascination with geology.

Still, Hutton and Clerk never quite found what they were looking for on Salisbury Crags. They did establish the hill had a structure hardly to be guessed from its outward appearance: the superficial stratum of igneous rock, formed from volcanic lava, rested on sediment. The finding ran counter to conventional geological wisdom, which assumed rock must lie below and sediment above. That was how the Flood would have left the Earth's surface, according to the account in Genesis. Could Salisbury Crags defy both common sense and the divine plan for the universe?

In fact the crags had aeons ago been shaped by the intrusion of molten rock between two existing masses, of which the upper mass in time eroded away. This turned out to be just one of many geological processes Hutton was able to define during his decades of patient investigation, observation and reflection. It also became clear to him how the ensemble of these processes could not possibly have been completed within the 6,000 years since God was supposed to have created the Earth by the accepted reckoning. Whatever the planet's exact age might be, it had to amount to much more than that. We ought to think in terms not of mere thousands but of millions or hundreds of millions of years; even then 'we find no vestige of a beginning – no prospect of an end'.[1]

Hutton's researches at length led him to evidence making the true history of the Earth clearer than Salisbury Crags could have done. Down the coast from Edinburgh, Siccar Point was a site where successive layers of rocks of the greatest antiquity rose in cliffs above the breakers of the North Sea. These were not just tidy layers, but vertical as well as horizontal, folded and creased and crushed. Hutton one day took some friends to land near the inaccessible headland, pitching in a small boat. A member of the party, John Playfair, later professor of mathematics at the University of Edinburgh, recalled the solemn silence which fell on them as Hutton's commentary instilled an awareness of what they were looking at:

> We felt ourselves necessarily carried back to the time when the schistus on which we stood was yet at the bottom of the sea, and when the sandstone before us was only beginning to be deposited, in the shape of sand or mud, from the waters of a superincumbent ocean. An epocha still more remote, when even the most ancient of these rocks, instead of standing upright in vertical beds, lay in horizontal planes at the bottom of the sea, and was not yet disturbed by the immeasurable force which had burst asunder the solid pavement of the globe. Revolution still more remote appeared in the distance of this extraordinary perspective. The mind seemed to grow giddy by looking so far into the abyss of time, and while we listened with earnestness and admiration to the philosopher who was now unfolding to us the order and series of these wonderful events, we became sensible how much farther reason may go than imagination can venture to follow.[2]

It was the start of the intellectual revolution by which the human race has come to a more realistic view of its obscure place in the cosmos – though even now, since we still do not know the answer to every question, the revolution is incomplete. Nor should we forget with what stubbornness older orthodoxies, however absurd they appear today, resisted the revolution, especially as their overthrow seemed so often to come at the hands of dour Scots too clever by half. A Victorian successor in the national school of geology, Hugh

Miller, recalled how 'the prejudices of the English mind' reacted 'with illiberal violence against the Huttonian doctrines. Infidelity and atheism were charged against their supporters, and had there been a Protestant Inquisition in England at that period of general political excitement, the geologists of the North would have been immured in its deepest dungeons.'[3]

※

If Hutton was the father of a new science, Edinburgh formed its cradle. Not many places on the planet enjoy such a visible and intimate relationship with their geology, where buildings seem sometimes to be grown out of the rock, rather than erected on top: Athens and Rome compare, but hardly another city of any size. Edinburgh stands amid a spectacular landscape fashioned by the powerful forces of the Earth. There are few better examples of how these can shape a vista and give it character. The seven hills of an eventful terrain have been formed by the action of fire and water, ice and wind on a surface that rose and fell, buckled and twisted. Today the city rests on a geological jigsaw of complex sedimentation, extinct volcanoes, flows of lava and igneous intrusions. The history is brought out by the differential weathering of hard and soft rocks. And it offers the setting for a superb built environment, where the hand of man completes the work of nature.

About 300 million years ago, before the movement of tectonic plates pushed this section of the Earth's crust so far north, the site of Edinburgh lay in the tropics. Warm, shallow seas and hot, humid forests left sediments that would at length turn into coal. Their transformation came under the pressure of fresh layers deposited on top, thrown out from eruptions along the geological faults. This matter forms the elevated ground in the centre of the city: the Castle Rock was a plug of basalt in the feeding pipe of an ancient volcano, which survives after erosion of the rest. Down the coast are yet finer examples, Bass Rock, projecting from the sea, and North Berwick Law, landmark of its town. In the hinterland, flows of lava and falls of ash built up the Pentland Hills and the Braid Hills. Igneous intrusion shaped Salisbury Crags and Corstorphine Hill. All these still stand high because the rock is harder than the sedimentary deposits surrounding them today at lower levels, laid down by water once the volcanic activity ceased. Rivers draining the mountains carried sand and mud into shallow lakes below. A look at almost any one of the sandstone buildings in Edinburgh will show this origin of the stone in traces of cross-bedding and ripples, or darker streaks of dead algae. My own house has them.

Indeed, the sandstones provided the main building material for Edinburgh until well into the twentieth century. Their names turned into bywords: Binny, Craigleith, Hailes, Ravelston. Some names came to imply particular qualities rather than the actual source, for even in a single quarry the sandstone can vary in composition, colour and durability. Uniform weathering has brought to the buildings constructed of different stones, and to the city as a whole, a pleasing harmony of aspect, silver-grey overall; but the harmony is deceptive. The stone's weathered outer layers may hide a range of colours inside, not often grey: Craigleith is pinkish, Hailes yellowish brown, Binny greyish orange and Ravelston dusky brown. The range results from several factors. Iron in the stone forms compounds with other elements, so even a tiny amount of it, less than one per cent, may produce shades of yellow, brown, red or even green. Any internal grey arises rather from vegetable matter in the original sand or mud: dead algae have given as much as airborne soot to the dark surfaces in the centuries since Edinburgh was built of stone.[4]

In one sort of Scottish mind, however, the desire for uniformity runs deep. Towards the end of the twentieth century pressure grew in certain quarters for the city's stone surfaces to be cleaned up, so as to get rid of all that gloomy silver-grey and reveal authentic colours underneath. These efforts in practice went further than removing soot or other superficial matter – the weathered stone was also chemically bleached. And this did not always show up the original colour, but brought to the surface iron oxide, which produced a shade never seen before, a strident orange. The champions of uniformity concluded they had not tried hard enough. They applied more chemicals, even resorted in effect to scraping the surfaces away, until the whole process became self-defeating. It has sometimes altered for the worse the internal structure and future durability of the stone without giving it a more pleasant appearance. Melville Crescent in the West End used to be a typical harmonious composition. Now it is almost garish, individual houses contrasting with one another and with the still prevalent silver-grey of Melville Street running through: a mess, in other words, expensive if well-intentioned, saved from disaster only by the dignity of the classical architecture.

※

Yet Edinburgh is a romantic as well as a classical city, made that way not just by its architecture but also by the rugged, diverse landscape where the buildings arise. This, after the long and fiery prehistory, took on its final form from the shorter, colder conditions of the Ice Ages. Starting two million years ago, enormous ice-sheets accumulated and moved out, west to east, from what are now the Highlands, down the long depression due to become the Firth of Forth. Within the city's present area, the ice shaped the crag-and-tail of the Castle Rock and Royal Mile, among similar geological structures. The crag consists of solid rock protecting a tail of glacial debris in its lee. Hollows also gouged out by the ice on either side, today the site of Princes Street Gardens and the Grassmarket, accentuate the resulting ridge. A glacial lake, the Nor' Loch, was left under the Castle Rock, while another covered the Meadows and a third the lower part of Corstorphine.

The last ice-sheet, 2,000 feet thick, may have reached its fullest extent about 15000 BC. Deglaciation then went on in irregular stages, with meanwhile some fresh advances of the ice. It did not vanish until 8000 BC. Scotland then would still have been hard to discern, with climate, fauna and flora all different from those of today and the whole shape of the country unrecognizable. Vast volumes of water were yet to be released from the more northerly ice-sheets in Scandinavia or Canada, so the surface of the world's oceans had some way to climb and the shorelines stretched far out from where they lie now. In fact the British Isles remained joined to the mainland of Europe across what has become the southern part of the North Sea. Once the huge weight of ice lifted some ground rose quite fast, such as the upper stretches of the Firth of Forth, only to be inundated again at the melting of the continental ice-sheets. Shorelines advanced and receded alternately, as can be seen from the raised beaches in many parts of Scotland: Leith Links rest on one a little above the present level of the firth and so, higher up, do Bruntsfield Links.

At least the climate warmed, and for good. The tundra left by the retreat of the ice was transformed through gentler conditions into steppe, later into scrub. The species of insects multiplied, then the species of plants. By about 4000 BC forests covered much of Scotland. In the mildest areas, as around Edinburgh, juniper gave way to birch and hazel, then to oak and elm.

Into the forests came animals. Scotland is rather poor in vertebrate species compared even with those parts of continental Europe on the same latitude. One reason lies in the isolation of the country since the eventual rise in the level of the sea – in general, islands support fewer species than continents. Impoverishment of the fauna comes about through local extinctions which are harder to redress. First the climatic changes were to blame and then, later on, man's deliberate alterations of the habitat together with his hunting and persecution of lesser species.

As the tundra in Scotland gave way to scrub and woodland, mammals dependent on tundra died out. Woolly mammoths had lived on it. They roamed what is now the valley of the Forth, and their tusks or teeth have been dredged up from the bottom of the firth. They had withstood warmer conditions during previous retreats of the glaciers but they did not withstand the end of the last Ice Age. Another Arctic species, the ringed seal, left its remains in deposits of clay around the shores of the firth. Once upon a time the lemming must have thrown itself from the cliffs, for its bones have been found on Corstorphine Hill. On the dry land the wild horse survived, if only as long as its open habitat. So did the reindeer, again until forests covered the country. A single denizen of the tundra managed to adapt to the novel conditions, the mountain hare, which is still there today after evolving in isolation into a distinct subspecies, *Lepus timidus scoticus*. In the hills it can be disturbed by walkers and surprise them in the spring with its still white coat as it races, always up the brae, to seek fresh shelter.

Before the land-bridge to Europe sank beneath the waves there was a limited time, about 1,000 years, for new species to colonize a more temperate, forested country. Yet a surprising number did so.

Some are still with us, such as the wildcat (just about), while others are extinct, the aurochs long ago and the polecat as recently as 1912. For evidence of certain later incomers we can rely on more than finds of their bones. The Gaelic language has words for the moose, *lon* or *miol*, so that beast must have been present when the Gaels arrived in Scotland during the Dark Ages. Pictish standing stones appear to depict the brown bear (though it is possible they represent imported dancing bears). In the Borders remains can still be seen of the dams, pools and lodges built by beavers; these charming animals are not recorded in Scotland after 1550. Slightly later the wild boar died out, and the last wolf was killed in 1743. All this came at the hand of man, by accident or design.

Man possesses no such dominion over the birds of the air. In any event it is harder to determine, or indeed define, if an avian species has become extinct on a particular territory. Even when a breeding population dies out or is eradicated, vagrants turn up and sometimes winter; as often in Edinburgh on Duddingston Loch, during modern times a paradise for bird-watchers. Within or around the city different species have certainly come and gone. The white stork nested on the tower of St Giles in 1416, a fact remarkable enough to have been recorded for posterity. The hand of man was again brutally at work on the flightless great auk, which used to breed on the Isle of May but was hunted to extinction there in 1840 (in this instance Scots need not blame themselves too much, for it had vanished from the whole planet by 1844). Yet the hand of man can also make species prosper. For centuries the fulmar was confined to St Kilda. Now it is common in the Firth of Forth and indeed on any coast with cliffs (which means most of Scotland), shaped like a torpedo, effortlessly gliding: an elegant bird, only disobliging when it spits a foul oily liquid at any other creature it sees as a threat. Its spectacular colonization of the coastal mainland followed the rise of the fisheries in the nineteenth century, producing waste for it to feed on.[5]

※

After animals and birds came human beings. By 5000 BC they were wandering the woods or scrub of the Lothians in search of game. A few weapons of flint they left behind at caches or camps are the only evidence of their passage. They presumably arrived from the south, perhaps first on seasonal forays which revealed the abundant wildlife of the Forth. It may have been the vast beds of shellfish, surviving until the nineteenth century, that offered enough staple food to encourage durable human occupation. Prehistoric middens of oyster-shells on the island of Inchkeith conceal traces of fires and hearths, but whether from seasonal visits or permanent sites is hard to say.

Human beings finally colonized the Lothians in about 3000 BC. They furthered natural changes going on in the landscape, notably the thinning of forests. No actual settlement has been found, just the implements with which these first farmers formed clear-ings or cut firewood for themselves and fodder for their animals. Most of the evidence comes from near the shorelines, where admix-tures of sand made the soil lighter to work. Bone or pottery in scatters of material from middens show the existence of settlements around Gullane and North Berwick in East Lothian.

Within the present boundaries of Edinburgh there is no such evidence; the arrival of a population has to be guessed from the distribution of its rude monuments. The biggest standing stone is the Caiystane at Fairmilehead, a rugged monolith decorated with cup-marks. A single prehistoric cairn survives nearby at Galachlaw, though several burial mounds have been destroyed in modern times. Further west, at Newbridge, lies an earthen barrow surrounded by standing stones, but not concentric in the ceremonial manner of a later era.

The Stone Age gave way to the Bronze Age as knowledge of metalworking spread through Europe from its pioneers in the Near East. This was a slow process, perhaps because the new technology's inventors remained possessive of it or perhaps because older societies resisted change. Certainly it did not reach Scotland before 2000 BC. Nor does the appearance of bronze always make the pattern of human settlement or its adaptation clearer, for bronze is a portable material. Still, axes found by the Water of Leith may point to the existence of a port or trading post between the Dean Village and Stockbridge; the first voyagers from afar could have arrived. Remains elsewhere show people living in small though permanent hamlets, just clusters of round timber houses and barns, probably undefended; there are no traces of ramparts or stonework to betray their presence, which is discovered only by accident.

Metalworking represented the first great technological break-through in human history. It made every task of farming or building easier, and opened a high road to faster development in many directions. Either new ways emerged spontaneously within the existing cultures, or else they arrived as more advanced invaders imposed their own. In either case, the archaeological evidence we have to rely on comes now in monuments implying social organization much greater than the family or small group.

A complex on Cairnpapple Hill in West Lothian, a dozen miles from Edinburgh, represented something new to the region: a permanent site of visible importance. In its earlier phase it was a ritual centre or meeting place and in its later phase the ground for monumental burials, commanding a broad vista. At about the time the building of Stonehenge started 400 miles to the south, a similar set of standing stones, if less impressive, arose at Cairnpapple.

A second period saw the site extended. Here too a henge was built, that is, an earthwork with ditch and outer bank, entered by causeways. Inside stood an oval setting of twenty-six standing stones and possibly a further, central setting now only to be traced by hollows in the ground. Beside one stone lay buried an early example of the type of bell-shaped pot known as Beaker ware, so designated by the founder of the chair of archaeology at the University of Edinburgh, James Abercromby. Beaker ware is found over much of western Europe, alongside other evidence of a common culture: metalworking, crouched burials and round barrows. The beakers were probably used for ritual consumption of mead or beer (Scotland's hard drinking started long ago). Vere Gordon Childe, inaugural holder of the Abercromby chair at Edinburgh, described the Beaker folk as 'warlike invaders imbued with domineering habits'. It is tempting to link all this with the Celts, but we have no proof.[6]

Larger structures spread across the Lothians during the first millennium BC. While some were still ceremonial or memorial, others served a military purpose as strongholds for powerful chiefs: it was a warlike, aristocratic society. Excavations at Kaimes Hill, near Dalmahoy, revealed how complex the history of such sites might be. At the centre lay the stone footings of a big hut-circle, 30 feet in diameter, which would have supported walls of timber and a roof of turf. Its inhabitants had first surrounded it with a single stone-faced rampart; behind the facing, the core consisted of just earth and rubble stabilized by a lacing of timber beams. When in time it collapsed for some reason, the defences were rebuilt with a new rubble wall, probably strengthened by the addition of two outer ramparts built to enclose a larger area. These had further protection in a line of pointed stones outside, set upright in the ground to hinder attacks. The purpose of the *chevaux de frise*, as they were later known, was to keep horsemen and possibly chariots at a distance from the defenders.

Not all places needed such ingenuity and labour to render them secure. The natural defensive advantages of the Castle Rock were already noticed and exploited; a settlement stood on top of the rock by about 900 BC. This makes it the longest continuously occupied site in Scotland, though so overlain by later settlements that little can be said about the first one except it was timber-built and metal-working was practised there.[7]

࣒

After the Bronze Age followed the Iron Age. Use of the harder metal came in for edged tools, implements and weapons. In Scotland this began in about 250 BC, a couple of centuries behind England and almost a millennium behind the Mediterranean region. Now, for the first time, we can put a name on the people living in the Lothians: the Votadini. They get a mention, among seventeen Scottish tribes, in the description of the known world by Ptolemy, the Greek 'father of geography' who lived at Alexandria in Egypt during the second century AD. This is a relatively late date, but the archaeological record offers little room for doubt that the same people occupied the Lothians for several hundred years beforehand and for some centuries afterwards. They belong otherwise to prehistory in the sense they left no written records of themselves, just enigmatic images on standing stones.

Yet what we know of the Votadini does tell some kind of story. They held sway in the Lothians from long before the Romans came until a little after the Romans left. For this period the historians of Scotland have tended to treat Rome's imperial stratagems and strongholds as the central topic, with the mere natives as marginal. The account here will take things the other way about.

Native power had shifted east from Cairnpapple. Some of it may have shifted to what is now Edinburgh, where forts surmounted several of the seven hills. Around Arthur's Seat lay a cluster of four, which suggests either that this was the area of densest occupation or else that settlement here proved not too successful, since none of the sites would be modified or rebuilt over any length of time. In effect the chieftains might have had to choose between Arthur's Seat, striking for height and mass, and the Castle Rock, craggy and impressive too, but lower in altitude and so more comfortable and convenient. The Castle Rock won the contest, with permanent results for the shape of the future city.

To judge from the excavated contents of its midden, rich in fragments of pottery and jewellery, the Castle Rock witnessed a good deal of conspicuous consumption. It is possible the finery came from craftsmen at Duddingston Loch, where the finds of quantities of bronze indicate a local centre of metalworking. This had now become not just a utilitarian but also an aesthetic activity: a sign of cultural advance. At other sites in the city archaeologists have dug up, beside the usual pots and tools, examples of artistry – and of a superlative kind, such as a bronze armlet from Wester Craiglockhart Hill or a scabbard from Mortonhall. The latter's decoration, brought out by being forged with two alloys of different colours, shows the high skills of Celtic smiths.[8]

A second place where native power had shifted lay twenty miles further east, at Traprain Law, on a hump the shape of a whaleback rising 300 feet from the Lothian plain beside the modern A1. It may not be lofty yet it is so conspicuous that, far in the future, local people would come to see in it the hub whence their culture had spread – and in fact, if for reasons they had not thought of, this is not far wrong. One of their myths can be easily disposed of. On the law is a standing stone, the Loth Stone, seven feet high, said to have marked the grave of King Loth, after whom the Lothians are supposed to be named. But excavation revealed no burial and the tradition of the king cannot be traced back before the sixteenth century.

In this case the reality is more interesting. Traprain, ten times the size of the site on the Castle Rock, formed in all probability the capital of the Votadini (assuming they had a single capital).

What has made it famous today is its buried treasure, discovered in 1919 and now on display in the National Museum of Scotland. To judge from four silver coins it contains, they were put in a pit on the law some time between 410 and 425. The rest of the treasure consists of fifty different objects, weighing 54 pounds in all, of no single or definable origin. Few remain entire; most had been cut into pieces and flattened. The largest number are silver pieces for service at table – jugs, goblets, bowls, dishes and spoons. Their motifs depict gods, goddesses and heroes: Pan, Venus and Hercules. But others exhibit Christian iconography, including a silver-gilt flask decorated with biblical scenes, Adam and Eve, the Adoration of the Magi, Moses striking the rock. For what reason did all this come to Traprain, and to be buried there? One theory is that it was loot stolen by the Votadini, another that it made up a votive offering to some Celtic god, a third that it had been sent by the Roman government of Britannia to pay for mercenary services. Possibly an attack on Traprain prompted its concealment – and the man who buried it never survived the conquest of the law by an unknown aggressor.

The treasure does not exhaust the riches of Traprain. Fresh excavations in 2004 revealed further facets of its long history down to the middle of the first millennium. Over that period it was endowed with ever more elaborate lines of defence while ever more dwellings crowded behind them. It became something greater than a fortress, in fact a densely peopled town. The hundreds of artefacts dug up show it carried on an ample trade with the Romans, ampler than any other place discovered in Scotland. It also boasted its own workshops, where craftsmen cast jewellery in bronze or carved bangles and beads out of oil-shale, a local resource. In exchange for the benefits of civilization it probably sent out the products of nature, for the Romans loved exotic merchandise with a whiff of the barbaric about it, coming from the fringes of the known world – shaggy skins, hunting dogs and so on. In short, Traprain supported the kind of complex community, with division of labour, which could only have been organized under political leadership. Yet somehow it all came to an end here in the middle of the first millennium.[9]

Altogether we can say Edinburgh sits amid both a complex geological and a rich archaeological landscape stretching from Cairnpapple to Traprain. Through seven centuries on the cusp of prehistory and history, fortresses on hills dominated this landscape – just as they dominated the contemporary landscapes of Andalusia or Tuscany under the sway of the Tartessians or the Etruscans. A difference is that in those kinder climes with more advanced civilizations we have a better (if by no means full) record of how a warlike caste of aristocrats lorded it over underlings. But we can argue by analogy, as the Scottish Enlightenment taught we might do, that contemporary life in the Lothians bore some resemblance to the life of these other peoples, even if nature's gifts here were more niggardly. In Andalusia, from the hot but fertile alluvial plain of the River Guadalquivir there arise ancient strongholds, Carmona or Antequera, which can still overawe travellers approaching from afar. So too, from among the vineyards of Tuscany, can some of the Twelve Cities of the Etruscans, going today under the names of Siena or Perugia. They may remind us of the Scotland of Cairnpapple and Traprain.

They were heroic societies. Their rulers' values defined them, in a martial code for noble warriors and valiant victors. These spent their time fighting, hunting or feasting, with more humdrum needs catered for by the toil of bondsmen in the villages at the gates or on the flatland beneath. The rude comforts of a few in the fortresses on hills could still never persuade the Romans their life was anything other than barbarous. Yet finer qualities did temper its primitive traits (which were in any case surely not so much more revolting than those in an imperial culture of amphitheatres and crucifixions).

While heroic societies had savage hearts, they found a saving grace in their arts. Later contempt or neglect has destroyed much, yet the Celtic artefacts we still possess leave no room for doubt that, in the fortresses on hills, aesthetic qualities counted for a great deal. Poetry formed the other ornament of the culture – oral poetry vanishing into the air with the bards' breath but so loved as to be remembered through generations. It lived on in the minds and mouths of those bards, the masters of a labyrinthine prosody but also, by extension, the keepers of ancient wisdom. A time at length came when it might be written down, if often much changed meanwhile by transmission through so many individuals.

A defining work by Maurice Bowra on *Heroic Poetry* (1952) shows how this art arose in many places at similar stages of human development. In Europe it ranges from the Homeric epics to the Norse sagas to the *Nibelungenlied* to the *Chanson de Roland* to *El Cid*. And heroic poetry may be common not just to Europeans but also to much of the rest of humanity. Bowra passes on to us from the ancient geographer Strabo a report that in Andalusia the Tartessian race sang songs about their ancestors' deeds; these can hardly have been anything else but heroic and may have recorded something of the history of what the Bible called Tarshish, which was also a promised land for Greek sailors. To the opposite end of the known world, several centuries later, the ferocious Huns swept in from the Asiatic steppes. The name of their leader, Attila, appears as Etzel in the *Nibelungenlied*, but he did not lack his own bards. When in 446 the Roman senator Priscus visited him on an embassy from the Byzantine Emperor, Attila summoned two of them to recite verses on his victories, while his hardy warriors listened in delight as they relived their old battles in the poetry. Bowra traces further epics among the Asian peoples, the Kalmuks, the Kara-Kirghiz, the Kazakhs, the Ossetes, the Uzbeks and the Yazuts.[10]

The Celts partook of this heroic culture. In their case, too, its literary monuments survive. In the British Isles the Celtic languages divided into two branches: the Brythonic spoken in Great Britain and the Goidelic spoken in Ireland, later in Scotland as well. The two branches are also more helpfully known as P-Celtic and Q-Celtic, after a sound-change distinguishing them. They took over the Greek and Latin term for Easter, *Pascha*, as a loan-word; in Irish and Scots Gaelic it became *Caisg*, so the sound-change must have happened after the Gaels' conversion to Christianity in the fifth century. The earliest Goidelic literature, the Ulster Cycle, takes us back to this late Iron Age. The cycle is in prose, but shares with Homer a gruesome realism: war is necessary, yet also terrible. The earliest Brythonic literature dates from the sixth century. Then two bards, Taliesin and Aneirin, sang in Britain. Neither lived in Wales, where the modern descendant of their tongue has become confined. Taliesin hailed from the kingdom of Rheged, with a capital at Carlisle. Aneirin was the bard of the Votadini.

In fact Aneirin's epic is named after his people, in the Brythonic rather than Latin form, *Gododdin*. It may be scarcely recognized, or recognizable, as the first work of literature from Scotland: that is what it is, all the same. The fact it survives only in a medieval Welsh version does not alter this. Before it was written down, it had over seven centuries been changed by bardic oral transmission. But traces of its remote origin reveal themselves in the extant text by the metre of certain sections and other clues. Kenneth Jackson, professor of Celtic at Edinburgh, described its highly inflected language in 1969 as 'very early Welsh', though 'so full of obscurities' that it could probably never be translated entire. Yet three versions in English appeared by 1997, the most complete and scholarly from the hand of John Koch. Hugh MacDiarmid, the national bard of the twentieth century, had already found in the poem an essential Scottishness: 'It is not the glory, but the pity and waste of war that inspires its highest passages.'[11]

The *Gododdin* is about the Battle of Catterick in 598. It marked the first stage in the gradual loss of the Lothians' Celtic character. The capital of the Votadini is Edinburgh by now, not Traprain. And Edinburgh here for the first time in history bears a name, or names, cognate with its modern one: Din Eidin or Eidyn (meaning the fort on the hill-slope), Eidin Vre (the hill-fort of Eidin), Cyntedd Eidin (Eidin's capital) or simply Eidin.

A further point about Edinburgh is made with a heroic epithet. Like 'cloud-capped Ilium' or 'Athens crowned with violets', it was 'Eidyn of the goldsmiths', a place where the Celtic craftsmen wrought under royal patronage – and so each of the warriors riding away for the battle wore a golden torque around his neck. King Mynyddog the Wealthy had beforehand feasted them for a whole year in his great hall on the Castle Rock. He did not in the event accompany their expedition for some reason, so the poem starts off in praise of a different chief, possibly Cynan of Traprain, destined not to come back. Another warrior mentioned, just once, is Arthur, who evidently has yet to embark on his career as the greatest defender of the

Britons against Germanic invasion; he may have been at Mynyddog's
feasts because he lived hard by at Arthur's Seat.[12]

The warriors, like future generations of young men in the Lothians, spent much of their time drinking and fighting:

> *Mynog Gododdin traethiannor;*
> *Mynog am ran cwyniador.*
> *Rhag Eidyn, arial fflam, nid argor.*
> *Ef dodes ei ddilys yng nghynnor;*
> *Ef dodes rhag trin tewddor.*
> *Yn arial ar ddywal disgynnwys.*
> *Can llewes, porthes mawrbwys.*
> *O osgordd Fynyddog ni ddiangwys*
> *Namyn un, arf amddiffryt, amddiffwys.*

> A lord of Gododdin will be praised in song:
> A lordly patron will be lamented.
> Before Eidyn, fierce flame, he will not return.
> He set his picked men in the vanguard:
> He set a stronghold at the front.
> In full force he attacked a fierce foe.
> Since he feasted, he bore great hardship.
> Of Mynyddog's war-band none escaped
> Save one, blade-brandishing, dreadful.[13]

The collective noun used by Aneirin for his heroes is *Brythonaid*,
Britons. These set off to attack a ruler of a different race, Aethelfrith
the Twister as they called him, King of Bernicia. Covering modern
Northumberland and County Durham, his was a kingdom of the
Angles, who had crossed the North Sea from what is now Schleswig-
Holstein in Germany; the *Gododdin* referred to them as (among other
things) English or Saxons. Their capital lay at Bamburgh, also a
fortress on a hill but one rising straight from the sea, visible from
miles away along the coast. It had been captured from the Votadini
only about fifty years before, probably by a band of pirates. Now
came the time for vengeance on the aliens.

The battle took place south of the River Tees at Catterick on the
old Roman road, Dere Street, down which the Celtic force no doubt
advanced. Though the Celts seem to have won the encounter, Aneirin
says the slaughter was so terrible that he alone survived – or almost

alone (the detail varies and may be hyperbole typical of the genre). He sits down to tell the tale and sing the deeds of the dead heroes. Most of the poem is a lament, or series of laments, for them. It offers the first example of this most enduring of Scottish literary and musical genres.

The *Gododdin*, composed for oral recitation, exhibits the typical literary devices of heroic verse the world over, which need not detain us further here. In psychological interest it is vastly inferior to Homer; but it yields some fascinating factual detail. The attackers appear to have been mainly armoured cavalry, skilled in throwing spears and fighting with the sword from horseback; Julius Caesar had seen just the same tactical skills among the tribes he encountered in the Gallic Wars. The Votadini were Christians (though their allies, the Scots and Picts, were not) while the Anglian foe was heathen. Once the Celts reached Catterick, the Christians among them did penance in preparation for the carnage to come. After, rather than before, the religious rites, presumably, the whole lot of them got drunk and in that condition launched their assault (as Scots regiments still did in the First World War). Bards urged them on, like the pipers of a later age.

৵

If this detail is reliable, how had the Votadini become Christians? There is no direct answer in the *Gododdin* or anywhere else. But a couple of possibilities suggest themselves. One is that contact with the Romans had, after the conversion of Constantine in 336, carried the empire's new official religion across its northernmost frontier. Romano-British Christianity is recorded even before this date. Early converts included the father and grandfather of St Patrick, who was born in about 372 at a place that could have been in Scotland, called Bannavem Taberniae. If this Christianity collapsed after the retreat of the legions, however, the country might have had to be re-evangelized.

That brings us to a second possibility. The earliest known preacher of the gospel in Scotland, at about the turn of the fifth century, was St Ninian. He sailed from France to Galloway and erected a stone structure with the help of masons he brought with him, since the natives could build only in wattle and daub; his white church, shining across the Bay of Wigtown, was called Candida Casa. The Venerable Bede's history mentions Ninian as a 'most reverend bishop and holy man of the British nation, who had been regularly instructed at Rome in the faith and mysteries of the truth'. Ninian also has a biography written 800 years later by Ailred, abbot of Rievaulx in Yorkshire. In it, early attainments in Rome win Ninian the favourable notice of a pope who sends him on a mission to convert the British pagans, in particular the Picts. Ailred tells us that, on Ninian's first foray from Candida Casa, they rushed to 'renounce Satan with all his pomps and works and to be joined to the body of the believers by faith, by confession and by the sacraments'. Ninian 'ordained priests, consecrated bishops, distributed ecclesiastical dignities and divided the whole land into parishes'.[14]

Actually there were no parishes in Scotland until much later. Other points cast doubt on Ailred's narrative. Ninian was not a novice but a bishop, and it would have been unusual for a bishop even in the Dark Ages to be sent to a permanent posting beyond the bounds of civilization, unless to a community of Christians already there. It sounds as if he and his masons knew in advance where they were going and what they were doing: perhaps following an established route for trade from France through the narrow seas off Great Britain to where a missionary base stood ready, sited among existing converts. To put the matter another way, neither the economic nor the religious legacy of Rome had been altogether lost in these parts.

In none of this has anything been said about the Votadini. Yet it is not impossible Ninian had established contact with them. He came for the sake of the Picts, and the nearest Picts to Candida Casa lived in central Scotland, a borderland contested among the indigenous peoples; the Pictish presence is revealed by the prefix Pit- on certain place-names (such as Pittendreich in Midlothian).[15] The one spot specifically commemorating the missionary lies in this stretch of country, at St Ninian a mile or two south of Stirling, where he may have founded a church to evangelize the local fortress on a hill. The Votadini were almost neighbours further down the Forth, so it ought to have been easy for a keen preacher to reach out to them too.

Whatever disdainful Romans thought, it never proved hard to bring the Celts within the pale of civilization, in a religious or in a more general sense. During the Middle Ages their culture would fuse with Christianity into a rich literary mysticism. It nourished itself from what was called the Matter of Britain, the corpus of native legend transmuted from its primitive origins into poetic enchantment for all Europe, not just in the medieval era but right down to modern times. It consists mainly of Arthurian romances, though there is a parallel if less copious tradition of Tristan and Isolde.

This particular tale rests on a classic triangle of doomed love – doomed by King Mark, to whom Isolde is betrothed even while being swept off her feet by Tristan. It arose in the Celtic countries, but the modern versions allude only to Ireland and Cornwall: Mark is King of Cornwall, Isolde is said to have come from Chapelizod, today a suburb of Dublin. Yet one source, an anonymous Welsh text of the fifteenth or sixteenth century, sets the tragedy in Celyddon, or the Caledonian Forest.[16] The fact this is a single source does not discredit it. All these old legends persisted in many variants, most now lost, and it is matter of chance which survived. More to the point, a Caledonian origin for Tristan looks plausible because his is a Pictish name: there are numerous Drusts or Drustans in the king-lists of his people. He could have come south, among the Votadini for example, through the Celtic custom of fosterage, which placed young sons of a chief in the care of another, to be brought up by him and to cement an alliance. The custom would endure for centuries ahead, into the dawn of the modern era. The *Gododdin* refers to a foster-son or brother as *cimelt* or *comelt*; the Scots Gaelic for fosterage is *comhdhaltas*, an abstract noun from the same root. Tristan's shortest road to Cornwall from Pictland would have run through the territory of the Votadini. Perhaps he grew to manhood during fosterage at Traprain or Din Eidyn.[17]

※

A conjectural history of the Votadini has been pursued here so far as it can be, even a little further, with scant reference to the stock starting point for Scottish history: the Roman occupation of territory up to the isthmus between the Rivers Forth and Clyde. To justify the switch of focus it may be pointed out that the presence of the legions in fact consisted of a series of brief incursions – though the historical record is patchy and the dates are often less than certain.

The Emperor Claudius had led an invasion across the English

Channel in AD 43 to found the province of Britannia, but the Romans did not reach Scotland until 79. Gnaeus Julius Agricola, their governor, then mounted an offensive to the River Tay. He built forts along the way, before forming a chain of military outposts across from Forth to Clyde. Campaigns north of this frontier continued, until in 82 he brought the Celtic tribes to decisive battle at Mons Graupius and crushed them. Their defeated leader was the first native whose name we know, Calgacus the Swordsman. All these events found their historian in Agricola's son-in-law, Tacitus, who ascribes to the Celts far finer moral qualities than any the Romans can show.

The annals of Britannia then peter out: Agricola just says the province was at once thrown away. By the end of the first century, in any event, the Romans had retreated to the line of Hadrian's Wall, along the River Tyne and over to the Solway Firth in England. They did not come back until 138 in the reign of the Emperor Antoninus Pius. He sent his governor, Quintus Lollius Urbicus, on campaign to reoccupy the south of Scotland. A new imperial frontier was fixed at the Antonine Wall, built from the present Bo'ness on the Forth to Old Kilpatrick on the Clyde. Guarded by nineteen forts with milecastles in-between, it consisted of a barrier of turf 10 feet high and 15 feet wide, with a still wider ditch, 40 feet across, on the northern side. Less elaborate defences extended from the ends of the wall proper along the southern shores of both the Clyde and Forth – in the latter case with garrisons at Cramond and at Inveresk. From here also, out of moorings at the mouths of the River Almond or River Esk, fleets could pursue and punish the barbarians beyond the cordon of military occupation.

Yet the toil and trouble of constructing such a salient imperial frontier soon turned out to have been wasted. The name the Romans called their new territory behind it, Britannia Barbarica, underlines their difficulties. About this time the historical murk is thick, but what we can discern seems to show subdued tribes south of the wall in grumbling rebellion and untamed tribes north of the wall penetrating it whenever they bothered to exert themselves. Before long the Romans had had their fill. After two or three decades they pulled out again.[18]

A policy had failed. But on Roman frontiers, as on many others' frontiers through history, policy was ambiguous. It veered on the one hand from the concept of a clean, clear difference between what was empire and what was not, marked on the ground by a wall, to, on the other hand, the concept of a buffer zone, of defence in depth, of a cushion between barbarism and civility with scope both for absorption of attacks and for preparation of offensives, without disruption to the *pax Romana* further south. From Berlin to Kabul, modern Europe and modern Asia have found themselves between the same two military minds.

⚜

It is from this short phase of occupation in the middle of the second century that Roman remains in Scotland are richest. The Antonine Wall itself survives in some shape over quite lengthy stretches. Excavations around Edinburgh have revealed more about the eastward extension of its defensive system. They show Cramond had a stone-built *castellum* with a small settlement outside the walls and probably a harbour at the mouth of the Almond, though no trace of this remains. It was a bog-standard military base and depot, full of storehouses and workshops, made somewhat more comfortable by the perquisite of warm baths for the troops. Gaulish legionaries occupied it, according to the inscriptions on its altars.

Inveresk was different, with a far bigger civilian presence. The settlement outside its walls represented the nearest thing to a Roman town in Scotland. Villas with hypocausts lined streets leading to the gates of the fort. Beyond lay fields, enclosures and tracks wandering off into the countryside. No doubt it was the proximity to the Votadini at Traprain that accounts for an impression of bustle. Resident at Inveresk was an imperial procurator, an official of the Roman state, by the name of Quintus Lusius Sabinianus; he dedicated an altar to Apollo, god of the sun, or of the light and reason he had come to spread here in the dark, wild north.

What were his duties? One probability is that Sabinianus regulated relations between the occupying power and the local chiefs. He seems to have made a good job of it, so long as Pictish marauders from beyond the Antonine Wall could be kept at bay. Inveresk and Traprain after all exhibit every sign of peaceful coexistence, of amity between the Romans and the Votadini. The tribe became not a little romanized, its eagerness to learn proving as important in this respect as the imperial example. To become romanized meant, in one basic sense, to establish durable order. The realm of the Votadini was durable, which must have meant it was in some degree ordered, independently of the legions' fitful presence.

Of course, the Votadini may have been paid to stay quiet, a common enough imperial practice. Then they would have counted as clients of Rome rather than allies. Negative evidence of the more commendable kind of relationship lies in the fact that there are few Roman sites elsewhere on the territory of the Votadini, apart from the roads crossing it: in other words, no need existed for military installations on the scale of the Antonine Wall to the west. In the peaceful hinterland the Romans could stick to routes leading straight to the bases and leave the Votadini to their own devices in the fortresses on hills.

The line of the main Roman road, Dere Street, followed the modern A68. Coming up from Hadrian's Wall by way of Jedburgh and Melrose, it swung into Lothian over Soutra Hill. When its extant remains disappear, by the traffic lights at Nether Liberton, it is on a heading to take it along the southern side of the Meadows (in Roman times the shore of a loch) towards a crossing of the Water of Leith near Dean Village. So the Roman road and the Castle Rock, with a fortress of the Votadini crowning it, stood within immediate sight and reach of each other: something surely unlikely unless the relationship on both sides had been easy.

An easy relationship was not what other tribes sought or found. The Romans, even after their withdrawal from the Antonine Wall in about 160, still mounted punitive expeditions. A major encounter took place under the Emperor Septimius Severus in 208–9. But a few years later all the legionary and auxiliary garrisons were gone from Scotland once more, and gone for good. In fact it appears the Roman Empire had long given up hope of permanently occupying territory north of Hadrian's Wall. Rather, the tables were now turned as barbarians threatened its territory to the south. The Picts again proved particularly troublesome. In 296 and in 306 they assaulted the frontier of Britannia. In 367 they joined Scots and Saxons in the Barbaric Conspiracy, which overran the province as far south as London. Restoration of order took two years. By now the final Roman retreat to the Continent lay less than half a century away.

We are looking, then, at just about five decades of the Romans' presence in one region of Scotland, out of the four centuries they ruled Britannia. Even so, we ought not to underrate the reach of imperial power or its flexible response to native society. The legions' comings and goings in the south of Scotland during the four centuries might have masked relative stability in the north of Scotland – here, too, there could have been some semblance of *pax Romana*. It is perhaps no accident how in the Northern and Western Isles the brochs, the natives' massive round towers of stone, fell into disuse during the period, to be replaced by less obviously defensive types of settlement. For tribes nearer at hand, the economics of cooperation with Rome must have offered a better deal than the fickle fortunes of war. A new plenty does seem to have been the reward for spells of peace in these parts, with comparative security fostering nascent development. Cohesion – political, religious and military – was Rome's gift to the peoples who would fuse to form the first kingdoms in Scotland: an achievement beyond the reach of their still tribal cousins in Ireland, where the legions never went.[19]

❧

The Dark Ages followed. With the prop of Rome removed, native chiefs were no longer strong enough to hold off foreign marauders hungry for territory and power. These had put in an appearance even before the legions went home. Now they swarmed around like packs of ravening wolves. Among other aggressors, the Gaelic-speaking Scots from Ireland colonized Dalriada, comprising much of present-day Argyll. On the opposite side of the country, the Votadini had to face the Germanic assault from across the North Sea.

According to the *Gododdin*, the Battle of Catterick inflicted terrible casualties on both sides. But in the end it clearly weakened the Votadini more than the Angles. Soon Aethelfrith of Bernicia recovered enough from his defeat (if that was what it had been) to expand his realm, and fast. In 603 he beat the Scots of Dalriada at the Battle of Degsastan. In 605 he attacked a rival Anglian kingdom to the south, Deira, covering most of Yorkshire. He expelled its ruler, Edwin, and fused both Anglian realms into Northumbria. Here Aethelfrith, 'a very powerful and ambitious king' according to Bede, reigned until his death in 617.

Then Edwin, a man of 'proud mind', made a comeback aided by Saxon allies. Seizing the throne of united Northumbria, he ushered in a golden age. He converted to Christianity in 627, having been moved by a parable of human life that one of his warriors told him – of a sparrow that flutters out of the winter's night into the warmth and light of a lord's great hall then in a moment flutters out into the cold and darkness once more. Yet Edwin also continued to wage war, now northwards into Tweeddale. When he was killed in battle in 634, Northumbria for a time fell apart again. But the setback hardly sapped the vigour of the Angles. Aethelfrith's son Oswald had taken refuge on Iona, so he spoke Gaelic; more to the point, he too had converted to Christianity, turning 'humble, kindly and generous to the poor'. Now he made his own comeback with help from his friends, the Scots of Dalriada. He invited an Irish monk from Iona, St Aidan, to found the monastery of Lindisfarne on Holy Island. At the same time, aggressive expansion resumed. In 638 Oswald's army of Bernicia besieged and captured Edinburgh.[20]

That marked the end of the Votadini as an independent people. One chieftain, Cunedda, had led a band of warriors off to Wales, where he helped to repel an invasion of Scots from Ireland. He was able to set himself up in a new home on distant soil, a little like Aeneas coming to Latium from the fall of Troy. Cunedda's dynasty ruled in Gwynedd for several centuries. Out of it arose the native Princes of Wales.

※

Edinburgh meanwhile was no longer a Celtic capital but the northern bastion of a kingdom which at length would merge into England. One way and another, it retained a frontiersman's role for the next millennium. Its site is strategic, after all. The Castle Rock, if second in altitude to Arthur's Seat, offers the most defensible position of any among the heights rising out of the coastal plain of the Lothians. Here it is at its narrowest where the ranges of Moorfoot and Pentland Hills approach the firth, before the terrain opens out again into the central belt of Scotland. Edinburgh would in a more distant future defend the gap against attacks coming across a frontier to the south. For the present, with a frontier to the north, it stood sentinel over the way into England. For either task the Castle Rock offered great advantages: natural security, visual prominence, ready control of passing traffic, supplies from a fertile hinterland. The advantages were reinforced by a further, detailed military consideration – girt on three sides by cliffs, the summit could be reached from the fourth side only up a long, narrow slope growing steeper towards the top. This was fine as a fortress; but scarcely promising as the site for a city.

On the Castle Rock no trace remains of the Anglian occupation. For the Kings of Northumbria, Bamburgh took precedence as the first seat of their monarchy, conquered by their heroic ancestors. But it was a feature of the new barbaric order in Britain, as in the rest of Europe after the collapse of the Roman Empire, that the kings resided from time to time at any one of several strongholds. Right into the Middle Ages, they would progress around them through the year, at each one exercising power and authority, dispensing justice, offering hospitality or patronage, with their hangers-on getting through huge quantities of food and other provisions. From the surrounding countryside they commandeered what they wanted – cattle, corn, services in kind – until a time came for them to move on and drain the resources from some other community. At their pleasure they even set limits to where the people might live and work. Beyond its farmland Midlothian was stern and wild, a country of hills and moors. Such ground would later be termed forest: a Scottish technical term still in use, meaning not necessarily a landscape of trees but rather one reserved for hunting. This was how the king and his warriors spent their days, before they retired at night to the Castle Rock for rest and recreation. There the middens now filled up with bones of deer or boar.

Behind the northern frontier guarded by Edinburgh, deeper changes went on. Lothian lost its pure Celtic character as it was settled by the Angles, who spoke a Northumbrian dialect of Old English. W. F. C. Nicolaisen, the historian of Scottish place-names, concluded on linguistic grounds that Whittingehame and Tyningham in East Lothian were among their earliest settlements, followed by Carrington and Haddington, then by Morham and Oldhamstocks. The progression indicates how the Angles came first to the coasts and the valleys of important rivers, before moving on and up to wherever they could find fertile ground – but not into the hills, the refuge of the Celts. The Northumbrian dialect of Old English was the ancestor of modern Scots. The precise quality of the vowel-sounds may have changed since, but the people used words like bairn for a child, daur for dare, swallie for swallow, neep for turnip and bleeze for blaze, all still to be heard on the streets of Edinburgh today. Robert Burns's line in 'To a Mouse', when he offers the terrified little animal 'a daimen icker in a thrave' (the odd ear in twenty-four sheaves), is Northumbrian.[21]

A fresh society took shape. The king or his officers on the Castle Rock claimed their supplies and services from a group of settlements that would by this tribute be taught to think and act together. That way they at length turned into the county of Midlothian, stretching from Kirkliston in the west to Inveresk in the east, and from Cramond by the sea to Penicuik at the foot of the hills. To the eastern side of the Castle Rock lay fine arable land, which teams of oxen had from time out of mind ploughed for cereal crops: oats and bere (the northern six-rowed barley) with a little wheat and rye. Some place-names here, such as Dalkeith, 'wooded valley', date back to before the coming of the Angles; pockets of Celts might have managed to survive displacement of the rest. To the western side of the Castle Rock the land was more rolling and less fertile. Its people lived rather from grazing cattle and sheep over meadows by the rivers and on slopes above them, or from fattening pigs on acorns and beechmast in the woods. Here, on inferior soil, there are more Celtic place-names, as well as mixed ones: Cramond 'fort on the Almond', Corstorphine, 'cross of Thorfinn'.[22]

Edinburgh itself acquired its hybrid name from the Anglian overlay of a Celtic past. The Edin- element, for the hill-slope, is well attested by the prime Brythonic source, the *Gododdin*, at the end of the sixth century, before the Angles got anywhere near the place; the same element is found in Edinbane, Edingight and other undoubtedly Celtic place-names around Scotland. What happened now was addition of an Anglo-saxon suffix, -burh, which (like the Din of Din Eidyn) means fortress. The idea it was renamed after King Edwin of Northumbria (dead by the time of its capture and the foe of its captor) is demonstrably false.[23]

Societies on frontiers develop in robust ways. This one for now formed part of Northumbria, the strongest Germanic kingdom in

Britain, expanding on every hand. To its south it overcame another
Anglian rival, Mercia, though at the cost of death in battle for
Oswald, the conqueror of Edinburgh, in 642. Because he had been
a Christian and the Mercians were heathen, he counted as a martyr
– and so a pious warmonger won sainthood. His triumphant
enemies dismembered his corpse but others rescued the bits, which
were venerated as religious relics for centuries ahead. Under his
brother and successor, Oswy (also brought up on Iona), Northumbria
advanced against the Celts too. To the west, Oswy acquired their
realm of Rheged by marriage in about 645. That carried his power to
the Solway Firth on the opposite side of Scotland. He pushed yet
further into Galloway. By 720 an Anglian bishop held the see of
Whithorn; the Northumbrian name, *hwit aern*, 'white house', merely
translates Candida Casa.[24]

Northern expansion proved tougher. The Forth made a logical
and defensible frontier but Oswy's son, Egfrith, was too rash to rest
content with this. He sought to extend his sway over the Picts on
the opposite shore. His forward policy was not crude: it had a
religious or cultural as well as military dimension. About 680 he
erected a bishopric and monastery at Abercorn on the upper reaches
of the firth under one Trumwin, so-called Bishop of the Picts. But
these proved unreceptive to his missionary blandishments. So in 685
Egfrith set out to subdue them by force, only to meet crushing defeat
at the Battle of Nechtansmere (Dunnichen in Angus). Here Brude,
King of the Picts, halted Egfrith's advance and killed him. Trumwin
and his monks fled Abercorn, though a religious establishment of
some sort seems to have survived on the spot.

Northumbrian power had overreached itself and went into
decline. A respite came during the peaceful reign of Egfrith's successor, Aldfrith. But his death in 704 opened decades of dynastic
struggle, chronic instability and general mayhem. As if that were not
enough, Vikings sacked Lindisfarne in 793, the first of many grievous
depredations. It marked the beginning of the end for Northumbria.
In 867 the kingdom was absorbed into the Danelaw after being
ravaged by the brothers Halfdan Ragnarsson and Ivar the Boneless.[25]

❧

Yet the influence of Northumbria proved not so transient as its political history suggests. Its vivid culture would in the long run outshine
the military prowess that had fused it in the short run. Both
combined a native energy and a gift for fruitful reaction with the
alien environment into which they had moved. Close contact with
the Celts, indeed rule over Celts, made Northumbria the least Germanic of the Anglo-Saxon kingdoms.

Above all, Northumbria's religion was Celtic. King Oswald had
after the conversion of his people called on the spiritual resources
of Iona, the monastery off the faraway western coast of Scotland
founded in the previous century by the Irish prince St Columba. The
men of God who answered the call brought their own form of
divinity with them. Long cut off at the edge of the known world,
Celtic Christianity had developed a character deviant from that
found otherwise in the western Christendom directed from Rome.

Minor procedural differences existed (how to reckon the date of
Easter, how to cut a tonsure) of which too much was made at the
time and later. A more important distinction lay in the less hierarchical nature of the Celtic Church. It set great store by monastic life, yet
its religious communities were not closed. Members of one order of
monks, the Culdees (*Céli Dé*, servants of God), combined their
vocation with the kind of ministry to the faithful that elsewhere was
carried out by the secular clergy; since Culdees could marry, they no
doubt gave better advice than a celibate priesthood would have done.
For any religious who were reluctant to submit to monastic rule the
Celtic Church countenanced, just as happily, the hermit's life of
solitary contemplation. This was quite different from Rome's growing
obsession with authority and hierarchy. The Celtic Church more
truly renounced the world, demanding greater and greater severities
of its ascetic monks and hermits. But it gave the world back its
devotion to learning and the arts.

In Northumbria this made for a culture deeper and more complex
than in the Saxon kingdoms to the south, even those that Rome's
emissary, St Augustine, had meanwhile converted to Christianity.
Northumbrian art was rich. It survives in metalwork, in stone
carvings, especially crosses, and in illuminated manuscripts. It com-
bines Celtic and Anglian elements with possibly others. The art of

Celts and Angles alike had started out from traditions of fine metal-work, adorned by animal or abstract figures and used for personal adornment by their chiefs. For their part the Picts had stonecutters who produced intricate, not to say exuberant, monumental carving. At Abercorn, the missionary site on the frontier, the three material cultures may have come together. The present medieval church there (dating from the twelfth century) holds pieces of the lofty standing crosses that had earlier adorned the site. To judge from their admittedly fragmentary remains, they combined the indigenous styles so as to cover every available surface with complex patterns and pictures, barbaric and fantastic but mixed with Christian motifs as well. The kings or abbots who patronized such meticulous labour of decoration wanted to see at the end of it objects of dazzling virtuosity in order to overawe a society of no other visual sophistication. Their legacy lies not so much in the specific stylistic features as in a fundamental departure from anything that might be called classical. The barely controllable energy of their northern style, spiralling across formal partitions, mixing the figurative with the ornamental, would become a feature of later medieval art, especially Gothic art. In the Lothian region mere shivers of all this survive but at least there is a complete example, in the Ruthwell Cross, from another far-flung Northumbrian frontier.

The Ruthwell Cross is now housed within its local church in Dumfriesshire, across the Border hills from Edinburgh. Dating from the eighth century it is, at eighteen feet high, the finest remaining Scottish example of its type. Presbyterian iconoclasts smashed it in 1664 but in 1818 the Reverend Henry Duncan, the versatile phil-anthropist who also founded the Trustee Savings Banks, restored it. Made whole again, it revealed how the original stonecutters had carved, as well as the crucified Christ and other sacred images, an inscription in runes, giving in their Northumbrian dialect a couple of lines from 'The Dream of the Rood'. To appear in such a context this anonymous poem must have been widely known to the Ger-manic peoples of Great Britain. Its complete text (preserved else-where, notably in the Vercelli Codex), offers insight into the culture behind the Cross. Its vocabulary comes out of the heroic corpus: *ealdgewyrhtum*, in the brave days of yore; *aergewin*, hereditary enmity; *middangeard*, 'Middle Earth' or present reality; *wyrd*, Fate. Yet in the poem old heathen words acquire new spiritual meanings. And they are, extraordinarily, spoken by an inanimate object, the Rood itself; it is suddenly hard to overlook that, fifteen miles away from Ruthwell at Ellisland, Burns was a millennium later the author of poems, 'The Brigs of Ayr' or 'The Humble Petition of Bruar Water', which also let the inanimate join in creation's song. The inscription at Ruthwell reads:

> *Krist wæs on rodi. Hweþræ*
> *þer fusæ fearran kwomu*
> *Æþþilæ til anum.*

> Christ was on the cross. Yet
> The brave came there from afar
> To their lord.

If the poem was moving simple pilgrims' hearts here in a remote outpost of Northumbria, we need hardly doubt it also gave pause to great men on the Castle Rock of Edinburgh. The blend of the Celtic and the Germanic set in motion the culture of the future city.[26]

🏵

Northumbrian religion left other enduring memories and traditions in Scotland. One was of its best-loved figure, St Cuthbert. He had been born in 635 into a poor family near Melrose (which also lay on the frontier of Anglian settlement, to judge from its Celtic name: *maol ros*, 'bare moor'). No doubt it, too, was a place where two cultures mixed, enriching the life of a man destined to attain heroic sanctity. At the age of sixteen, while keeping sheep, he had a vision of the soul of St Aidan being carried to heaven by angels, though it did not at once impel him into religious life. He spent a few years as a soldier of King Oswy in the English campaigns. Only then did Cuthbert enter the monastery at his birthplace. He soon impressed his superiors. When monks from Melrose were sent to found a new monastery at Ripon in Yorkshire, it was he who led them.

By now the Celtic Christianity fostered under the Kings of Northumbria was coming to a crisis. Oswy had a Kentish consort, Queen Aethelburga, who followed the Roman usage introduced by St Augustine at Canterbury. No doubt for the sake of a quiet life,

Oswy decided to resolve the differences. Probably he put the pressure first on new religious foundations: in 661 Ripon fell into line with Rome. Cuthbert and others preferred to go back to Melrose, where in 664 he became prior. But in the same year the Synod of Whitby was summoned to settle the disputes between Roman and Celtic Christianity. St Wilfred of York took the lead for Rome. He urged the synod to accept not just a different calendar and style of tonsure but also a centralized diocesan structure. The Celts were defeated. Led by Bishop Colman of Lindisfarne, they trailed back to Iona. But this time Cuthbert recalled his vow of obedience and acquiesced in the new order. For his proven qualities of leadership and holiness, he was sent to take over at Lindisfarne and smoothe a painful transition. Still, he did not forget the old ways; in 676 he retired to live as a hermit on Farne Island. There he stayed, with brief interruptions, until his death in 687.

Cuthbert won a lasting place in his people's hearts, Celts and Angles alike. In fact, he was at length adopted as the patron saint of Edinburgh. The church with the most ancient tradition in the city is dedicated to him. It stands at the western end of Princes Street, picturesque and unrelated to the Georgian formalities nearby, below the level of the modern roadway, a refuge from commerce and commotion, its trees shading the graves where dead generations sleep. It is there because it occupies the site of its medieval fore-runner, first mentioned in 1127 (and possibly founded during the previous century). The churchyard then formed one shore of the Nor' Loch, already a haven of peace under the stern visage of the Castle Rock.

Later, at the Reformation of 1560, people called to mind once again the ancient tension between the Celtic and Roman strains of Scottish Christianity. Protestantism represented in one way a con-scious effort to restore primitive purity to religion. That was a special enthusiasm of George Buchanan, first lay Moderator of the General Assembly of the Church of Scotland and tutor to James VI and I, in whom the Union of Crowns between Scotland and England would take effect in 1603. Buchanan claimed the old Culdees as Protestants before their time, defenders of the Celtic Church against Roman corruption. Whether true or not this proved a potent myth, revived once again when Scottish Christianity faced another great crisis at the Disruption of the Kirk in 1843.[27]

A problem with the Scottish appropriation of Cuthbert is that he could scarcely have regarded himself as a Scot. Indeed he was not: despite Lothian's political and economic importance to the future Scotland, before the Middle Ages descendants of its Anglian settlers would never be thought of as Scots. In the days of Cuthbert the Scots formed only one of several kingdoms at the northern end of Great Britain, and the nearest lived some way from Edinburgh.

To be sure, these Scots, after invading from Ireland in the fifth century, had extended their original realm of Dalriada eastwards. They ran up against the Picts and warred with them for a couple of hundred years. The King of Scots, Kenneth MacAlpine, inflicted a decisive defeat on the last King of the Picts, Drust IX, in 843 – the date by which later generations marked the beginning of Scotland as a monarchy and a nation.

Even then the resulting fusion of Gael and Pict, ruled from Scone on the Tay, covered no more than the central parts of the country and, notably, not the Lothian region of the Angles. Nor could the future expansion of the Kingdom of Scots have been a foregone conclusion. On the contrary, an evolution is not hard to envisage by which Edinburgh would have become part of England rather than Scotland – if in that case Scotland could ever have coalesced into a nation at all.

Yet, while the political geography of the future remained veiled amid the current congeries of kingdoms, in Great Britain as a whole the differences between the English and the rest already existed and were already sensed. Scotland began to discern a threat from the south, from Wessex in particular, far away though it was. The Kings of Wessex set about demanding, and getting, homage from lesser rulers. That was how in the end they created England. They could conceive of this national entity long before its actual formation, while the Anglo-Saxons still lived in separate kingdoms or were being ravaged by the Vikings. But they would only be able to form England and Englishness by excluding what was non-English, in particular what was Celtic. The southern part of Great Britain would as a result see the rise of two nations, the English and the Welsh, with the latter pushed off among their mountains and valleys. The northern part of Great Britain saw the rise of one nation, the Scots – formed haltingly and out of more diverse origins, yet in the end one nation all the same.

That is to say, the making of Scotland turned out to be qualitatively different from the making of England. This fact has left its mark down to the present. Scotland took longer to weld into one because she could only ever be put together from a motley mix of peoples – the Britons, the Gaels, the Picts, the Angles, later the Vikings and the Normans. Nor without Edinburgh could the nation have become what it is, or even have existed at all. In the end the various elements, the original Celtic stock along with the incomers, learned to live together. An idea of Scotland emerged to which all could subscribe. Scottishness was slow to crystallize but was inclusive, rather than sooner-formed but exclusive after the English manner.

One consequence, for good or ill, was that Scotland still bore marks of her remote origins a millennium after the country came into being. The names of the petty kingdoms where her indigenous peoples had dwelt – Lothian, Moray, Fife, Galloway and more – survived up to and beyond the Union with England in 1707; another, Strathclyde, was to be resurrected in the late twentieth century as a monstrous local authority. On several occasions the patchwork might have dissolved. Scotland did manage to maintain her independence into the dawn of the modern era, but she was always a nation more untidy, precarious and provisional than others, than her southern neighbour especially, and never able to efface her variegations through any durable centralizing force: all the better for that, Scots would say. But this came at a price.

❧

While from the time of Kenneth MacAlpine the fates of Scotland's peoples would be linked, in harmony or discord, two more centuries were needed for his dynasty to extend its rule to them all. It is true his grandson Donald II (889–900) already used the Gaelic title *rì Alban*, King of Alba, implying dominion over the whole northern end of Great Britain. The aspirations may have been fired by the collapse of Northumbria, by a turn of the tide against the Vikings and by the fact that English resurgence was starting up safely far away under the House of Wessex. Even so, the title as yet represented ambition rather than achievement. It would take time for the House of MacAlpine to feel at home anywhere else than in its Scoto-Pictish heartland. Its kings cast, however, jealous eyes on Lothian, the most fertile part of the future Scotland. They began to probe forward across the Northumbrian frontier on the Forth.

A detailed account of the political ebb and flow would become tedious, even if its history were fully known (which it is not). One signpost appears in 973, when several other rulers in Great Britain did homage to King Edgar of Wessex at Chester, in token of which they flexed their own royal muscles to row him down the River Dee. At this point he seems to have recognized, in some form, the claim to Lothian by Kenneth II, King of Scots. In reality the claim remained far from sure. The next King of Scots, Malcolm II (1005–34), almost forfeited it again when after his accession he led a hasty invasion of Northumberland, now a mere English earldom, and got as far as Durham before being beaten back with great loss. He would soon learn better, to be remembered in the end as a pious Christian and powerful commander.

All came right for the Scots by 1018. The English had been under attack from King Canute of Denmark, who managed to seize their throne. Malcolm II, in alliance with Owain, King of Strathclyde, saw an opportunity in England's difficulty. They assailed and defeated Uhtred, Earl of Northumberland, at Carham on the southern bank of the River Tweed. As a result the Scots could turn their temporary occupation of Lothian into permanent possession. The old Northumbria was partitioned in effect along a fresh frontier on the Tweed. Edinburgh's role in defending it remained as important as when the Castle Rock had stood guard behind the previous frontier at the Forth. The new one would still be disputed for two centuries: the Kings of Scots coveted Northumberland too, while the English fought back. But Scotland now included, and would forever include, Edinburgh.

❧

The House of MacAlpine brought Gaelic ascendancy to its enlarged realm – if for a matter of decades only, until the culture and tongue of the dynasty changed and set off the decline in Gaeldom which has continued ever since. The Gaelic language was for the time being spoken everywhere in that realm except among the Vikings of the far north and in the Lothians just annexed from Northumbria. Here too, though, an elite of Gaels moved in. We can tell as much from the place-names in Edinburgh's suburbs, Comiston or Gilmerton, dating back to that era. From the Anglian peasantry the names took one element, the Northumbrian -ton, meaning a fenced settlement. But by the other element they also commemorate the incoming Gaelic lords: Comiston for Colman (or Columba), and Gilmerton for Gilmour, devotee of the Virgin Mary. The Gaels did not just drive out the incumbent Northumbrian lords, however. There was room enough for everybody. The basic mixed Celto-Germanic stock of the population, descended from the Votadini and the Angles of Bernicia, merely mingled with the new Gaelic (perhaps we should say Scottish) or indeed Viking blood which arrived, as shown up by the personal names in the surviving records. It was a racial rainbow. The Lothians' leaders all the same developed solidarity and staying power, future proof against both royal encroachment and foreign aggression.[28]

Malcolm II further cemented his monarchy. His ally Owain had died at the Battle of Carham or soon afterwards. The astute King of Scots took the opportunity to win the succession to Strathclyde for his grandson, Duncan. Following his grandfather's death Duncan would be recognized as the ruler of all Scotland, apart from the Viking earldoms. This still guaranteed no absolute stability or security for the House of MacAlpine. In 1040 Duncan felt obliged to assert his authority in the north of Scotland, only to suffer defeat and death at the hands of Macbeth, mormaer or sub-king of Moray. Macbeth was at once accepted as King of Scots instead. He drove Duncan's two sons, Malcolm and Donald Bàn, into exile, and by 1050 felt safe enough to make a pilgrimage to Rome; there, with a remote barbarian's anxiety not to seem scrimping, he gave more money to the poor than he could afford. But after his return to Scotland the dynastic uncertainty reared its ugly head again. And it provoked intervention from England, not for the last time.

The English earldom of Northumberland had meanwhile been granted to one Siward. He may have been Duncan's brother-in-law, for the dead king's heir, Malcolm, took refuge with him. The young prince had obvious political value, so was passed on to the court of the English king, Edward the Confessor – usually thought of as a dove, not to say a wimp. Yet Edward ordered Siward to invade Scotland, drive out Macbeth and install Malcolm on the throne. In 1054 at the Battle of Dunsinane, near the Scots' capital of Scone, Malcolm and Siward led an army from both sides of the border to victory over Macbeth.

Malcolm III, nicknamed Canmore, 'Big Head' (1058–93), became King of Scots. He had a head not only big but also uneasy, for like most other rulers of Scotland he found endless problems in uniting or defending his realm. These took on new, fearsome dimensions when, after the Battle of Hastings in 1066, he faced the mightiest warrior-king of the age, William the Conqueror, now with the power of both England and Normandy behind him. Between the pair of them sour mistrust alternated with pure spite.

One reason lay in Malcolm III's continuing friendship with the House of Wessex (or now its remnants), which had helped him on to the throne of Scotland. Half a century before, the resistance of that house to Canute's conquest of England had been led by Edmund Ironside, who was killed or murdered in 1016. Two sons, Edmund and Edward, survived him. Whether or not Canute expelled them or they fled, they somehow reached Hungary, where they were out of harm's way, if almost forgotten. Not until 1057 did the younger Edward return to England, summoned by his uncle, Edward the Confessor, who probably saw in him an heir to the throne, as indicated by the title he assumed, the Atheling. But this younger Edward soon died, leaving a son Edgar, also known as the Atheling, with two daughters, Margaret and Christina. Margaret had brought back with her the legacy of a Hungarian upbringing, among a people only just converted to Christianity: she combined missionary passion and devotion with hieratic certainty and zeal.

Englishmen refusing to bow to the Conqueror after 1066 tried to rally round Edgar the Atheling. He and Margaret, still living in England, could as members of the House of Wessex hardly be thought safe. In 1068 William the Conqueror, finished with subduing the south of the country, marched north pillaging, burning and killing. Northumbrian diehards fled into Scotland, taking Edgar and his sisters with them. John of Fordun's *Scotichronicon* tells how

Malcolm III sent a messenger to meet the refugees. This man felt impressed by a lady not yet identified, 'whom, by reason of her incomparable beauty and pleasantness of speech, I took to be the chief of the party'. It was Margaret. Once she reached the court of the king he, a widower, fell in love with her and married her. He brought down on himself the suspicion, not to say wrath, of the Conqueror.[29]

In 1072 William invaded Scotland and pursued Malcolm III as far as Abernethy on the Tay. Here, right in the ancestral Scoto-Pictish heartland of his kingdom, Malcolm bowed to the Conqueror and became his vassal. Not surprisingly, English propagandists would long afterwards recall the ceremony as proof of Scottish subjection. Against this has to be set the fact that William never conquered Scotland as he had conquered England, being shrewd enough to see what a daunting task that must be for any English king. For his part, Malcolm invaded England four times, in 1061, 1070, 1079 and 1092. While the last of these expeditions ended with betrayal and death for him and his heir, at least this record shows how, as between the two realms, the superiority did not lie wholly on one side. In any case, the medieval mind had no trouble with the idea that a man might be king and vassal at once. For example, the Kings of England were vassals of the King of France for lands they held across the Channel; this did not mean the French monarchs ruled or could rule England.

❧

More important in the long run was how the marriage of Malcolm and Margaret radically redirected Scottish society. By birth, upbringing and inclination she looked to England and Europe. Influences from both bore in on Scotland, most obviously in the life of the Church, but not only there. The steering of the country on a fresh course proved decisive enough to withstand Celtic resurgence and challenge from Donald Bàn, Malcolm III's brother and successor in 1093. At the behest of galled native lords, he threw out all the foreigners and their weird ways. That did not last long, for he soon met a sticky end of his own. After further dynastic struggles, three of his nephews, Edgar, Alexander and David, ruled as successive Kings of Scots from 1097 to 1154. These younger sons of Malcolm and Margaret defined the medieval Scottish monarchy. Each showed in his life, above all in his Christian ardour, the stronger influence of his mother.

How did Margaret impress herself so? We can understand more about her than about other royalty of the age because she became the subject of an official biography by her confessor, Turgot. She was intelligent. She could even read. She won over Malcolm III an influence rare in what we know of medieval marriages at this highest level. Her Celtic warrior husband was a lion not a lamb, needing nothing by way of personal culture, so he remained illiterate. Yet he once found a manuscript she liked and had it encased in gold, ornamented with jewels, just to please her. She otherwise raised the life at his court far above its previous uncouth level to a magnificence Scotland had never known before. Still, her humble piety impressed everyone. She prayed for hours on end. She was charitable. She fed the poor and washed their feet. She ordered humane treatment for English prisoners-of-war enslaved to Lothian households. She took charge of nine orphans and saw to their schooling. She decreed for pilgrims a free passage across the Forth, still commemorated by its two termini at North and South Queensferry. On the further side she saw to the building of a great priory at Dunfermline, where she and the king had wed and where they were to be buried. She behaved altogether just as the medieval mind expected of someone both holy and royal.

Margaret was to be canonized in 1250. Her people had felt her sanctity already proven by the scene at her deathbed in Edinburgh Castle. There she lay while her husband and eldest son were away warring in England, on an invasion she had foretold would come to no good. As she felt her end approaching, she asked for the Black Rood to be brought to her. It was the most sacred of all the relics she had kept by her in her long life's journey from Hungary to England to Scotland, a golden crucifix with an ivory image of Christ, enclosing a piece of the True Cross. While she pressed it to her lips, a younger son burst in with the evil tidings of his father's and brother's deaths at Alnwick. At first, seeing her condition, he thought better to say nothing after all. She begged him by the cross to tell the truth, and then she cried, 'I thank thee, Lord, that givest me this agony to bear in my death hour': spoken like a saint.

And Margaret, in a sense, left Edinburgh its oldest building.

Chronicles of her life make of the Castle Rock a colourless stage-set, though it was perhaps in her time that it won its mysterious medieval epithet, *Castellum Puellarum*, Maiden Castle, even if with her six sons she was, whatever else, no virgin. But from those sources we do learn some facts. The place was fortified. Its main defence lay to the east with a second wall to the west, where climbing the cliff is not easy yet not impossible. On top stood a royal residence with an oratory as well as a church, St Mary's, possibly an earlier Northumbrian foundation. Nothing of this survives except the small, simple chapel dedicated to St Margaret at the north-western corner of the ramparts. It was erected in the twelfth century and a couple of hundred years later people regarded it as the chapel where she had worshipped. This cannot be true: architectural evidence rules out a date earlier than 1100, and she had died in 1093. It would have been built in tribute to her by one of her sons.[30]

Scotland had under Malcolm and Margaret begun to turn from a barbaric into a civilized kingdom. Not the least part they played came in changing the character of the royal house, bringing in new blood and preparing its mind for furtherance of the work they started. Its Celtic heritage slipped into the past, if never to be quite lost. That can be viewed not with regret but rather as the precondition for the deeper enrichment of Scottish life. It would continue with contributions from several cultures, including Celts, though no longer confined to them. Scotland was, and is, a small country, but had already grown remarkable for its diversity. Her character was now mirrored in her ruling dynasty, to which fell the daunting task of forging out of diversity some semblance of unity.

Perhaps a capital had to be part of this. The Scottish monarchy in its wandering way already made use of Edinburgh Castle along with other castles. There was as yet no place of residence, or at least not much of one, for which they could show a penchant even if they had wanted to, in what time they found free from hunting and feasting and mulcting their subjects. That began to change under the best of the three younger sons of Malcolm and Margaret, King David (1124–53).

❧

If it were not for Robert Bruce, who saved the nation from premature extinction, King David would be recalled as Scotland's greatest
medieval monarch. Already in his time he faced English pressure.
Though he proved wily in fending this off, unlike Bruce he did not
have to fight in the last ditch and come back from it, or anything
like that. In fact King David was capable of the friendliest relations
with the English court of the Norman kings, where he had spent
some years of his youth while the dynastic rumples at home got
ironed out. He was treated there as just another member of the royal
family; his experiences made him, for example, at home in the French
language he would bring back with him. Later the relations grew
rockier. One of this royal family's apparent aims was to mould the
inherited range of Celtic, Anglo-Saxon and Norman allegiances in
Great Britain in such a way that all its parts might in some sense
come to form a single monarchy. The royal family was already
English enough to assume the single monarchy must be England's,
to which others would owe fealty.

Yet King David's allegiances had to be wider. Through his father
he was the legitimate heir to the House of MacAlpine. Through his
mother he was the legitimate heir to the House of Wessex, which
beyond her generation had no descendants in direct male line
(Margaret is the link between today's House of Windsor and its
remotest Anglo-Saxon ancestors). True, David united this blood with
the Conqueror's; his mother-in-law was William's niece. Indeed he
strengthened the connection by marrying off his sister to William's
son, Henry I of England. All the same, his aim was to secure the
independence of Scotland.

We can tell this from the way King David never scrupled to
exploit any English weakness. He wanted to resolve in Scotland's
favour one open question, where her bounds would be set. Already
the monarch of a Northumbrian minority north of the River Tweed,
he sought to push those bounds south of the river. During his spell
at the English royal court he had been granted a title, as Earl of
Huntingdon, with a domain from which he drew revenue; a later
phase of benign relations with that court brought his son another
title, as Earl of Northumberland. This earldom David made sure not
just to tax but to govern himself. In effect he shoved his border to

the River Tees. The son's early death in 1152 doomed the stratagem. In the next reign the Kings of Scots would be robbed of all the land they held south of the Tweed. So there the border stayed.[31]

Not every scheme could come off even for such an energetic and resourceful monarch. Contemporaries recognized his qualities all the same and wished to record them for posterity. One was an Englishman, the chronicler Ailred of Rievaulx. Ailred had started his clerical career in the Scottish royal court and left a lively, if rosy, picture of life there. He records how the king made a point of sitting by the door of the hall in whatever castle he happened to be staying, so as to hear and deal in person with grievances brought to him by the poor, sick and suffering. Painstaking in his approach to government, he wanted his country to flourish in every other way too. His favourite pastime was gardening; he enjoyed working with his hands and making things grow. In wider spheres, he set others to the same kind of productive tasks. He was a fine fellow yet as a ruler of men with ambition he had to exhibit a streak which, if not exactly nasty, at least showed a resolve to make his subjects do things they might not otherwise want to do for themselves.[32]

One of King David's policies was to set over the heads of the people a new class of mostly foreign feudal lords. He provoked dismay, alarm, even rebellion. He was never put off. He granted much of the Lothians and the rest of the south of Scotland to incoming tenants-in-chief who held their land of him in return for military service, with a right to bequeath it to their sons or other heirs. Many arrived from Normandy, or nearby provinces of France. In this era such men seemed to be on the way to forming a supranational military caste committed to chivalry (or so they said) rather than country. Such frenchified thugs had already conquered the kingdoms of England, Sicily and Jerusalem, would soon overrun Ireland and before they finished have a go at Hungary and Poland too. To Scotland at least they ventured in peace, invited by the king. The natives might be put out but got used to the idea in the long run: they had no choice. The Scottish feudal system, transmuted by time into something rather different – and of prime importance to the history of Edinburgh – would last in law until 2001.

The process of making Scotland feudal and making feudalism Scottish can be traced back to the earliest charter surviving from

King David's reign, granted at Scone probably on the occasion of his enthronement. One of his old companions from the English court, Robert de Brus, had turned up for the celebration. In return, under the charter's provisions, he got the lordship of Annandale, 200,000 acres of it between Carlisle and Dumfries. The Brus this Robert hailed from, now spelled Brix, is a small village near Cherbourg in Normandy. While he had by this stage of his life won favour from two kings, of England and of Scotland, he could hardly have thought of himself as either an Englishman or a Scotsman. But his family of Bruce would hold Annandale for 200 years, and long before that period elapsed they became Scots; indeed they were the ones who saved the nation from the English. So the Norman influx had its good sides and its promise too.

Some material remains around Edinburgh serve to show what the Normans brought with them and why King David wanted them. As military men they imported their own design of castle with motte and bailey, though hardly any example outlasted in its original shape the later wars that ravaged the region. One that did stands at Dirleton in East Lothian. The land was granted by the king to the family of de Vaux, who on it built and steadily extended a castle of enclosure set about with a ditch crossed by a drawbridge, around a cluster of towers rising straight from the bedrock. Not far away, nestling in the shadow of Traprain Law, Hailes belonged to the Earls of Dunbar, once Northumbrian refugees from the Conqueror, later assimilated here and then raised in feudal rank. Their tower and curtain-wall still perch today on the bank of the River Tyne. Their pit-prisons, like the subterranean Goblin Ha' nearby at Yester, are a reminder how unpleasant life could be made for anyone defying the new order.[33]

※

Kindlier motives appeared in other novel policies. One included the foundation of the royal burgh of Edinburgh about 1130. Here we see again King David's instinct for making things grow. Until his time Edinburgh was a fortress on a hill and little more, except perhaps for some humble settlement at the gates. From his foundation the outline of the later city at once starts to emerge – notably in two landmarks that are landmarks still, if not inside their original fabric.

It tells us much about the king that they are religious, but it also speaks for his secular practicality that they even yet measure out the shape of the Old Town, and its progression of the High Street, or Royal Mile, down the long eastward slope from the Castle Rock.

Halfway along stood and stands St Giles, the burgh's parish church – it would remain the only one throughout the Middle Ages. The building was doubtless started as soon as possible after the foundation of the burgh, certainly well before the earliest written reference to it in 1178. From the original structure a single scallop capital survives. But until 1796 a large portal dating back to the twelfth century formed the northern entrance to the nave. Drawings before its removal show it to have been decorated with many of the same favourite medieval motifs as are yet to be seen on an extant contemporary door of St Cuthbert's church at Dalmeny, now a western suburb of the city. In its Northumbrian intricacy, a local stonecutters' style flourished still. Here they let their imaginations run riot. They liked to carve masks, fantastic beasts, tangled interlace, reliefs of warriors, signs of the zodiac – oh, and a Lamb of God, just to show how devout they could be too. St Giles, apart from that surviving portal, would be rebuilt in the two centuries before the Reformation on a scale to match the growing importance of the burgh. So we otherwise see nothing today of what was first erected on the site.[34]

Then, down at the foot of the Royal Mile, there arose the abbey of Holyroodhouse, Holyrood for short. King David founded the abbey in 1128. He gave it to the Augustinian order of monks, who dedicated it to the True Cross of Christ, in this age an object of popular devotion all over Europe. The abbey's proximity to an ancient royal castle and a new royal burgh endowed it from the beginning with prestige. Soon councils of the Church and of the nation met there. By the end of the century it was being rebuilt on the scale of a cathedral, so that, again, the original fabric has vanished, apart from one doorway and the excavated plan, which was quite modest. The splendid new edifice replacing it would also suffer the ravages of time, but the whole nave survives. 'Work here is of the highest order aesthetically,' says the authority on the subject, with 'tall, elegant proportions and a fastidious clarity of articulation.'[35]

Architecture of such grandeur and distinction was new to Scotland: it is no surprise that legend gathered around it. The legend exactly dated the foundation of the abbey, or at least the idea of it, to 14 September 1128. Then, in fine weather, King David and his retainers left the Castle to hunt in the forests beneath. The chase somehow separated him from them and he found himself near the foot of Salisbury Crags. A giant white stag, maddened by the pursuit, turned at bay and attacked him. He defended himself with his sword, but things were not looking good. All of a sudden there appeared above him a cloud with a silver lining, whence a hand emerged and handed over a sparkling cross. The king waved it at the stag, which ran away and was killed afterwards. He felt impressed but had no idea what to make of it all until that night, when St Andrew appeared to him in a dream. The saint commanded the king to build a monastery on the spot where his life had been saved and to dedicate it to the holy rood.

It was a miracle by any definition, the importance of the message underlined by the status of the messenger. St Andrew had been one of Jesus Christ's disciples, after all – though why a swarthy Mediterranean type, rather than a good local saint such as Cuthbert or Oswald, should perform a miracle here in the back of beyond was something of a puzzle. In any case, in King David's time or a little later a Scottish cult of St Andrew started up, inspired not least by his relics. These had been kept in Constantinople until a Greek monk, St Regulus (or St Rule in the Scots' sloppy articulation), was told by an angel to take them 'to the end of the earth'. The monk set off and decided he had reached the end of earth when he got to Fife. Shipwreck cast him ashore at the Pictish settlement of Cill Rimhinn, promptly renamed St Andrews in honour of the precious cargo he brought with him.[36]

※

All the spin can be seen in more serious light as part of King David's campaign to raise the status of his country and of the Church within it. In particular, he wanted St Andrews to become a metropolitan see no longer subject to York, as it was then reckoned to be. Its subordination arose because the archdiocese of York, founded in 625 by St Augustine's companion, Paulinus, covered after the Synod of Whitby the entire old Northumbrian realm and more. Nothing had ever been done to make the Church in Scotland as independent as the state. The matter would not be resolved until 1472.

King David began by currying papal favour. That surely formed one purpose of his huge bounty to the Church, whatever real personal piety may also have inspired it. His successor, King James I, would gaze on David's tomb in Dunfermline Abbey and regret how much royal land he had given away to priests, monks and nuns. David had, said James, been a 'sair sanct for the Crown'. The poor old Culdees did not figure in his plans, though; they seem, for example, to have been just chucked off their hermitage on Inchkeith by Augustinian interlopers.

This was typical: King David imported from England and Europe the newest monastic orders, now flourishing in a Church Militant. He granted them sites for their abbeys right across Scotland, complete with lands, properties and privileges. His list of benefactions just in and around Edinburgh is long. Beside the Augustinians at Holyrood, Cistercian monks came to Newbattle Abbey, Cistercian nuns to Haddington, North Berwick and Manuel (near Linlithgow). Of the recently created crusading orders the king granted to the Templars a place now named after them, Temple in Midlothian, and to the Hospitallers a preceptory at Torphichen in West Lothian. The Carmelites received one friary at Luffness and another at South Queensferry, where their plain church still stands. Trinitarians were assigned a priory at Dunbar, of which the steeple is today a doocot. The king brought in monastic orders just as he brought in a feudal aristocracy, to modernize his country by furnishing it with institutions for which its peoples might cast off old loyalties and acquire new ones, or be made to. He had to work in a high-handed way because, while he laid up his treasures in heaven, his policy often unsettled his subjects.[37]

King David wished the monks at Holyrood, for example, to enjoy outright and absolute possession of their lands with all chattels down to the most trifling. So we find him forbidding the people of Midlothian to cut peats from or graze beasts on the land thus granted – they must have earlier enjoyed some customary entitlement. He felt concerned not so much about petty theft or nibbling encroachment on monkish assets as with the problem of fitting a new kind of institution on to an age-old framework of common rights and expectations: here he did it in effect with a clean sweep of the latter. The natives could have seen little in it for them, though they did benefit in the long run from the cultural and economic stimulus given to Scotland by the monastic orders, often through links to mother orders in Europe. Cistercians could keep in touch with what went on there because they had to attend general chapters on the Continent. This probably helped the monks at Melrose, where the king had founded them a new abbey, to build up their huge trade in wool to England and Flanders. On the other hand, it did not stop them getting into a long and bitter wrangle over grazing rights with the people in the hills of Midlothian, at Stow. These simple peasants prayed for help to the image of the Virgin Mary in their church that King Arthur was said to have brought them back from Jerusalem; it was the men of God who seemed materialistic and ruthless. Such were the tensions of a new order.

But another of the religious reforms did directly benefit the people rather than impose on them. This was the creation of a national system of parishes, first in the Lowlands; in the whole of Scotland there would eventually be more than a thousand of them. Popular religion had so far been accommodated in countless shrines, chapels, hermitages or other small places of worship bearing ancient dedications to a huge variety of saints, mostly Celts. Now in every parish there was to be a stone-built church, its nave constructed and maintained by its flock, its chancel by its priest and reserved for his use. Some turned out grand, as when modelled on the Dunfermline Abbey that King David rebuilt: his nave and west front still stand, the central monuments of the Romanesque style in Scotland. Of imitations in the Lothians, St Cuthbert's at Dalmeny comes closest, though St Baldred's at Tyninghame cannot in its time have been far behind. Most survive only in fragments: Borthwick, Duddingston, Gullane, Haddington, Kinneil, Kirkliston, Lasswade, Uphall. But such ambitious structures were greatly outnumbered by the modest churches now rising all over Scotland, often mere boxes behind thick walls of rubble, with small windows and sometimes no tower. Though Catholic, their plainness would render them wholly acceptable to Presbyterians four centuries later.

No other social institution served the Scots people so long as the parish and its church.[38]

※

King David made yet more things grow, not only castles and churches but also burghs. The foundation of Edinburgh in about 1130 formed part of a general policy of creating burghs as another spur to progress. By the end of the thirteenth century they would number thirty-six. The record of Edinburgh's particular foundation is lost – or may never have existed, for the first grants of rights to burghs were quite possibly made by word of mouth in a ceremony before witnesses. There had been earlier models at Berwick and Roxburgh. Edinburgh again followed a new scheme.

The scheme was elaborate and tailored to the peculiar site. The High Street or Royal Mile formed a single thoroughfare all the way down from the Castle Rock to Holyrood, by which point it had entered a smaller burgh of Canongate created specially for the monks. Over the middle stretch it widened out into a marketplace. Uniform, however, was the way the ground to its north and south came divided into 'tofts', strips running to the bottom of the ridge on each side. They were to be allocated to burgesses who within a year and a day had to build a house on them. This made sure merchants and craftsmen disposed of a basic facility for business. Such business would also benefit from royal privileges – though at a cost, so it was necessary to prevent evasive smuggling into or out of the burgh. For an economic as well as defensive purpose, then, the whole place required enclosure, perhaps by just a palisade at first, but a West Gate is mentioned before 1160 and a South Gate in 1214.[39]

The aim was to promote commerce. Why had Edinburgh been selected for that? The burgh was not exactly accessible: it had no river running through and the sea lay two miles away, at a time when trade in bulk could only go by water because of lack of roads and means of transport. It would long remain less important than the more senior burghs of Berwick and Roxburgh. Probably some lesser places – Aberdeen, Dunfermline, Haddington, Perth or Stirling – were already building up manufactures and trade because of their natural advantages. Edinburgh had none. Indeed, if position and topography could have decided the matter, no burgh would ever have arisen on the Castle Rock. Leith or Musselburgh surely offered better sites; even as things stood, Edinburgh had for the future to spend time and money on killing their competition.

The key lay in the fact this had been for time out of mind a centre of power. It was a strategic spot where kings had built a fortress on a hill to use while roving around their realm. They were coming to favour it over others, and saw the advantage in having merchants and artisans gathered close by. They granted what royal privileges they needed to ensure as much. It was the first of many triumphs over nature that made Edinburgh.

Those royal privileges regulated life in the burgh so as to foster an exchange: the burgesses would develop manufactures and trade while the king would draw an income from the rent on their properties or the customs on their products. They might hold a market protected by his peace and form a merchants' guild. They could charge tolls but themselves remained free of tolls in Scotland. They enjoyed a collective monopoly on foreign trade out of Edinburgh and Midlothian, exchanging the fruits of nature for finished goods from overseas, most now from Flanders and Germany. It was not a bad deal.

Overall the burgesses prospered, yet in crucial respects their economy could hardly have differed from that of the fortress on a hill at Traprain Law a thousand years before. The basic, not to say primitive, livelihood of the Lothians remained tied to animal products, to wool, hides and so on, processed in the household, and in a backyard rather than a workshop. Perhaps any inkling of a more commercial society met with local suspicion; nor could new skills and products be conjured up out of thin air. So King David gave an especially warm welcome to foreign immigrants to his burgh, with reliefs on their rents to entice them. All burgesses – whether native Scots, or else English, Flemish or French – were to be free men in the sole sense the mind of the age admitted, that is, free tenants of the king. He set up a burgh court where they could safeguard their privileges. There they had a right to plead before their peers, their fellow burgesses. To this as yet limited extent they began to govern themselves.

The burgh was favoured in other ways. Since trade could never develop far in the form of barter, currency was needed. King David's reign saw Scotland's first silver pennies minted in Edinburgh, as well as at Berwick, Perth, Roxburgh and Stirling; they bore his head, with a sceptre. Nor could trade develop far without some sort of legal framework. Scotland as yet had no single code of laws; the several constituents of the nation still followed their own, Celtic or Germanic, inherited from their fathers. This at least meant there was no problem in adding on a new code specially for the new urban constituent of the nation. It was the Laws of the Four Burghs (Edinburgh together with Berwick, Roxburgh and Stirling) that came to govern Scots civic life in the Middle Ages. Berwick and Roxburgh had doubtless already regulated themselves in some ways, but for the rest these laws represented still another innovation of King David's. He took the oldest of them almost word for word from a corresponding charter at Newcastle-on-Tyne, while it yet stood on the brink of becoming a part of his kingdom as he governed it in right of his son from 1136 to 1152. With much else, that aspect of the novel urbanity of Scotland was owed to him. Scotland's thoroughly modern monarch bolstered her security and independence so as to place her on a par with other European kingdoms.[40]

※

Cultural benefits, too, flowed from that security and independence. The Scots seem always to have been what they still are, a male chauvinist society, at this stage with values running from barbaric brutality to a heroic ideal. But, if only at the topmost level, at least some notice began to be taken of the other half of the human race. In noble circles courtly love blossomed, the social and literary conventions of an idealized feminine virtue matched by an idealized masculine gallantry. If this sounds soppy, it did improve on what had gone before. Courtly love would in fact spread through Europe from these improbable sources in the British Isles recently subjected to Norman militarism. Even knights in shining armour needed a little time off from conquest and slaughter. Now they might swoon with scarce a qualm into the embrace of their damsels.

Whatever might have happened in real life, courtly love inspired literature that was enriched also because it drew on the Matter of Britain, on Arthur, Tristan and the other legendary figures. Tristan emerges out of a presumably oral prehistory in the poem named after him and written in Old French, about the time of the Norman Conquest, by Thomas of Britain. It survives only in fragments. Nothing is known of the poet, but he was imitated in France, Germany, Italy and Scandinavia with works counting among the finest of medieval European literature. In Scotland, if Tristan had been forgotten meanwhile, he made a comeback now. Workmen digging at Perth in 1921 discovered an old well in which they found, dropped ages ago, a medieval mirror-case decorated with human figures. These were named: Tristrem, Isoude and Marcius.[41]

Even the tradition of Tristan hardly compares with the huge, to this day undying, appeal of the Arthurian romances. One of them, the *Roman de Fergus*, originated in Scotland. Somebody calling himself Guillaume le Clerc wrote it, also in Old French. Scholars think it was composed to entertain the court of King David's son, William the Lion, by William Malveisin, a royal clerk who rose to be Bishop of Glasgow and of St Andrews. The poem goes out of its way to praise the qualities of folk in Galloway, so it may have been meant in particular to please Alan of Galloway, a friend of the king; they could have listened to it together in the great hall of Edinburgh Castle. Yet it has a popular flavour too, so might also have been aimed at those immigrant burgesses who, when Edinburgh began, made it in part a French-speaking community.

At any rate, the *Roman de Fergus* is the first piece of non-Celtic vernacular literature from Scotland. Like its counterpart in Old Welsh, the *Gododdin*, it is hardly known today because of its exotic language. It survived in two manuscripts, now held in Paris and at Chantilly. Published in 1841 by the Abbotsford Club, it came out in the original Old French without translation or commentary, so was not easy to identify as part of the national literature. It made no impression before a flurry of scholarly interest in it arose towards the end of the twentieth century. All the same, Scottish it is.

The Fergus of the title is a folk-hero, a poor, simple man who rises to be a knight of King Arthur. The tales of his trials, troubles and travels do ramble, yet in the cause of subverting the courtly virtues they seem on the surface to extol. Both nobles and peasants are sent up. Parody is the great virtue of the text. In that Fergus originates a Scottish type. It is not hard to find other such characters in the future literature of Edinburgh: in Sir Walter Scott, say Caleb Balderstone in *The Bride of Lammermoor* (1819), or James Hogg, say Robin Ruthven in *The Private Memoirs and Confessions of a Justified Sinner* (1823), or Robert Louis Stevenson, say David Balfour in *Kidnapped* (1886).

The *Roman de Fergus* is useful to history, too. Its plot takes Fergus from Galloway in the south-west of Scotland to Dunnottar Castle in the north-east, by way of Edinburgh:

> *Tout Lodian a trespassé*
> *A un manoir est ostelé*
> *C'on dist le Castel as Puceles...*
> *Par le matin dou castel s'en ist*
> *Et vient à un port desour mer*
> *Que jou oï molt apeler*
> *De plusieurs le Port la Roïne.*
> *Illucques Lodian define*
> *Et Escoce est de l'autre part;*
> *La mer ces deux terres depart.*

> He passed right through Lothian
> And lodged at a hall
> Which is called the Maiden Castle...
> In the morning he left the castle
> And came to a port on the sea
> Which I have often heard
> People call Queensferry.
> This is where Lothian ends
> And on the other side is Scotland;
> The sea separates these two lands.[42]

Since the poet shows everywhere a mastery of local detail, he can be trusted when he says that in his time Lothian and Edinburgh with it were not yet thought of as belonging to Scotland, which only began at the Forth. The old frontier of Northumbria still ran in people's minds. But Scotland would soon become synonymous with the whole realm of the Kings of Scots. At length they would settle on Edinburgh for their capital.

CHAPTER TWO

'PRECIPITOUS CITY'

(Robert Louis Stevenson)

ON 20 AUGUST 1769, the philosopher David Hume wrote to the economist Adam Smith announcing that, after years away in France and England, he was back home in Scotland. Paris he would always miss but London not at all, with its 'barbarians . . . by the banks of the Thames'. Anyway, he was to stay for the rest of his days in Edinburgh. He meant to devote his time to what he unabashedly called 'my great talent for cookery'. Ever since being feted by the French he had fancied himself as a chef – and not through any slavish imitation of their *haute cuisine* but through taking homely Scottish fare to unexampled heights, applying to it the culinary techniques he learned in the mecca of gastronomy. While adept at recipes from the classical repertoire, he actually preferred to pep up traditional Scots specialities: 'For beef and cabbage (a charming dish) and old mutton and old claret, nobody excels me. I also make sheep's head broth in a manner that Mr Keith speaks of it for eight days after, and the Duc de Nivernois would bind himself apprentice to my lass to learn it.' The invitations to Hume's elegant dinners, matchless for food, wine and talk, were soon like gold-dust in the Scottish capital.[1]

Hume, aged fifty-eight, felt happy and grew fat. Another friend, Adam Ferguson, mocked him in his essay 'An Excursion into the Highlands'. This is supposed to tell the tale of how Ferguson once led a party of the enlightened from Edinburgh on a hike through his native Atholl, at the southern edge of the Grampian Mountains. Of Hume this must strike the modern reader as an improbable idea. A glance at any portrait of him, with his jovial jawline and tubby tummy, will show a man little given to climbing hills and probably unable to. Ferguson's fiction is, rather, the peg for a philosophical discussion that he would better have set in some agreeable salon. Amid such surroundings Hume looked so content that others in Edinburgh would not believe it. He was an atheist, after all: did his conviction of an inevitable end to mortal felicity cast no shadow over him? The question so nagged at the shameless literary gadfly, James Boswell, that he would turn up beside Hume's deathbed in 1776 and ask 'if the thought of annihilation never gave him any uneasiness. He said not the least, no more than the thought that he had not been.'[2]

This was the home life of Edinburgh's men of letters: native sagacity mixed with cosmopolitan wisdom, whether from the philosophy of the past, acquaintance with great minds of the present or revolutionary insights for the future. Some writings can come across as a trifle bloodless, with arguments conducted at a level of high theory. Yet often the approach is softened by a human touch and by the authors' actual or implicit reference to the ordinary life they knew best, that of their own Scotland – and not least in the eight volumes of Hume's biggest though not greatest work, his *History of England* (1754–62, often revised in later editions). He embarked on the project for fear he was failing to make it as a philosopher, so he had to generate income somehow.

While called *History of England*, it often brings in Scotland – much more than any such history by an Englishman would have done, then or now. In itself that casts light on some ambiguities the Scottish Enlightenment had to face, not least concerning its own country (which in fact it often preferred to ignore, passing quickly on to more exalted and less tricky themes). Now and again the *History* strikes a patriotic note, yet elsewhere sympathy for a Scotsman's point of view is quite lacking. Seeing how Hume supported the Union with England of 1707, it may be all the more peculiar that he chose not a British but a narrower Anglocentric approach. Odder still is the way he treats his country with ill-disguised contempt in some of the passages he does devote to it. For example, after an encouraging overture on 'the curiosity of all civilised nations' about 'the exploits of their ancestors', he takes the Germanic forebears of the Scots as the only ones worth talking about. In fact his sole comment on the early history of Scotland deals with the incursion of the Northumbrians:

How far [their] dominions extended into the country now called Scotland is uncertain; but it cannot be doubted that all the Lowlands ... were peopled in great measure from Germany; though the expeditions by the several Saxon adventurers have escaped the record of history. The language spoken in these countries, which is purely Saxon, is a stronger proof of this event that can be opposed by the imperfect, or rather the fabulous annals which are obtruded by the Scottish historians.[3]

Hume finds nothing whatever to say on the rest of the peoples of that time, neither Britons nor Picts nor Gaels. An alliance of the last two in the end got the better of the Northumbrians, yet he has them appear only as colourless 'other inhabitants of the island'. On the precise racial make-up of modern Scots, he merely remarks: 'We shall not enter into any detail on so uninteresting a subject.'[4]

But how does Hume approach the episode most crucial to the existence of his nation, the Wars of Independence? 'If the Scots ever had, before this period, any real history, worthy of the name, except what they pick up from scattered passages of the English historians, these events, however minute, yet bring the only foreign transactions of the nation, which might deserve a place in it.' The text later notes in passing how most early records of Scotland had been destroyed during struggles with the English, usually by the English. This hardly troubles Hume the historian: 'It is not probable that a nation, so rude and unpolished, would be possessed of any history, which deserves much to be regretted.' Thus did enlightened Edinburgh look back on, not to say down on, medieval Edinburgh.[5]

❧

In that Edinburgh (to be precise, on 18 March 1286) Alexander III, King of Scots, sat in the castle drinking his blood-red wine.[6] He was the great-great-grandson of King David. His grandfather, William the Lion, had reigned for half a century (longer than any other Scottish monarch), growing ever more saintly. His father, Alexander II, had sought to extend his effective rule over the Highlands and islands (he died on Kerrera in 1249) and maintained good relations with England by marrying again into its royal family. Alexander III came to the throne aged eight. This succession of a minor was untroubled,

which is more than can be said of several English successions in
the Middle Ages. Scotland in the thirteenth century had been on the
whole a peaceful, prospering country.

To some, the dawn of 18 March 1286 portended an end to peace
and prosperity. The sun rose on a wild, windy Scotland, in other
words on a northern springtime, but to the superstitious the tempest
confirmed old wives' tales that this would be the Day of Judgement.
Alexander III had heard such tales and jested about them as he later
sat down to dine after a meeting with the lords of his council. The
conclusion of official business let him think, though, about sex
rather than sin – marital sex, that is to say, with the young French-
woman, Yolande of Dreux, who was his wife of less than six months.
He had left her at the royal manor of Kinghorn on the other side of
the Firth of Forth, twenty miles away by bad roads and the ferry. He
was the sole survivor of his first family, a wife, Margaret of England,
two sons and a daughter who had married King Eric II of Norway.
Alexander III's blood now ran only in his granddaughter Margaret,
the three-year-old Maid of Norway, far away across the North Sea.
The Scots nobles had accepted her as his heir but it would be easier
for him, them and the nation if he could father a sturdy boy on his
new wife, and as soon as possible – like tonight. He suddenly wanted
to go to Yolande. His counsellors told him not to: there was a gale,
it would snow. But political necessity stiffened physical desire, and
he set off into the gathering dusk with just three esquires for
company.

When Alexander III reached Dalmeny the ferryman, too, urged
him to turn back. The king asked if he felt afraid. This cryptic
Charon replied: 'I could not die better than in the company of your
father's son.' As darkness fell they rowed across the rough waters of
the firth to the royal burgh of Inverkeithing. There they were greeted
by a member of the king's household, Alexander le Saucier, master of
his sauce-kitchen, doubling as bailie of the burgh. He in his turn
begged Alexander III not to go on but to stay the night at his house.
Already Scots of whatever rank, nobles, burgesses or peasants,
addressed their monarch as an equal; it would astonish Englishmen
in later times. Alexander the cook now said to Alexander the king:
'My lord, what are you doing in such weather and darkness? How

many times have I tried to persuade you that midnight travelling will bring you no good?'

Alexander III ignored the plea and pressed on with his escort, guided by two local men, along the rough coastal road towards Kinghorn. What happened then is unknown, except that the escort and guides lost him in the storm. Next morning searchers found him on the shore, dead of a broken neck. His kingdom now lacked a king, a state for which its feudal constitution knew no remedy. During more than a century virile monarchs had led and bound it together by exacting the fealty of its turbulent nobles and, through them, of the people below. As the crown passed to a sickly infant in a foreign land, all stood in peril.

※

The first task was to see to the government of the country while it awaited the arrival of the Maid of Norway. To Scone, historic seat of the monarchy, was summoned an assembly of earls, barons and clergy, which defined itself in its acts as 'the community of the realm'.[7] It chose six guardians, two from each estate, as caretakers until a new sovereign could be enthroned in due form. Meanwhile their authority stemmed in effect from the nation as a whole, so they felt entitled to hold Parliaments, see to security, send out embassies and exact an oath of allegiance. One of their aims was good relations with King Edward I of England, who seemed to share their wish. In fact he would propose in 1284 that Margaret should marry his own heir, Edward, whom he had just created Prince of Wales. The guardians felt not averse so long as they could be sure of their country's future independence and integrity. They thought to have got the guarantees they wanted with Edward I in 1290 in the Treaty of Birgham, which set up the marital alliance he proposed, yet affirmed Scotland would remain 'separate, apart and free in herself without subjection to the English kingdom'. She would still live by her own laws under her own sovereign (even if, as consort of the King of England, this sovereign would often be absent). The treaty certainly contained no hint of English overlordship. And Edward I ratified it at once in a Parliament summoned to Northampton. But within months the worst possible news reached the guardians: on the voyage over the North Sea, Margaret had died in Orkney. Her body, taken back to Bergen, was already buried in the cathedral there.[8]

What now? Scotland had to have a monarch yet there was no undisputed successor, only (in the end) fourteen rival claimants. Some proved to be more serious than others but from the outset two led the field, Robert Bruce and John Balliol. Bruce was the fifth lord of Annandale in succession to his namesake who had been the friend and favourite of King David. The family stood so close to the royal house that the fourth lord of Annandale had married into it, to Isabel, King David's great-granddaughter. This was the basis of Bruce's claim. A still vigorous man of over sixty, he could, in addition to everything else, offer a secure succession of his own. He had a son, another Robert, Earl of Carrick by marriage, and a grandson, Robert again, future liberator of his nation, then sixteen years old, having just attained the formal status of knight, with his own horse, armour and esquires. Balliol, lord of Galloway, could boast a superior claim. He, too, had been born to a female descendant of King David's, Devorguilla, foundress of Balliol College, Oxford, but in a line senior to that of the Bruces, also with sons in the next generation.

Scots feared not so much a victory by either leading candidate as the risk that a dispute between them might degenerate into civil war. This was why the guardians took the fateful step of turning to Edward I as arbiter. He had so far worn sheep's clothing, but now the wolf inside cast it off. He manoeuvred Balliol on to the throne of Scotland under terms reducing him to a vassal of his own, Toom Tabard ('empty surcoat'), as the people said. The train of events tore the community of the realm apart, with the nobility all at odds and the commoners fearing the worst, which they would indeed soon suffer. Edward I carried out, in effect, a bloodless conquest of Scotland. In 1291, having ensured that he was recognized as her feudal superior, he made by way of Edinburgh a short, triumphant progress round the country. Then he left Balliol to it.

Balliol sought to be a good King of Scots, but Edward I proved so unreasonable that a breach between them was not long coming. War followed. The Scots had taken the precaution of turning for support to the French: this was the Auld Alliance. Edward I had to fight on two fronts, then, but affected not to mind. He tackled

Scotland first and advanced in the spring of 1296 to Berwick, still the nation's biggest and richest burgh. He besieged it for a month, stormed it and massacred its citizens. He moved on to rout the Scots army that met him at Dunbar on 27 April. A week later he occupied Edinburgh.

By midsummer Balliol surrendered. Edward I now set out on a much more radical policy of expunging Scotland's nationhood and statehood. This was how most of her early records vanished, into the flames. What the English chose not to destroy they stole, bearing back a huge booty: treasury, jewels, plate, regalia. It included St Margaret's Black Rood from Edinburgh and the Stone of Destiny from Scone: the stone would be held in Westminster Abbey, inside St Edward's throne, until a government in London more worried about Scotland returned it in 1996. Into that castle Edward I put a garrison; as he did also at Berwick, Roxburgh, Stirling and other strongholds.[9]

🌂

Yet the fight had not gone out of the Scots. Hardly a year passed before they rose up under William Wallace, who gathered enough support to defeat the English at Stirling Bridge. While his rebellion had started north of the Forth, he seems to have reckoned Lothian was above all where he had to win. At any rate his military manoeuvres most clearly menaced Edinburgh or the other occupied citadels. And it was in this region he risked another battle with the English, once they came after him with a big army, at Falkirk in 1297. His defeat reduced him to guerrilla warfare, which would end with his treacherous capture and gruesome execution in 1305. All these events had in the end served only to strengthen the enemy's hold on the Lothians.

Robert Bruce, seventh of Annandale and second of Carrick, the knightly novice of 1290, took over as the leader of national resistance – and as King of Scots. Reviving his family's claim to the succession, he descended hastily on Scone to get himself enthroned in 1306. He soon transformed the military situation so as to push the English on to the defensive, though not before a disheartening prelude of setbacks. The enemy at first pursued him into the northern or western fastnesses of Scotland and finally offshore to Rathlin Island

– where he regained the will to win as he watched a spider spinning and respinning its web. He at length ventured back to the mainland, to his own Carrick. Here, too, the English had moved in as conquerors. But, with long lines of supply across rough country, their hold over the outlying regions of Scotland was slacker.

In May 1307 King Robert won his first big victory at Loudoun Hill in Ayrshire, against Aymer de Valence, Edward I's deputy in Scotland. By skilful choice of field he forced the English to fight on a narrow front where their superior strength counted for nothing. The Scots attacked them so fiercely that they turned and ran. It was not a tactic the king would repeat, however. On the contrary, in future he avoided pitched battles where he would have to fight against the odds. Instead he too waged a guerrilla war, surprising his adversaries, raiding their resources, unsettling their forces and, if need be, scorching the earth of Scotland at whatever cost to her own people.

It helped that the arch-enemy now passed from the scene. In July 1307, Edward I died aged sixty-nine at Burgh-on-Sands, just short of the border, as he prepared another expedition into Scotland. There was no mistaking the change from him to his son, Edward II. The campaign planned by the old monarch had got only as far as Ayrshire when the new monarch abandoned it: he would not be seen again in Scotland for three years. That left King Robert the scope to embark on a long march round the outer regions of the country, with many cheeky raids on unwary foes. He aimed to put heart in the Scots and to wear the English down until they decided that they had had enough, that this war could not be won, that they had better go home. Almost from the first he met with success.

Straight after Loudoun Hill the people on Bruce's own, formally forfeit lands in Annandale were ambushing English convoys as they moved across country. By the end of 1307 lords and peasants alike in the central Borders had 'traitorously joined Robert de Brus'. This meant he already dominated the south of Scotland from the coast of Ayrshire over to the English strongholds at Roxburgh and Jedburgh. As for the north of Scotland, soon only castles and defensible burghs held out against him. In the summer of 1308 the Scots captured Aberdeen. That denied the port to English ships and reopened Scottish traffic with Europe. By the spring of 1309, the king could call his first Parliament at St Andrews, which sent to Philip IV of France, renewing the Auld Alliance.[10]

English control of Scotland depended on the occupation of castles. At his zenith Edward I had held forty of them, big and small. Only slowly could the Scots retake them. By the end of 1310 King Robert is known to have seized and destroyed no more than nine lesser strongholds. According to tall tales Scots would tell by their firesides long after the war had ended, the castles were often surprised by the tricks of folk-heroes. True or not, two things can be read into such stories. One is that the king, though setting out from nothing, found no trouble winning the loyalty of the Scots people wherever they felt free to give it. The other is that he still did not have the men or means to storm a castle or fort of any strength. If he did manage to, he would order its demolition. At least each of these rare prizes marked a milestone, making it harder for the enemy to restore and maintain the occupation at the previous level. This may help to account for Edward II's long torpor in the face of Scottish resurgence. There was little he could do to win back initiative or territory without a programme, costly and toilsome, of building or rebuilding castles.

In its strategic situation Edinburgh was the most crucial castle of all. The English, though ensconced in it for over a decade, now found it harder to supply, since it had no harbour. But even then they could scarcely have seen much reason to suppose their hold on it would be less than permanent, here in the heart of the region where the Kingdom of the Scots had reached its full extent before being smashed. At a maximum, 325 of Edward II's soldiers manned the ramparts; they would have to do no more than sit out the following years of guerrilla warfare, their defences being far too redoubtable to fall to what force the Scots could muster, or so it seemed. Inside the Castle an English constable held the command and in the burgh below an English sheriff laid down the law. They were two among the swarm of alien officials sent to control this cowed country for its conqueror. They acted, or sought to act, as if their government was unquestioned, and for that it had to wear a formidable face.[11]

Edinburgh guarded, along with counterparts at Berwick, Roxburgh and Stirling, a Fortress Lothian, a close grouping of strongholds at the points of an irregular quadrangle – the bastion of English rule in Scotland. Large castles round the edge were supported inside, especially on the main routes, by smaller ones at Cavers, Dirleton, Dunbar, Haddington, Linlithgow, Livingston, Luffness, Selkirk and Yester: this was defence in depth, by any standards. The complex could be supplied out of the food, stores and weapons held in security at Berwick, the gateway from England. If transports overland were harassed, or even vanished into insurgent hands, Edward II's ships still ruled the waves. All this came together to create a powerful position, constantly reinforced and consolidated.[12]

❧

Yet the position would not prove impregnable. On the contrary, it crumbled as King Robert drew near. Once the people made their true allegiance clear, English garrisons had to take their security into their own hands. They could not be overwhelmed yet they needed to strike deals with the locals hemming them round if they were to follow their orders from London and hold out. The term used in documents of the time for the currency of the deals they struck is *tributa*. To translate this as tribute, in the normal modern sense of what is paid in submission by one party to the other, hardly conveys its sense; these garrisons did not think to recognize the King of Scots. What the term really means is blackmail for a temporary truce.

Edward II was tempted into authorizing the truces because he had no other means of supporting his commanders as they sought to shore up shaky positions. The lords of his council even wrote out a definition of the policy in 1308. They ordained that, while their royal master should not himself enter into truces with a mere rebel like Sir Robert de Brus, 'wardens of Scotland may take such as long as possible, as they have done hitherto of their own power or by commission'. The council kidded itself it was dealing with temporary accords on a small scale in a faraway country of which it knew nothing. Tactical trade-offs could not impugn English sovereignty, of course, but amounted to no more than a regrettable military necessity winning time for supplies to be dispatched or garrisons to be reinforced. It was not even as if the king could be bound by his own truces, as the opposite parties to them would have to accept:

'He may break the truce at leisure, if others will yield this point; but if they will not, the truce is to be made without it.' It was all wishful thinking. Edward II had to have truces because he was incapable of effective action. He did not need to pay for them, so they were cheaper than campaigning. And, as he did not need to pay for them, he was not obliged to raise taxes for them; otherwise he would have had to turn to his Parliament and make all sorts of concessions on domestic issues to his ever stroppier English subjects. He preferred to tolerate and even encourage truces.[13]

This strategy was a bit too easy for a king 400 miles away who did not have to face the consequences on the ground. In fact he was making a big mistake. In the first place the truces gave King Robert legitimate authority in Scotland – and among English occupiers, let alone native Scots. Whatever Edward II and his council might have had to say, they could no longer claim to be acting on some transcendent constitutional or political principle; for them it was now a matter of taking what they could get, of compromise in other words. In the second place the truces gave King Robert the things he most lacked, a steady flow of food and funds for his fighters. He had from the outset shown no scruple in extorting the resources he needed for a war of liberation, if only because at first it amounted to little more than his personal struggle to survive. The results justified his behaviour to himself and to others.

In sum, the truces could not solve Edward II's problems. After a year or two he even turned to the alternative they were meant to avoid: again it made no difference. In 1310 he mounted another invasion to consolidate his hold on Lothian and chase the Scots forces away. This in itself showed how King Robert had by now more or less cleared the English from the North and West of Scotland. Anyway, Edward II set out too late in the campaigning season, then spent his time on a leisurely progress round his garrisons to replenish and reorganize them. He got as far west as Renfrew, before retiring by way of Linlithgow and Edinburgh and taking ship to Berwick at the beginning of November. It was hard for him to venture forth again because he had run out of forage for his horses and because most of his soldiers went home, being required by feudal law to serve only for forty days. Faced with all this, King Robert had followed his normal tactic: he retreated northwards and would not be drawn into a fight. He reappeared once the English withdrew. With what force was left to him Edward II again chased away the Scots. They still would not offer battle, so he settled in at Berwick. He would stay there until the summer of 1311, when he was obliged to turn south, with nothing achieved, to meet an English Parliament.[14]

※

King Robert then found his chance to close in on Lothian. Probably the region had not recently suffered as much as other parts of Scotland. Some historians have supposed it assented to alien occupation because its people spoke a dialect of English. But they had never belonged to the kingdom of England as such (rather to the old Northumbria). Nor had they ever been subject to the Norman Kings of England, those forebears of Edward II who came over from France only in 1066, half a century after Lothian was annexed by Scotland; they could have felt no hereditary fealty to Edward. On the contrary, when their allegiance was tested by crisis from 1290, they remained true to Scotland right through the first phase of war, largely fought out round them.

This patriotic allegiance had become harder to maintain, of course. The English occupation did not spare the custom of the country: Scots landowners refusing to truckle to it were forfeited in favour of English incomers on the make. Feudalism imposed on the lieges an obligation to follow the lords, yet the injustice of what went on aroused some unprecedented defiance, not to mention great courage, on the people's part. In a case where records survive at Ballencrieff and Luffness in East Lothian, a new English superior had to resort to the eviction of tenants suspected of sympathy for the resistance.[15]

Edward II might have found the situation hard to grasp, but a Cumbrian source, the Lanercost Chronicle, had no trouble understanding it:

> In all this fighting the Scots were so divided that often a father was with the Scots and his son with the English, or one brother was with the Scots and another with the English, or even one individual was first on one side and then on the other. But all or most of the Scots who were with the English were with them

insincerely or to save their lands in England: for their hearts if
not their bodies were always with their own people.[16]

King Robert not only harassed the forces of occupation but also
carried the war into their own country, on raids far across the border.
In Northumberland and Cumberland the people were soon offering
him their own allegiance, not because they wanted to become Scots
but because it was their one way to ward him off. For his part he
never distinguished between the Scots still under English rule in the
Lothians and the actual English across the border. On both alike
he waged a guerrilla war where nobody was safe.

Away from Edinburgh or the other strongholds, then, the hapless
people of the Lothians could not count on English deterrence, let
alone protection. Isolated and unarmed, they were sitting targets for
intimidation. No wonder they and their lords also began to offer and
to take truces, in other words, to seek guarantees that King Robert's
forces would not attack them. Little information about these truces
in the region has come down to us: details of who entered into them,
how much they cost and how long they lasted remain sketchy. But
in the three years up to the Battle of Bannockburn in 1314 there
were at least five.

One lasted four months, in the winter of 1311–12, after Edward
II had headed south from Berwick. King Robert pursued him in the
sense of mounting in his wake a long and ruinous raid, 'destroying
everything', down as far as Corbridge in Northumberland. He black-
mailed the locals for immunity from fire and sword, exacting his
price in money and cattle (which might be moved back north with
ease). If they could not or would not pay he let his fighters loose on
them to loot, wreck and burn – though as far as possible he spared
their lives.[17]

But in this campaign King Robert wrought just as much havoc
on the Lothians. The English after all still ran the civil administration, such as it was, in the sheriffdoms of Edinburgh, Berwick and
Roxburgh. Where local landowners, including Scots, supported the
regime their tenants normally felt bound to follow. Among those
landowners figured Patrick, Earl of Dunbar, who had submitted
to Edward I in 1291 and who afterwards refused to renounce this
allegiance (even though others who swore fealty at the same time,

notably the Bruces, had done so). For his stubborn loyalty he now paid a high and rising price. Yet he would maintain it until he died, and only with the Battle of Bannockburn did his son come over again to the King of Scots. Dunbar had a neighbour and kinsman, Adam Gordon of Gordon, who followed the same course – and was still alive after 1314 for his misguided chivalry to be appreciated at least by King Robert, his new sovereign. He gave here an example of his often incredible generosity, making Gordon an ambassador to Rome.

That lay in the future, however, and in 1311 neither Dunbar nor Gordon felt their lands and people could suffer again what they had just suffered as King Robert rampaged through on his way south. So they sought to come to terms with him. As a result, until February 1312 'those of the earldom of Dunbar ... who were still of the King of England's peace, were very heavily taxed for a truce'. This implicitly specified, in a salving of the two lords' consciences, that they were not and should not become subjects of the King of Scots; their action was later justified as essential 'for the safety of the country and their allegiance'. Both sides got something out of the truce, then. In fact Edward II would authorize Dunbar and Gordon to renegotiate it for a further term. This they evidently managed, though we do not know how long the fresh truce lasted. Later in the year, English sheriffs and constables in the Lothians were ordered to contribute cash to what was probably a third agreement, with Edinburgh paying one-quarter of the total; at any rate a truce of unknown duration came to an end in June 1313. A shorter one of fifteen days followed. Another, lasting five months, came after; it cost the earldom of Dunbar 1,000 quarters of corn.[18]

Under these pressures the life of the Lothians, the farming and the markets, began to break down, even where the occupation held: an inquisition of 1312 showed falls of one-half in the value of the estates forfeited by Scots to Englishmen. Yet the hardships the people felt forced to sign up to by the truces failed to give them the protection from violence they expected in exchange. On the ground, the English commanders would not be bound by anything agreed among mere Scots. Their soldiers seized the crops meant as the currency of the truces and sold them for profit. Demoralization was one motive here, to be sure. Some garrisons had been cut off and could not be paid for months on end. The soldiers took out their frustration and resentment on the nearest targets, not on invisible guerrillas but on innocents in the wrong place at the wrong time. The commanders seemed ready to condone this, being probably in the same state of mind themselves. When Edward II told them off for oppressing the people still in his allegiance, they merely claimed his orders had never got through. The people of the Lothians not only had to pay for the Scots resistance to stay away; now they also had to pay for the English occupiers not to molest them.[19]

❧

Soldiers from Edinburgh's garrison were among the worst behaved. They abused, beat and robbed the townsfolk, or slammed them in jail and demanded ransoms. This all had a drastic effect on the economy: in the last full year of English rule the burgh could cough up a paltry £35 in taxes, less than what was paid by the smaller Roxburgh. There the people had to fend off both sides. In a plaintive petition, they complained of being forced to find one ransom for the release of abducted locals, then another to avoid Scottish reprisals for an English breach of their truce. When the burgh's aldermen went to complain to the commander of the castle, they were locked up as well. Gordon of Gordon remonstrated so fiercely that he, too, was detained. At least a big landowner could get redress. Gordon went to Westminster to protest in person to Edward II, who sacked the commander and issued the troops with fresh orders to desist from any action likely to put truces at risk. The king made up their arrears of pay. But all he sent the local loyal Scots was an official letter of thanks. Matters stood no better at Berwick. Here the soldiers picked on 'upland people' who came into the market; if unable to pay protection on the spot, they were killed and their bodies thrown in the River Tweed. This reign of terror could not hide the fact that, if security had to be bought, it was better bought from King Robert than from Edward II.[20]

The English were losing, yet still held on to Lothian's castles. These the Scots could hardly besiege. They had none of the latest weaponry, like siege-engines to hurl rocks at the fortifications, nor skilled operatives to work such machines if they had had them, nor even food to feed soldiers sitting round the walls for weeks on end.

But Scots take pride in their ingenuity and bravado. With nothing better to hand they fell back on the mere tools of their civilian trades, on rope to make scaling ladders and iron hooks to fit to the ends. The makeshift *matériel* was light enough to be toted about by a couple of men who could sneak beneath the walls of a fortress during a long winter's night, snoop round until they found a good spot and hurl the ladders on to the parapet. Their mates could then scramble up and over the defences. The first attack mounted on this rough and ready plan would have been sensational if it had succeeded. Berwick, hard by the border, was the base-camp for the entire English occupation. On the night of 6 December 1312, King Robert sent his soldiers to break in. But a dog barking within the walls alarmed the English and frustrated the Scots. Berwick would become Scottish again, but not until 1318.[21]

Stirling was the next target. King Robert's brother, Edward, besieged the town in the spring of 1313, though he preferred to rely on conventional methods. He, too, was a chivalrous man, if headstrong. Instead of resorting to ladders and hooks, he committed the Scots to a pact menacing their cautious strategy of the last seven years. This would indeed change the whole course of the war as they had fought it so far, in avoidance of pitched battle with the English. Edward got a reprimand from Robert, but it was too late. The deal with the commander of Stirling – himself a Scot, Sir Philip Moubray – gave the garrison a year's grace up to Midsummer's Day, 1314. If by that date no English army had come within three miles of the castle, Moubray would accept his position could not be held and surrender. Perhaps Edward Bruce thought he was buying Stirling cheap, for in England relations between the monarchy and the nobility had by now more or less broken down. Yet neither party to that domestic dispute would hesitate to turn and meet a foreign foe – least of all the Scots who might be forced on to a field where, of course, they could be beaten once and for all. That field would be Bannockburn on 23 June 1314.

The Scots' genius for improvisation meanwhile came good at Roxburgh and Edinburgh. Both were equipped to withstand long sieges, yet they fell within a month of each other. In the night of 19–20 February 1314, a force led by the king's boon companion, James Douglas, the Black Douglas, crawled on all fours up to the walls of Roxburgh wrapped in dark cloaks to hide their armour. They carried their rope ladders, here fashioned by a man called Sim of the Ledows, who had the honour of being first over the top. The clatter of the grappling hook alerted a sentry who came to inspect just as Sim clambered over the rampart. With a knife he skewered the Englishman and the Scots swarmed in. Since it was Shrove Tuesday, the garrison was having a party to prepare for the privations of Lent. The Scots killed or captured them before they knew what had happened. The castle was slighted.

Edinburgh Castle fell three weeks later to Thomas Randolph, Earl of Moray. He had been besieging it for a while. The English troops' morale had sunk so low they came to suspect their commander, Piers Libaud, a French mercenary, would betray them; and they might have been right, for after the Castle was taken Libaud entered the Scots' service, only to be shortly executed for treason. For now, his men clapped the shifty Frenchman in irons and found another officer to take over. The siege wore on until March 1314, and still Moray made no progress. Then, spurred by Douglas's feat at Roxburgh, he offered a reward to anybody who could scale the wall. Though this rose straight from the lofty Rock, a man for the moment appeared. He was William Francis, a son of Edinburgh brought up in the Castle, where his father had served. As a lad, seeing a girl down the High Street, Willie had often climbed in after dark, so knew just how to do it. On the night of March 14 the Scots staged a mock attack before the fortifications, which the garrison rushed to repel. Meanwhile, Willie and the real assailants inched their way up the precipice on the northern side and swung their rope ladders over the parapet. At the top they dealt with the sentries, headed for the gates and opened them to the force of Scots on Castle Hill. They killed all the English. King Robert, in line with his usual policy, had the Castle levelled to the ground. For a couple of decades cattle grazed on the Rock.[22]

❧

The war would go on for another dozen years and more. Not until 1327 did both sides seek peace. In England a new king, Edward III, had been put on the throne by the coup of his mother, Queen Philippa, and her lover, Roger Mortimer. They locked Edward II up in a castle where he would meet a grisly end. But a new monarch meant the old one's rubbish could be thrown out. For his part, King Robert now wanted a settlement all the more eagerly because he sensed he was dying, and would have to leave his country to his four-year-old son, David. So the terms he proposed looked generous to a fault. They would be written into the Treaty of Edinburgh that brought to an end three decades of the national struggle for liberation.

The prime provision was for King Robert to be recognized as sovereign in Scotland without qualification; that is, Edward III had to surrender all claim to the country. Otherwise the Scots met the English on whatever terms might stick. For example, young David was offered in marriage to Edward III's little sister, Joan, so the royal families could be conjoined again; the English avidly agreed. There was even to be some sort of alliance between Scotland and England. That would prove a dead letter, but meanwhile the terms salved English pride.

King Robert made sure all the same that to sign the treaty the English would have to come to him rather than he go to them. Beforehand he opened a Parliament in Edinburgh in February 1328. It was the twelfth of his reign: a creditable tally seeing how much else he had had to do, but he valued this representation of his people. He summoned 'bishops, abbots, earls, barons, freeholders and six sufficient persons of the various burghal communities specially empowered for the purpose'. He had invited burgesses to Parliaments before, if not invariably. From now on their presence became normal, and sealed an exchange of royal favour for commercial sustenance of the state. Two weeks later the English envoys arrived with authority to settle all outstanding points at issue. King Robert was ill, indeed bed-ridden by now. The two sides signed the peace on March 17 'in a chamber within the precincts of the monastery of Holyrood in Edinburgh where the lord king was lying'.[23]

Edinburgh at this point was more of a capital than ever before. Even so, King Robert did not tarry. He was a man of the West, of the Gàidhealtachd. There he returned to end his days. Just over a year later, on 7 June 1329, he would die in the rustic retreat he had built himself at Cardross by the River Clyde, within sight of the mountains.

But before King Robert died he did Edinburgh a last great service. While it had been playing the role of capital for the treaty, all the action took place at Holyrood. The case could scarcely have been otherwise, since the Castle lay in ruins. And it seems unlikely the burgh had yet recovered from the English occupation. Now, on 28 May 1329, ten days before his death, the King of Scots in effect refounded Edinburgh by granting it a new charter. Such was his status as liberator and hero that the burgesses would hardly have objected if he had strengthened royal control over them. Yet, on the contrary, he offered them more freedom: what a great man!

᠅

By the charter of 1329 the burgh was 'given, granted and to feuferm let' to its burgesses. It also made over to them a port at the mouth of the Water of Leith. Thrown in were mills and other pertinents, in 'all their right meiths [boundaries] and marches, with all the commodities, liberties and easements' they had enjoyed in the time of Alexander III. 'Feuferm' was novel to the Scots feudal system (the only other notable example having come in a charter to Aberdeen in 1319). It meant the burgh would pay the crown a fixed annual amount in lieu of the sundry rents, customs and other dues collected previously by royal officials – which had given scope for dispute and abuse. Under the new deal, Edinburgh was liable for a flat fee of 52 merks a year in equal instalments at Whitsun and Martinmas.[24] The sum seems modest beyond belief: Berwick was assessed for 500 and Aberdeen for 320 merks. But the very fact of the grant of feuferm must have expressed confidence that Edinburgh would rise again. Feuferm certainly had a future. In Scots legal parlance the money paid can be called feu-duty, and this survived into my own lifetime. When I bought my flat in 1976 I was entitled under a recent amendment of the law to redeem the feu – that is, by a single payment on taking possession to relieve myself once and for all of the annual sum. It was an oblique introduction to the role feudalism has played in the history of Edinburgh.

King Robert saved his country, yet his peace did not last. Guerrilla war is never pretty and some Scots had ended up on the wrong side through no fault of their own. Others disputed the Bruces' pretensions even yet. Such were the Balliols, unlucky winners of the

competition for the throne back in 1290. They still felt cheated.
Toom Tabard was dead, leaving his claim to a son, Edward. Since
Scotland now had a boy for a king, in 1332 this Balliol and other
malcontents mounted, with English connivance, a seaborne expedition from the River Humber to the Firth of Forth. The Scots
hit back by invading England the next year, to little purpose. By the
Battle of Halidon Hill they lost Berwick again; it would change hands
four times during the next 200 years. Yet its unstable status proved a
boon to Edinburgh, which took over as the main Scottish port on
the North Sea, even for Berwick's own hinterland of Tweeddale.
Meanwhile, however, Edinburgh also fell to the invaders. In 1342 it
was said to be waste and had to miss at least a year's payment of
feuferm.[25]

Again the Scots would bounce back from appalling reverses.
Relief came with the outbreak of the Hundred Years' War between
the English and the French. In 1346, Edward III of England crossed
the Channel and won the Battle of Crécy. David II, King of
Scots, had as a child been carried for safety to France but by now,
a headstrong twenty-one-year-old, he was home again. Eager to be
worthy of his father, he broached the border so as to confound the
common foe with a classic war on two fronts. Alas, he bungled
the Battle of Neville's Cross in County Durham. The enemy cut up
his army. He himself was wounded and taken captive, if still able
to knock a couple of teeth from the jaw of the Englishman who
cornered him under a bridge as he tried to get away. He would
remain a prisoner-of-war for eleven years. This did not at all deter
the Scots from striking again at England in 1355, when Edward III
invaded France in the campaign leading to his victory at the Battle
of Poitiers. Then, in 1356, Edward appeared with an army in Scotland
to ravage Edinburgh during the 'Burnt Candlemas'. Yet in 1357 he
freed David II for a ransom of 100,000 merks payable in annual
instalments over ten years (the ransom never was paid in full).

By 1385 Scots and English were at each other's throats once
more. England had a new monarch, not a good one, in Richard II.
He was another destined for a sticky end, progressing steadily
towards it from a bad start. He could not hold the territory his father
had conquered in France. The French saw here a chance to reopen
war on two fronts and sent an expeditionary force to Scotland. The

chronicler Jean Froissart wrote up an account of it. He probably culled his information from compatriots who took part, though he had the necessary background for the task, having himself visited Scotland some years before. He thought of the Scots what they thought of themselves: they were 'ardent, fiery and proud' and in battle 'terribly strong, brave, hard and bold'. But to him Edinburgh, with its 400 houses, had looked no better than a French provincial town such as Tournai or Valenciennes. Now he felt struck by a difference in the reception his countrymen were given by the Scots – from the nobility a gracious welcome, from the people a surly question: 'Who the hell has sent for them? What are they doing here? Can't we fight England well enough without their help? We'll get nowhere with them here. We are strong enough in Scotland. Show them we can take care of ourselves. Let them drop dead.'[26]

After that it was little surprise the 500 French knights on the expedition could find no room in Edinburgh but had to be billeted out to castles in the surrounding countryside. They thought themselves ridiculously overcharged for food and other supplies. Servants they sent out to forage for firewood were waylaid, beaten and robbed. The French decided it was a dismal country, where gentlemen like themselves 'shall find no iron to shoe their horses, nor leather to make harness, saddles or bridles, for all such things come to them ready made out of Flanders'. And the poverty shocked these courtly Frenchmen. They went home saying 'they had never suffered so much in any expedition ... they had never seen such wicked people, or such ignorant hypocrites and traitors'. Richard II answered their intervention with reprisals, crossing the border to sack Edinburgh. But the people said: 'Let the Englishmen burn our houses. We could not care less. We can make them again cheap enough. We need just three days to do that, if we get four or five stakes, and boughs to cover them.'[27]

%

The fifteenth century saw less desperate struggles, though that is hard to tell from some of the earliest literature in Scots written at the time. Blind Harry's *Wallace*, composed in the 1470s, seethes with a hatred of the English that is absent from John Barbour's *Bruce* of a hundred years earlier. When a papal legate, Enea Silvio Piccolomini, the future Pope Pius II, arrived in Edinburgh he discovered 'nothing pleases the Scots more than abuse of the English'. He too felt appalled by the privation: 'I saw the poor, who almost in a state of nakedness begged at the church doors, depart with joy in their faces on receiving stones as alms'; this was the coal of the Lothians, donated by the charitable to let them heat their huts. At least the randy Italian found Scots lassies easy to lay.[28]

War had now mainly been reduced to small stuff on the border, often waged by proxies of the two monarchs, so it never really stopped. Pedro de Ayala, Spanish ambassador to the Kingdom of Scots, said: 'They spend all their time in wars, and when there is no war they fight with one another.' The most serious casualty was King James II, who lost his life besieging Roxburgh in 1460. 'Mair curious nor became him or the majesty of ane king', he got blown up by the explosion of one of his own cannon. Roxburgh fell to the Scots, but Berwick went to England for good after 1482, during the century's most serious invasion. At one time larger than Edinburgh, it remained a mighty fortress on the common frontier, yet sank in every other respect into a backwater.[29]

The English won their biggest victory over the Scots at the Battle of Flodden in 1513. King James IV fell with the flower of his nobility, not forgetting the provost of Edinburgh, Sir Alexander Lauder. Fought and lost just fifty miles away, it threw the capital into panic. The hurried building of the Flodden Wall, still standing today over lengthy stretches, was one consequence. Yet the new defences would never be tested, for the English did not bother to follow up their success. Inside Scotland the episode yet had an effect in the formation, durable if not permanent, of a party that was pro-English (bearing in mind all things are relative). At any rate it sought to resolve the endless feud by means other than battle. Scotland and England had been locked into a conflict neither could win, driven forward also by the alliance of Scots and French, so the Anglo-Scottish wars might seem to have been of a piece with the Hundred Years' War. Yet this was deceptive. When the English were finally expelled from France in 1453 their fight with the Scots just ground on in its sporadic, destructive way, each side able to damage the other without ever defeating it once and for all. Further battle there would be in the mid-sixteenth century. But a way had opened – and gradually widened – leading towards peace and in the end unity between the two nations.

❧

In other words, Scotland had still after the death of King Robert faced a stupendous fight for survival. It is the more remarkable that Edinburgh appears for the rest of the fourteenth century to have enjoyed one of its great building booms – and not only, as Froissart might lead us to think, because the English kept burning the place down. The Castle's ramparts were repaired in 1335 and then furnished with stone-throwing machines. David II's return from captivity in 1357 ushered in its golden age as fortress and royal residence. He would die on the Rock in 1371 before seeing a finish to the first stage of reconstruction, which marked just the start of works stretching two centuries into the future.

David II remodelled the Castle to make it mightier than ever before. Additions of the era still to be seen are the Wellhouse Tower of 1361, which defended the supply of water, and a gateway through the Constable's Tower at the north-eastern tip of the curtain-wall finished in 1375–9. Inside, the ancient St Mary's Church was rebuilt in 1366. Royal residence necessarily involved ceremony, so required some suitable space within the walls. Next to the church a court (now Crown Square) was laid out as a terrace over tiered cellarage below – a foretaste of the spectacular underbuildings in the later, classical Edinburgh. Lower down the Rock there probably ran a second circuit of walls. Indeed the Netherbow Port, built in 1369 right at the opposite end of the High Street, half a mile from the Castle, might be counted as just such an outer work, seeing that defence of the burgh and the Castle went together, in certain conditions at least. This huge but narrow gateway guarding the main entry to the High Street stood until 1764 when it was demolished to improve the flow of traffic; only its clock survived and today adorns the Dean Gallery at the western edge of the New Town.[30]

The defences of the Castle proper were also concentrated at the eastern, most vulnerable side of the Rock. The Victorian cultural critic John Ruskin, judged that 'the grandeur of Edinburgh Castle depends eminently on the great, unbroken, yet beautifully varied parabolic curve in which it descends from the Round Tower [Half

Moon Battery] on the Castle Hill to the terminating piece of independent precipice on the north'.[31] So he advised us in surveying the
scene to cast our eye from east to west. But in the fourteenth century
the eye would have been drawn to and fixed at the lofty structure
jutting forward belligerently on the east so as to command the slope
down into the burgh: manmade peak rather than natural curve. This
was David's Tower of 1368–77, with five storeys on massive foundations. Like the first King David's buildings, it made the values of its
time clear – now of defensive intransigence rather than of religious
devotion.

Yet David II meant to live there as well: his tower contained his
private apartments, compact and no doubt all the cosier for being so
safe. If it had not formed part of a vast citadel and the elaborate
fortifications going with that, it could without hesitation have been
called a towerhouse – a prime example of an architectural genre
that is one of Scotland's gifts to the world. It set a tone for the
picturesque, if finally mannered, baronial style which flourished for
several centuries ahead until it gave rise to Balmoral and many other
modern imitations, including countless suburban villas, not only in
Scotland but also as far afield as North America and the Antipodes.

Tourists today flock to see Glamis in Angus or Craigievar in
Aberdeenshire, but David's Tower must have been quite as awesome
and was arguably the original of them all. Mere fragments of it
remain, buried under the Half Moon Battery. Excavation has shown
the lower storeys had the same blank walls, cunning arrow-slits and
diminutive doors as the northern examples, beneath the living space
that opened out above. The rest is gone but at least, not far away at
Crichton in Midlothian, a fine local example of a towerhouse built
just a little later can be viewed. Within the present boundaries of
Edinburgh is another from the fifteenth century, Craigmillar, which
may have been a copy of David's Tower; the two could be seen the
one from the other. The new works on the Castle Rock were above
all geared to making sure no future siege could succeed. And none
did until 1573 when David's Tower crumbled under a sustained
barrage by modern artillery. But for a couple of centuries it was the
foremost feature of Edinburgh's skyline.[32]

❦

Down the High Street, St Giles had to be rebuilt too. Though the dating is unclear, fresh work on it was indispensable after the English sack of the burgh in 1385. The basic fabric must have survived this vandalism, for just two years later the town council paid three masons to add a row of chapels to the southern wall of the nave. In their contract the nave was said to have five bays west of the central tower, as it still has. This suggests that it arose earlier: 1370 has been proposed as the approximate year of its construction. Transepts existed by 1395 when a chapel was added to the northern one. The cruciform plan of the church was then in place. The council finished it with the choir by 1419 when, claiming to have spent 5,000 gold crowns for the purpose, it applied for St Giles to be made collegiate, that is, to be served by more than one priest. At first the idea went nowhere. By the time it did, in 1467, the choir had been again remodelled. And now the central tower looked too squat. So it, too, was raised in height, though it still seemed and seems compact. It was topped by its most famous feature, a pinnacle carried on eight flying buttresses springing from the corners and centres of the sides: the crown spire.[33]

Next to St Giles, in the middle of the long marketplace laid out under the first plan of the 1120s, the Tolbooth was built. The perversity of this development half-blocking the High Street had its reasons. The Tolbooth was in origin the municipal office where people paid charges due to the burgh under its chartered privilege for use of the commercial facilities. As collection of revenue accounted for much of local government, the Tolbooth soon in effect acquired the function of a town hall. And because any wretches who defied the by-laws might be locked up there, it turned into a prison as well.

That did not exhaust the tally of the Tolbooth's uses. Edinburgh still lacked sites for larger gatherings of a secular kind; David II cannot have wanted to see too many scruffy lieges in his nice new tower. So, by another odd twist, the Tolbooth also became a seat of the Scots Parliament if it happened to meet in Edinburgh. King Robert (1306–29) held two of twelve Parliaments there, David II (1329–71) one of sixteen, Robert II (1371–90) one of seven, Robert III (1390–1406) one of five, James I (1406–37) two of sixteen (most of the rest at Perth, which in his reign looked like a rival for capital of the country). But James II (1437–60) held all except two of his thirteen Parliaments in Edinburgh. From now on this was the normal place of its meetings, though excursions elsewhere continued at the royal pleasure.[34]

The Parliament must have gathered on the ground floor of the Tolbooth, which was roomy enough if airless. It also lacked a supply of water and so any sanitation. Waste got thrown into a hole under the stair, but inadequate hygiene has never put Scots off. 'Its black stanchioned windows [opened] through its dingy walls like the apertures of a hearse,' wrote Robert Chambers who saw the last of it in the nineteenth century. During legislative sessions, did the prisoners remain in durance vile, clanking their chains in the politicians' hearing, on the floor above? This storey, too, comprised a single room with an iron bar along the floor where the inmates lay or sat in heavy manacles. In the middle was a square box of plate-iron, called the cage: the condemned cell, the legendary Heart of Midlothian. The Tolbooth, from time to time rebuilt and added to, stood until it was pulled down in 1817; Sir Walter Scott took its doorway and keys away to his country house at Abbotsford. Its site is even yet marked by a heart laid out in the cobbles of the street just to the west of St Giles's main door – usually covered with gobbets of sputum because the vulgar spit on it, as a symbol of authority, whenever they walk past.

❧

To the eastern side of St Giles stood and stands the Mercat Cross. There public proclamations of all kinds – dissolution of Parliament, accession of the monarch – were made and still are. More to the point for the Middle Ages, the Cross marks the spot where goods imported into the burgh had to be displayed for sale. If landed at Leith, they would have been received and valued by municipal officers. But they could not yet be sold: they had to be carried to the Cross and deposited there. Freemen of the burgh then got first refusal. Only afterwards could others look and buy, still at the favourable price fixed in advance, on an understanding they were not to resell what they bought. The burgh remained intent on absolute control of its markets.[35]

Today the Cross is an octagonal shaft topped by a capital and a frisky unicorn. It dates in this form only from 1885, though it incorporates older work. The man who recreated it then, Sydney Mitchell, was able to include a capital of the fifteenth century carved with shapes, now eroded, perhaps meant as dragons, perhaps as foliage. The capital and its shaft had been used in a previous reconstruction of the Cross in 1617; they were saved (if with the shaft broken) when the time came in 1756 for renewal of that Cross. It had carried the coat-of-arms of Edinburgh too, with its stylized depiction of the Castle; this was copied on to the Cross of 1885, though other panels with human heads were not. Scott also took the panels of 1617 to Abbotsford, where they can still be seen.[36]

Further down still stood the Tron, in origin a weighing machine provided by the burgh to ensure customers at its markets got good measure. Food-stalls gathered round and the whole space became known as the Tron. Not only was the price of wares fixed but their quality had to be vouched for too, by tasters of beer or wine, inspectors of bread, meat and everything else. Inferior produce was destroyed or given to lepers who, if shunned by the rest of the population, took to hanging about here. The Tron had a second, seamy side: the post of the weighing machine could serve as a pillory for petty criminals, and rotten vegetables lying about came in handy to pelt them with. Under the perennial pressure of space in the Old Town, in 1636–47 the medieval site was covered with a new church for a flock ejected from St Giles; secular the name of Tron may have been but the church, today a museum, still bore and bears it. A final use evolved nobody knows when. At the Tron the people of Edinburgh gather on Hogmanay to welcome in the New Year – to hear the bells in local parlance, though the Tron in fact has no bells. The assembly must have been customary by 1812 when, in a vicious riot, a mob of drunken thugs broke it up.

Finally, the entire middle stretch of the Royal Mile got cluttered, again until wholesale clearance in 1817, with Krames and Luckenbooths, rows of permanent covered stalls. Krames stood against the walls of St Giles while Luckenbooths were erected in the middle of the street. Once more, all this seems to carry inconvenience towards the height of absurdity. Yet on its strange site, a mere 140 acres in area, the burgh could not expand far outwards. It would soon expand upwards, but all available space within the walls meanwhile got filled in these resourceful if eccentric ways.

By 1500 the High Street had continuous frontages on either side. Behind, the old tofts were being subdivided to the point of congestion. Most now contained several 'lands' (buildings), either 'forelands' on the street or 'backlands' down the sides. The foreland could be built across two tofts and the entrance to the backlands then went in by a 'pend' through the ground floor of the building. The crowding caused hazards of both fire and water. Lothian was being denuded of trees but construction in stone could not by itself offer protection against fire in such a close-built place: the last great conflagration in the Old Town would break out as recently as 2002. The second hazard arose because of primitive sanitation, which was deteriorating. Once there had been room for middens behind the houses; now the tofts were being built up, and nothing could be done with human waste but throw it out of the windows. Nobody knows when the cry of Gardyloo (from the French *'Gardez l'eau!'*) was first raised, but it could have been in this medieval period of greatest Gallic influence. With people living amid their own filth, sickness was rife. The Black Death arrived in 1349 from across the border, belying the Scots' fond notion that God had sent it to punish the English. Three further epidemics followed by 1401, and more later. Disease found here a rich breeding ground right up to the visitations of cholera and typhus in Victorian times.[37]

❧

For several reasons suburbs seemed desirable. Beyond the walls, rebuilt in 1450–75, lay the Canongate and the Cowgate. The Canongate had been part of the original master-plan of the 1120s, and by now held buildings in every toft. It throve by the comings and goings at Holyrood. The Kings of Scots often used the abbey's guesthouse, for the Castle could be 'windy and richt unpleasand', as poet and prelate Gavin Douglas said. Holyrood turned more and more into a royal residence. To James II it was home: born there in 1426, crowned there in 1437, he was married there in 1449 and buried there in 1460. James IV, planning his own wedding to Margaret Tudor in 1504, in effect changed the primary purpose of the place from monastery to palace by adding apartments, a gallery, a gateway and a private chapel. James V made the change yet more manifest when he elbowed aside the abbey's Romanesque front to start building the new facade, reminiscent of a towerhouse, which looks up the Royal Mile today. Inside, the rooms were not just cosy, in the way of towerhouses, but stately. As a quadrangle emerged behind, next to the monks' cloister, the modern Holyrood arose.[38]

If the Canongate was old the Cowgate was new. It developed in the long hollow running below the steep southern flank of the Royal Mile, out of which the ground on the opposite side rose again. The hollow offered a track for cattle kept in byres in the burgh to go back and forth to pasture on the Meadows – hence the name. In 1477, James III banned 'all quick beasts, kye, oxen' within the walls; whether or not he did get rid of them, the name stuck. The Cowgate then turned modish, with desirable residences built along it from the east. They enjoyed a pleasant outlook across to monasteries and gardens stretching up the low ridge to the south: of the Blackfriars or Benedictines, of the Greyfriars or Franciscans, and of the Kirk o' Field of Our Lady, belonging to the Augustinians at Holyrood. The Flodden Wall would bring all this within the burgh. The fortification seemed imperative in 1513 but it enclosed ground that could and would be built up once the monasteries disappeared later in the century. The fetid, teeming Cowgate of the future turned out far different from the flowering, tranquil Cowgate of the past.[39]

And Edinburgh owned the port of Leith, two miles down the hill. In 1329 this had consisted of just the natural harbour on the waterfront at the Shore, but as business bounced back from war a settlement extended to the rear. This, after the loss of Berwick to Scotland, faced no serious trading rival between the Rivers Tay and Tweed. It became the entrepot for a wide hinterland, above all the sheep-rearing region of the Borders. In the fourteenth century Edinburgh already carried on a third of Scotland's trade in wool, by the mid-fifteenth century half of it and by the end of the sixteenth century almost all of it. In absolute terms, the exports of animal products grew several times over, from 44,000 sheepskins, 29,000 other skins and 24,000 hides in 1499, to 197,000 sheepskins, 205,000 other skins and 37,000 hides in 1598. The share of Scottish customs that was paid here over the same period rose from 60 per cent to 72 per cent. Edinburgh would never lord it over Scotland as London lords it over England or Paris over France, in a political as well as an economic sense; but for now it was in the northern kingdom commercially supreme.[40]

The bulk of the traffic went through Leith. Yet even as the main Scottish port Leith was an unfree town with no rights of its own, and Edinburgh took a perverse delight in oppressing it. By the feudal charter under which all property was held in Leith, no resident could take part in trade. Burgesses of Edinburgh tempted to set up house by the Shore would have found themselves in trouble with the town council. Of course they needed to go down there on business from time to time. But then they used municipal offices built for the purpose (after which Burgess Street is still named) and went home again up the hill once they had finished. Locals could only find work as dockers and sailors, or in the army of porters and carters that passed up and down Easter Road, the main thoroughfare between the burgh and its harbour. So Leith remained poorer than Edinburgh – and was meant to stay that way. Relations between the two have never quite got over the unfortunate medieval start.

※

The great medieval building boom still could not make of Edinburgh anything other than a cramped place, crouched on the tail of the Rock and stinking to high heaven. The people were driven from house and close to spend their waking hours in the High Street. Already in 1500 the council complained of a 'great confluence of sempill peipill' on the Royal Mile. While usually they faced there nothing worse than a boisterous climate, crowds in Scotland often mean trouble. Records of later periods show urban violence to have been routine and it is hard to believe this was not true of the medieval era too: it had its own word, 'tuilzie' (pronounced tooly), for a brawl on the street.[41]

The worst tuilzie of all, in the distracted years after Flodden, may be taken as standing for the rest. In capital and country there had arisen two political factions. One, under James Hamilton, Earl of Arran, and James Beaton, Archbishop of St Andrews, stood fast by the Auld Alliance with France. The other, under Archibald Douglas,

Earl of Angus, wanted to be nicer to the English so that the English might be nicer to the Scots. For the time being the pro-French party remained in charge. Arran ran the government during the minority of James V, serving for good measure as provost of Edinburgh. Still, the situation remained tense and trouble easily got out of hand.

Most years there were disturbances of some sort, and in 1520 they began with the arrival at the Shore of a shipment of timber from Holland. This caused a row between the Leithers, led by one Robert Barton, and the burgesses of Edinburgh laying claim to the cargo. For the government, Arran took the part of the Leithers. He aroused the ire of the burgesses, who turned for support to Angus. Feelings ran so high that by 30 April the two noblemen's clans, the Douglases and the Hamiltons, were ready to settle the contention with cold steel. Archbishop Beaton owned a house in Blackfriars Wynd, where on that day 1,000 men – including the archbishop himself in his armour – fought a battle. The Douglases got the better of it and beat the Hamiltons out of town. Arran and his son saved themselves only when they jumped on a passing packhorse and rode for their lives through the shallows of the Nor' Loch. Beaton had to be rescued by a brother cleric, Gavin Douglas, as he was about to fall victim to a murderous mob that chased him to the altar of Black-friars. The clash became known as Cleanse the Causeway, after the mess of blood and brains and guts needing to be mopped up afterwards: that the sanitary operation seemed more worthy of note than the public carnage tells us much about Edinburgh.[42]

⁂

But there were peaceful diversions on the High Street too, religious or secular, from the colourful commotion of the markets to the pious processions on saints' days. Things never got so perilous that spectators might not even bump into the king, assuming they could penetrate his disguise. Handsome, debonair James IV loved nothing so much as to wander about the burgh listening incognito to the voices of the people. A prince of the Renaissance, patron of art and science, perhaps he wished to know what they thought of his urban improvements. Or else he was just interested in ordinary folk: the humanist Desiderius Erasmus, who tutored one of the king's bastards, recalled that 'he had a wonderful intellectual power, an astonishing knowledge of everything, and unconquerable magnanimity, and the most abundant generosity'.

His son James V inherited the royal taste for camouflage. He was the 'gaberlunzie king', who acted the beggar or tramp. Sometimes this led him into trouble. He was on his own one day heading back to Edinburgh from Cramond when robbers set on him. The local miller, Jock Howieson, saved him, then took him home to get cleaned up. The victim described himself as the gudeman of Ballencrieff, that is, tenant of a royal farm near Stirling. He invited Jock to come to Holyrood and see his landlord the king; he would be able to make him out as the only man in the room wearing a hat. When Jock, with a cap on his own head, took up James's offer and together they entered a chamber in the palace, all the courtiers uncovered themselves and bowed. Jock turned to stare amazed at James, saying: 'Then it must be either you or me!' He was rewarded with the freehold of the farm of Braehead, hard by the bridge at Cramond, on condition his descendants should always receive the sovereign's successors when they crossed it with a bowl of water and towel. This reception was last afforded to George VI in 1937. There is no way of telling if these later legends of the Kings of Scots are truer than some earlier ones already related. What they do show is a popular tradition of familiarity and ease between monarch and people which only such an intimate capital as Edinburgh could have fostered.[43]

※

Standing in disguise at the Cross, the king might have eavesdropped on the merchants gathered to whisper and shake hands on their deals. But here he would certainly have risked being recognized, for friendship flourished between the royal house and this elite of the burgh. Given that the nobility was so anarchic – and seldom had any money – the burgesses proved far more useful and reliable to the state. From early anonymity their names start to emerge in its service about the middle of the fourteenth century. The most prominent then was Adam Tore, or Torrie, who acted at home as master of the mint and went abroad on an embassy to reopen trade with Flanders during an interlude in the wars. His greatest contribution came, with his fellows Adam Gylyot and John Goldsmith, in raising the ransom for David II.[44]

Among themselves merchants were uninterested in competition. On the contrary, their guild punished members who competed on the sly, for example by forestalling, or buying up goods before they had been exposed to common view at the Cross. Merchants had to contend more and more, however, against people from outside their inner circle. This reflected growing complexity in the urban economy. In the twelfth century a burgess might himself have kept animals on his toft, slaughtered and processed them there and exchanged the products on the High Street or further afield. By the fifteenth century merchants no longer had to do any dirty work (at least with their hands). There were professional craftsmen for this purpose, ranging from fleshers (butchers) to skinners for the beasts, from cordiners (leather-workers) to websters (weavers) for animal products, from masons to wrights for buildings and byres. As in other successful trading communities, there had been a division of labour.

This paralleled the evolution of cities all over Europe. What followed was also common to medieval society: the combining of individual craftsmen into closed corporations. In Edinburgh these proved resilient, their grip not being finally broken until 1846. When the craftsmen had first tried to follow the protectionist example of the merchants, the latter resisted – and had the power to do so because they manned the magistracy of the burgh. Yet regulation for a common purpose was what they practised themselves. Before long they saw that unwashed artificers, if allowed privileges of their own, might turn into pillars of society too, which could even strengthen the burgh's collective ability to defend and promote its interests. So the balancing act needed to neutralize the rise of these social rivals modified to some extent the despotism of the elite.

꘎

These complexities found expression in some parliamentary legislation of 1469 and 1474. Its response looked paradoxical, however: to all appearance the one Act closed down municipal life while the other Act opened it up.

One Act regularized the hitherto customary procedures of the town council in order to limit control to as small a group as possible. In particular, the outgoing council was from now on to elect the incoming one. This allowed the men in charge to stay there by repeated re-elections of themselves or of relations and friends. From such a breathtaking imposition of oligarchy some compensation came the craftsmen's way. They were let through the strait gate of municipal power for the first time, though grudgingly – a couple of them would be allowed to join the dozen merchants who sat as members of the council.

The other Act offered the craftsmen more of a sweetener by giving them their own apparatus of economic privilege. They were empowered to set up 'incorporated trades', on analogy with the merchants' guild. A craftsmen's incorporation would have the same functions of professional club and benefit society for its members, then of commercial cartel and detective agency to keep others out of its business. Just as, since the days of King David, the merchants had enjoyed the sole right to distribute goods within the walls, so the craftsmen now enjoyed the sole right to make anything there. The activities of these two groups would define what the burgh was and what it did.

This basic law of the burgh, which had four centuries of life before it, followed a gambit by ten hatmakers who turned up at the Tolbooth one day asking the magistrates to ratify draft regulations for the structure and discipline of their craft: terms of entry, of apprenticeship and so on. After some shilly-shallying they were approved. A string of formal incorporations on similar lines followed: of skinners in 1474, of masons and wrights in 1475, of websters in 1476, of hammermen in 1483, of fleshers in 1489, of waulkers and tailors in 1500, of surgeons and barbers in 1505, of cordiners in 1510. In the last case the move was justified by the canny argument that 'multitude but reull makis confusion' – confusion arises from a lot of people working without rules: an early statement of Edinburgh's values.

But the craftsmen's incorporations, fourteen in all, were, like the merchants' guild before them, tempted to overdo the regulations. Some verged on the oppressive. Apprentices had, for example, to sign up for seven years. Even after serving their time they could not become masters of their craft with a right to employ others unless they were also the sons or sons-in-law of an existing craftsman, or else paid a stiff fee. In Edinburgh this brought about the emergence, below the crafts, of a class of skilled but unprivileged workmen with no more rights than the unskilled labourers below them. Like rustic serfs or Highland clansmen, medieval townsfolk were born to a station in life which only great determination or luck could alter.

It was not even as if jumping through the hoops of incorporation always protected a craft in the way its members intended. During the century or so after the websters and waulkers had achieved this, their status declined and their numbers within the burgh shrank. They migrated instead to new suburbs along the Water of Leith. This seemed like a good idea at the time: they escaped Edinburgh's regulations and taxes, while also finding the supply of running water they had really needed all along while choosing to ply their craft in such a crazy place as the tail of the Rock. What they did not know was that they had also opted for further slippage in the economic pecking order. The men who made money in Edinburgh laid it out for, among other things, capitalist investment in textile factories along the Water of Leith. There they offered regular jobs to the websters and waulkers – and by the same token turned them from a craft into an industrial proletariat.

Yet some who made money in the burgh remained themselves, in legal technicality, craftsmen. Hammermen offer an example of an incorporation that managed by financial success to raise its real social status. Work with a hammer was about the one thing at the outset uniting a group of trades actually rather disparate, or getting that way: armourers, blacksmiths, buckle-makers, cutlers, goldsmiths, lorimers (makers of bits and bridles). Goldsmiths in particular diversified early on. Edinburgh was the seat of a royal mint, cunyie-house in Scots, which with economic growth became all the more of an asset. The coinage expanded. To King David's pennies the later monarchs added groats, nobles and lions. The Scottish state took its monetary seignorage seriously: in 1398 a counterfeiter was boiled alive on the High Street.[45]

Still, there was nothing to stop Scots coin being exported or foreign coin being imported, because no concept of legal tender existed; coin, being one form of precious metal, and the most portable, just followed flows of trade. On the burgh's markets that fact required men, ideally goldsmiths, with the discernment and experience to value the coins brought to them for inspection, to assess their purity and mark if they had been worn or clipped. Some set up shop in the Luckenbooths where, to guess from the fortunes they made, they did a roaring business. They would come to rival the merchants in wealth. And they would form a separate incorporation of their own in 1581. In hindsight we may say this was the origin of the financial industry, which later carried Scottish canniness round the globe and forms today an essential basis for Edinburgh's post-modern economy.

Sometimes different fates awaited members of the same incorporation, as in the case of surgeons and barbers. Their coming together in 1505 is often claimed as the foundation of that eminent professional body of the present day, the Royal College of Surgeons of Edinburgh. But the link is not quite direct. At first surgeons and barbers could combine because their trades required the same nimble fingers. Both approached customers with sharp instruments in hand to chop bits off them, whether long hair or crushed limbs; the difference lay in the fact that customers would usually survive a meeting with a barber, less often one with a surgeon. In time the two diverged further. The surgeons succeeded in 1583 in taking one of the seats assigned to the crafts on the town council. They justified this by their rising status – which did not, however, yet reflect any genuine advance in surgical skills. To be sure, a master surgeon had to 'knaw the nature and substance of everything that he werkes, or ellis he is negligent'. The apprentices were taught a little anatomy, such as the whereabouts of veins – though since the circulation of blood had yet to be discovered this knowledge might not have been all that useful. The fact the youngsters also had to learn astrology is a clearer sign of the intellectual level of their instruction.

The actual purpose of the professional humbug was to suppress competition, while the incorporation sought to pass from being a mere craft to being, in its own words, 'a learned society'. In the end that meant getting rid of an ever more embarrassing bond with the barbers. In 1648 a majority of the incorporation, now surgeons, banned further entry into it by men who were no more than barbers, unqualified in surgery. This only caused a shortage of barbers in the burgh. People complained they had to go to the suburbs to get a haircut, until during the Cromwellian occupation English officers, roundheads in need of constant croppings, refused to put up with such vexation. The surgeons were not to be deterred: in 1657 they joined with the more genteel apothecaries, yet could not shake off the barbers until 1722. Only then did the surgical profession attain the self-esteem to which it felt entitled. Edinburgh had turned snobbish.[46]

※

Economic change and growth always produce social strains, which took their own form in the small setting of the Scottish capital. In the Middle Ages kings, burgesses and craftsmen found common interests they did not share with the nation's horrible aristocracy. An example came when Scotland got into more than her usual turmoil in 1482. James III was a flawed monarch: a prince of the Renaissance in patronage of music and architecture, but not in statecraft. He fought running battles with his noblemen and preferred to consort with his commoners. Virtual rebellion broke out in an incident at Lauder Bridge in the Borders, which ended with blue-blooded bully boys stringing up his lowborn favourites. Wicked uncles, the Earls of Atholl and Buchan, kidnapped him and shut him up in Edinburgh Castle. He feared for his life. On top of all that, the English invaded.

In Edinburgh a distracted Queen Margaret enlisted help from the provost, Walter Bertram. He and the townspeople solved the immediate crisis by raising 6,000 merks for the king's ransom. In gratitude James III granted the Golden Charter, which made Edinburgh a sheriffdom in its own right and the provost its sheriff, entrusted with the power to enforce the law of the land inside the walls. Bartram and his lady also got a royal pension. And, as a memento of the craftsmen's loyalty, the king presented them with a banner bearing the thistle of Scotland. This became known as the blue blanket and is to this day preserved (or at least a later copy is) at the Trades Maiden Hospital. Round it a tradition grew up. The trades raised the blue blanket – that is, bore it at the head of a popular demonstration – whenever they considered themselves in serious contention with the state (as opposed to just going on a drunken rout). The tradition was to last three centuries, until the advent of industrial society changed the nature of such conflict.[47]

Medieval Edinburgh managed, despite its many trials and tribu-
lations, to give in crucial respects durable shape to its mode of life in
both a material and an immaterial sense. In a material sense, either
the stones of what was then built up still stand today, or else the
remains can be identified, or at least a site has been commemorated.
The great immaterial legacy of the Middle Ages lies in the literary
culture of Edinburgh, which, like the place itself, grew richer with
the centuries and helps to fill in the story of what sites and stones
cannot tell.

                                ❧

Poetry was and is the prime form of that literary culture, not least
because it is linked with the fate of the Scots language in which the
people expressed their most intimate thoughts. As in other European
capitals, the presence of a royal court may have fostered the first
flowering of the local vernacular and raised it to a literary standard.
James I himself composed a long poem, *The Kingis Quair*. This has
nothing to do with Edinburgh, only with an Englishwoman he loved
from afar, but it introduced a certain literary ethos to the city.
Medieval writers thought of their writing as a kind of craft: in their
view, a creative artist and a manual worker in essence engaged in the
same activity. A long poem was like a big building, the language like
its building blocks and writers themselves like the builders. Poets
mastered the skill of poetic composition in the same way as a mason
learned to dress stone or a hammerman to forge metal. This differs
from the later romantic conception of the artist as innate, spontaneous genius. In the Middle Ages there could be no art for art's
sake. Nor indeed could there be realism, for all art was inevitably
contrived; it would be foolish, perhaps sinful, to suppose otherwise.
Yet a wordsmith might rejoice in his command of the means for
construction in his own medium, just as a master builder might
rejoice at the skills he brought to his raising of a cathedral.

It would be idle to claim Scotland possessed any unique sense of
these medieval values, which were common to the whole of Europe.
But the Scots language did have a special term for a craftsman in
literary skills, just as it had quaint names for the trades. It might
have borrowed the term poet, as English and French did from Latin
and Greek. Instead it coined the term 'makar', meaning just the same

as the Greek ποιητης, a man who makes things, in this instance verses. It implies surely (and implies better than the term 'poet' can) a man who makes things for others and casts them in a form they may appreciate. It is a fine term to stand at the fountainhead of Scots poetry.

❧

The first makar, during the final quarter of the fifteenth century, was Robert Henryson. He lived at Dunfermline but knew Edinburgh and some of his work was linked with events there. He wrote a series of poems he called *Fables*. These were animal tales, modelled on Aesop and popular traditions, with a moral relating ordinary life to deeper experience. One of them, 'The Lion and the Mouse', is believed to be a tribute to the people of Edinburgh who saved James III in the crisis of 1482. Like the king a cultured man, Henryson sympathizes with him. The lion (the king) falls into a trap set by hunters (treacherous noblemen):

> *The lyoun fled, and throw the ron rynnand,*
> *Fell in the net and hankit fute and heid;*
> *For all his strenth he couth mak na remeid.*

> The lion fled, and running through the undergrowth,
> Fell in the net and entangled himself foot and head;
> For all his strength he could not get out again.

But mice happen along and nibble through the mesh:

> *Now is the lyoun fre of all danger,*
> *Lows and deliverit to his libertie*
> *Be lityll beistis of ane small power.*

> Now is the lion free of all danger,
> On the loose and delivered to his liberty
> By little animals of small strength.[48]

❧

The makar of greatest reputation, William Dunbar, was a chaplain to James IV. He never rose high in the Church but was often at Holyrood because the Kingdom of Scots relied on clerics for its administration; perhaps he worked in the royal secretariat. The court gave him not only his livelihood but also his audience and his material. He wrote of actual people too, and he composed a vivid poem about Edinburgh. Its theme is the absence of public spirit (a common trope of medieval literature across Europe), especially in the merchant elite. But what comes over most powerfully is Dunbar's word-picture of the din and dirt and smell in the streets. The burgh has become unbearable

> *For stink of haddockis and of scattis,*
> *For cryis of carlingis and debattis,*
> *For fowsum flyttingis of defame.*

> For stink of haddocks and of skates,
> For the cries and quarrels of old women,
> For foul-mouthed and abusive disputes.

It is not even as if the merchants, when minding their own business, offer desirable goods on the markets:

> *At your Hie Croce quhar gold and silk*
> *Sould be, thair is bot crudis and milk;*
> *And at your Trone but cokill and wilk,*
> *Pansches, pudingis of Jok and Jame.*

> At your Mercat Cross where gold and silk
> Should be, there are only curds and milk;
> And at your Tron only cockles and whelks,
> Paunches [by which haggis may be meant]
> And puddings of Jock and Jamie [black and
>   white puddings].

> *Your burgh of beggeris is ane nest,*
> *To shout thai swentyouris will not rest;*
> *All honest folk they do molest,*
> *Sa piteouslie thai cry and rame . . .*
> *Through streittis nane may mak progress*
> *For cry of cruikit, blind and lame.*

> Your burgh is a nest of beggars,
> Scroungers who never stop shouting;
> They molest all honest folk,
> So piteously do they cry and beg . . .

Nobody can get along the streets
For the cry of the crooked, blind and lame.

Yet none of this seems to bother the mercantile fat cats:

Your profit daylie dois incres,
Your godlie workis les and les . . .
Thairfoir strangeris and leigis treit;
Tak not over mekill for thair meit,
And gar your merchands be discreit.
That na extortiounes be, proclame
All fraud and schame.

Your profit daily does increase,
Your godly works get less and less . . .
So care for strangers and the king's subjects;
Do not take too much for their food,
And make your merchants act sensibly.
So that there should be no extortions,
Denounce all fraud and shame.

In the end, though, Dunbar has little faith any of this will come
to pass:

Singular proffeit so dois yow blind,
The common proffeit gois behind.[49]

❧

A makar of different kidney was Gavin Douglas, a son of the Earl of
Angus. He too went into the Church and, being of noble blood, rose
high. In 1503 he became provost of St Giles and in 1515 Bishop
of Dunkeld. But he ended up on the wrong side in the troubles of
the time and was exiled to England, where he died in 1522. Unlike
Henryson and Dunbar, Douglas does not write poetry of primarily
popular appeal; his concept of his art is learned and exalted. He turns
to classical literature for inspiration. And the craft he sets out to
master is translation. Alas for him, nothing could have been more
likely to rob him of renown in later epochs of reverence for the
romantic artist, by whose lights he is unoriginal. If he has a saving
grace in modern Scotland, it lies in his contribution not to literature
but to language, to the evolution of Scots. All over Europe, linguistic

pioneers were enriching the vocabulary and extending the range of vernaculars by adding to them from classical sources, so that they became capable of saying things they had not said before. Douglas did for Scots what François Rabelais did for French or Angelo Poliziano for Italian. Douglas also figured in another sense as a nationalist. Until his era the language of Lothian was called English or rather Inglis; the term Scots in linguistic usage, translating Latin *lingua Scotica*, meant Gaelic. He was the first to call the language he used Scottis.

Douglas's great achievement lies in his version of Virgil's *Aeneid*, the longest piece of verse of any kind in Scots. It is one of those rare examples of how translation (in English the Authorized Version of the Bible springs to mind) can attain the status of literature in its own right. Scots was not as rich as classical Latin, and it hardly disparages Douglas to say Virgil still outranks him as a poet. But Douglas gives us more of Virgil than is to be found in any other version in any variant of our language, and also gives us a great poem.

Despite the classical model, at times it is hard to believe the poem has not been set in Scotland, in Lothian and in Edinburgh. Here is a description of winter from the prologue to the seventh book (the prologues are not translations, but original work):

> *Soure bittir bubbis, and the schowris snell*
> *Semyt on the sward ane similitude of hell,*
> *Reducyng to our mynd, in every steid,*
> *Goustly schaddois of eild and grisly deid.*
> *Thik drumly scuggis dirknit so the hevyne,*
> *Dym skyis oft furth warpit feirfull levyne,*
> *Flaggis of fyir, and mony felloun flame,*
> *Scharp soppis of sleit and of the snypand snawe.*
> *The dowy dichis war all donk and wait,*
> *The law vaille flodderit all wyth spait.*
> *The plane stretis and every hie way*
> *Full of fluschis, doubbis, myre and clay.*

> Sour bitter blasts, and the biting showers
> Seemed on the ground a bit like hell,
> Bringing back to our mind, in every place,

Ghostly shadows of old age and grisly death.
Thick gloomy clouds so darkened the heavens,
Dim skies often threw out fearful lightning,
Flashes of fire, and many an evil squall,
Sharp soaking sleet and smarting snow.
The dismal ditches were all dank and wet,
The low valley flooded all in spate,
The level streets and every highway
Full of marshes, puddles, mire and clay.

At any rate, none of this sounds much like Rome or the Campagna.

𝕏

Douglas's was learned literature, more than Henryson's and Dunbar's, but other makars had a popular bent too – necessarily so when it came to drama, for example. Of course a play could be performed specially for the royal court, and often was. Yet it would more likely come alive before an audience of all classes. Medieval Edinburgh did see such performances. An official 'playfield', or open-air auditorium, had been set aside by 1456. It appears that, as in the rest of Europe, the spectacles were often put on about the time of the feast of Corpus Christi in June. They might have originated as religious pageant, but they evolved into mime and mummery. Whether they developed further is unclear, since no text has survived.

More certainly, religious pageant was left behind by the time we get to the first extant Scottish play, Sir David Lindsay's *Ane Satyre of the Thrie Estaits*. The premiere took place at Cupar Fife, in his home county, but there is evidence it was then staged in Edinburgh on 12 August 1554, in a new playfield at Greenside on the northern side of Calton Hill (where a performing tradition continues today, in some sort, at an ugly cinematic complex). Lindsay spent his life in the service of the crown, first looking after the boy James V, finally becoming Lyon King of Arms, in charge of heraldry. Courtier and king remained friends not least because both were makars (James V wrote poetry himself and a long pastoral, *Christ's Kirk on the Green*, has been attributed to him). In vivid language, with stinging sarcasm, *The Thrie Estaits* exposes corruption and vice in high places. Though

Lindsay does not let secular authority off lightly, his prime target is the Church.

The popular flavour arises in part from local reference, as when he compares small Scots burghs with large European kingdoms:

> *Ranfrow and all the realme of France,*
> *Yea, Rugland* [Rutherglen] *and the toun of Rome,*
> *Castorphine and al Christendome!*

Lindsay reinforces the local reference by playing it for laughs:

> *I will get riches throw that rent*
> *Efter the day of Dume,*
> *Quhen, in the colpots* [coalpits] *of Tranent,*
> *Butter will grow on brume!*

Knowledge of national history is a less expected side of that popular consciousness Lindsay appeals to, going back even beyond the obvious point of reference in the Wars of Independence. John the Common-weill, the everyman of the play, asks:

> *Quhat gif King David war leivand in thir dayis,*
> *The quhilk did found sa mony gay abayis?*
> *Or out of Heavin quhat gif he luikit doun*
> *And saw the great abominatioun*
> *Amang thir abesses and thir nunries*
> *Thair publick huirdomes and thair harlotries?*

> What if King David was living in these days,
> The man who founded so many fine abbeys?
> Or what if he looked down from Heaven
> And saw the great abomination
> Among these abbesses and these nunneries,
> Their public whoredoms and their harlotries?[50]

Despite all the local interest, *The Thrie Estaits* is not a parochial piece, in space or in time. It represents a milestone in European drama, looking backwards to medieval morality plays, sideways to contemporary courtly masques and forwards as well – less to the classical European drama than to the political theatre of still later ages, say to Bertolt Brecht, who is not so much interested in individual psychology as in public personae and the movement of the masses. A wide linguistic range reflects this, from parody of the makars' Latinity to echoes of the idiom of the streets, including the bawdy and obscene. Lindsay uses terms not again allowed on stage until the Lord Chamberlain's censorship in Britain was lifted late in the twentieth century. A count of Lindsay's 'fowll wourdis' shows little change in their incidence between his Edinburgh and ours:

> *Bischops are blist, howbeit that they be waryit* [cursed],
> *For thay may fuck thair fill and be unmarryit!*

> *Behauld some prelats of this regioun . . .*
> *Thay swyfe* [copulate with] *ladies, madinis and uther mennis wyfis*
> *And sa thair cunts thay have in consuetude!*[51]

Since Lindsay's era the literature of Edinburgh has seldom been squeamish about frank expression of physical detail. *The Thrie Estaits* proved its enduring appeal when revived by Tyrone Guthrie for the Edinburgh Festival of 1948, and again since.

❧

With populist irreverence towards the Church we approach the Reformation. Yet the substance of what Lindsay says does not take him beyond the position of Erasmus, for example, who while a reformer never broke with Rome. Both were in the first place humanists, concerned with the education, preaching and spiritual regeneration that the corrupt Church neglected. It is difficult to know how far such learned attitudes spread down into the population, just as it is hard to assess the general state of religion in Scotland at this stage. Enquiry before the twentieth century tended to get lost in Protestant polemics; the modern nation feels rather guilty about this and lends an ear to Catholic apology. So no settled view about religious conditions in the mid-sixteenth century has yet been reached. Something known for certain is that English Bibles and Lutheran tracts were smuggled in. A Catholic government took steps to defuse, rather than suppress, such defiance of orthodoxy, perhaps because this was all it could do. The Parliament of 1543 legalized the reading of vernacular Bibles, 'baith the New Testament and the auld in the vulgar tongue in Inglis or Scottis'. Provincial councils of the Church between 1549 and 1559 sought to curb clerical abuse and lay heresy at once.

At all events, within five years of *The Thrie Estaits* being performed at Greenside the Reformation hit Scotland. Nothing, not even the vindication of national independence a quarter of a millennium before, has so marked Edinburgh's character.

Conceivably, Protestantism might have come by English arms. On the death of James V in 1542, Henry VIII attempted once again the conquest of Scotland that had eluded his ancestors. This was his Rough Wooing, to force a marriage to his own heir, later Edward VI, of the infant Mary Queen of Scots. If he had succeeded, Scotland would no doubt have got a Henrician Reformation with an Anglican Church to boot. Henry was no advertisement for this. His army burned down the abbeys of the Borders, Dryburgh, Jedburgh and Melrose, which were never to be rebuilt. In 1544 the army reached Edinburgh and sacked the town, though, as in former times, the English could get no further. The French sent aid, but the Scots took fearful punishment in a war that went on until 1551. It ended when France beat England on the other side of the Channel, to leave Henry VIII's foolish foreign policy in ruins. The king was by then dead in any case, and a humiliating peace forced the withdrawal of his troops from Scotland. At this point the two neighbour nations were more at daggers drawn than they would be ever again, not only in a political or military sense but also in the confessional contrast of a newly Protestant England and a still Catholic Scotland.

That revived the Auld Alliance one last time. In fact, during no other period were Scots and French so closely tied as now, just before they broke up for good. Scotland was governed by regents affirming the link: by James Hamilton, Earl of Arran, also a peer of France as Duc de Châtelherault, uncle of the late James V; then by the king's widow, Mary of Guise, who treated Scotland as part of France. She put Frenchmen in public office and defended the country with French troops. A small, backward economy seemed ripe for bringing into dependence on a bigger, richer one; in the 1550s more than 60 per cent of Edinburgh's trade was going to French ports.[52]

Intellectual stimulus followed. The Kings of France, if Catholics, followed the spirit of the age in liberating learning from the Church, notably by the foundation in 1530 of the Collège Royal, later Collège de France. The purpose was to sponsor new, secular branches of learning. Mary did just the same in Edinburgh, which as yet had no university (the classes she provided for were held at St Mary Magdalen in the Cowgate, chapel of the hammermen). In 1556 she made Alexander Sym and Edward Henryson royal lecturers in Roman law and Greek respectively – here was the culture of the Renaissance. Perhaps economic structure indeed determined cultural superstructure in the classic Marxist sense: even the Scottish Reformation, when it came, would turn out in essence to be French.[53]

※

French government and Catholic religion seemed not to bother Edinburgh meanwhile. But the Scottish reformer John Knox hailed from nearby, having been born in 1514 at Haddington, the county town of East Lothian. He studied at St Andrews, probably under the theologian John Mair, himself a native of East Lothian, who had come back from an academic career in Paris where he may also have instructed St Ignatius Loyola, founder of the Jesuits. Mair damned abuses in the Church, the idle pomp of Rome for example, though this was by now nothing out of the ordinary. He proved less predictable in the attention he paid to the theological implications of the discovery of America. He argued that the natives there, cruelly abused by the *conquistadores*, had a right to overthrow the colonial regime. God chose rulers yet their authority derived from the people: this would soon come to be seen as a Scottish doctrine.

Of young Knox no more is known until in 1540 he appears as a notary apostolic in East Lothian, dealing with legal affairs of the Church and secular matters it governed, marriages, wills and so on. He does not reappear in the record until 1543, when employed as a private tutor. It is usually assumed he had abandoned the earlier career because of his conversion to Protestantism. He next took to the road with a travelling preacher, George Wishart; Knox would go on ahead brandishing a sword to deter troublemakers. Wishart was, all the same, arrested and executed. Knox found refuge at St Andrews, where a gang of Protestants who in revenge had killed Cardinal David Beaton were holed up in the castle. Here Knox began his ministry in the sense of preaching for the first time.[54]

The government in Edinburgh saw these Protestants as an

English fifth column. In July 1547 it sent a French naval squadron under the Florentine admiral Leone Strozzi to St Andrews. Strozzi bombarded the castle until the rebels gave in. They were transported to France and condemned to the galleys. Knox managed to escape to England, to be accepted there as an Anglican vicar; the Duke of Northumberland gave him the parish of Berwick in 1549. Through that connection he preached before Edward VI. He was offered the bishopric of Rochester, but declined it.

When in 1553 Bloody Mary succeeded as Queen of England and restored popery, Knox fled to Geneva. There John Calvin, ever since himself arriving as a refugee from Paris in 1536, had turned the city into a citadel of his own radical Protestantism. He set out its basis in his *Institutes of the Christian Religion* (1536), the first work of theology in French. It struck a tone different from the crabbed Latin texts he meant it to displace. Its rationalism, rigour and clarity of exposition helped to found a fresh intellectual tradition: the classical tradition of France. Yet it did so by bringing back to life some older Christian teachings, notably those of St Augustine, lost from view under medieval accretions: salvation through faith, not works; the utter corruption of fallen man; the logical necessity of predestination. Knox became a disciple of Calvin.

On the Continent Knox stayed until 1559, except for a visit home in 1555–6. He lodged then in Edinburgh with a merchant, James Syme. He met others among the urban elite: successful, literate, self-confident burgesses such as James Barron, dean of guild, or David Forrest, master of the mint. Knox made contact also with aristocrats who might shape up as lay leaders of a Scottish Reformation, John Erskine of Dun and Archibald Campbell, Lord Lorne, heir to the Earl of Argyll – and even with a royal bastard, Lord James Stewart, later Earl of Moray. Knox preached in private houses to people likely to be aware of developments in Europe – as he put it, to merchants and mariners 'who, frequenting other countries, heard the true doctrine affirmed and the vanity of the papistical religion openly rebuked'. This prelude to the Reformation was important in implanting a Calvinist rather than Lutheran concept of reform at the summit of Scottish society.[55]

Such activities did not escape official attention. In 1556 Knox was summoned to appear before a court of the Church on a charge of heresy. This could have brought a sentence of death, but Mary of Guise intervened. In an age ever more intolerant she remained a *politique*, to use the French term, not a bigot. During twenty years in Scotland she had learned like a true Stewart how to reconcile the various elements of a disparate nation – now even to include Protestants. At any rate she did not want a trial of Knox to spark off unrest, so she had the charge against him dropped. He carried on preaching until he received a message from Geneva asking him back. He had formed no favourable impression of the prospects for reform in Scotland, and there was always a risk of fresh prosecution. He left for Geneva that summer.[56]

❧

Knox could, then, hardly have been at the root of the religious violence that all of a sudden burst on Edinburgh in 1558. Elsewhere in Scotland anti-clerical protesters had been smashing images. They planned a trip to the capital for the feast-day of St Giles, 1 September. Then, by tradition, dignitaries of the burgh would lead a procession bearing the saint's statue from his church in the High Street down the Canongate, to the beat of the drum and the blare of the trumpet, with banners flying overhead. This year, before that happened, a mob stole the image, bore it to the Nor' Loch and ritually drowned it, then fished it out again and threw it on a fire.

The Catholic clergy, though outraged, were not deterred. Greyfriars kirk also owned an image of St Giles which could serve just as well. It was borrowed and on the saint's day the procession set off as if nothing had happened – with Mary of Guise, no less, at its head. It got as far into the Canongate as the house of Sandy Carpenter, a burgess who had invited her to dinner. Once she entered, Protestants shoved their way through the crowd to where the statue lay while its bearers took a break. They lifted and shook it to shouts of 'Down with the idol!' Then they bashed it on the ground until the head and hands came off. The first sectarian brawl in Scottish history erupted. Protestants got the better of it. Priests and friars fled. Mary looked on from a window but did not venture out again until later, when she could be hustled back to the safety of the Castle. Attempts to identify the miscreants failed.

Protestantism had so far been the interest of a minority, if with the advantage that it was a wealthy, even noble minority. It now came into the open as the Lords of the Congregation, a sort of pressure-group demanding tolerance of reforming opinions. Soon the Lords grew more ambitious. They began to plot some kind of coup. Those who had met Knox saw him as the man to lead a Reformation in Scotland. They wrote to Geneva asking him to return home: he landed at Leith in May 1559.[57]

Reformation could still not be led from Edinburgh, however. Knox spent just two nights there before leaving for Perth, where the Lords of the Congregation mustered their strength. On 11 May he preached a sermon 'vehement against idolatry' in St John's kirk. A mob rushed out to wreck the local monasteries. Knox rode with the Lords when they marched on Edinburgh and entered the city on 30 June. Here, too, the rabble indulged in an orgy of destruction; for example, of all the stained glass in the whole town a single example survived, at the Magdalen Chapel in the Cowgate, where it survives to this day. On 7 July the Lords assembled in the Tolbooth to elect Knox minister of St Giles.[58]

❧

It was a moment of triumph, yet it could not last. Mary of Guise was sure to call on help from France. She had retreated to Dunbar, where the castle offered refuge until that help should arrive. She was the kind of woman who would fight back. She accused the Lords of the Congregation of using religion as a pretext for overthrowing lawful government and ordered them to leave Edinburgh. When they ignored her she advanced towards them with what force she had, just 1,700 men. Her goal was Leith.

Mary of Guise had been showing remarkable foresight in her favours for Leith, after its long oppression by Edinburgh, and almost made it an alternative capital. She hinted she would erect it into a royal burgh and bring the nonsense of its feudal burdens to an end. To this end she had bought the feudal superiority, with the charter imposing them, for £3,000 raised by the people themselves. She moved the seat of the parish into the port from an ancient holy well at Restalrig a mile away (the nave of her new building remains inside the present church of South Leith). She furnished herself with an official residence in Water Street (the same church still houses a panel with her coat-of-arms, sole remnant of that residence). Overlooking the Water of Leith, on Coal Hill, she raised a building for the royal council whence, if need be, the government of Scotland might be run (today commemorated in the name of Parliament Street).

But Mary of Guise's biggest boon to Leith had been her building of fortifications round a large rectangle of ground back from the Shore. There she was not just doing the place another good turn: this represented the most advanced defensive system in the British Isles. As part of a chain of citadels at Eyemouth, Dunbar and Inchkeith, it could have served to make the Firth of Forth a French naval base for control of the North Sea. The plan came from the hand of an avant-garde engineer, Piero Strozzi, brother of the admiral who had captured Knox. Strozzi understood how the technological advances in modern artillery and the tactic they allowed of firing in barrages must also change the nature of fortification. Instead of walls and towers vulnerable to being knocked down, there had to be bigger but flatter angular bastions capable of absorbing the enemy's ordnance or making cannonballs bounce off, while supporting one another with crossfire. Thanks to Mary, Edinburgh's port by now boasted a full circuit of such fortifications. In this crisis she occupied them.

The Lords of the Congregation deployed their forces down Easter Road but did not in fact want a battle at this stage, any more than did Mary of Guise. On 23 July, on Leith Links, a compromise was reached providing for the religious partition of Edinburgh. Protestants could hold services in St Giles, mass could be said at Holyrood. Neither party would interfere with the other. Mary moved up to the Castle again. Knox preached from his pulpit in the High Street. People were free to choose which form of worship they liked. In return the Lords evacuated their army and promised to respect royal authority in future.[59]

Still, this was an uneasy truce, destined to be upset almost at once. On 7 August news arrived of the death of King Henry II of France in an accident, leaving Francis II, his brother, king in his stead and making Francis's wife of a year, Mary Queen of Scots, also Queen of France. What was more, they would share both crowns, so Francis would be King of Scots too. With two teenage sovereigns, it would be their uncles that wielded all power: the Duke of Guise and the Cardinal of Lorraine, who were also brothers of Mary of Guise. Government and policy in France and Scotland became in effect one.[60]

The outlook was alarming, to say the least, to the Lords of the Congregation. They reacted by attempting a fresh coup. They declared Mary of Guise's commission as regent suspended and set up a junta under Châtelherault. But Mary kept cool, sure they were overplaying their hand. She was right. The Lords bickered as their unpaid soldiers drifted home. All at once, their morale crashed. On the night of 5–6 November, they fled Edinburgh for Linlithgow. Mary ruled the roost again. She had St Giles reconsecrated by her priests and herself heard mass there.

꩜

Only such straits could have persuaded the Lords of the Congregation to ask for aid from England, even while protesting loyalty to the new sovereigns. The crisis suited the ruthless but subtle Queen Elizabeth I. In January 1560 she sent envoys to Berwick, who signed a treaty with the Lords. One aim was to establish Protestantism in Scotland, though the text said not a word concerning religion. Instead it rambled on about a plot to subvert the nation and unite it to France. Out of the goodness of her heart Elizabeth felt bound to intervene. She would send an army to expel the French, though not to impose an English occupation.

The army arrived and linked up with the Lords of the Congregation in March. They proceeded to lay siege to Leith and its Franco-Scottish garrison. On 7 May they launched an assault which proved the worth of the marvellous fortifications, for it ended in farcical failure. But Mary of Guise was still not necessarily looking for military victory.[61] She worked away from Edinburgh Castle for a negotiated deal. She had next to no time left. Dying of dropsy, she called in deputations of Protestants who found her propped in a chair, physically failing though mentally as sharp as ever. She argued with them that, for Scotland's sake, a French alliance must be better than an English one. By the time she died on 11 June, she had got nowhere. In her own cause Elizabeth I remained as untiring. She bothered not so much about the Scots as about the French. With them her faithful, discreet servant Sir William Cecil conducted secret talks at Newcastle-on-Tyne. Once Mary of Guise had died, he crossed the border and brought the crisis to a close.

Under the Treaty of Edinburgh in July 1560, English and French troops were alike to be withdrawn from Scotland. Military works would be slighted, so Leith ceased to boast the most modern fortifications in the British Isles; their site was left waste for two centuries until it offered space for the eventual construction of Great Junction Street, Constitution Street and Bernard Street (this last among the finest urban compositions in Scotland, so the wait was worthwhile). Something of what Leith lost can still be seen outside Eyemouth; the fort there, too, was slighted but not so thoroughly. Leith's independence vanished with its bastions. The feudal superiority would soon be sold to Edinburgh by a cash-strapped government, and Leithers were never to see again their £3,000. Meanwhile, under the treaty, the country's religion was to be decided in the Parliament. Knox had been drawing up a constitution for the Church of Scotland, the *First Book of Discipline*. It was approved in January 1561.[62]

So the work of Reformation went on even as, in November 1560, the political environment changed yet again. In Paris, Francis II came back from a day of hunting and fell ill of fever. Though his wife, Mary Queen of Scots, and his mother, Catherine de Medici, nursed him tenderly, he died on 5 December. Now there would be no children of Mary and Francis to rule both Scotland and France. The prospect of a union between the two nations dissolved.

Scotland's leaders invited Mary Queen of Scots to return. Whatever her religion, she was their lawful sovereign; and they hoped to convert her to Protestantism. Her reaction was wary. She would rather have found another royal match – Spaniard, Englishman, anybody really – than come back. But in six months not a single suitor appeared for the teenaged dowager. She had nowhere to go but home.

On 14 August 1561, Mary Queen of Scots boarded a great white galley at Calais. Five days later she sailed into Leith in a dense fog at eight o'clock in the morning. Nobody expected her and nothing was prepared. But she was warmly received. Later she went up to Holyrood and in the evening the townsfolk lit bonfires as they gathered beneath her windows to serenade her with psalms. They rejoiced to see the tall, lovely young queen with the Stewarts' red hair. The nobles welcomed her for various reasons of their own. Knox, however, was filled with foreboding as he stared out at the fog falling again overnight: 'The very face of heaven the time of her arrival did manifestly speak what comfort was brought unto this country with her, to wit, sorrow, dolour, darkness and all impiety.'[63]

CHAPTER THREE

'PERILOUS CITY'

(G. K. Chesterton)

ON 10 MARCH 1762, the Reverend William Robertson, a minister at Old Greyfriars Church in Edinburgh, was elected principal of the city's university. In the three decades he would have to direct its affairs he turned it into the powerhouse of the Scottish Enlightenment – indeed, into the best seat of learning in Europe, a status it sustained until the rise of the German universities in the nineteenth century.

Edinburgh was a municipal college, for which the main appointments had to go to the town council. At times there was intense competition for these. Rumours abounded in the spring of 1762, also, of a contest between Robertson and Adam Ferguson, then the university's professor of natural philosophy and the future father of the modern science of sociology. But it told against Ferguson that, while an ordained clergyman of the Church of Scotland, he had scarcely followed a ministerial vocation: who could say, in such a sceptical age, what his true opinions might be? In the end, then, Robertson went forward as the sole candidate and the councillors chose him without dissent.

Still, of greater influence in the process than any local bigwig was John Stuart, Earl of Bute, the first Scot to be Prime Minister of Great Britain. Mutual friends had asked him to step in on Robertson's behalf. Bute sent his orders to minions in Edinburgh who passed them down the municipal line. It was this kind of jobbing that, while unexceptionable and natural in Scotland, aroused the ire of the English and made them say rude things about the politics of the northern kingdom – the first line in an old song that has not ceased since.

Some Englishmen claimed Bute was a closet Jacobite (he had the right surname) intent on undermining the Hanoverian state. A swelling chorus of such innuendo would before long force him to resign. Yet the accusations were absurd. Bute, lacking any parliamentary base of his own, had to rely on his friendship with King George III as the sole prop of his power. Even if the Jacobite smear had been true, it would scarcely have made Bute favour Robertson, a veteran of the volunteer force raised on behalf of the British government against Prince Charles Edward Stewart's rebellion in 1745. It must be assumed Robertson had then been ready to die in defence of Edinburgh, except that no defence of the city was ever attempted. The Scots had their reasons, of which the English knew nothing, for the way they chose to work inside the Union. What counted here was that the selection of Robertson would prove by any standards sound, indeed brilliant.[1]

꽃

The University of Edinburgh always had a minister for its principal – it was therefore helpful in this clannish country that Robertson came of a clerical family. Born and brought up in his father's parish of Borthwick in Midlothian, he had found his own first charge in a rustic spot just as humble, Gladsmuir in East Lothian. Old Greyfriars was a big step up. The capital's clergy ran the Kirk and Robertson moved into its elite. Yet the laurels he sought were literary rather than religious. An advantage of Gladsmuir had lain in the fact his duties there took up little of his time while he worked away on a *History of Scotland*, which came out to critical acclaim in 1759. Not obviously a money-spinner (as it was by no means clear that anyone but Scots would want to read about the subject), in fact it opened all other doors to its author. Without it the post at the university would hardly have come his way. It must, then, have been history with special qualities. Nothing better exhibits these qualities than its treatment of Mary Queen of Scots. Robertson wrote the first modern account of her; in a sense she made his career.

This was as intended. Robertson wasted no time on the less sexy bits of his material. Two millennia of the nation's early history, the Wars of Independence included, merited a brief introduction. Recent stuff was consigned to a conclusion quite as curt. In between, the narrative dwelt on the years from the middle of the sixteenth century to the Union of Crowns in 1603. It seems clear Robertson's principle of editorial selection was to point up issues still hot in his own time: Reformation, Anglo-Scottish relations, above all Mary Queen of Scots.

About these things Robertson's countrymen continued to feel strongly enough not just to give a rousing send-off to his own literary career but also to salvage that of the flagging philosopher David Hume. Hume had set the pace in Marian studies with a sympathetic account of the doomed queen in his own *History of England*. It is an open question whether he wrote that account out of scholarly conviction; just as likely he sought to goad godly Presbyterians. The suspicion is fed by a story the novelist Henry Mackenzie told about him. Hume once wanted to borrow a book from the Advocates' Library, then under the care of Walter Goodall, an antiquarian who had published vindications of Mary. Goodall was a drunkard to boot. Hume came along with a friend to find him fast asleep in his chair. They could do nothing to wake him until Hume leaned over and bellowed in his ear, 'Queen Mary was a strumpet and a murtherer.'

'It's a damned lie,' grunted Goodall, starting out of his slumber – and Hume soon had the book he was looking for.[2]

Such was the literary scene on which Robertson launched his own account. It posed a test of his political as well as his authorial skills, which he was by temperament well fitted to face. To one side of him stood the Whigs, who had won most of the political victories in the last couple of centuries and crowned them by bringing Scotland into the Union of 1707. The Whigs thought Mary Queen of Scots an evil creature who had tried to restore popery and ordered her husband's murder. To the other side stood the Tories, clearly history's losers after the Battle of Culloden in 1745. For them Mary had been the innocent victim of Protestant bigotry and of jealousy from her ruthless English rival, Queen Elizabeth I. How did Robertson deal with all this? He split the difference. A plague on both Whigs and Tories, he said: Mary 'neither merited the exaggerated praises of the one, nor the undistinguished censure of the other'. She might have made mistakes, as in her choice of husbands and her means of disposing of them. But at heart she had not been a bad woman.[3]

The account was a studied exercise in impartiality, appealing beyond raucous partisans to the people Robertson really wanted to reach, the thousands of general readers who might buy his book and make his fortune, both monetary and professional – as they soon did. His impartiality began to approach the level of genius when he applied it also to the queen's diametric opposite, John Knox. Robertson was a Presbyterian too, and entertained no doubt that reformers of the sixteenth century had been right to cast down 'Romish superstition'. Still, he himself was tolerant, an advocate in his own time of Catholic emancipation. And in the book he went out of his way to stress, if somewhat improbably, the 'moderation of those who favoured the Reformation'. Even when obliged to describe how severe Knox had been at times, Robertson let him off on the grounds that 'those very qualities, which now render his character less amiable, fitted him to be the instrument of Providence for advancing the Reformation among a fierce people'. Providence was always useful to Robertson when he wanted to glide from one awkward position to another by a route not on the face of it obvious.[4]

※

It would be fair to say this view of Knox and of his relations with Mary Queen of Scots has not stood the test of time. The queen is more often depicted as the victim in a real-life nightmare, Knox as one of the horrors lurking in the shadows. Yet there could be something to Robertson's alternative approach. Of course it rested on Knox's own *History of the Reformation in Scotland* (1559–64). It had to, for that book is the prime source for all his dealings with the queen whether they were written up by Robertson or anybody else. Only through Knox, in fact, do we gain some inkling of the finer traits in Mary's character – for example, that she was, whatever else, intelligent and charming. The *History* is a personal memoir, though couched in the third rather than first person, yet almost more of a drama than a memoir; and no drama can be any good if too one-sided. It is also among the greatest works of Scots literature. Readers may begin to wonder about Knox's grim reputation if they reflect that the logic of the story as he himself tells it is what leads them to sympathize with woebegotten Mary.

Knox had four interviews with his sovereign, and the point most remembered about them is that in the last one he made her cry. The interview takes place amid rumours that she, the French widow, is about to remarry. He feels incensed with certain Protestant courtiers who accept her new husband may be a Catholic. At St Giles he has harangued his flock on the subject. This in turn has stung Mary, who summons him to Holyrood. Blue-blooded supporters come with him, and John Erskine of Dun accompanies him into her chamber. She is in 'a vehement fume'. She starts with the angry remark that 'never prince was handled as she was'.

The queen goes on: 'I have borne with you in all your rigorous manner of speaking, both against myself and against my uncles; yea, I have sought your favour by all possible means; I offered to you presence and audience whensoever it pleased you to admonish me; and yet I cannot be quit of you. I vow to God I shall be revenged.' Already beside herself, she bursts out in tears. A page hands her a handkerchief.

Knox waits until the queen is calm and admits they have had their differences: 'But when it shall please God to deliver you frae that bondage of darkness and error in the which you have been nourished, for the lack of true doctrine, your Majesty will find the liberty of my tongue nothing offensive.' If he is not preaching, he insists, he seldom gives offence. But if he is, 'I am not master of myself, but maun obey him who commands me to speak plain, and to flatter no flesh upon the face of the earth.'

The queen now comes out with the question weighing most on her mind: 'But what have you to do with my marriage?'

Knox will need to answer this question twice. His first answer comes from a minister of religion. God tells him to preach a gospel in two parts, repentance and faith. Preaching repentance starts by pointing out what sins people commit. Noblemen, for example, are so enchanted by the queen 'that neither God's word, not yet their commonwealth are rightly regarded; and therefore it becomes me to speak that they may know their duty'.

But the queen shows no interest in Knox's job description. 'What have you to do with my marriage?' she demands once again, 'Or what are ye in the Commonwealth?'

The second answer comes from a man of the people. What is he in the Commonwealth? Why, 'a subject within the same, Madam.' The rest makes this a famous answer, on behalf of a form of religion holding all believers to be equal. The Church of Scotland puts Knox and an aristocrat on an identical footing:

And albeit I be neither earl, lord nor baron within it, yet has God made me (however abject that ever I be in your eyes) a profitable member within the same; yea, Madam, to me it appertains no less to forewarn of such things as may hurt it, if I foresee them, than it doth to any of the nobility, for both my vocation and my conscience crave plainness of me.

This is the reason he will not dissemble to her:

Whensoever that the nobility of this realm shall consent, that ye be subject to an unfaithful [Catholic] husband, they do as much as in them lieth to renounce Christ, to banish his truth from them, to betray the freedom of this realm and perchance in the end do small comfort to yourself.

Here the queen goes into hysterics again. Erskine tries to calm her down with 'many pleasing words of her beauty, of her excellency and how that all the princes of Europe would be glad to ask her favour'. He just throws fuel on the flames. Knox meanwhile stands silent for a long time, before astonishing us with this:

Madam, in God's presence I speak, I never delight in the weeping of any of God's creatures; yea, I can scarcely abide the tears of my own boys, whom my own hand corrects, much less can I rejoice in your Majesty weeping. But seeing that I have offered no just occasion to be offended, but have spoken the truth, as my vocation craves of me, I maun sustain (albeit unwillingly) your Majesty's tears, rather than I dare hurt my conscience or betray my Commonwealth, therefore my silence.

Now, though, the queen is all the more offended. She orders Knox out. In an anteroom he finds everybody but Lord Ochiltree, a junior scion of the Stewarts, pretending not to know him. Nothing daunted, he turns to some ladies of the court, sitting there in 'gorgeous apparel'. And 'merrily' he says to them:

> O fair ladies, how pleasing was this life of yours, if it should ever abide, and that in the end that we might pass to heaven with all this gay gear? But fie upon that knave Death, that will come whether we will or no, and when he has laid in his arrest, the foul worms will be busy with this flesh, be it never so fair and so tender; and the silly soul, I fear, shall be so feeble, that it can neither carry with it gold, garnishing, targating [tasselled borders], pearl nor precious stones.

This is not quite small talk: it would clear most rooms. Yet Knox chats up the ladies until Erskine emerges to take him home.

The interview and its sequel were clearly important to Knox. If he had wished just to set out his own point of view, he need never have told the story in so much detail. On the contrary, however, he wants to demonstrate the complexity of his exchanges with the queen. It is true he dramatizes himself so as to appear, like Martin Luther before him, the honest pastor who refuses to hide the truth from one unwilling to hear it, or even the loving father who hates beating his children. And he depicts the queen as quite irrational and out of control. Yet he leaves us scope to feel for her, as a young woman with a heart and a conscience given pause by the words of a grave, forceful man. But why does Knox also find it necessary to report that, once dismissed, he dallies with the ladies of the court? It may give him another chance to run through his sanctimonious patter. How, though, can he do so 'merrily'? And how does it connect with what has gone before? Instead of lavishing praise on these birds of paradise, as the flatterer Erskine might have done, he tells them all flesh is grass – yet, while he is shunned by the rest of the court, they still sit there and talk to him.[5]

※

It is seldom recalled that Knox was rather a gallant. For all his stern demeanour, his taste ran to raffish pastimes, to music, dancing, theatre – and to women. In fact he seems to have felt more at ease with women than with men, being himself a little insecure and nervous, or at least beset by humility and doubt. His liking may have gone further. There is the notorious passage in a letter to Elizabeth Bowes: 'Call to mind what I did standing at the cupboard in Alnwick. In very deed, I thought that no creature had been tempted as I was.' Contemporaries sniggered at his frequent visits to this lady, legitimized after he married her daughter. He then confessed to his new mother-in-law how, among other failings, he had committed adultery in his mind and his heart was prey to 'foul lusts'. Among American evangelists of the present day, fervent faith has been found to go with carnal compulsions: why not in Knox too? As for the appetites of Mary Queen of Scots, we shall come to them below. Should the tension between her and Knox have been also in part sexual, it is easy to see how mortified he could have been that she did not respond to him. It would have made their relations worse than necessary. Suppressed attraction, if this is what it was, may have flipped over into its opposite: uninhibited loathing.[6]

The Scottish Reformation in the end set about controlling every human tendency to err. Edinburgh is often held up as a place which built this outlook into its way of life, with its cold weather, cold stone and cold heart. There are those who regret that John Calvin rather than Martin Luther triumphed here, even that King Henry VIII never imposed Anglicanism at the Rough Wooing. Whether this estimate should be laid at Knox's door is another matter. It is after all unlikely he could simply have brainwashed his parishioners of St Giles, let alone the rest of the nation. In fact, in an age of extremes, he was not the most extreme. It took the bitterness of civil war, caused by the failings of Mary Queen of Scots, to bring out Calvinist fanaticism in her people. In doctrine and government of the Kirk the radical victors in that conflict went beyond Knox, who was dead before it finished; rather they fulfilled the ambitions of a younger militant, Andrew Melville of Glasgow (always, compared to Edinburgh, a city of bigotry). The Reformation had its own roots in the capital, in a social order already prizing virtues of literacy and thrift while combining a sense of responsibility with a commitment to personal dignity – as given voice by Knox when, to his regret, he made his queen cry. All this, along with the sanctimony, also formed part of Edinburgh's Calvinism.

The resulting ambiguity towards Mary Queen of Scots was typical not just of Knox but of the capital and the nation; it still is. Even in August 1561, when she landed from France, initial rejoicing in Edinburgh gave way within days to ugly violence. But the Scottish Reformation was unlike Reformations elsewhere. For one thing it came last of them all in time; that is, no effort to introduce Protestantism to any other country proved successful after 1560. For another thing it made the sole exception to the contemporary principle of *Cuius regio, eius religio*, 'The ruler determines the religion of the state'; Mary remained a Catholic in a Protestant country. It was from the start an awkward, angular, even schizophrenic mix.

※

Before the queen ventured back to Scotland she had doubtless struck bargains, yet she could hardly have expected to see them tested so soon. She arrived on a Tuesday, and on the following Sunday she and her household went to mass in her private chapel at Holyrood: she had started as she meant to continue. But Protestant hotheads from the town managed to penetrate the palace and tried to disrupt the service. No less a personage than James Stewart, Earl of Arran, one of the proto-reformers of the 1550s, had to bar the door of the chapel. To Knox this meant that Arran was deserting the cause of truth. The Sunday after that he preached a ferocious sermon in St Giles claiming a single mass was more dangerous than the landing of 'ten thousand armed enemies'. The government had to respond. On the Monday it issued an official statement of the queen's position: neither to bring back Catholicism nor to make any kind of change in the nation's religion unless authorized by Parliament.

This was not a final solution. Meanwhile, it seemed only in order that, after arriving out of the blue and missing any kind of official welcome, Mary Queen of Scots should make a ceremonial entry into her capital. The pageantry might head off the problems. Plans had been made for 2 September, two days after Knox's sermon. But then, as now, Edinburgh housed pernickety people who could not let a chance go by to make their point. The queen attended a banquet at the Castle and afterwards led a procession down the Royal Mile. She marched along with a gold-fringed purple canopy held over her head. Fifty youths dressed as Moors, in black masks and yellow suits, capered before her. By the Cross girls in diaphanous dresses posed as mythological figures, while wine flowed from the fountain at its foot. When Mary reached the Tron a child came down out of a painted cloud and presented her with the keys to Edinburgh, then with two books in rich velvet bindings. She opened them. One was a copy of the Bible in English, not Latin, the other a book of psalms: symbols of Protestantism. She handed them without a word to the Earl of Huntly, a Catholic nobleman standing next to her. He later reported that, as she had moved off again, he felt obliged to stop some people about to burn the effigy of a priest.[7]

Could Edinburgh's town councillors have had something to do with this impudence, by any chance? It was not beyond the bounds of possibility. The rulers of Scotland did not lightly countenance dissent in their capital, but its council had become a scene of sectarian strife because the rulers of Scotland kept changing. Mary of Guise and the Lords of the Congregation had fought for control of the council. When Mary held the upper hand, a Catholic, George, Lord Seton, served as provost; when the Lords were in control a Protestant, Archibald Douglas of Kilspindie. The two regimes alternated during the year up to the election of Michaelmas 1560, which unlike previous ones is supposed to have proceeded 'by normal and due process'. This resulted in a Protestant victory, repeated in 1561. On 5 October the incoming councillors threw down a challenge to Mary Queen of Scots, just to show how glad they were to see her again. They reissued the anti-Catholic ordinances passed by their predecessors. Perhaps they had not reckoned with her accepting the challenge. She told them to sack Douglas and bring back Seton. And they did; they might send childish cherubs to act out charades in the High Street but, when it came to the crunch, they dared not yet disobey a direct royal command. This would change.[8]

❧

But the queen saw off the early threats to her authority. Things never went too badly wrong before her marriage to Henry Stewart, Lord Darnley, in 1565. That she had to remarry nobody doubted. Yet all the possible foreign consorts seemed likely to cause as many problems as they might solve. After much toing and froing it was this other Stewart, a cousin of hers, that seemed the best match available.

They fell in love (at first). Their union made political sense as well. It promised an independent, patriotic monarchy.

Official jollification was once more obligatory, no doubt reflecting the nation's sentiment. On another level it gave a boost to the literary revival Mary Queen of Scots had sparked off since arriving back from the most cultured court in Europe. A bright young lawyer, Thomas Craig of Riccarton, brought out his *Epithalamium*, a Latin song of praise summed up in the line *'Tu vero, o coelo iuvenum gratissime, Nymphes connubiis (junguente deo) dignate superbis'* ('You, indeed, oh most pleasing to heaven of young people, God unites while nymphs prepare a sumptuous marriage-bed'). The Protestant George Buchanan, home again in a hurry from being fingered by the Inquisition in Portugal, wrote in hopes to Darnley: *'nos quoque pendemus de te, sol noster'* ('We too depend on you, our sun'). When Scots were not showing off their Latinity they turned to their own homely tongue. The makar Alexander Scott had addressed Mary:

> *Welcum, oure rubent roiss upoun the ryce!*
> *Welcum, oure jem and joyfull genetryce!*
>
> Welcome, our ruby rose upon the twig!
> Welcome, our gem and joyful genetrix!

Now the romance of a royal wedding created a fashion for love poetry, seldom cultivated before by gruff, bashful Scots. When in 1568 the merchant George Bannatyne fled from the plague in Edinburgh, he would while away his rustic idleness by writing out a huge collection of vernacular verse, containing more love poetry than anything else, in the Bannatyne Manuscript (preserved at the National Library of Scotland).[9]

But, spontaneous as it may have been in the hearts of the people, the flamboyant flattery seemed to go to the heads of the young couple, and in the matter not so much of love as of religion. Darnley was a stupid, sottish, sex-crazed lout, vacuously handsome and doubtless without belief in anything much. His bride felt too smitten with him to mind when, though they had a Catholic wedding, he refused to attend the nuptial mass. He continued to go to St Giles on Sundays, so Knox could rage at him; one time, said Darnley, it put him off his dinner. But then at Christmas he goaded Presbyterians –

who had ceased celebration of the old religious festivals – by returning to the mass. Later, on 2 February 1566, he chose Candlemas, feast of the Purification of the Virgin Mary, to be invested with the Order of St Michael, the most exalted honour in the chivalry of France, after a high mass at Holyrood in the presence of the European diplomatic corps. There could scarcely have been any clearer sign of a will to reunite the Scots crown with French power and Roman religion, just as under Mary of Guise. The solemn ritual did not stop Darnley, drunk as usual, swaggering afterwards up the Royal Mile with boorish boasts of how he had brought his country back to the true faith. Soon he was writing to the pope to complain his wife had not done enough for Catholicism.

Protestants, who in 1560 had come out on top by main force, were never going to stand for this. Still, their reaction fell not on Darnley, rather on another Catholic close to the queen, her Italian servant, David Rizzio. On the evening of 9 March a gang of noble thugs led by Patrick, Lord Ruthven, penetrated Holyrood, burst in on her chamber and dragged a screaming Rizzio from her, in their excitement already plunging daggers into his body. Outside they finished him off. Scots relish such gruesomeness. An English traveller, H. V. Morton, would visit the spot in the 1920s to be told by a guide: 'They used to put raddle [red ochre] down here at the head of the steps and tell people that Rizzio's blood would never wash away. But now we have a brass plate.'[10]

The remarkable element in this was that Darnley joined the assassins in Holyrood. They left his dagger in the corpse to make the point that he was the most eager to be rid of Rizzio. Quite why is a puzzle, but the end of marital relations an obvious possibility. Rumours ran of the queen seeking solace in the arms of another, though the lickspittle Latin seems a doubtful candidate. More likely was James Hepburn, Earl of Bothwell, just back from France; he at once found favour with her, to which she gave concrete expression by granting him the castle and lands of Dunbar. Still, this does not itself explain the brutal murder or Darnley's complicity. Perhaps he was indeed a lush who hardly knew what he was doing. His wife decided enough was enough.

The crime was compounded by the fact that the queen was pregnant at the time, and might have suffered a miscarriage from the shock. Her son, James VI to be, was born on 19 June 1566, at Edinburgh Castle, the last King of Scots to arrive in the world there. Darnley came to see him an hour or two later. The queen took the baby in her arms and held him out saying: 'My lord, here I protest unto God and as I shall answer at the great day of judgment, this is your son, and no other man's son; and I am desirous that all here, both ladies and others, bear witness, for he is so much our son that I fear it may be worse for him hereafter.' Darnley fed the suspicions it could be some other man's son by refusing to attend the baptism.[11]

The birth had been difficult, but in October the queen felt well enough to go on a royal progress round the Borders. By 20 November she was back at Craigmillar Castle, where she stayed for a fortnight. Here she is supposed to have laid her plans to murder Darnley, who fell sick on a visit to Glasgow. The queen went to visit him and persuaded him to return to Edinburgh. She had him quarantined at Kirk o'Field, in the provost's house just inside the southern section of the Flodden Wall, on the site of the later university.

The evening of 9 February 1567 was busy in the royal household. The queen gave a dinner for the Savoyard ambassador. Then she went to her husband's bedside for a couple of hours, returning to Holyrood at midnight for a masque to celebrate the marriage of a favourite French servant. At two o'clock in the morning there was a huge explosion at Kirk o'Field, so loud that the revellers in the palace thought it was cannonfire. Townsfolk sprang up and rushed to the scene. It was one of utter destruction. Of the provost's house nothing remained but rubble. When soldiers searched the grounds they found the body of Darnley, not frazzled by flame but strangled by hand.[12]

※

Bothwell had grown closer to Mary Queen of Scots as her relations with her husband broke down. He had been at Holyrood the night of Rizzio's murder and escaped from a window at the back. While the queen was in the Borders that autumn he went on raids round the region to hunt down reivers. A clash left him wounded, and she so exerted herself in riding to be with him that she herself took ill. Like her forefathers she was a poet, and she wrote a sonnet about the awakening of her love for Bothwell:

> *Pour lui aussi je jette mainte larme.*
> *Premier quand il fit de ce corps possesseur,*
> *Duquel alors il n'avait pas le coeur . . .*
>
> *Pour lui j'ai hazardé grandeur et conscience,*
> *Pour lui tous mes parents j'ai quittés, et amis,*
> *Et tous autres respects sont apart mis.*
> *Brief de vous seul je cherche l'alliance.*
>
> For him also I shed many a tear.
> First when he possessed this body,
> Of which he did not yet have the heart . . .

But in the end she had fallen head over heels in love:

> For him I have risked greatness and conscience,
> For him I have left all my family and friends,
> And have put aside every other consideration.
> In brief I seek the bond with you alone.[13]

Bothwell was an obvious suspect for the murder of Darnley. Inquiry brought to light that his men had been shifting barrels of gunpowder into the cellars of Kirk o'Field while the victim lay ill upstairs. Darnley's father, the Earl of Lennox, got Bothwell arraigned of the crime before the privy council. But the trial turned out a farce and he was acquitted on 12 April.

Then, on 24 April, Bothwell abducted the queen. She was on her way back to Edinburgh from Stirling after a few days with her son. As her party approached the capital, Bothwell rode out to meet her at the head of an armed force. Seizing her horse by the bridle, he claimed it was too perilous for her to go on into town. He would instead take her to safety at Dunbar. Her escort drew swords but she stayed them, saying she would have no more bloodshed; some suspected she was colluding in her own capture. So to Dunbar she went, and Bothwell may have raped her there. They were married in a Protestant ceremony on 15 May.

Now, even for such a turbulent nation, things had gone too far. On 15 June, rebel lords confronted Mary Queen of Scots and Bothwell at Carberry, just outside Musselburgh. There could have been a battle but the two sides chose to parley. The lords told the queen to leave her latest consort. A deal was struck: he would get a safe conduct out of the country while she would place her trust in them. And so, Bothwell went to Denmark, to die in a dungeon, while she was led off to Edinburgh, then four days later to custody at a castle in the middle of Loch Leven in Fife. As she rode into her capital, then out again, the mob jeered.

The queen's captors held her on Loch Leven until she escaped in May 1568. Enough Scots rallied round to let her face her foes at the Battle of Langside. There she lost and gave way to panic. She fled across the Solway Firth into England. She was again taken into custody, where she would stay until her execution at Fotheringay Castle in 1587 for plotting against Queen Elizabeth. But at the moment of her desertion the nation did not know it had seen the last of Mary; on the contrary, it expected her quick return. Her friends fought on against her enemies, these deeming the infant James VI already to have succeeded to a vacant throne. While he yet mewled and puked, they crowned him at Stirling. Five years of civil war followed.

This was called a war of the king's men and the queen's men. First fought out in distant regions of the country, it steadily closed in on the capital, which, within the walls, was held for Mary, while her foes skulked beyond. The conflict then became also a war of Edinburgh and Leith, with two town councils and two kirk sessions trying to assert their authority, and both factions claiming to be the legitimate government of Scotland. They not only battled against each other but held their own Parliaments as well. Sometimes two Parliaments sat at once, legislating to seize lands and goods from men of the opposite party. There was nothing amusing about this: it descended into brutalism, with captives slaughtered and sufferings inflicted on innocent civilians as the Lothians were again ravaged.

By late 1572 the king's men were getting the better of the queen's men and laid siege to Edinburgh Castle. Inside, the garrison hoped against hope that a Spanish army led by the Duke of Alva, at the time massacring the Protestant Dutch, might cross the North Sea and do the same to the Protestant Scots. What arrived instead was English artillery, courtesy of Elizabeth I. For a month in the spring of 1573 it pounded the castle so relentlessly that squads of besieging soldiers were sent round the foot of the Rock to look for cannonballs which had bounced back off the walls and might be recycled; the sentries on the ramparts used these scavengers for target practice. The game was up when the topmost storeys of David's Tower collapsed into its well. A soldier-poet, Robert Sempill, saw it happen:

> *By weirlyk volyis thocht the wallis wes wycht*
> *Yit dowbell batterie brak thame all in inchis.*
> *Of Davies toure, in all the toune menis sycht,*
> *Thay riggein stanes come tumland ovir the trinchis.*[14]

> Though the walls were defended by warlike volleys,
> Yet a double battery broke them all in fragments.
> From David's Tower, in all the townsmen's sight,
> The ramparts came tumbling over the trenches.

Surrender followed. Prisoners were murdered in cold blood. At least a time of woes ended. The Earl of Moray, regent for James VI, could now in the infant king's name secure a Protestant state.

❧

The fabric of Edinburgh had not come well out of all this. The greatest building on the Rock lay in ruins, along with the ramparts flanking it. Repair of the fortifications would take two decades. A new eastward defence of the castle with no pretence to style, the Half Moon Battery, was wrapped round what remained of David's Tower. Its gun-ports pointed down the High Street, though they would seldom be used. Elsewhere, internal destruction was the story at St Giles, with the medieval screens and furnishings all smashed. Nor had the building itself been held sacred: the western end underwent secularization, taken over as an annexe of the Tolbooth to be used for a courtroom. In 1581 walls would be thrown up inside the church, partitioning it so as to provide separate places of worship for three of the new parishes into which the burgh was divided; the medieval community, one since its start, split up. At the foot of the Royal Mile, Holyrood had yet to recover from being pillaged and burned by the English in 1544. The church was repaired, but in 1559 reformers dismantled the altars and left the monastery to crumble. Its abbot at the last was Robert Stewart, bastard of James V; two laymen followed him in the nominal office though this meant nothing except rights to the property, as in the other defunct religious houses of Scotland. Only the nave stayed in use as the Canongate's place of worship; even here, choir and transepts were demolished in 1570.[15]

But where there was ruin there might also be reconstruction, which often brings a quick return to prosperity. So it went also in Edinburgh. Long-term economic growth resumed, and one shape it took was in more solid buildings, with stone replacing timber in the fabrication. This is why, leaving aside the major monuments, the earliest survivals of the domestic architecture date from this period. In the High Street, John Knox's House had been started earlier but must have been finished by 1573, the year after his death. We know as much because the next owner, the goldsmith James Mossman, had his coat-of-arms carved into a wall facing the street, and he was one of those executed at the fall of the castle, having made the mistake of financing the doomed garrison. Off the Lawnmarket, in Riddle's Court, stands a house built a bit later for John MacMorran, wealthiest merchant of his time. Down in the Canongate, Huntly House is of the same era.[16]

The building boom resulted not only from the destruction of war but also from the needs of a soaring population. Estimates of the numbers living in Edinburgh vary, but credible is the conclusion they doubled between 1550 and 1650. A serious contemporary effort at enumeration came at the division of the burgh into parishes, when it was found to contain 2,239 households with 8,000 persons 'counted to discretion'. We cannot be sure the poor were included, all the same, and they may have made up a quarter or third of the true total. Edinburgh certainly boasted more people than any other place in Scotland; according to the assessments for tax, which may provide a proxy for population, it was as big as Dundee, Aberdeen and Perth combined. It rivalled the larger towns of England or the Swiss republics of Geneva and Zürich, though it still came far behind Amsterdam, Antwerp or London, which each had a population of 100,000, let alone Paris with its 200,000.[17]

But on the tail of the Rock more people led to more crowding, and those who could afford it began to seek some space. There were limits to where they could go if unwilling to abandon the burgh or the business they conducted there. What they could do was buy a bit of land in the Lothians and on it build a roomier residence. This was no social revolution: they never tried to rival the feudal nobility with its wide estates and covetous jealousies. Prosperous burgesses just wanted a place to bring up children in safety, where they themselves might relax over a long weekend before commuting back into town. Up to now the Lothians' landscape had contained castles for lairds or hovels for peasants. Now it was to be graced also by a novel style of bourgeois home on the scale of a villa (long before suburbia had been invented). The house would sit on a plot sometimes no bigger than a large garden, certainly not itself a source of income; rather, this was, for the first time among the wealthy of Edinburgh, an investment in style and ease.

The retreats were still baronial in architecture, while displaying none of those fantastic sprouts of turrets marking the final development of towerhouses, abodes of the Scots nobility. In Aberdeenshire and Angus, Craigievar or Glamis are contemporary but as from another age. The aim at Lothian's country houses was not refuge and defence but prestige and comfort. Owners built the walls thin, by earlier standards, and harled them: they were not expecting to be bombarded by cannonfire. Inside, they used the scope for interior design. They had beamed ceilings put up and painted with patterns of plants or animals; an example survives at Caroline Park, erected about 1585 on the shore of the Firth of Forth by the merchant Andrew Logan. Soon, as at the Brunstane begun by his colleague John Crichton, Scotland's tradition of exquisite plasterwork would emerge in profusions of foliage, flowers and fruit, interspersed with heraldry or emblematic human figures. Beyond the present boundaries of the city lie further examples at Fountainhall in East Lothian, Linhouse and Midhope in West Lothian.[18]

❧

For Edinburgh, a rise in population and quality of building reflected a rise in civic status too: no question now that this was the capital of Scotland. Political results followed. At the municipal level, the burgh got a new sett or constitution, the decreet arbitral of 1583.[19] One aim was to bring peace between the privileged merchants and the aspirant craftsmen after a century or more of feud. In fact the merchants again came off the better – or rather, the new deal required minimal adjustment by them. In the town council, where the crafts had been entitled to only a couple of members, they got more: six deacons from among their fourteen incorporations. That yet preserved a majority of ten merchant members plus, in any given council, the retiring office-bearers from the last (provost, two bailies, dean of guild and treasurer, nearly all merchants). So the merchants continued to control most business. They kept a bare majority even when this so-called ordinary council of twenty-five expanded into an extraordinary council of thirty-three, with the rest of the crafts' deacons, for special purposes: decisions on the common good (independent property and revenue of the burgh) or election of members of the Parliament. Since it was not a wider electorate but only each complement of councillors that chose its successors at the end of a two-year term, the ensemble remained an oligarchy. In effect co-option, not election, was what won a rising man his place among them.

The sole gesture made by the reforms of 1583 towards life outside the Tolbooth came in recognition that the medieval distinction between merchants and craftsmen was losing meaning, though the decreet arbitral relied on it still. But, from this point on, craftsmen could be admitted to the exclusive merchants' guild. Money was talking here. While goldsmiths counted among the richest people in town, until now they had been defined as mere craftsmen. On the other hand, lawyers had risen even faster, yet, being unincorporated, their municipal status remained equal to that of casual labourers – they were all alike 'unfree', as the burgesses crowed. The various categories of burgess made up perhaps one-third of the adult male population. They were the only ones with any say in the burgh's affairs.

※

Above the municipal level Edinburgh, while for over a century now the normal residence of the Kings of Scots, had so far lacked other normal attributes of a capital. It was never the metropolitan see of the country, which had been fixed at St Andrews from 1472. Nor had it until recently housed any central law courts, because the nation possessed none. And the three medieval universities of Scotland were sited elsewhere.

Now, with the Catholic dioceses abolished, the way opened for

Edinburgh to become in effect the religious capital of Scotland. A portent lay in the fact that, just ten days after Mary Queen of Scots had been taken into captivity in 1567, it was here the General Assembly convened, itching to launch a second, more radical stage of the Reformation. The first stage had also taken the shape of revolt against the crown; since the crown now rested on a baby's head, even less was it possible for a godly prince, as in other countries, to stand in the way. With more or less complete freedom the liberated Kirk set out to realize its own vision of pure apostolic Christianity.

This General Assembly proceeded to overthrow everything in medieval tradition with no sanction in scripture. It got rid of a top-heavy hierarchy, though Calvinist aspiration meant the new structure could not be kept simple either. The goal was to awaken faith in the bosom and bowels of the people rather than to pass down divine authority from on high. So in its completed form the structure would mount up from kirk sessions in every parish, by way of superintendents in bigger towns round the country, to provincial synods meeting twice a year and finally to the annual General Assembly with jurisdiction over all. The complexity, indeed cumber, of the Kirk's fabric was the price to be paid for its evangelical aims. From the start the General Assembly normally met in Edinburgh; the ministers of the burgh also held special powers to convoke it in any emergency. So far as the Church of Scotland had a Rome, it was here.[20]

茶

As for central law courts, Scotland's lack of them had found a remedy from James V in 1532 when he established in Edinburgh the Court of Session as the highest civil court. This rounded off the legal development of a century. Most law any ordinary Scot might encounter had fallen under the administration of the Church – the kind once dealt with by the promising notary apostolic John Knox, the law of family and property. Like Knox, young men wanting to practise law often did better to become priests first. Priests, if worldly (as many were), did better to study law than theology.

Yet there had always been greater matters that went up for decision to the Parliament or king's council. Their number rose as wild Scots calmed down and resorted to law rather than feud for the settlement of their differences. James I set up a 'session' to deal with the resulting flow of business. Then James III named regular Lords of Council to take it over. Since the king now usually resided in Edinburgh, the 'Lords of Council and Session' met there too, in the Tolbooth: the seed of a central civil court was sown. James V finally gave it a full-time salaried bench, under the grand title of College of Justice, more often known as the Court of Session, again sitting in Edinburgh. At the outset seven churchmen and seven laymen manned it, under a president who was also a churchman. The clerical majority seemed natural when most civil law derived from canon law. Only slowly did a secular system emerge, one better served by lay professionals.

A consequence of the Reformation was to free Scots law from its medieval constraints and set it off on that secular, but above all national, path of development. Lawyer-clerics had no more right to hog civil cases. Nor might the finer points of law be any longer referred to Rome, so appeals could not go higher than the Court of Session or privy council. Radical Protestants in any event sought stricter separation of the sacred and the secular. For the law, that meant courts of the Church were to have no part in deciding non-religious causes, even though civil magistrates ought to be guided by godly principles. However that all may have been, laymen displaced clerics in legal practice. Canon law was then bound to go into decline, and civil law to flourish in its stead. Edinburgh profited. As the regular meeting place of the Parliament and privy council, now of the Court of Session too, not to mention of its own sheriff or burgh courts, this became far and away the biggest centre for legal practice in Scotland – as it has remained ever since.

Legal practice required legal training. That had always been best obtained on the Continent, at schools in France and the Netherlands serving the whole of Europe. At the Reformation these schools, too, switched their focus from canon law to civil law by reviving for modern times the jurisprudence of the Roman Empire, a fertile source of intellectual inspiration and debate even into the era of Enlightenment. So, for another couple of centuries, Scots students still went to study with profit at the French and Dutch schools. Not everyone, however, followed that route. There was the alternative of serving an apprenticeship with a practising lawyer in Edinburgh. A

young man with legal ambitions might start by sitting in on cases at
the Tolbooth. There he could mix with advocates who after hours
would be able to give him private instruction. In time he might try
his own hand at pleading in a lower court. Once he had a track
record, he could hand in an account of his cases – perhaps with a
'specimen doctrine' to demonstrate his theoretical proficiency – to
the Lords of Session, who if satisfied would give him leave to appear
before them. In these ways Edinburgh's legal profession, so pregnant
for its future, emerged.[21]

※

Education in general followed a trajectory similar to that of law, of
secularization spreading its benefits among the people. We have met
the men who made up Knox's first private congregations in Edinburgh, well-informed and literate burgesses. The town now offered
them facilities to keep themselves so. Since 1507 it had housed a
printing press. James IV then gave a patent to Walter Chepman and
Andrew Myllar, merchant and bookseller, to 'bring hame ane prent'
from Rouen in France where they had been working. They set up
shop in the Cowgate. Their first productions, some of which survive
in fragmentary form, included works of the makars. Given that
Chepman and Myllar might have stuck to missals and chronicles,
their publishing policy looks progressive. Still, probably they made
their greatest profit from the monopoly they held for producing legal
textbooks and Acts of Parliament.[22] Like much else in a small, poor
nation, Scottish printing suffered a discontinuous history. But the
Reformation was to transform the trade. The new order rested on a
literate ministry (not universal before) and on a literate people (quite
novel).

Knox's Presbyterian manifesto, the *First Book of Discipline*, ordered
all Scots children to go to school and, as the religious matrix for
their general education, to learn a catechism. It comes as no surprise he made this hard to learn. The first question put to a child in
the English catechism was a feeble, 'What is your name?' The Scots
catechism began with a bang: 'What is the chief end of man?' By this
and other means the true faith was to be instilled under competent
instruction into every Scot.

For that purpose Edinburgh already offered reformers a foundation, whereas in much of Scotland the edifice of reform needed to be built from scratch. Since the burgh's foundation there had been at Holyrood a school, later to be known as the High School of Edinburgh. It taught the monastery's novices, no doubt along with other boys, the reading and writing that led on to religious vows or to lay careers. Not much else is known about the school before David Vocat became its master in 1519. The next master, Henry Henryson, was tried and convicted of heresy in 1534. But the classes can hardly have been nests of subversion, for William Robertson, master during the Reformation, remained Catholic and defied all efforts to oust him, up to and including a case that went to the Court of Session in 1569. As the abandoned abbey at Holyrood decayed, the school moved out to the late Cardinal Beaton's residence in Blackfriars Wynd, then into a second disused religious house, Blackfriars, on the other side of the Cowgate. There it was re-launched under Hercules Rollock – but he could not stop his pupils absorbing, along with their lessons, the turbulence of the time. In 1595, in a row over the length of their holidays, the boys barricaded themselves inside the school. The town council had to send in heavies to deal with them, led by John MacMorran, the richest man in the burgh and bailie to boot. The pupils jeered at them as 'buttery carles'. MacMorran ordered the door to be broken down with a battering ram. One lad, William Sinclair, leaned out of a window and shot the bailie through the head.[23]

The medieval schooling had seemed to meet the burgh's needs, but for higher studies bright youngsters always needed to leave. Most went to university at St Andrews or Glasgow, a few abroad. Now people began to think the capital ought to have its own university, on a more modern plan than any set out in the episcopal charters of Scotland's more ancient foundations. Even before the Reformation that thought had struck Robert Reid, bishop, judge and diplomat for Mary of Guise. When he died in 1558 he left money to found a college in Edinburgh. Although a cleric, he stipulated it should not come under the control of the Church. It would have three schools: a grammar school for children, a school of arts for more advanced studies, and a school of law.[24] Not all this came to pass, and another benefactor was equally influential in giving the college its eventual character. He was Clement Little, who in 1580 bequeathed 200 books to form the nucleus of an academic library, most of them on religion and philosophy. He had made his living as an advocate, and gave an early example of how in Edinburgh the members of his profession were already starting to form an intellectual community of prime importance for the city's culture. An elder of the Kirk, alike concerned with the plight of the poor and the education of the young, he was typical of many who found their way from the European Renaissance to the Scottish Reformation.[25]

Nothing more could be done about a university for Edinburgh in the reign of Mary Queen of Scots or the civil war following. It was the town council that afterwards took up the idea again. The councillors knew what they wanted, a college to supply the spiritual and intellectual needs of a reformed burgh, one they could support and in some degree control – but without spending too much money. They secured in 1583 a royal charter allowing use of any of the collegiate kirks or friaries, 'now waste and vacant places', to house 'professors of the schools of grammar, humanity and the languages, philosophy, theology, medicine and law, or any other liberal sciences'.[26]

The site at length chosen for the University of Edinburgh was Kirk o'Field, lying yet in ruins after being blown up over Darnley. Repairs still left it with a makeshift appearance, which visitors would deride for decades ahead. Nor were the councillors over-generous to the inaugural principal, Robert Rollock, recruited from St Andrews. They made him also serve as a minister at Greyfriars, on a stipend of 300 merks. Economical as the joining of academic and clerical functions was, it would have its uses down to the time of Principal Robertson and beyond. As for the rest of the staff, no specialist professors were employed at the outset: so-called regents did all teaching, each to a class of his own, throughout the curriculum of arts and divinity. The first students matriculated in October 1583. Among the forty-seven who entered then and graduated in 1587, at least fifteen chose careers in the Church. For the better part of three centuries ahead, the council would get here what it wanted.[27]

❧

Church, law and university (together with the schooling for higher education) were the institutional pillars of the new civil society of reformed Scotland, the visionary aim of Knox and his fellows. The new civil society would grow robust enough to outlast Scotland's statehood and preserve her nationhood down to the present, after being also – at the Scots' insistence – guaranteed by the Treaty of Union with England in 1707. These pillars of the new civil society were built, or at least began to rise, in 1560, overlaying the structures of the medieval nation with the foundations of the modern one. And all were sited in whole or in important part in Edinburgh. They justified its status as capital of the kingdom, and would keep it as capital even after the independence of the kingdom came to an end. In earlier ages the survival of nation and monarchy had relied on the heroic patriotism of the Scots people, with those of Edinburgh playing their part, if not always a central or decisive part. The new civil society would be maintained by different means, in which Edinburgh's role proved crucial.

The new society ordered the everyday life of burgh and nation, though not all the many changes met a universal welcome. To traditional royal and feudal authority the authority of the rising institutions was added – and authority in Scotland had few effective constraints.

With new courts and new laws came new crimes. Confession and penance had formerly been enough to efface minor moral faults among the people; and as the confessional remained secret, all was a matter for penitent and priest alone. There had been exceptions, however. In 1547 Janet Bruce's priest told her to go on to the High Street of Edinburgh, donate a wax candle to a chaplain, seek out Isobel Carrington and say to her, in front of witnesses and in good Scots: 'I grant here before three honest persons that I have fairly and wrangfully injurit and defamit you, sayand and allegand you are ane common bluidy whore. I knaw nathing but ye are ane honest woman and keeps guid pert to your husband.' Janet was to say also to Isobel's husband, Robert: 'I failit far to you and your wife calling you ane cuckold, whilk I confess is nocht of verity for your wife is ane honest woman.' For the sake of satisfaction on every side, Isobel was then to go to Janet and say: 'Ye are ane honest woman, I never knew that ever ye swiffit [copulated] with the auld official, and insofar as I rehearsed the samen I ask God forgivance and you.' The penance was public but aimed at conciliation, not punishment, so as to soothe sore feelings rather than harden hearts.[28]

⚘

The old easy-going response to all manner of mischief comes over more generally in a long poem by Alexander Scott, 'The Justing and Debait at the Drum'. This is literature rather than reportage, to be sure, and it may expose a certain degree of condescension in the courtly poet towards the great unwashed – though more likely it once again shows the intimacy among different levels of this small society, something destined to survive the huge changes now bursting on to it. In literary terms, the poem mixes several genres favoured by the makars, mock heroics with depictions of peasant brawls. Its subject is the people of Edinburgh as they enjoy a holiday at the Drum, a leafy spot on the main road south (now occupied by a classical mansion). A tournament is supposed to be held there but, because of various ludicrous muddles, it does not take place. The people have to seek a different festive expedient, further out in the country:

> *Than to Dalkeith thai made them boun,*
> *Reidwod of this reproche.*
> *Thair wes baith wyne and vennisoun*
> *And barrellis ran on broche.*

> Then to Dalkeith they set out,
> Furious at this reproach.
> There was both wine and venison
> And barrels ran on tap.

Everybody gets drunk and then, because Scots like fights and there is little else to do, young men spar with each other to entertain themselves and the crowd. This goes on until evening:

> *Be than the bowgill gan to blaw,*
> *For nycht had thame ourtane,*
> *'Allais,' said Sym, 'for falt of law*
> *That bargan get I nane.'*

> *Thus hame with many crak and flaw*
> *Thay passed every ane,*

Syne pairtit at the Potter Raw,
And sindry gaitis are gane.

By then the bugle began to blow,
For night had overtaken them,
'Alas,' said Sim, 'because of the law
I do not get a fight.'

So home with many a joke and boast
They passed every one,
Then parted at the Potterrow
And went their separate ways.

In other words, as they enter at curfew through the southern gate of Edinburgh they all agree they have had a wonderful time. The poem cannot be precisely dated either to the period before the Reformation or to the period after it. Beyond doubt is that this was the sort of behaviour the reformers set out to stop.[29]

The changes were never going to be instant and only rigour – not to say fanaticism – could enforce them. There was a stern reaction against what the former clerical laxity had winked at. But the reaction affected more than religious observance: it targeted the whole tenor of life in Edinburgh and elsewhere. Public plays, carnivals and processions were banned successfully. Prostitution, drunkenness and other personal vices were banned unsuccessfully. Repeated thunderous proclamations from the town council suggest human nature remained the same. Yet the reformers did exert a real effect in turning Edinburgh glummer. Sir Richard Maitland was a judge of a family connected with the regime of Mary Queen of Scots. He had retired and gone blind by now but the fact he could see the merry old Scotland only through his mind's eye made his memories all the more poignant:

Quhair is the blythness that has bein
Bayth in burgh and landwart sein,
Amang lordis and ladyis schein,
Dauncing, singing, game and play?

But now I wait noght quhat thai mein,
All mirriness is worn away . . .

> *For now I heir na wourde of yule*
> *In kirk, on cassay nor in scule . . .*

> *I saw no gysaris all this yeir*
> *But kirkmen clad like men of weir.*

> Where is the happiness that has been seen
> Both in the burgh and in the countryside
> Among fine lords and ladies,
> Dancing, singing, game and play?

> But now I don't know that they mean,
> All merriness is worn away . . .

> For now I hear no word of Christmas
> In church, in the street or in school . . .

> I saw no mummers all this year,
> Only clerics clad like men of war.[30]

❧

Reformers would not rest content with public rectitude but pried into personal morals as well, supported by a spate of laws from the Parliament. Adultery was banned in 1563, witchcraft also in 1563, fornication in 1567, sabbath-breaking in 1579, adultery again together with swearing and fashionable dress in 1581 (a peak of zeal), then drunkenness in 1617. Not until the restored Parliament of 1999 would there arise a second such gale of legislative wrath against the bad habits of the Scots people.

In the sixteenth century the practical prying into these sins was carried out by the kirk sessions, the lowest tier in the reformed structure of the Church, manned by ministers and elders. They had the mission of bringing fundamentals of the new faith to bear on everyday life in everything from enforcement of social discipline to relief of the poor. The sessions could be presumed to know their flocks, or at least be able to find out about them; that godly impartiality might guide them was only to be hoped. But in Edinburgh, if not everywhere, they carried on their work free of wider tension, and the town council could support them without intervening in what they did.

An obvious reason was that the Reformation won the hearts and

1} James Hutton (1726–97), the 'father of geology', explained the history of the Earth from the topography of Edinburgh.

2} The Cramond lioness, which symbolized imperial power at the Roman naval base on the Firth of Forth.

3} The Traprain Treasure, found in a Celtic fortress in East Lothian, dates from the final phase of contact with the Romans in the fifth century.

4} St Margaret's chapel in Edinburgh Castle, erected about the turn of the eleventh century, is the oldest extant building in the city.

5} The philosopher David Hume (1709–76) looked back, and down, from the elegant Edinburgh of the Enlightenment on the rough vigour of its medieval past, portrait by Ramsay.

6} The ornate doorway on the northern side of St Giles survived from the original building of the twelfth century until replaced in 1797.

7} The finest medieval structure in Edinburgh was the chapel of the monastery at Holyrood founded by King David I in 1128.

8} The hero-king and saviour of the nation, Robert Bruce, surveys the scene of his triumph at the Battle of Bannockburn (1314); he also gave Edinburgh its royal charter.

9} The fortifications of the embattled Scottish capital: fronting the Castle the Half Moon Battery (1573–88), built on the bombarded ruins of the taller and more imposing David's Tower (1368–77), and to the right the Flodden Wall (1513).

10} St Giles with its graceful crown spire of the late fifteenth century and, on its southern side, a Parliament Square peopled with cartoon characters from the Scottish Enlightenment.

11} Until 1817 the medieval Tolbooth stood in the middle of the High Street, an all-purpose building used alike as prison and Parliament.

12} With a face and mind full of craft, William Robertson (1721–93), portrait by Raeburn, ruled both the Church of Scotland and the University of Edinburgh in the spirit of the Enlightenment.

13} It was the enlightened that made out of Mary Queen of Scots a tragic heroine, painted here in white mourning by Clouet, rather than a bigoted bogeywoman.

14} It was the Victorians that restored John Knox as hero of a Presbyterian nation, dramatically depicted by Wilkie preaching to the Lords of the Congregation.

15} In the New Town the fine arts attained an exquisite virtuosity comparable with the best in Europe, as in the plasterwork of the Cullen Room at the Royal College of Physicians.

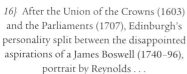

16} After the Union of the Crowns (1603) and the Parliaments (1707), Edinburgh's personality split between the disappointed aspirations of a James Boswell (1740–96), portrait by Reynolds . . .

17} . . . and the ruthless opportunism of a Henry Dundas (1742–1811), portrait by Lawrence.

The Maiden.

18} Those with more dangerous ambitions, religious or political, might finish up under the Maiden: the Scottish guillotine.

19} After the Stewart Restoration of 1660, Holyrood was remodelled into a delightful blend of medieval towers and classical columns. The flock of figures on the fountain in front 'have all the charm and much of the appearance of garden gnomes' (*Buildings of Scotland*).

minds of the people. From the Canongate comes good evidence. The Kirk kept communion infrequent; to take it was a declaration of commitment to the new order, easily made by those who wanted to, and understood by others. The session in this suburb of the capital recorded, for instance, that 1,000 took communion on Sunday, 25 February 1564. This must have included most of the adult population. The Reformation was giving the people what they had been waiting for.[31]

❧

There were, of course, backsliders. One matter in which the kirk sessions felt forced to take close, if not obsessive, interest was their parishioners' sex lives. In the Canongate sexual offenders came up for censure at an average rate of one a week. At one extreme of the spectrum of sin, adultery was harshly punished. Culprits had to stand in sackcloth with bare heads and feet, first at the door of the kirk, then on a stool of repentance in front of the congregation every Sunday for months or even years. They might be whipped and fined too. Across five centuries we can still feel the fury of the session at a case of sexual contumacy. A hatmaker, John Millar, and his girlfriend, Beatrix Morris, had already been condemned and expelled from the Canongate when they were caught 'continuing in the same filthy crime, without fear of God or punishment of the magistrates' (the equation is interesting). John now had to stand at the cross in the branks, an iron gag and halter, with a shaven-headed Beatrix beside him. Afterwards they were to be slammed up in the Tolbooth – and the tone of the record does not give an impression they were going to get out soon. Such people had to be really careful, for under the new law anybody guilty of 'notour and manifest adultery' who did not stop when found out by the Kirk could be put to death.

So draconian a law created as many problems, not to say trage-dies, as it solved. There is no case in the Canongate's records, during the decade after the Reformation, of infanticide. But ruthless punish-ment of fornication must in time have made the consequences of an illegitimate birth so fearful that fallen women sought drastic solu-tions to their problems. One was to smother the baby. Edinburgh in the next century saw a steady, pathetic procession of such cases. The girl was always hanged.[32]

But in the 1560s, at the start of its policing, the Canongate's kirk session had shown some inclination to leniency, or at least a little understanding that a wholesale change of morals could not be brought about among common folk just by legislating for it. James Hert found somebody new after his wife left him, but later he and she wanted to get together again. He explained this when hauled up for adultery in 1565, and 'the haill kirk decerns willingly and heartfully to receive the said James to repentance that he be noght swallowit with desperation ... specially because the act and fault was committit afore any Act of Parliament was made for punishing of sic vices'.

Still, an iron will to alter popular custom, if it lacked scriptural sanction, was unmistakable. Thomas Russell, gardener, asked if he could end his betrothal to Christine Weddell and marry Janet Anderson, after Christine fell in love with another lad at Linlithgow. Betrothal, rather than marriage, had been the usual point at which couples started living together; to this day, in Scots law, they can be legally married not just by religious or civil ceremony but also 'by habit and repute'. Yet William Falconer and Margaret Moorhead were forced to confess to having had intercourse before they got leave to wed. Legislation could change the conduct of people who were surprised when told that the usage of generations now broke the law, but not overnight.[33]

For some the new order made things easier. In a society where those higher up routinely oppressed those lower down, oppression might be sexual. Masters often seduced maidservants, for example. Now the girls had a kirk session to complain to if they got pregnant. In 1565, John Hunter claimed he had had sex just once with Janet White, and then only fifteen weeks before her baby's birth, so he could not be the father. She came back with a battery of facts: 'As I will answer in God's present, the said John had deill with me three sundry times, the first time upon Saturday after Lammas in his awn bed, the second time upon the Monday was aucht days therefter into that same place, the third time upon the Tuesday afore his marriage, into his own boucht [sheepfold].' John must have feared failing to convince the session for, while still denying paternity, he offered to pay Janet an annual £4 until the child was five years old. The elders accepted, but did not believe his protestations of innocence: they also made him spend a night in the Tolbooth.[34]

What with the Parliament and the law courts and the foreign ships at Leith and now the General Assembly of the Church of Scotland, there were always single men hanging round Edinburgh far from home and with little to do. Whether or not this had a magnified effect in the swish suburb of the Canongate, the kirk session claimed as much: 'the haill gait abounds with harlotry'.[35] This was not the sole reason why the problem of prostitution seemed so perilous: another was the risk of syphilis. The effect of its arrival in Edinburgh in 1497, just five years after Christopher Columbus's crew brought it back from the New World to the Old, had been virulent. The town council ordered all those suffering from the 'grandgore' to gather on Leith Sands for shipment to isolation on the island of Inchkeith. There is no record to state whether or not this drastic measure worked, but in the long run the disease spread. For example, modern analysis of the symptoms suffered by both Darnley and Bothwell has diagnosed in the one the onset, in the other the progress of syphilis.[36]

Sex went on anyway. The French ambassador, resident in the Canongate, seems to have shared his bed with many a bonny lass. In 1565 Katherine Lenton confessed before the kirk session to sleeping with him. She was sentenced to be put in the branks, to be cut on one side of the head and clipped on the other, then to stand for three hours at the Cross before being banished from the burgh. If she came back she would be branded on the cheek and whipped. From the nature of her punishment and quality of her clientele we might guess she had been a pretty girl. A further step was to attack the madams. Margaret Sempill felt picked on. She protested to the session, 'I get the name but others the profit.'[37] She accused several women of practising the oldest profession, two in Janet Reid's house, then May Aitchison, 'midwife, plain bordellar', more of them in George Black's house behind the Cross, 'common bordel', not to speak of Margaret Thomson in John Aitken's house. In fact, 'I sould take twenty men's wives in the Canongate by the hand that has playit the huris by their guid men.' The session lost its temper, ordered her to be whipped for her own harlotry and made to prove her charges against the rest, or else she would be whipped again. She was to be expelled from the Canongate and whipped once more if she came back. Male customers were supposed to perform some penance too, but it seems unlikely the French ambassador did.[38]

Spending so much energy on sex, kirk sessions had less to spare for the other duties laid on them. However good the intentions, Edinburgh made little progress with its poor. These had once been a charge on the monasteries, but monasteries no longer existed. Knox pinpointed the need for a new system, but even in his own parish this was easier said than done – and a tall order if he expected canny burgesses to pay for something of no benefit to themselves. Here was a conundrum of Calvinism: those instilled with its godly sense of personal responsibility might take an unchristian view of those with none.

So Edinburgh felt ill at ease about the poor. While they were proper objects of Christian charity, it might be wasted on them if their poverty was their own fault – better for them in that case to get off their backsides and fend for themselves. Knox himself wrote: 'We are not patrons for stubborn and idle beggars who, running from place to place, make a craft of their begging ... but for the widow and fatherless, the aged, impotent or lamed ... that they may feel some benefit of Christ Jesus now preached to them.'[39]

But when the town council tried to raise a poor rate in 1575, it failed because 'people will no ways liberally or willingly disburse money for ... sustentation [of beggars]'. All that could be done was to restrict begging to those issued with 'the town's mark upon their hats, bonnets or shoulders'. Beggars from beyond the burgh would be locked up, fed on bread and water, then expelled. The only kindness allowed them was that through the barred windows of their cells they might 'hang forth ane purse to beg for their sustentation' (so saving the council the cost). A later effort to raise a rate fell foul of the craftsmen's incorporations, which promised to care for their own members. But they were supposed to do that in any case, and the poor did not on the whole belong to the crafts (or they might not have been poor).

It took the fear of death to change minds. In a year of plague, such as 1584, the burgesses felt even less happy than usual to be pestered on the High Street by beggars who might pass on their fleas. The town council wielded carrot and stick. It raised a rate to hand out to beggars but ordered them all off the Royal Mile. What, though, when the plague passed? The council resolved that beggars who had taken its money must stay off the Royal Mile. It even frowned on 'little bairns begging and lying all the nicht at honest men's doors'. But where else were street kids to go? The system in Edinburgh remained mean. The mendicant swarms would haunt the town for a long time to come before any measure of effective public relief could be devised. The meanness would not be cured until the British state took full responsibility for welfare in the 1920s.[40]

❧

The poor were not the only losers from the Reformation – the social standing of women was depressed too. In the Middle Ages women had already been subordinate to men, of course, yet a few won economic independence or some other advantage even from the adverse conditions of the time. A factor in their favour was that, given the closed shop of the merchant guild in Edinburgh, marriage to a burgess's daughter offered the easiest entry to its privilege for a go-ahead young man. Such daughters became eligible and sought after: in 1405 one had even been made a burgess herself on her brother's death, presumably in the absence of male heirs to the family's fortune. There was not much chance of that once the Reformation came. The town council banned single women from setting up households on their own, on the grounds only the 'idle and licentious' would want to.[41]

Was not baking cakes a harmless enough female pastime? But the town council turned its beady eye on this too, lest 'women and unfree persons' put bread in the oven with the cakes and then sell it – so breaching the baxters' privilege. Still, there was the craft of brewing, legitimate but unincorporated, dominated by women because done at home and easy to combine with housework. It was an activity that found a ready market in a burgh which, by the peculiar geology of the site, always risked running short of water. And beer did not carry disease. So Edinburgh enjoys a tradition of formidable female publicans. They had not just brewed beer. In 1557 the bailies ordered Bessie Campbell to stop distilling whisky, or even selling it 'except on the market day' (not, then, a very stringent prohibition).[42]

After 1560 the tide turned against drink as well. In its usual fulminating fashion the town council sounded off that 'the iniquity of women taverners within this burgh has been ane great occasion of huredom within this burgh, so it appears ane bordel to be in every tavern'. Twenty years later the council was still sounding off against 'the filthy vice of fornication, drunkenness and all kind of pollution daily increased through the great multitude of women taverners who entices the youth and insolent people to such filthiness'. Not until we read the full text of this by-law banning them do we find it applies only to those who are not the wives or widows of burgesses: economic privilege is masquerading as moral indignation. But advances in brewing technology made it less suitable for domestic production, so that a woman's trade ceased to be one. In 1596 the council stood on its head and voiced concern about a decline of brewing. A society of brewers was set up to revive the industry, but they would be men. Perhaps no other development did so much to depress the economic status of Edinburgh's women.[43]

❧

Starting from the confrontations of Knox and Mary Queen of Scots, the reformed burgh and nation seemed altogether to take on a misogynist slant. At its extreme it appeared in witch-hunts. Warlocks suffered too, but women made up the vast majority of those tried for the witchcraft that reformers had promptly turned into a capital crime. This was a change from the older attitudes in Scotland. There had been witches before, so called by themselves or by others, but seldom were they persecuted or killed. To the still half-pagan mind of the medieval Scot the air was full of good and evil presences, from saints to sprites. Any effort to get rid of them would be at once perilous and futile. Better by far was appeasement, with little gifts left out overnight or something of the sort. Only a handful of witches had been executed before the Reformation; again, after the Union with England, numbers would fast sink away to nothing. Between 1560 and 1707, however, hundreds of Scotswomen suffered horrible deaths, burned at the stake, for alleged witchcraft.

In an odd way, then, belief in witchcraft was a facet not of ancient but of modern Scotland. It mirrored a change all over Europe. Calvin insisted: 'The Bible teaches us that there are witches and that they must be slain. God expressly commands that all witches and enchantresses shall be put to death and the law of God is a universal law.' In Edinburgh the Parliament upheld the opinion of the Kirk in its literal reading of the Mosaic text, 'Thou shalt not suffer a witch to live.'[44] The politically correct Scots of the time seemed to think they had to root out witchcraft just as the politically correct Scots of today think they have to root out racism; whether either problem has ever been a serious issue in Scotland is another matter. But in the sixteenth century such unsavoury self-righteousness easily swung over into something much darker and crueller, into an irrational hysteria mixed with perverted pleasure. This, too, would take its place in the life of Edinburgh.

The rot started at the top. King James VI personally egged on one of the great witch-hunts, in 1597 at North Berwick, down the coast from his capital. He was wondering why his recent voyage across the North Sea to fetch home his bride, Anne of Denmark, had been beset by storms. He suspected witches of casting spells against him in collusion with his cousin Francis Stewart, fifth Earl of Bothwell, nephew of the last spouse of Mary Queen of Scots. When the king heard of a coven unmasked at North Berwick, he drooled in fascination. Under questioning the witches confessed to defiling themselves in various sordid rites. More to the point, they described how the Devil (or Bothwell – the distinction was none too clear) had commanded them to make a waxen image of the king and to chant over it, 'This is Jamie the Saxt, orderit tae be consumed by a noble man.' At that the Devil 'did greatly inveigh against the King of Scotland . . . the king is the greatest enemy he hath in the world'. The witches were commanded to dig up buried corpses and wrench off their limbs, tie them to cats and throw the whole lot in the sea: this would raise storms to sink the royal ship.[45]

James VI felt flattered at the Devil's personal attentions. He made himself an expert in this enemy's ways and published the results of his researches, as detailed as they were fantastic, in a tract, *Daemonologie* (1597). Here, among other things, he argued that more witches than warlocks existed because women were frailer than men. The Devil, the seducer of Eve in Eden, had been 'homelier with the sex'

ever since. This turned into a hackneyed theme. Like his ancestors a
poet, the king wrote 'A Satire against Women', which ended with the
lines:

> Some craft they have, yet foolish are indeed
> With lying whiles esteeming best to speed
> [When they think to advance their interests by lying]

The king did his regal and conjugal duty by blowsy Anne of
Denmark, but showed no further interest in the opposite sex. He had
been brought up without maternal love, or even female company,
under the tutelage of the austere Prebyterian humanist George
Buchanan. This ideologue of the second phase of the Reformation
did not balk at beating and berating the boy for being his mother's
son. The poor mite, quaking at his mentor's every approach, sought
what affection he could find from other young men. Among the first
was his cousin, the handsome and debonair Esmé Stewart d'Aubigny,
brought up in France as the opposite of a forbidding Presbyterian
(though, when he came to Scotland, he converted at the king's
insistence and became an unforbidding one). In 1582, by which time
James and Esmé were exchanging kisses and cuddles in public, stern
Scots forced the pair to part and the Frenchman to go home for
good. The inconsolable king wrote a poem to a phoenix, his symbol
of consuming loss:

> And thou, o Phoenix, why was thou so moved,
> Thou foule of light, by enemies of thee,
> For to forget thy heavenly hewes, whilkis loved
> Were baith by men and fowlis that did them see?[46]

❧

James VI grew up not just queer but peculiar: an example of how
Presbyterianism, for all the virtues it instils, can warp personalities.
The king may stand as the first of the cranks and crackpots who, as
they lurch between amiable eccentricity and tortured schizophrenia,
enliven the history of modern Edinburgh. While he was unlucky in
his own parentage, his family, the Stewarts, had been an intelligent
dynasty. James turned out the most intelligent of all, if with a mind
shrewd and pedantic rather than creative. A precocious childhood

and a bizarre education of censure mixed with flattery gave him a high opinion of his own abilities – which were without doubt well above average, served by a retentive memory and including a command of several ancient and modern languages. His education let him get the measure of the huge problems facing him: a long minority, maternal plots, a turbulent nobility, an insolent clergy, the poverty of crown and country. The achievement was undoubted, but we are still left wondering at the character of this 'wisest fool in Christendom'.

The king did not lack a range of other odd vices, from a weakness for gluttony to a terror of assassination or kidnap. In culture he was a control freak. He espoused the ornate, formal culture which, across the courts of Europe, flourished in the Renaissance. At Holyrood he created a circle of poets dubbed the Castalian Band, after the mythical fountain on Mount Parnassus sacred to the Muses. He wrote out guidelines for the group, *The Reulis and Cautelis to be observit and eschewit in Scottis poesie* (1584; *cautelis* means devices). He minutely instructed the members of his band both as to their manner – 'that ye ryme ay to the hinmest syllable (with accent) in the line' – and as to their matter – 'gif your purpose be of landwart affairs, to use corruptit and uplands wordis'.[47] He ordered one Castalian, Thomas Hudson, to translate the French poetry of Sallust du Bartas; another, William Fowler, to translate the Italian poetry of Francesco Petrarch. By such means the king earned a European reputation as patron of the arts. A French poet, Guillaume du Peyrat, wrote a panegryric to him:

> *O bien-heureuse Ecosse, o trois et quatre fois*
> *Bien-heureuse Edimbourg, le siege de tes rois!*
> *On t'appelait jadis le Château des Pucelles,*
> *Tu l'es ores vraiment, puisque de tes douceurs*
> *Ton Prince y entretient les neuf pucelles soeurs,*
> *Filles de Jupiter, les Muses immortelles.*

> Oh most happy Scotland, oh three and four times
> Most happy Edinburgh, the seat of your kings!
> You used to be called the Maiden Castle,
> Now you really are, since with your delights

> Your prince there entertains the nine maiden sisters,
> Daughters of Jupiter, the immortal Muses.[48]

The modern eye is more likely to see here a lot of self-seeking creeps jumping to the whims of a bumptious boy. This may explain why the Castalian corpus of poetry fails on the whole to attain the vitality of what had been written by the makars at the same Holyrood. The language is still vigorous and enriched from diverse sources, yet Castalians seem distanced from the real life throbbing through the lines of Robert Henryson, William Dunbar, even Gavin Douglas. It is true that Robert Aytoun, secretary to Queen Anne, appears to have been the original author of 'Auld Lang Syne', than which there is no better-known Scots song in the whole world. Others strike too often a note almost of apology for what they are doing. Perhaps it is the nation they apologize to for having to grovel before the king; more often they look as if they are apologizing to him for the inevitable uncouthness of native subject matter compared to the classicism he has instructed them to ape. One of the band, John Stewart of Baldynneis, writes of a boating trip on the Firth of Forth:

> *The noble nymphs likes not thir wavering jaws*
> *That hants the valleys and the seemly shaws,*
> *Nor yit the Muses with thair michty spreit*
> *Upon this Forth has no delight to fleit.*
> *Great difference is betwixt fair Helicon*
> *And this salt sea quhilk seik we sail upon.*

> The noble nymphs like not these choppy waves
> That rim the valleys and the pleasant woods,
> Nor do the Muses with their mighty spirit
> Delight to float upon this Forth.
> Great difference lies between fair Helicon
> And this salt sea we seek to sail upon.[49]

The bard bringing up the rear of the Castalian band, William Drummond of Hawthornden, went a stage further. He had not long ended his studies at the University of Edinburgh when in 1610 he inherited his estate in Midlothian. There he secluded himself with a large library. He was hospitable enough to welcome the playwright Ben Jonson, who walked all the way from London to visit him in

1618. Jonson was typical of one type of English tourist to Scotland in showing no interest whatever in the life of the country. He spent his time discussing with Drummond the finer points of classical prosody. Record was kept of their exchanges. They demonstrate Drummond to have had a liking for foreign rather than native models. That was no bad thing in itself, but what he also shared with his fellow Castalians was subservience to James VI. He wrote of the Union of Crowns in 1603, which had taken the king away from Edinburgh to London:

> That day, dear prince, which reft us of thy sight
> (Day, no, but darkness and a dusky night)
> Did freight our breasts with sighs, our eyes with tears,
> Turned minutes in sad months, sad months in years.

And he implored the king to return:

> Ah why should Isis only see thee shine?
> Is not thy Forth as well as Isis thine?
> Though Isis vaunt she hath more wealth in store,
> Let it suffice thy Forth doth love thee more. [50]

Drummond marked an end of the makars' era in a pregnant sense: he composed in English, the first Scottish poet to do so. In itself this might have added to the linguistic resources of Scotland, which always drew on classical or modern tongues to enrich the vernacular. The literature of Edinburgh was as a result polyglot. Drummond's choice of language took the first step towards making it monoglot, that is, using only or overwhelmingly English for literary purposes. A prime reason was that James VI of Scotland had meanwhile become James I of England; the influence of the court on language and literature in Scotland remained huge, if now exerted at long distance.

❦

It had been late on Saturday, 26 March 1603, in bleak and windy weather, that a lone horseman came galloping along the high road from the south and at nightfall found the entrance to the palace of Holyroodhouse. It was already locked up, and he had to hammer at the doors to get in. He gave his name, Sir Robert Carey. The guards seemed to know, without his saying in his strange accent, who he was and what he wanted.

Carey was led to the chamber of the King of Scots, who started up at the intrusion. There was a moment for Carey to take him in, an ungainly but otherwise typical Scotsman of thirty-six, of middle height, with short sandy hair, reddish beard, ruddy complexion and blue, staring eyes, slobbering a little in agitation: not a regal figure to an English eye.

But Carey was already on bended knee, saluting him as King of England. The last of the Tudors, Queen Elizabeth I, had died aged seventy at three o'clock in the small hours of the previous Thursday at Richmond Palace in Surrey. Her chief Minister, Sir Robert Cecil, as always a model of cool, meticulous, devoted efficiency, had everything ready. At eleven o'clock the same morning, James I was proclaimed in Whitehall. It remained to inform him as quickly as possible, even before any official notification. That was what Carey had come to do, after thirty hours of breakneck riding, interrupted only by an ugly fall. Carey was expected. There had been breathless excitement in Edinburgh throughout the Queen of England's final illness. James VI, seething with impatience, hardly left Holyrood in case of news from London. He was in touch with Cecil, had sent down a warrant to let all English Ministers stay on for now as caretakers in their posts, and had vetted a draft of the proclamation to be made in Whitehall. Meanwhile, Cecil ordered Berwick and Carlisle along with other strategic garrisons to be reinforced, and a few potential troublemakers to be arrested.

James could still not believe his luck. Elizabeth had kept him on tenterhooks and never named him as her successor, for there were other possible candidates. But when the English ambassador, George Nicolson, came to Holyrood he treated everything as settled. The king, anxious yet, decided just for safety's sake to send officials of his own to take possession of Berwick, lost to Scotland more than a century before. They were welcomed there with joy, and he breathed a sigh of relief.

Now the king was keen to be gone. He had to borrow money to get to the border, and spent a week on feverish preparations for the departure of a large entourage. The next Sunday, 3 April, he went to the service in St Giles. After the sermon, he himself stood up to say farewell to the people of Edinburgh.

Their mood had changed, and they no longer felt exhilarated that one of their own was taking such a step up in life. They understood an epoch in the history of their city and country had come to an end, and they were sad. The King of Scots would not be there to stand in St Giles and speak to them in future. Edinburgh would see no more the colour and commotion of the royal court. Politics and power were moving elsewhere. Some even wept.

James VI misjudged their feelings a little with a rather priggish address. He said he was touched by their sorrow, which he could well understand, but begged them not to take his departure too much to heart. Though he would be far away, they could still benefit from his rule. While he would be a mightier monarch, he could not love them more. He promised to come back every three years to see them. Some wept again when, two days later, he and his party rode out and took the road for the border. But he failed to keep his promise. He left it until 1617 before he came back, driven, as he said, by a salmon-like instinct to see once more the land of his birth. And this was not just the first time he returned but also the last.[51]

🐝

The Union of Crowns could have been a catastrophe for Edinburgh. The presence of the royal court was what had first raised it from commercial community to national capital – and now the royal court was gone. Yet Edinburgh had so grown into the role of capital that it would not just survive and adapt but flourish too. It also remained the seat of government, despite James VI's absence. Typical of the odd mix in him of sense and perversity was how he yet wanted to bring its capital status to an end and stride straight on from the Union of Crowns to a Union of Parliaments between Scotland and England. The Scots were used to the bees in his bonnet but the English would have none of it – which, for a century ahead, put a stop to that brilliant idea.

By way of compensation James VI boasted of his 'government by pen', his ability to send orders 400 miles to the dutiful privy councillors he left behind in Edinburgh and to see his will obeyed.

For these men the king's departure was not so much a blow as a chance for sensible discretion. Bloodcurdling commands – say, to exterminate some insolent Highland clan – still arrived from time to time. Now the councillors, on the pretext of needing to find means and money, could postpone obedience until the king's always short attention-span switched to something else. Yet it was his own earlier exercise of authority and imposition of order that had made his bureaucracy effective when he was no longer on the spot. He had prompted Scotland to start modernizing, and this paid off.

One crucial thing needed in a modern state was revenue. Most came from the merchants of Edinburgh. About 300 rich men made up less than 2 per cent of the capital's population yet paid half the nation's taxes – and lent the government any difference between income and expenditure. Never before or afterwards was the solvency of Scotland in the hands of so small a group.[52]

The merchants of Edinburgh won this status because of their booming business. Leith had long been the most bustling port in Scotland. By exploitation of privilege and vigilance against rivals the merchants meant to keep it so. Wherever they could they extended control over potential competitors, however puny. Beyond the bounds of the burgh some craftsmen had escaped its tight regulation by setting up in the humble suburbs of Potterrow, on the main road south, or Portsburgh, on the main road west, or Broughton, at the other side of the Nor' Loch; and then there was the Canongate, where royal or noble patronage could make up for lack of civic and commercial rights. Edinburgh moved to suppress such dodges. By 1648 it won, through purchase or commutation of debts, the feudal superiority over each of these adjoining places. They were now to be ruled by officials appointed from Edinburgh, who would supervise economic activity in them.

In fact, economic policymaking for all Scotland came to be dominated by the merchants of Edinburgh. With relish they took to a role beyond municipal politics, to serve as commissioners to the Convention of Royal Burghs (founded to serve common interests in 1581) or as members of the Scots Parliament. They could then bend laws and regulations and contracts to their own advantage. Soon the merchants of Aberdeen, for example, found it easier to conduct foreign trade through Leith rather than from their own harbour 100 miles north; much the same held true of other burghs in the eastern Lowlands and Borders. The trouble with this capture of public policy by private interests was that it tended towards the haphazard. Protectionist purposes produced too much random or indeed contradictory legislation, usually forbidding the export of raw materials rather than encouraging development. The ensemble lay far from anything that could be called rational commercial strategy.[53]

That still did not stop Edinburgh's business booming, for the European economy remained buoyant. Oceanic traffic stemming from the age of discoveries brought in treasures of the Orient and wonders of the Occident. In their modest way Scots could profit from all this too, if supplying in exchange little more than the products of nature to their neighbours within easy sailing distance. But even such a poor country could respond to the rise in demand from its biggest markets in France and the Netherlands. England, too, in earlier times closed to Scots by war, had been opened up at the Union of Crowns.[54]

The merchants of Edinburgh adapted with resource. Overseas traffic remained risky and one way of minimizing risk was to form partnerships for the transport of cargoes. No merchant put all his freight in one boat. No boat sailed without consignments from several merchants. As a result, shipping and chartering turned into sidelines of the capital's commerce too. Means had besides to be found of financing the foreign trade, in a period when no mechanisms existed for transfers of funds apart from sending gold and silver in the ship's hold; a problem of piracy in the North Sea counselled against that. Instead the merchants of Edinburgh made friends of correspondents in the ports they trafficked to, so each party could carry balances for the other. This instilled both the basic principles of foreign exchange and a desire for amity in foreign relations (Scotland fought no external wars between 1560 and 1639). It would be armed conflict at home and abroad in the mid-seventeenth century that brought the phase of prosperity to an end.[55]

From all this activity the merchants generated a surplus of capital. Another part of their income could then come from lending money. The rate of interest had hovered round the 10 per cent sanctioned in holy writ (though not in Scots law). By 1633, the country was flourishing enough for the rate to be lowered to 8 per cent by Act of Parliament. From a base in Edinburgh, the economy was monetized: a huge step forward from a system of mere subsistence and transactions in kind. Still, no banking existed as such – all was financed in specie, in gold and silver. Jinglin' Geordie, Edinburgh's richest man in the later reign of James VI, won his nickname from the sound made by the coins he carried about him as he walked the streets. Today he is commemorated in the name of a pub, or more especially by the school and charity he founded under his real name, George Heriot. Heriot was a goldsmith, five times deacon-convener of the trades. He became jeweller to Queen Anne, then in 1603 followed the royal couple to London to supply the cascades of gems that kept her contented while lubricating the king's relationships with his male favourites. They were always slow to pay; Heriot still made a fortune. Because he died with no legitimate heirs, he left his estate to establish Heriot's Hospital for orphans and the education of the poor. His name lives on in the Heriot's School that grew out of this foundation. Its buildings offer the best example of Jacobean architecture in Edinburgh.[56]

⚹

From the prosperity, capitalism began to emerge. Production in Edinburgh had so far amounted to little more than the output of the individual craftsmen working from home, who needed next to no capital investment. Out in the Lothians extractive industries, coal-mining or salt-making, existed on a larger scale, and now they could expand. But major change came through merchants' ventures into manufacturing. These also exposed the snags in the medieval system of regulation.

The earliest factory in Scotland was for woollen goods, built at Bonnington by the Water of Leith in 1587. The factory needed skilled workers who were brought over from the Low Countries, and so caused trouble with Edinburgh's crafts. In 1590 the merchants Mungo and Gideon Russell, father and son, opened a paper-mill at Dalry, again operated by foreign labour. In 1619 the town council itself, admitting in effect that Flemish technology was superior, invited more weavers across to start a factory at Paul's Work, on the northern bounds of the burgh; its products had still, in the accustomed way, to be displayed at set prices and could be exported only by consent of the merchants.

But now the merchants found a cuckoo in their nest. Nathaniel Udward, son of a former provost, decided he was fed up of the petty restrictions in the burgh and started a factory for soap, a product so far always imported from the Netherlands. He set it up at Leith, where contrary to regulations he also insisted on living. He guarded himself by obtaining a royal privilege, which even included a right to import fish and their oils from Greenland. He seems to have been one of nature's enterpreneurs, forever dreaming up ways to make money. Burgesses complained he was 'like ane rolling stone now here now there living upon projects' – but projects were what the development of Edinburgh needed.

Others, too, chipped away at the old restrictions. The cordiners of Edinburgh and the Lothians complained to the privy council about the poor quality of leather they got for their shoemaking from local tanners. The government decided to attract English tanners and grant them a monopoly; which led to further dispute with the capital's trades, and the idea foundered. Innovation went on all the same, just in the way of the world. In 1629 William and Thomas Dickson started the manufacture of golf-balls at Leith. By 1642 Gilbert Fraser and Robert Tait were making tobacco-pipes in Edinburgh. And in 1645 a partnership of the city's merchants set up what appears to have been the first manufacturing plant in Scotland on an industrial scale, a factory for woollens at Newmills, near Haddington.[57]

❧

Change affected not just the buildings of the burgh or the behaviour of its economic agents but also its more basic allegiances. A striking feature of the burgh's earlier life had been the affection and loyalty between the people and their kings, often in common cause against Scotland's appalling aristocracy. In return for their support the House of Stewart gave the burgesses freedoms. But benefactors are often put out when beneficiaries use the favours granted to them in ways never reckoned with. On the evidence from Edinburgh, for example, it seems clear that Scots shaped their own religion, if not initially at the national level then certainly afterwards, and more intensely, at the local level. When later called on to choose, their resolve to uphold their religion had grown strong enough to loosen their links with the royal dynasty – in the end fatally.

In other words, the people of Edinburgh defended the Kirk from the king if they had to. The need arose quite soon. As the young James VI took up the reins of government he was already finding presbytery offensive to his own conception of his divine right. His eventual solution would be to insinuate bishops loyal to him into the structure of the Church of Scotland, complex enough though it already was. Once in England after 1603, with the direct example of Anglicanism before him, he stepped up his efforts.

James VI returned to Edinburgh in 1617 meaning to finish the job. Beforehand Holyrood had echoed to the sounds of English workmen, sent on ahead, hammering and sawing. An organ arrived by ship. The carpenter who came with it said he had been better treated earlier in life as a prisoner of the Turks than he was now by the Scots. Rumours ran that gilded statues of apostles and patriarchs were to be set up in the royal chapel. Even the king's new Scottish bishops thought this went too far, and wrote to tell him so; the popish baubles never appeared. James himself, the day after arriving at Holyrood, went to a service in the chapel conducted according to the English ritual, with choristers, surplices and music from the organ. When the moment came for communion, the king commanded all to kneel. Not all did: even one bishop remained seated. James said he would overlook their fault for now, but they must conform in future.

Soon communicants in the whole burgh were ordered to kneel. The Reverend David Calderwood left an account of what followed at St Giles. Many parishioners refused to obey. At the kirk session following, a merchant, John Inglis, announced he and other elders or deacons would no longer serve the bread and wine: 'Ye know that they were aye ready before, but this novation is the occasion of men's unwillingness now. Men cannot serve contrary to their mind.'

The Reverend William Struthers, one of the ministers at St Giles, interrupted: 'John, we thought something of you before, but now we know what is in you.'

Bartle Fleming joined in to support Inglis: 'Think ye men will serve contrare to their conscience?'

Struthers turned on him, too: 'Bartle, we thought something of you before. Now we count nothing of you. Bartle, hold your peace. When ye are stillest ye are wisest.'

A third parishioner, John Mein, piped up: 'This is a strange thing. Ye will have us to serve whether it be reason or not.'

Mein nettled a second minister, the Reverend Patrick Galloway, who told him off: 'Sir, let us alone. I suffered enough of you last day. I say to thee, man, thou art a very Anabaptist.'

Struthers backed Galloway: 'What, sir! Know ye the office of a deacon? I will examine you presently.'

'Yes, sir, I trow I know something,' answered Mein.

'What is it?' demanded Struthers.

'To serve the tables,' answered Mein.

'What is the cause ye do it not then?' demanded Struthers.

'Because ye have left Christ's institution, for ye will be wiser than Christ in setting doun a better form of your own.'

At this a third minister, the Reverend Thomas Sydserf, could not contain himself: 'Oh horrible blasphemy! Oh horrible blasphemy! If ye would serve, wherefore have ye left us?'

Mein answered, 'We left you not till ye left the truth.'

The argument grew ever more heated. Struthers decided to pull rank (Calderwood adds that he looked proud and lofty). 'Know ye,' he challenged Mein, 'the Sixt of Acts, what the word "deacon" means? Know you the Greek word? I say, man, you are our servants' [the Greek word means servant].

In scorn Struthers went on, 'We know nothing. We must go down to John Mein's booth and buy books and get a lesson from him ... They will learn us what we sall do.' He turned on Fleming with the same pompous question: 'Have ye read the Sixt of the Acts? Ye would serve at tables. Ye think yourselves very wise. Would to God we had as mickle wisdom amongst us [ministers] as every one of you thinks ye have.'

Fleming just replied: 'We served aye before till ye come in and took our place over our heads and would serve yourselves.'

Galloway lost his temper. He grabbed the roll of elders and

deacons and shouted, 'I sall keep this. The king's majesty sall be informed. There cannot be a king in the country if this be suffered.' He ordered the clerk to call the roll to find out who would serve at communion and who would not. When Mein was called and refused to answer, Galloway screamed at him in reproach.

Mein kept his nerve: 'We know now who are our persecutors.'

Bailie Alexander Clerk joined in: 'Hold your tongue. There is too much spoken. I command you silence, sir.'

Mein replied: 'Ye may not command me silence in this place.'

'What say ye, sir?' challenged the bailie, getting to his feet and repeating louder, 'I command you silence.'

'Ye may not command me silence in this place,' said Mein.

'What say ye?' Clerk repeated, 'May not I command you silence? I command you silence.'

'Sir, ye may not lawfully command me silence in this place. Ye are but a sessioner here, sir. Ye may not reign over us.'

'What say ye?' demanded Clerk. 'I sall let you wit, sir, I am more than a sessioner. Ye are but a very false knave. Ye are but a gowk. I sall fasten your feet, sir.'

Mein retorted: 'I can bear all that, sir, and all that you can do to me, and more too, sir. But I will not hold my tongue.'

'My joy, John, hold your tongue,' said Clerk.

Calderwood concludes: 'So endit that session.'[58]

Alas, even a willingness to kneel could not make Scots good at it, so far had the practices of popery fallen into disuse. At Easter 1622 the pastors of Edinburgh, before offering communion to their flocks, were themselves required to receive the bread kneeling. Galloway of St Giles did so and remained on his knees for a moment in prayer. He was now getting on in years, so when he stood up he took hold of the communion table for support. On it stood several cups full of wine. He pulled over the table and spilled all the wine. The sacrament had to start again. Somehow, kneeling did not suit Scots.[59]

❧

The rumbles under James VI formed just a prelude to the storm that broke after his death in 1625. His son Charles I, though born at Dunfermline, knew nothing of Scotland. After the Union of Crowns he had gone as an infant to London and grown up an Englishman.

Now sovereign of three kingdoms in the British Isles, he wanted unity among them. But to him this meant Scotland and Ireland must become more like England.

Charles I's policy still did not wear quite the same face in each kingdom. To Scotland he at first offered at least a little goodwill. In his view the divine right of kings, to which he held yet more firmly than his father, endowed other national institutions, the Parliament and the Church, with a dignity requiring physical expression. Edinburgh should get a proper Parliament House, then, so the nation's laws need no longer be made in the cramped, smelly old Tolbooth. Next door, behind St Giles, stood the manses of its ministers, which at the back overlooked its graveyard running down to the Cowgate, long hopelessly overcrowded. From 1632 all was swept away to make room for building the new Parliament House, with its wonderful hammerbeam roof of Danish oak fashioned by John Scott, master wright to the town of Edinburgh. Space became available inside this complex for law courts as well. St Giles could then be quit of the courts' earlier encroachment on the western end of the nave. No longer profaned, the high kirk of the burgh might also be cleared of its clutter of internal walls, together with two of its three reformed congregations (one to the Tron, the other to Lady Yester's kirk on the other side of the Cowgate). After that it would be fit for erection into the cathedral of the diocese of Edinburgh, with a bishop named by the king, which would also raise the status of the capital from burgh to city.[60]

The policy was in its way benign, and Charles I perhaps felt amazed at the resistance it met. But here, as in all else, he never tried to understand or reconcile those differing from him, only ignore or overbear them. In Scotland he had inherited competent, diligent servants of the crown, largely left to their own devices since his father went to England. They in their turn showed themselves flexible, sensible and willing to delegate, not least to the influential town councillors of Edinburgh. Charles was much more remote yet much more meddlesome. He got rid of men who thought for themselves and tried to bludgeon the rest into obedience. In Edinburgh he wanted to nominate the council himself. While that had been a practice in the previous century, then the King of Scots and the burgesses all knew one another; now they were strangers.[61]

Charles I returned to Edinburgh in 1633 to be crowned. As the advocate for order and dignity in what he saw as chaotic Presbyterian worship, he set an example by following English ceremonial in St Giles. Scots rejoiced to see their king again, but his rites made their flesh creep. Back in London, in 1637, he ordered the Kirk to adopt a prayer book which not only took kneeling at communion for granted but also babbled on about ornaments in church and celebration of saints' days. He seemed to be softening up Scots for a British Church on Anglican lines – and of a type, with smells and bells, obnoxious to them.

❧

On Sunday, 23 July 1637, lords, ladies and gentlemen, bishops, judges and town councillors turned out in force for morning service at St Giles. The prayer book would be used here for the first time. The establishment was ordered on parade to show support. Inside St Giles, however, a far from hushed and reverent atmosphere reigned. The Reverend James Hannay, formerly its minister, now its dean, began to read out: 'Almighty God, unto whom all hearts are open, all desires known, and from whom no secrets are hid . . .'

After he had, as he hoped, prepared the congregation's minds for communion, he recited the Ten Commandments. In the novel liturgy, the worshippers were meant to respond to each with the words: 'Lord, have mercy upon us, and incline our hearts to keep this law.' Instead, scabrous comments rose from the body of the kirk. 'False antichristian,' cried even a few of the doucer citizens. Others, raucous stallholders from the High Street, or loudmouthed harridans from the closes, or rowdy apprentice lads, bawled out some of the seventeenth century's saltier insults: 'Beastly belly-god! Crafty fox! Ill-hanged thief! Judas!'

The hubbub grew so loud that the Bishop of Edinburgh, the Right Reverend David Lindsay, intervened and called for silence. When he got it, more or less, he told Hannay to go on and read the collect for the day. According to legend, this was too much for Jenny Geddes, an old woman who sold herbs by the Tron. She started up and shouted: 'Out, thou false thief, dost thou say mass at my lug?' Then, taking the stool on which she rested her creaking bones in church, she hurled it at the bishop's head. Modern historians have decided Jenny never existed. In that case, it was necessary to invent her: she represented a people who would put up with no more corruption of their religion.

Bedlam followed. Stools rained through the air. Some worshippers staged a walk-out to join hostile crowds outside. Others stayed to carry on barracking. Scuffles spread as the magistrates tried to eject them. The priests struggled through the order of service, but the protesters had not finished. They assaulted known conformists when the congregation emerged on to the High Street. They chased Hannay up into the steeple, where he had to hide for the rest of the day. They scooped turds from the closes and pelted Lindsay with them.

This was the sole occasion the liturgy would ever be heard right through in St Giles. For the evening service, the priests gabbled a truncated version behind barred doors. They still had to face the mob outside in the street. Lindsay was again roughed up and only saved by the Earl of Roxburghe, who bundled the bishop into his own carriage and sped away towards Holyrood. Showers of stones chased them down the hill. Inside a week the government felt obliged to announce the prayer book was being abandoned.

With that the king's religious policy collapsed. Soon his whole rule in Scotland began to dissolve too. His privy council merely squabbled. By October it had to decamp for its own safety to Linlithgow, leaving the capital to a mob swelled with people from all over the Lowlands come to petition against the prayer book. They hung about the streets plotting, arguing, demonstrating, awaiting events. Institutions of the state closed down. Revolution was in the offing.[62]

꾼

Revolution began in earnest when the estates of the realm (noblemen, lairds, burgesses, ministers) moved into the political vacuum. They had to do so, if any semblance of authority and order was to be maintained. With no legal Parliament or General Assembly in session, they set up what later ages would call a provisional government. Each estate chose delegates who in November started sitting together as the so-called Four Tables, sixteen men in all. It remained unclear what status they had, or what they were supposed to do. But one initiative they took was to authorize a National Covenant, setting out the people's claims as a religious and political community against their lawful king.

Among those entrusted with drawing up the Covenant was a rising young lawyer from Edinburgh, aged twenty-seven, Archibald Johnston of Warriston. The son of a fiercely Presbyterian mother, and from merchant stock, he might have chosen to enter the ministry himself but his own family warned him he was too intense. Even to them he must have come across as a grim Calvinist zealot, rigid, callous, bigoted, implacable. Yet he had a way with words. His were to be some of the most sonorous phrases hailing the Covenant, as 'the marriage day of the kingdom with God'. Scotland then showed herself to be the new Israel, they being 'the only two sworn nations of the Lord'. The Kirk might have been 'gadding after strange lovers', but now there was a 'honeymoon betwixt the Lord and his runaway spouse'.

Nuptial metaphors came easily to Johnston. Like Knox, he was probably oversexed. In his diaries he kept a count of his 'carnal supposed lawful contentments', performed after the foreplay of pious discussion with his wife. He recorded these details of his life because he believed God guided and controlled every moment of it. He agonized at length, in painful emotion, about what the Creator meant by this or that stroke. But once Johnston thought he had worked things out, nothing could change his mind. He was insufferable yet prepared to work hard without fee, and he knew the law affecting the Kirk backwards.[63]

While Johnston and others grafted away on the Covenant, a typical reaction came from Charles I. After months of passivity he suddenly issued a ferocious proclamation. It rejected all compromise over the Kirk, ordered dissidents in Edinburgh to disperse on pain of treason and forbade them to return without his privy council's consent. But his threats were empty. He had no means to enforce them.

One thing Charles I did do was provoke the publication of the Covenant. This turned out to be long and disjointed. Whole sections of it cannibalized previous declarations or statutes, yet its aims sounded out loud and clear. It appealed to the people by condemning the evils of popery and standing firm for true, godly religion. It signed off with a 'national oath and subscription inviolable', setting out Scotland's right to spiritual and civil liberty – but always in due form, by the principles of the Reformation and in deference to legitimate authority. The Presbyterian militants sought to demonstrate how the weight of the law lay behind them so that this represented no challenge to royal prerogatives as such, only to the king's misuse of them. They demonstrated this not only to their own satisfaction but also, in the event, to the nation at large.

By 28 February 1638, the document was finished and was then read out from the pulpit of Greyfriars. The Lord Advocate, Thomas Hope of Craighall, vouched for its legality. People of all classes, starting with nobles and going on through ministers to ordinary citizens, began to sign it. Among the tombstones of the wintry kirkyard they did so for two days. A copy of the Covenant afterwards went to every parish in the land. In each case it was again to be read out from the pulpit – which took half an hour – and to be signed by the people.

Johnston recorded in his diary for 1 April the ceremony at the Trinity church in Edinburgh. The minister was the Reverend Henry Rollock, who had among his fashionable flock several peers of the realm. After he read the Covenant, he asked them all to hold up their hands and swear by the name of the living God. 'At the which instant of rising up, and then of holding up their hands, there arose sic a yelloch, sic abundance of tears, sic a heavenly harmony of sighs and sobs, universally through all the corners of the church, as the like was never seen or heard of.'[64]

๋

The Presbyterian militancy of the Covenant snowballed into a popular movement. What motivated the many was no doubt a fear the Reformation could be reversed. That might not have been enough to win over the few, the merchants of Edinburgh who by means of their money had to keep the covenanting show on the road and who stood to lose most if it careered off. With Charles I they had been warily cooperative, whatever covert sympathy they might have felt with the resistance to him. They carried on paying taxes while the wars into which he led England ruined trade. The richest made loyal contributions when he sought to raise money without a Scots Parliament from 1633 to 1639. Yet all this had led in the end to the flight of his government from his capital. What else was there to do now but support the Covenant?

The richest man of all, the equal of John MacMorran and George Heriot in earlier generations, gave an example of the shift in thinking. William Dick, lord provost 1638-40, had a townhouse which still stands in Advocates Close, a building of four storeys, its lintels inscribed with Latin quotations from Horace and Ovid. Outside town he owned the estates of Grange and Braid on the rising ground and hills to the south, today among the city's most desirable suburbs. He now adopted a political position which, though apparently contradictory, appealed to many as the ideal solution to Scotland's problems if only it could be brought off.

Dick was one of the merchants who had given large sums to Charles I, and in reward he was knighted: to that extent, a great extent, he remained a royalist. Now he also lent £200,000 to raise a covenanting army; the sum would soar to £474,000 in the conflict that shortly ensued. How were the two aspects of his munificence to be reconciled? He supported both king and Covenant. To be precise, he wanted Charles I to take the Covenant, to follow his subjects in swearing on something greater than monarchy or nation and then to govern by its principles. Dick and others would hold to the ideal of a covenanted king right through the years of civil war to come, and at times felt close to realizing it. It appealed to the urge in Scots to confront and overcome the contradictions always at work in them, a feeling so different from the bland English preference for compromise.[65]

Charles I prepared to invade, though no English troops had fought the Scots for a century and the plans needed preparation from scratch. With some difficulty he assembled a force on the border. The Covenanters, on a surge of popular support, attracted streams of eager recruits. General Alexander Leslie took command of them, after returning from Germany, where he had organised the signature of the Covenant by the thousands of Scots mercenaries serving in the Thirty Years' War. Now he marched out from Edinburgh and took his stand on Duns Law. In the event, neither side was spoiling for a fight. Talks began and after a fortnight concluded in the Pacification of Berwick. The king gave way; the people won. A free Parliament and a free General Assembly would be called to ratify the results of this Scottish Revolution. Edinburgh felt sure, in the long, balmy days of June 1639, that God was smiling on it.

Within six years God rather gave evidence of his wrath, in the most terrible visitation of the plague Edinburgh ever suffered: perhaps a third of the population died. In other respects, too, the Covenant was turning out a cruel self-deception. It led on to a supposed fulfilment in the Solemn League and Covenant of 1643, negotiated at Westminster and providing for Presbyterianism to be extended all over Great Britain – needless to say, the false English soon abjured it. When Charles I fell to the axe in 1649, Scots wanted to ensure that next they got a covenanted king. They proffered the Covenant to the martyred monarch's son, Charles II, who took it. But this only brought, after crushing defeats at the Battles of Dunbar and Worcester, English conquest for the first time in 300 years. Confusion followed, though with one deep change that marked Scotland and Edinburgh for good: from now on it was to be not the king but the Kirk that claimed the first loyalty of city and nation.

CHAPTER FOUR

'CITY OF PALACES, OR OF TOMBS'

(William Hazlitt)

ON 30 JULY 1774, at his flat on the fourth floor of James Court, Edinburgh, James Boswell woke up with a terrible hangover. It was a Saturday morning and, in his time as in ours, Scotsmen often spent Friday night getting drunk. Boswell followed this national custom with enthusiasm. The previous evening he had dined with fellow lawyers at the house of Andrew Pringle, Lord Alemoor, a judge in the Court of Session known for his liberal hospitality. 'I was well warmed with wine here,' Boswell would record in his journal. Then he had let himself be persuaded by a more senior colleague at the bar, Robert Macqueen, and by a second judge, Francis Garden, Lord Gardenstone, to press on to greater things at the house of yet another advocate, David Moncreiffe. 'I determined to go. I did so, and was flashed away. I was really excellent company,' Boswell modestly recollected. Again, 'there was very hard drinking. I however did not exceed a bottle and a half of old hock. But, with what I had taken at dinner, I was far gone.'

Boswell still managed to stagger down to the law courts in the High Street by nine o'clock in the morning. There he bumped into the Solicitor General of Scotland, Henry Dundas, whom he also remembered from the night before. Now he found Dundas 'standing in the outer hall looking very ill. He told me he was not able to stay, so he went home. He had struggled to attend to his business, but it would not do.' A second advocate up early that day, Peter Murray, recounted how he had already seen Dundas come out of a dram-shop in the Back Stairs, where he was trying to settle his stomach, in all his formalities of large wig and cravat. Boswell observed: 'In some countries such an officer of the crown as the Solicitor General being seen in such a state would be thought shocking. Such are our manners in Scotland that it is nothing at all.'[1]

The two men knew each other well, for circumstance had seemed to mark them out for a similar course in life. Born eighteen months apart – Boswell in October 1740, Dundas in April 1742 – both were scions of old though not wealthy families. Both their fathers owned merely middling estates, yet dwelt amid the splendour of a house built in the magnificent Palladian style. So both had to earn a living in the law, and they ended up sitting on the bench, respectively as Lords Arniston and Auchinleck. Arniston was the superior in professional ability, the outstanding judge of his generation; at the climax of his career he became Lord President of the Court of Session. It was Arniston who had recommended Auchinleck for a gown. Each adopted the same terrifying demeanour whether in front of their households or presiding in court.

The sons were expected to follow in their fathers' footsteps. While no evidence confirms as much, they might already have known each other in boyhood. They certainly became classmates studying law at the University of Edinburgh, whence they qualified as advocates, Boswell in 1762, Dundas the next year. Boswell formed the impression, and never lost it, that he had the better mind, an impression which from his side determined their relationship. Yet if Dundas was not a deep or original thinker, the professional gifts he did have he used to better effect than Boswell.

The similar backgrounds worked differently on the two lads. It was perhaps of advantage to Dundas that Arniston had died in 1753, leaving him to develop free of paternal approval or disapproval. His true father-figure was his stepbrother, his senior by thirty years, who in due course became the second Lord President of the Court of Session with the judicial title of Arniston. Dundas's relationship to him was less fraught than it might have been to a real father, to judge by the example of Boswell and Auchinleck. The Dundases stood on the best of terms, the elder colluding in the younger's advancement at the bar. He could altogether count on a degree of support from his family that was withheld from Boswell, if largely through his own fault.

This offers us a clue why Dundas would rise high in his profession while Boswell hardly got off the ground. Unlike Boswell, Dundas followed his family's expectations. Scotland was in the throes of headlong material and intellectual change, yet it had started out as a traditional, close-knit society where the extended family formed the prime economic and political unit. Clannishness might not only dictate that sons or brothers should in their choice of career follow a path laid down by parents or siblings, but also demanded of them along the way a deliberate exertion to advance the interest of the family as a whole. This was, not least, an unspoken assumption at the bar in Edinburgh. Legal families existed because their webs of connections offered a way to success. For an advocate, it was especially helpful to have a relation on the bench, solicitors being eager to ply such a man with work. Boswell would later note with amusement how he prospered when his father sat, though all rapport between them had by then evaporated. That only showed to what extent he undervalued the social discipline binding together the landed and legal class which, from Edinburgh, now led Scottish public life. In a rather closed, somewhat stern society such discipline was reckoned vital, even amid the new freedom offered by the enlightened thinking of the age.

Dundas, by contrast, proved quite a prodigy at the bar. Colleagues admired his sound though never extravagant eloquence, the pains he took with his briefs, the concision and competence of his pleading. Soon he was handling sensational murders and other big cases. With rising renown came rapid reward. In 1766, three years after finishing his studies, Dundas was appointed Solicitor General, the second highest post in the crown's legal service in Scotland. His ability attracted favourable notice from the Lord Chief Justice of England, Lord Mansfield, a Scot who had spent his career in London and built up there a wide political influence. Before another year passed, Dundas became involved in Scotland's greatest civil lawsuit of the century, the Douglas Cause, as counsel for Archibald Douglas, the successful claimant to the disputed lands and fortune of his uncle, the Duke of Douglas. In 1775 Dundas was promoted to Lord Advocate, the highest non-judicial post in his profession, also in effect chief officer of government in Scotland.[2]

Boswell lagged far behind. Early on the despair of his father, he also earned the disapprobation of others when at the end of his studies he went swanning off to the Continent to hobnob with

Rousseau and Voltaire – impressive, if unlikely to lead anywhere in Edinburgh. That thought never bothered him, but even he felt struck at his return home by the widening professional gap between himself and Dundas. On the latter's first official promotion, Boswell wrote to a friend from college, William Temple: 'Do you remember what you and I used to think of Dundas? He has been making £700 as an advocate, has married a very genteel girl with £10,000 fortune and is now appointed His Majesty's Solicitor for Scotland.' Yet Boswell would not exert himself enough to close that gap, even after his father insisted on his settling down to the law. The Douglas Cause, for example, offered rich pickings to advocates, and Boswell would make a little out of a subsidiary case. In its main phase his contribution was merely literary, however, writing allegories and ballads about the Cause – or downright scandalous, when he capered with the yelling, gesticulating mob that stoned his father's windows after the austere old judge disdained to join in popular celebration of Archibald Douglas's victory. Boswell was still trailing by the time of Dundas's second and greater step up in 1775. 'Harry Dundas is going to be made King's Advocate – Lord Advocate at 33!' Boswell howled to Temple. 'I cannot help being angry and somewhat fretful at this. He has, to be sure, strong parts. But he is a coarse, unlettered, unfanciful dog. Why is he so lucky?'[3]

Enlightened Edinburgh was a place of paradoxes, private and public. This city, no longer the capital of an independent kingdom, yet widened rather than narrowed its horizons and raised its aspirations rather than suffered its hopes to sink. The Scotland that had renounced her statehood at the Union of 1707 compensated by imagining a universal realm of progress; she formed, so to speak, a parallel universe to the degraded reality, with Edinburgh at its core. Having brought down the curtain on the dark drama of her past, Scotland might then still pursue a destiny of her own, intellectual and material. The paradoxes worked themselves out in striking individual ways, too. Dundas and Boswell, so sharply contrasting with each other, serve as excellent examples.

※

Dundas made the best of the opportunities the Union offered. He was a son of Edinburgh, born and bred to its legal establishment, which during the eighteenth century had replaced the old merchant oligarchy in leadership of the city. He was educated at its High School and university. He launched his career from its Parliament House. He took care of its municipal government and architectural adornment. He returned from his official duties whenever he could. He spoke to the end of his days (even in the House of Commons) in the accents of the Lothians. He never disowned the social habits of Edinburgh (chiefly drinking). And he would die in Edinburgh, which afterwards erected to him a triumphal column topped by his statue, still standing in the middle of St Andrew's Square.

Even when Dundas needed to linger in London, it was as if he had never left Edinburgh. He surrounded himself with his countrymen and got them good jobs. To him being Scottish was an asset in itself, and he cared not a fig about English complaints of his favouritism. While legislation for Scotland took up little time at Westminster, he made sure it went through. He spread Edinburgh's ideas, above all by introducing the father of economics, Adam Smith, into the highest political circles and setting off there the process of education that would make the British state the global pioneer of free trade. He pursued an enlightened concept of empire, not of conquering, occupying and colonizing alien territory but of opening up peaceful commerce with autonomous native powers. He exploited every avenue to make Scots richer, happier, more respected and honoured in the world.

Dundas rose higher in the counsels of the new United Kingdom than any other Scotsman of the eighteenth century (leaving aside the Earl of Bute in his atypical, calamitous but mercifully short premiership). Dundas's career at Westminster spanned four decades, and he was a kingmaker there. Yet he never deluded himself that he could, faced with English prejudice, head a government himself – the second Scot to achieve this (one of Dundas's protégés, the Earl of Aberdeen) would have to wait until the 1850s. Instead, Dundas, serving loyally under his Prime Minister, William Pitt the younger, made himself an indispensable member of the inner cabal that saw the country through the worst perils of its wars with revolutionary France, up to the point – say, the Battle of Trafalgar in 1805 – where the British could no longer lose, even if their final victory would still be long delayed. This was a global war, too, and Dundas directed a second front in the Orient. He changed India from being in the first place an economic interest of Great Britain into one just as much political and strategic. He not only remained, then, a patriotic Scot and Briton but also became a citizen of the world. There are places named after him from Canada to Australia. He exerted an influence over five continents and seven seas.

In tandem with Dundas's personal role in Britain and the empire, his nation, after its earlier hesitancies and setbacks, became in crucial ways integrated with its southern neighbour. The Treaty of Union had not yet been greatly tampered with, so the structure of the native institutions guaranteed in 1707 remained more or less intact. But Scots no longer had to rely on them to protect their interests. That was done rather by their all-round success in the Union, at a personal level among countless individuals, at a national level through English acceptance of the Scots as equals (something the Irish never achieved during their own membership of the United Kingdom from 1801 to 1922), above all at an imperial level where fewest barriers existed to a poor yet resourceful people. Dundas, one of many for whom all this worked, was himself an embodiment of how the small capital of a small country could yet make itself count by the vigour of its personalities, the force of its ideas and the scale of its ambitions.[4]

⚜

Boswell might have died sooner than admit Dundas was setting him an example. Some of their differences remained glaring. In 1763 Boswell, 'much agitated', met his hero, Dr Samuel Johnson, for the first time. He introduced himself by saying, 'I do indeed come from Scotland, but I cannot help it.' This gave Johnson the chance to crush him, which was promptly taken: 'That, sir, I find is what a very great many of your countrymen cannot help.' They then became the best of friends, though this only reinforced the grovelling Anglophilia in Boswell. Yet it was he, if chancing to meet Dundas in London, who played the patriot's part. Once, in 1783, Dundas took it calmly as Boswell twitted him about his exercise of patronage, asking why he consented to be 'a salesman for us, like cattle'. The reply came: 'It was better for the country, better for individuals not. For when all could scramble, they would have a chance to get more for themselves and their friends without regard for merit. Whereas an agent for government must distribute to the best purpose. He has a trust.'[5]

Here was a politician in bland mode; the reader must judge whether he had not given more away in the 'very remarkable incident' recounted in 1778 by Horace Walpole. According to tittle-tattle at Westminster, Dundas was drunk with his cronies in the early hours one morning when he 'broke out into an invective against the English. He said he would move for a repeal of the Union, that any ten Scots could beat any ten English: and if there were any competition, he was, and would avow himself, a Scot.' Scotsmen normally keep such opinions to themselves; Dundas by now could get away with them. Compared with Boswell, then, he cultivated his Scottishness. Yet, at least when sober, he stood for the Union.[6]

Boswell could also wax quite nationalistic if provoked, yet he never thought of his upbringing and education as anything better than a springboard to the more exalted sphere of London, the true centre of his universe. A way of getting there and staying there would have been to win election as an MP, something Dundas did time and time again (in the end nobody bothered to oppose him in his constituencies of Midlothian, then Edinburgh). Boswell's political career by contrast never took off. On occasion he did exert himself yet all his efforts came to nothing. It was Dundas who, as electoral manager of Scotland, decided which potential candidates might go to Westminster and which not; and while he made soothing noises to Boswell he did nothing more, regarding him no doubt as too much of a gadfly (this was true). Another possible path for Boswell would have been through the law, but practice at the bar in Edinburgh meant by definition absence from London. It was an act of desperation on his part, when he had already passed the age of forty, to try his luck at the English bar and compete with men at least as able or diligent and half as old as he was – and not only an act of desperation but also a waste of time. Boswell at length got a consolation prize as recorder of Carlisle, which combined practice in England with proximity to Scotland; but this, among his many professional disasters, turned out to be the most humiliating of all.

Yet Boswell did in the end win the acclaim he craved. He won it as a man of letters – then and now, among the most difficult careers anybody can follow. And he won it, after a few earlier experiments, with a single work, the *Life of Johnson*. This offers a splendid portrait of a memorable character, who lives down the ages in large part through the truth and force of Boswell's depiction. It also stands at the fountainhead of the modern genre of biography in English literature, a bubbling well of riches probably never to be exhausted. To all their contemporaries, Dundas was beyond doubt a greater man than Boswell. Boswell is yet remembered to the present day despite or because of his failings, which were legion – while not one in a hundred, even in Scotland, recalls Dundas, the man or his achievements.

A big regret at the end of Boswell's life, when he died in London at the age of fifty-six, was that he had not been able to spend more time there. Yet it was Edinburgh that marked up in his generation the greater accomplishments, which to posterity have put it on a par with the Athens of Pericles or the Florence of the Medici. How could Boswell have been blind to this and instead have despised Edinburgh as a dull, provincial backwater? It is indeed a city of paradoxes.

❧

Edinburgh remained so despite a fitfully growing tranquillity in the century after the Union. It was hard to get over the inheritance of the century before: not halfway through it, the earlier prosperity of capital and country had issued in war with the English, first against their king, then against their Parliament. After Charles I's execution in 1649 the Scots, insisting on a sort of hopeless loyalty to the native House of Stewart, proclaimed his son Charles II. The next year Oliver Cromwell invaded, won the Battle of Dunbar and took Edinburgh. But in 1651 the young monarch landed from his Dutch exile and was hastily crowned at Scone before he dashed south to meet crushing defeat at the Battle of Worcester. Cromwell swept through the Lothians again, held up not for a moment by fresh fortifications built along the line that later became Leith Walk. Even Edinburgh Castle put up no fight. 'It used to be called the Maiden Castle, but henceforth call it the prostitute whore,' said one disgusted observer.[7]

English soldiers, too, might have been driven to strong language as they got to know the city. They felt appalled at its filth. They ordered a general cleansing of closes and wynds and put a ban on throwing excrement from the upper windows to a cry of Gardyloo! It made no difference. With their inability besides even to get a decent haircut in town, the roundheads preferred to run the country from Dalkeith. This became the effective capital or at least (what amounted to the same in a conquered nation) the military head-quarters. Politically, Scotland was united to England on humiliating terms.[8]

Whether royalists or Covenanters, the Scots remained downcast but mutinous. One faction of Presbyterians, with their genius for hair-splitting, still stood for both Covenant and king. They prayed for Charles II. The English liked this not one bit. When the minister of South Leith did so the local military commander locked up the kirk and told its flock to push off, he did not care where. They were soon pleading to the authorities that they had 'ever since had our meeting for the worship and service of God in the open field which, by the inconstancy of the weather, hath very much disturbed the exercise; besides many aged and infirm people cannot go so far, and such as have young children...'[9] This would become a common experience for Scots. Life offered no comfort otherwise. War caused a slump in the economy, so business in Edinburgh languished. Scant advantage could be taken of the free trade with England inside the Cromwellian Union. Yet Scots had out of their own pockets to pay for the occupation of their country, not least for construction of a huge citadel at Leith (of which one gateway survives). Feeble efforts at revolt came to nothing.

Suddenly, on 1 January 1660, the English commander-in-chief in Scotland, General George Monck, crossed the border and marched his army away south, to the alarm of other military leaders of the Commonwealth. Since Cromwell's death over a year before, the republican regime had been tottering. Monck would give it the final push and negotiate the return of Charles II. When the young king landed to reclaim the thrones of his fathers on 25 May, Monck was waiting to welcome him on the beach at Dover. An insubordinate gamble had paid off, and now he handed three kingdoms back to his sovereign.

※

Scots greeted the Restoration with as much joy as the other nations of the British Isles. Charles II was proclaimed in Edinburgh on 14 May. Bells rang, cannons boomed, drums beat and trumpets blew, while people danced in the High Street and a bonfire burned atop

Arthur's Seat. On the other hand Archibald Johnston of Warriston, author of the Covenant and councillor of state in the Commonwealth, saw 'great riot, excess, extravagancy, superfluity, vanity, naughtiness, profanity, drinking of healths; the Lord be merciful to us'. There was more of it all on 19 June when Edinburgh held a day of thanksgiving. Everybody toasted the king in wine running from the spouts of the Cross. At night fireworks on Castle Hill depicted Cromwell chased by the Devil and vanishing with his pursuer in a big bang and puff of smoke.[10]

The joy was not reciprocated. Charles II nursed only miserable memories of Scotland, in particular of the endless Presbyterian sermons he had had to sit through in 1651 after taking the Covenant, many on the subject of his own sins. Now he would treat the Scots with contempt. Left to their own devices since Monck's departure, they were obliged to go to London to find out what was to happen to them. So little account of their country did triumphant English royalists take that nobody bothered to say it had regained its independence. No proclamation or dissolution of the Cromwellian Union followed – nothing. Scots were expected to pick up where they had left off.

A new government in Edinburgh decided 1633 was the point for Scots to pick up where they had left off. The first Parliament of the reign, the so-called Drunken Parliament, passed an Act Rescissory repealing all legislation passed since that date. One effect was to bring back Episcopalianism, which had only been abolished with the National Covenant of 1638. But many refused to submit to the bishops set once more over them, and 270 ministers across Scotland were deprived, including seven of eight in Edinburgh and the Canongate. A few would be later reinstated, yet the aim even of this modest indulgence was to divide the Presbyterians. While moderates in the Kirk conformed, others were driven to extremes where the government expected to isolate and crush them.

That was still not enough for royalists. They outlawed the Covenant. And they wanted to see covenanting blood run in the High Street of Edinburgh. They wrought their first revenge on the leader responsible for many of those laws passed after 1633, the Marquis of Argyll. Arrested in London, where he had gone in an effort to see Charles II, Argyll was shipped back and tried before his peers at

Parliament House. His case did not at first seem hopeless. He had espoused the cause of a covenanted king and had with his own hands placed the crown on Charles's head at Scone. The charges against him were not easy to make stick. His lawyers began to speak of acquittal. Then a spectre from the past struck with a vengeance. Monck dug up some letters Argyll had written to him during the English occupation, pledging full support for the Commonwealth; the fact both men at that time concurred now counted not in the least. When the prosecution read out the letters, nothing remained to be said for Argyll. His judges sentenced him to death. On the day of his doom, 27 May 1661, he was calm, brave and dignified. Executions took place next to the Cross in the early afternoon. The victim had time for a last meal, and Argyll lunched cheerfully on partridge. On the scaffold he spoke for half an hour, first denying any complicity in the death of Charles I, then urging Scots to stand by the Covenant, finally forgiving his foes and submitting to his fate as the will of God. After prayer, he was strapped to the board of the Maiden, a sort of guillotine. The blade severed his head.[11]

Retribution was visited not only on the great but also on the less. The Reverend James Guthrie, with a dozen of his more unabashed Presbyterian brethren, had made so bold as to send Charles II a message. This tempered tepid congratulation on his return from exile with a sharp reminder he had once taken the Covenant – yet he was already bringing back Anglicanism to England, and God would punish him if he did any such thing in Scotland. For their cheek the ministers were arrested. Guthrie, the ringleader, faced a capital charge of high treason. He pleaded guilty because, he said, the indictment set out just those principles he held. He was condemned to hang on 1 June. He also tucked in with relish to a last lunch, above all the cheese; his doctor had told him to avoid it but now he need not worry. On the scaffold in the High Street he showed no fear and spoke for an hour as if in the pulpit. Pinioned for the noose, he managed somehow to shake off the cloth covering his head, so he went into eternity with his eyes open and at the very last moment 'lifted up his voice for the Covenants'.

After Guthrie came a soldier, William Govan, who was alleged to have been on the scaffold in Whitehall at the beheading of Charles I. Executed now for what counted by any standards as a minor role then, Govan gave the sort of witness that would turn out typical of Covenanting martyrs. 'As for myself,' he said, 'it pleased the Lord, in the fourteenth year of my life, to manifest His love to me and now it is about twenty-four years since; all which time I professed the truth which I suffer for, and bear testimony to at this day, and am not afraid of the cross on that account: it is sweet, it is sweet.' He turned to Guthrie's body dangling above him and went on: 'Otherwise how do I look upon the corpse of him who hangs there with courage, and smile upon those sticks and that gibbet as the gates of heaven?' And up the ladder he, too, clambered to the noose, saying he was happier than those who had changed sides against the Covenant.

The final figure on the government's immediate hit-list was Johnston of Warriston. A royal decreet had gone out for his forfeiture and death. But it went out in his absence, for he had fled the country and was at that moment in hiding at Rouen in France. The government of Scotland sent a spy who pretended to befriend Mrs Helen Johnston. Before long she innocently revealed her husband's whereabouts. The French extradited him. Back in Edinburgh he cut a wretched figure. He did not recognize his own family, and wailed aloud when he could not recall quotes from scripture. At the trial he fell on his knees and wept, cowering and incoherent: 'It was really a reproach to the government to proceed against him,' said a moderate Episcopalian, Gilbert Burnet. Johnston's condemnation sobered him, however, and by the time he came to be hanged, on 23 July 1663, he too had regained his composure.[12]

※

Persecution served only to fortify the Covenanters. In 1666 they even managed a rising, if one easily defeated at the Battle of Rullion Green in the shadow of the Pentland Hills a few miles south-west of Edinburgh. About 1,000 rebellious peasants marched there armed with pitchforks, scythes and staves. They had meant to advance into the capital but were turned away and found their road back blocked by Bluidy Tam, the royalist General Tam Dalyell of the Binns. They could tell him by his long beard, which he had let grow ever since hearing of Charles I's execution. Then he spent some years of exile in Russia, serving in the army of the Czar. Another nickname for him was the Muscovite Deil, because on his return at the Restoration he brought with him an ingenious Russian invention, the thumbscrews. Covenanters would now learn about them, too. Bluidy Tam routed, killed or captured the churls ranged against him. Many were tortured and hanged in Edinburgh.

Again the doomed faced death with dauntless courage, if not blithe indifference. One, twenty-six-year-old Hugh McKail, rejoiced from the scaffold: 'Farewell father and mother, friends and relations. Farewell the world and all delights. Farewell meat and drink. Farewell sun, moon and stars. Welcome God and Father. Welcome sweet Lord Jesus. Welcome blessed Spirit of grace. Welcome glory. Welcome eternal life. Welcome death.' David Arnot said he felt 'highly honoured to be reckoned among the witnesses of Jesus Christ, to suffer for his name, truth and cause; and this day I esteem it my glory, garland, crown and royal dignity to fill up a part of his sufferings.' Humphrey Colquhoun assured the crowd of onlookers that 'I bless the Lord again and again I die for this oath and Covenant.' John Shields apologized as 'an unlettered man and not accustomed to speak in public', but added, 'I cheerfully lay down my life for this cause.' John McCulloch, an old man, pointed out he and others were being 'put to death expressly for having taken the Covenant, and we are so far from being ashamed thereof that we account it our honour to be reckoned worthy to suffer for such a cause.' John Wodrow, a merchant, agreed: 'I bless the Lord, who hath counted me worthy to die for so good and honourable a cause.' John Neilson had been one of the few lairds at Rullion Green 'but was so far accounting that course rebellion that I judged, and still do judge, it was my duty to join therein, and my honour to suffer therefore'. Thomas Paterson thanked God 'who not only kept us steadfast in his Covenant, but has also accepted and dignified our offer with this public appearance ... and in midst of thee, O Edinburgh!' Alexander Robertson just regretted 'that so many in this city once made famous and honoured for harmonious owning of the cause and Covenant of God, and blessed above many other cities with solemn assemblies for worship and government, should have been ensnared to suppress the revival of the work of God within this land'. So it went on.[13]

The Covenanters are usually recalled as a rustic movement, gathering at armed conventicles amid hill and glen, ready at any time to break off their prayers or psalms and turn to fight royal dragoons hunting them down. But they were also present in Edinburgh, and not just on the scaffolds. Here conventicles took place in private houses. The fevered piety arising from a time of horrors thrust together people who wanted only to fortify one another's faith through common witness, often under a deprived Presbyterian minister. In Edinburgh the conventicles may have been invisible, yet we can tell they were there by efforts the government made to discover and suppress such 'secret nurseries of schisms and trouble'. In 1679 even the magistrates found themselves hauled up by the privy council for allegedly permitting a conventicle at the Magdalen Chapel. They were fined and told to be more vigilant in future. They could only plead in mitigation that they had acted already to prevent other conventicles, for example, in Lady Yester's kirk.[14]

❧

Outward conformists could not always be trusted, then, even if in one case it was for reasons quite other than the authorities suspected. In 1670 Edinburgh felt shocked by the case of Major Thomas Weir, captain of the town guard and former officer in the army of the Covenant. He lived in retirement in the West Bow with his sister Grizel. In the street he cut an unmistakable figure striding along with a black thornwood staff. He had a reputation as one of the city's most pious men, and he did go to private conventicles. There, too, he stood out by the fervour of his devotions and earnestness in urging repentance on his fellows. Latterly, however, as he prayed and witnessed, he could no longer hear the word 'burn' without showing signs of distress.

Then at one meeting Weir began to recite a list of crimes he had committed himself: incest, satanism, witchcraft. His sister confirmed what he said, adding that he drew demonic powers from the black staff. Fellow worshippers thought he was going off his head but reported the pair to the town council. The case was serious enough for the lord provost, Sir Andrew Ramsay, to question them in person. They said they had years ago made a pact with the Devil. It came to light they had as teenagers had an incestuous affair, found out and reported by another sister; their parents sent Grizel away. Later, in 1651, a horrified minister heard about a traveller seen nearby in an act of bestiality with his mare. A military patrol set off in pursuit but when the suspect turned out to be the godly Major Weir his indignant denials were believed, and the woman who reported him was whipped for her pains. Meanwhile he had started committing incest with his stepdaughter, who, when she fell pregnant, was married off to an English soldier. And Weir had his evil way with a maidservant for twenty years. After his wife's death he sent for Grizel, now keeping a school at Dalkeith. She came to stay in the West Bow.

The Weirs were tried for witchcraft, found guilty and sentenced to death. Thomas, after acting all his life as one of the elect, knew now he was one of the reprobate. He would not pray or let ministers pray for him: to what end, when he must by Calvinist doctrine have been predestined to eternal damnation? Even at the stake he refused to repent. The executioner put the rope round his neck and told him to say, 'Lord, be merciful to me.' But he retorted, 'Let me alone, I will not. I have lived as a beast and I will die as a beast.' He was strangled, and his body burned along with his staff. Grizel went to be strung up the next day. She declared she meant to die with all possible shame. On the scaffold she tried to strip herself naked, but the hangman restrained her and pushed her off the ladder.[15]

❧

As in Edinburgh the unspeakable history of persecution and its gruesome consequences unfolded, the Episcopalian regime in the Kirk found one leader who counselled moderation, if tempered by his own eye for the main chance. This was James Sharp, who had started his career as a regent at the University of St Andrews, became minister of Crail in Fife, then worked for Monck and left with him for England in 1660. Sharp was trusty enough to be sent to Holland with the party that negotiated the return of Charles II. Not many ministers of Crail had looked at a king. When Sharp returned to Edinburgh with a royal letter apparently favourable to the moderate Presbyterians, he came as the man of the hour, relieving doubts and fears at a time when legal government had yet to be restored in Scotland. These moderate Presbyterians hoped to win back what they saw as their rightful place in charge of the Kirk. Their hopes would be dashed. Instead, bishops rose again. Sharp popped up at their head, as Archbishop and Primate of All Scotland. Here was an example of that never popular figure, the Scotsman on the make.

Sharp's foes called him Judas, yet, while he got little credit for his efforts, he did try under impossible conditions to steer a middle course for the Kirk. There could be no doubt of its utter political subservience to the royalist regime. But on other matters of practice or doctrine Episcopalians were often not far from Presbyterians. For example, they kept communion infrequent. It was offered on just one or two Sundays in the year and in Edinburgh all the churches would offer it on the same date. One such date was 17 November 1661. Then a lawyer, John Nicoll, recorded in his journal how two boys went down to play on the ice just formed over the Nor' Loch. But it broke 'and they both fell down and were drowned miserably in the filth and dirt. Let this be ane document to all profaners of the sabbath,' gloated the delightful diarist. He was not alone in his sanctimony. The synod of Edinburgh declared it still had on hand enough 'work to sharpen the rod of discipline and Church censure against all sorts of scandals ... uncleanness, profaning of the Lord's day (as is usual) but likewise of drunkenness and profane swearing, slandering and reviling, mocking of piety'.[16]

Covenanters remained unimpressed. They repaid Sharp with attempts on his life. The first came one afternoon in the summer of 1668 when he was visiting Edinburgh with the Bishop of Orkney, Andrew Honeyman. As they entered their coach in the High Street they paused to scatter coins to the usual crowd of beggars. One pulled out a gun and fired at the archbishop. The bullet missed him but shattered Honeyman's arm. Their servants felt too shocked to do anything but stare as the disguised beggar took to his heels. And Sharp was by now so unpopular that nobody else tried to stop him. Some bystanders cried, 'A man is killed!' Others replied, 'It is but a bishop.'[17]

Still, the assassin's face must be hard to forget for the victim who survives. In the winter of 1674, Sharp was again in Edinburgh and during an idle moment looked in the window of a shop selling brandy and tobacco, to both of which he was partial. Staring back stood the shopkeeper, a 'lean, hollow-cheeked man of a truculent countenance', in whom Sharp recognized his would-be killer of six years before. The man was one James Mitchell, who had studied but failed to become a minister, and now ran this small business with his wife. Sharp had him arrested. The privy council examined him *in camera*. He denied everything until Sharp persuaded the government to offer him pardon in exchange for confession. He was sent to the Bass Rock in the Firth of Forth, a prison for Covenanters. Four years passed. Suddenly Mitchell was brought back to be tried for his life. When his counsel protested this broke the plea bargain, Sharp claimed there had never been one, though the register of the privy council showed he was lying. The judges ruled such evidence inadmissible, then tried and condemned the prisoner. The royalist leader, the Duke of Lauderdale, brutally quipped: 'Let Mitchell glorify God in the Grassmarket' – where a gibbet stood.[18]

Ruthless repression brought no peace. A second rebellion broke out after the cold-blooded murder of Sharp on his way to St Andrews in 1679. This had the same result as the first rebellion – the defeat of the Covenanters. But at the Battle of Bothwell Brig the royal commander, the Duke of Monmouth, showed relative leniency and executed just a handful of prisoners. He spared any promising not to bear arms again. Even survivors who refused were only to be transported to the West Indies, though most died in a shipwreck off Orkney. The rest, after confinement in the kirkyard of Greyfriars in Edinburgh, went free.

❧

It was a period of rage and despair, misery and uproar, persecution, violence and tyranny – or so historians have depicted it for 300 years. But there is another story that might be told, on telling evidence from Edinburgh. It contains a paradox absent from received views of the era, one pointing out that the savage cruelty was accompanied by a cultural flowering. Collapse of the quest for the Covenant and the division of the Kirk into warring factions brought a reaction which, in some circles, sought to strike out on another path, to forget the history of suffering and present a different ideal to Scotland.

If we look at physical memorials of the time, they do not at once convey the impression of a prostrate, bleeding country. In Edinburgh, on the contrary, some quarters and certain buildings were reconstructed in a lavish fashion fit for a restored capital. The best work came at Holyrood, which had been partly burned down while in use as an English barracks. From 1671 the king's apartments, dating from the time of King James V, were repaired and refurbished by the royal surveyor-general, William Bruce, and master mason, Robert Mylne, with later additions by James Smith. The Holyrood we see now largely dates from this period. Its careful classical style, novel in Scotland, proposed an aristocratic ideal for a new era.

The noblemen of Scotland interpreted the royalist ideal held out to them in different ways, to judge from the variety of townhouses they in their turn built on the Canongate. The grandest surviving is Queensberry House, today a portal to the Scottish Parliament. It was constructed between 1681 and 1685, when the Duke of Queensberry bought it. Its plan, with restrained centre and bold wings round a forecourt, recalls the sort of *hôtel particulier* with which King Louis XIV's aristocracy was at the time adorning Paris. In contrast, on the opposite side of the street, stands Panmure House erected by the Maules of Panmure, patriotic historians. Hailing from Angus, they put up this *pied à terre* not in a cosmopolitan but in a national style, most obvious in the crowstepped gables. Or again, compromise between modernity and tradition is found at suburban Prestonfield, in the 'compact but classy' mansion of Sir James Dick, a lord provost. It has gables at each end yet a flat roof in between and, of all things, a Frenchified balustrade. Finally, within the walls of the burgh, Tweeddale House showed renewal was possible even amid the thickets of the urban jungle. Bought and recast by Bruce before he sold it to the Earl of Tweeddale in 1670, it lay deep in a close, claustrophobic as it left the High Street but opening up at the end into light, space, even elegance. Nobody yet sought architectural harmony in Edinburgh. Rather, during this phase of reconstruction, cultural battles were fought out in stone.

Urban renewal came also from the town council, which took powers of compulsory purchase over property it wanted cleared. The biggest clearance created Parliament Close, now Parliament Square, in the gap between St Giles and Parliament House. It found room for a life-sized equestrian statue in lead of Charles II, the oldest of its kind in Britain. Renewal did not always imply grand scale: the council felt as happy to open up small courtyards back from the High Street, still surrounded by lofty walls and offering only a glimpse of sky above but a relief from congestion all the same. Off the Lawnmarket, Brodie's Close contained two such courtyards, of some architectural interest; this remains today 'from the south the most atmospheric of

Edinburgh's closes. At the northern end of the mansion [Roman Eagle Hall] is a gabled stair-tower, its moulded door cornice supporting a rounded turret which serves as a corbel for the jettied upper stages.'[19]

In 1674 the town council announced an exemption from taxes for seventeen years on any house of stone replacing one of timber; from 1677 new houses of timber or roofs of thatch were banned. The new houses of stone often followed exotic fashion with a 'piazza' (local usage for arcade) on the ground floor at the front. This created more space for upper storeys, which were not then bound by regulations on the width of the street. Given the later importance of the Palladian style in Scotland, it is tempting to see here a precocious influence of the Basilica Palladiana at Vicenza, with its courtly colonnades, or even of the earlier Palazzo di Venezia in Rome, which more Scots would have seen; the Place des Vosges in Paris was another conceivable model. In any event, the Royal Mile took on a more imposing aspect – all lost today except at Gladstone's Land in the Lawnmarket, built somewhat earlier. This possibly set the pattern for and certainly is the sole surviving example of a piazza (apart from an aggressive modern imitation by Basil Spence in the Canongate). There was the pleasing prospect of an arcaded Royal Mile, hard to imagine now unless we go to the High Street of Elgin in Moray where a provincial imitation has not yet been fully razed.

For sale to developers the town council created parcels of land that often cut across the closes still following the pattern of the medieval tofts. One aim was to allow roomier dwellings to be erected over bigger sites. As more and more people squeezed on to the tail of the Rock, tenements mounted on a gigantic scale. The so-called Babylon, highest of all, rose on one side fourteen storeys from the Cowgate, 'ane immense heap of combustible material' which would go up in a great fire of 1700.[20] Some speculative jerry-building went on, too, but the measures by and large prompted better planning of tenements in more durable and elegant form, as at the Milne's Court of 1690 on the opposite side of the Lawnmarket. Here flats had five or six rooms, some as many as a dozen, lavishly fitted out. The trend to height brought about the first social segregation within the walls. The rich lived on the middle storeys of tall tenements; the poor were relegated either to ground floors, next to the noise and stench of the street, or to top floors, at the end of a long climb.

❧

Further amenities appeared. A burgess donated swans to swim about the Nor' Loch and make it look prettier. They cannot have long stayed white. The town council banned the slaughter of beasts in backyards and set up a shambles on the shore of the loch. Blood oozing into the slime and offal mulching the muck nourished wildlife less attractive than swans. In general there could hardly be more refinement without more cleanliness, or more cleanliness without more pure water. The council at last saw to the supply. In 1672–5 it laid pipes from springs at Comiston, beneath the Pentland Hills, to five (later ten) cisterns within the walls. It felt proud of this feat, to judge from the care and expense it lavished on the wellheads where water was to be drawn. One still stands at the foot of the West Bow, designed by William Bruce and Robert Mylne, no less, with concave pyramid roof and classical urn on top. Alas, the system had hardly been installed when it broke down during an abnormally dry summer. In fact the city remained without running water until 1676. But a couple of years later there was so much of the stuff it could be piped to thirsty breweries in the Canongate, even to the covenanting prisoners in the kirkyard of Greyfriars. Perhaps the town at long last really turned a bit cleaner. Human waste was produced in such industrial quantities that it could be rouped (auctioned) to farmers of the Lothians to cart on to their fields. It brought amazing increases in crops, but as these were sold back into the city the problem became a circular one.[21]

Modernity began to emerge in other aspects, too. As urban life grew more complex, information had to be exchanged. From 1695 a postmaster held office in Edinburgh. Within the city, messages could be conveyed by 'caddies' who knew every address and appeared at a burgess's elbow the instant he needed to send a letter or parcel, and who accosted strangers in search of lodging or just looking lost on the High Street; they also acted as pimps. The caddies were in truth 'wretches that in rags lie upon the stairs and in the streets at night, yet they are often considerably trusted' (their descendants today have only to remember the topography of golf-courses). For tidings of the wider world, prototypes of newspapers had arrived in the shape of ephemeral broadsheets during the civil wars. The earliest recognizable as anything like the present equivalents were the *Mercurius Caledonius* and the *Kingdoms Intelligencer*, which appeared in 1661 and may have lasted a few years. The *Edinburgh Gazette* began in 1680 and was relaunched in 1699 by an old soldier turned entrepreneur, James Donaldson; it is still in existence but now prints only official notices. Then in 1704 Adam Boig brought out the *Edinburgh Courant*. The two organs competed, Boig coming off the better with his deeper coverage and wider circulation in the prelude to the Treaty of Union.[22]

To move about the city there was public transport, first in the shape of sedan chairs. The earliest appeared in 1661. There were only six by 1687 but dozens a century later; usually Highlanders worked as the 'chairmen'. Sedan chairs, while handy for penetrating closes and wynds, hardly counted as modern, but hackney coaches came closer. By 1673 there were enough to be numbered, one to twenty. In 1676 they got orders to stop their 'furious driving' in the High Street and to go at walking pace. A regular service to Leith began. In 1670 Adam Woodcock won permission to set it up, charging a shilling. In 1677 William Home was given a monopoly on the route for twelve years. The next try came from Robert Miller, who had a monopoly for nine years from 1702 and seems to have done better than the others, for the council began to make regulations for the coaches. In 1675, for the first time, streets outside the walls had been paved, the head of Leith Walk and what is now Lauriston Place.[23]

Shops opened, also as rather a novelty. Until now customers had always bought directly from craftsmen whatever these had a privilege to produce. For food they went to open-air markets, the names of which survive in Fishmarket Close and Fleshmarket Close. Otherwise merchants had always supplied and still did supply most of what was bought and sold. As they seldom specialized but dealt in any goods they got hold of, they needed no premises dedicated to sale of particular items. What shops there were tended to offer foreign luxuries. For example, in 1689 the town council gave permission for a perfumer fleeing the Irish troubles to shift his business to Edinburgh. In 1695 it let two Huguenots set up in the trades of japanning and gilding. In 1698 another was authorized to make mirrors. The burgh dealt altogether kindly with foreign refugees: by 1700 three Jews had leave to work in Edinburgh, probably in import–export business, and were told they might become burgesses if they converted to Christianity.[24]

Traffic in luxuries boomed so much that in 1704 a stern patriot, Andrew Fletcher of Saltoun, felt moved to collect statistics with a view to banning it. His survey shows the same goods on sale here as in other cities of northern Europe. This being Scotland, alcohol, tobacco and 'drugs' figured prominently. With few exceptions, all glass and metalware were imported, as was much of the earthenware, not to speak of more elegant furniture, mirrors and clocks, let alone porcelain, tea, coffee and chocolate, or prunes, dates, raisins, figs and currants, or olives, capers, anchovies and pickles. These things would be hard to find amid the tatty tourism of the High Street today.[25]

❧

The growth in retailing prompted the jealous merchants of Edinburgh to attempt a takeover. In 1681 they formed the Merchant Company with a sett providing for surveillance of its members, just as craftsmen's incorporations had of theirs. What may have inspired the move was the penetration by now of too many craftsmen into the old merchants' guild, a result of the decreet arbitral of 1583. The formation of the new company looks like an effort to seize back a more exclusive privilege. It was meant first to enforce a merchants' monopoly over the sale of clothing and manufacture of material for making it; from now on, anybody engaged in either activity would be forced to join the new company. We may guess quite a few townsfolk had begun to earn a living in the ways specified without bothering about the burgh's regulations. Now even the craftsmen objected that 'a society on the lines proposed, destructive of other people's liberties, is against all reason and without a parallel. The governors of such a company would be masters of the town.' The fears seemed to be realized when the Parliament then passed laws forbidding both import and export of textiles: the country was to become a closed market for home-produced garments under the thumb of the new company.

But the stratagem failed. In its first year, 139 retailers joined the

Merchant Company; in its second year, two. As late as 1704, when some radical opening of a stagnant Scottish economy seemed unavoidable (and desirable) the company petitioned the Parliament that the plethora of regulations already in place 'in no ways answered the design or obtained the end, for which they were made, which was to curb prodigality, improve our own product and discourage all foreign import'. For example, 'it is evident from practice and experience that foreign silks of all sorts, and stamped calico and linen were never more frequently worn and ... hundreds of ells are worn, for one ell made in the kingdom'. This was not just a commercial but also a moral problem, since 'the trade of silk from abroad is carried on by unfreemen, strangers and smugglers, of mean fortune, and desperate, who run the silk stuffs free of duties and all public burdens, to the ruin of merchants and retailers'. In other words, the traditional mercantile elite's refuge lay in trying to keep everything as it always had been.

Unable to turn the clock back, however, even the Merchant Company began to tire of its protectionist zeal. Its effort and failure to reinforce or maintain privilege can be taken as the first fall from that control of the burgh the traditional elite had held for half a millennium. The sett of the new company provided for the dues collected from members to be applied to charitable purposes. This came to seem preferable to flogging the dead horse of monopoly. Today, the Merchant Company's schools provide most private education in Edinburgh.[26]

❧

Renewed material advance also took on an immaterial or institutional form. Indeed this period saw the founding of several of Edinburgh's institutions. Since the times were hierarchical, the institutions themselves formed a sort of hierarchy. At the top has to be placed the Order of the Thistle, founded by King James VII in 1687 and, after being engulfed by revolutionary troubles, refounded by Queen Anne in 1702. Its original chapel was at Holyrood, fitted out under the king's personal supervision. In his own royal yacht he sent up from London an altar, organ, vestments and images, with a throne for himself and a dozen stalls for a new order of chivalry, the Knights of the Thistle. It was a high-class job: Grinling Gibbons did the carvings. But the mob sacked the chapel in 1688. To this day the order rewards the great and good; the present Thistle Chapel of 1909–11, by Robert Lorimer, is in St Giles. One step down the social hierarchy, though if anything even snootier, came the Royal Company of Archers. This was founded as a private club for sport in 1676, and still awards a silver arrow to the winner of an annual shooting match on butts set up at Musselburgh Links. It would evolve at the hands of Sir Walter Scott into the sovereign's bodyguard in Scotland. Only toffs need apply.[27]

Other new institutions were useful rather than decorative. Pride of place must go to the Advocates' Library. The Faculty of Advocates decided in principle to establish a library in 1680. When Sir George Mackenzie of Rosehaugh became dean of the faculty in 1682 he set out to realize the concept. He drew up the lease for a building and had the first volumes collected. The library opened in 1689. Nothing else like it existed in the British Isles. For over a century it remained among the finest in Europe. It turned into the National Library of Scotland in 1925. The present book has been largely researched there.[28]

※

Scotland uses the term institution also in a special sense, to denote systematic exposition of her law by authorities known as institutional writers. They may be cited in court, where they have the same standing as a bench of judges or as statute where no statute applies. A succession of institutional writers defined and revised Scots law during two centuries and more, until their work was overtaken, not to say overwhelmed, by a rising tide of detailed legislation from Westminster. Mackenzie had many talents but is best remembered as an institutional writer. His own work, *Institutions of the Laws of Scotland*, came out in 1684. One with the same title by Viscount Stair had preceded it by three years. Stair urged politicians to avoid passing too much legislation because it tended to make the law not clearer but less clear; his advice has gone unheeded.

What this feat did was sum up the development of Scots law as it had risen to autonomy since the Reformation. Older feudal law was adapted to changing conditions by that brilliant young Thomas Craig who had hymned Mary Queen of Scots in Latin. His *Jus Feudale*, finished by 1603 but not published before 1655, was a treatise on the feudal system, probing amid thickets of custom for unifying principles, and still cited until the abolition of feudalism in 2001. Older canon law fell into disuse, without losing all influence. A different kind of Roman authority entered Scotland and other reformed nations of Europe in quest of a secular basis for law. For inspiration they looked back to antiquity and the Emperor Justinian's *Corpus Juris Civilis*. In cases where no better law seemed applicable, Scots referred to this and its interpreters. By Stair and Mackenzie the entire range of sources of the law was welded into one system soon also an object of patriotic pride.

As Scots law became central to the life of the capital, so also the legal profession rose to pre-eminence. Professional men in general already formed a larger part of the population here than anywhere else in Scotland. Returns for a poll tax in 1693 revealed more than 500 individual professionals in Edinburgh; the same returns revealed fewer than 400 merchants, who on that evidence were already sliding into relative decline. Within the professions, lawyers made up the biggest group – 179 writers (solicitors) and 36 advocates. These numbers must have been out of all proportion to the burgh's needs; they reflected its status as capital and seat of government.[29]

※

Little less telling was progress by the medical profession. The returns for the poll tax showed thirty-three doctors of medicine (all with degrees from abroad), twenty-three surgeons and nineteen apothecaries, these two groups forming part of a craftsmen's incorporation. It preserved their past in its links to the town council, where its deacon sat. But surgeons had been looking to a future as a learned society. Now they created what became, under a charter of 1697, the Royal College of Surgeons. They built the Surgeons' Hall, which is still standing. It housed a library well-stocked with contemporary medical literature from Europe. It also housed a theatre for dissection, another key to advancing knowledge. For it a supply of bodies was needed, though only the council could authorize this. In 1705 the surgeons sought to move matters along by naming one of their number, Robert Eliot, as public dissector charged with regular teaching from cadavers on a slab. To a request for support in this delicate venture the council responded by appointing him professor of anatomy. An unintended consequence was owed to enterprising citizens: in 1711 the council had to make it an offence to dig up fresh corpses from their graves and sell them, at 40 shillings each, to the surgeons. For customers still alive there was a massage parlour by Surgeons' Hall. In 1723 John Valentine and his daughter would be named public 'rubber and rubberess'.[30]

While surgeons sought to establish higher status in the city, they had to deal with rivalry from the Royal College of Physicians, chartered in 1681. This was the brainchild of Robert Sibbald, Scotland's leading boffin, who counted Charles II among those consulting him for medical advice. Sibbald had in his choice of career sought an antidote to the tumults of the time: 'I saw none could enter to the ministry without engaging in factions. I preferred a quiet life, where I might not be engaged in factions of Church or state. I fixed upon the study of medicine, wherein I thought I might be of no faction and might be useful to my generation.'[31]

But why the distinction between surgeon and physician? At the time a surgeon's craft lay in violent, bloody, often lethal interventions in the human body, while a physician's craft lay in external treatment, in drugs, medicines or – more likely in the seventeenth century – herbs. To a superstitious age the latter craft was hard to distinguish from witchcraft, and Sibbald saw the need to place it on a less dubious footing. All over Scotland grew plants which were held locally to have curative properties. One of Sibbald's aims was to find a place where he could cultivate and test them. As he put it: 'I had from my settlement here in Edinburgh a design to inform myself of the natural history this country could afford, for I had learned at Paris that the simplest method of physic was the best, and these [plants] that the country afforded came nearest to our temper, and agreed best with us.' On part of the grounds of Holyrood he founded in 1677 what would become the Royal Botanic Garden of Edinburgh. From there it moved to a site later covered by platform 11 at Waverley Station, where a plaque commemorates it, and finally down to Inverleith.

Sibbald's third project was to start instruction in medicine at the University of Edinburgh. He envisaged the university as the teaching institution for physicians and his Royal College as their licensing authority. This was a good idea, not least in eventually helping to relaunch the university after its first century of catering just for local students of arts and divinity. In 1685 Sibbald won appointment as one of three inaugural professors of medicine, along with James Halket and Archibald Pitcairne. Halket was an obstetric surgeon trained at Leiden in Holland. That was where Pitcairne had studied too, and written a thesis on the circulation of the blood so distinguished that in 1692 he was offered a chair there. But he preferred Edinburgh. Beside his contributions to learning, he was an active and charitable general practitioner. He held a surgery in the Lawnmarket in a cellar so dark it was known as the 'grope shop' (in Scots the words rhyme); Pitcairne also tickled his patients with anti-Presbyterian jokes. By agreement with the town council he treated paupers free and got their corpses when they died. In the event, however, the three first chairs of medicine at Edinburgh remained titular. Sibbald did not succeed in establishing regular medical instruction; Dutch universities remained just too famous for any Scottish one to compete. At least that was now an aspiration.[32]

❧

In Scotland the keenest intellectual advance came for the time being in mathematics. James Gregory accepted the first chair in the subject at Edinburgh in 1674. He had previously spent nine years at the University of Padua, where he talked to former pupils of Galileo Galilei. In a fundamental branch of his discipline, the differential calculus, Gregory was one of three Europeans working at its furthest frontier, the others being Gottfried von Leibniz in Hanover and Sir Isaac Newton at Cambridge. No academic journals or conferences yet existed to publicize the results of research. The three kept abreast by personal correspondence, which had drawbacks: they could choose to be frank with one another or not, out of uncertainty or for some different reason. Gregory let Leibniz and Newton know when he was the first to solve Kepler's Puzzle, of how to determine at any given time the location of a planet in its orbit. But he did not care to divulge further results in which he suspected Newton had anticipated him, even if Newton himself would publish nothing short of the epochal *Principia Mathematica*. Scholarly scruples of the age could never, all the same, hold up its scientific revolution, of which the culmination came in Newton's discovery of gravity. This proved that nature obeyed laws. Edinburgh was one place the scientific revolution reached early.

James Gregory soon died but, when his no less brilliant nephew, David, succeeded him in the chair at the age of twenty-two, Edinburgh became the first university in the world to hear lectures on Newton's teachings. Not content with exposition, David Gregory and others would apply the latest discoveries to various branches of science, in the process extending the scope of theoretical advance so as to start changing human conceptions of reality. Gregory did that for astronomy, and remodelled the discipline. He cast off its theological past, its mumbo-jumbo of empyrean spheres and the like, to make it consistent with Newtonian physics. Vital to this was his interest in Greek geometry, manifested in his edition of Euclid in 1703. In the changing conceptions of reality, geometry no longer served as just a formal exercise, a part it had played in western learning since antiquity. With Newton's revelation that mathematical law related physical bodies to one another, Greek geometry became a key to reality. Newton had done much to revive it on his own account, and Gregory made it central to Scottish intellectual tradition.[33]

❧

In that tradition the Restoration's renewed royalism came to terms with the capital's rekindled culture so as to produce polymaths (leavened still by some eccentrics). On the Gregories, for example, the last in the line of enlightened Scots philosophers, Sir William Hamilton, would look back in 1838 and write that the renown of their chair had been owed 'not certainly more to the mathematical skill than to the philosophical ability and varied learning of its professors. The illustrious men who shed the first, perhaps the most brilliant, glory on the chair – James and David Gregory – they were not only great mathematicians but learned scholars.'[34] James, beside his work on theory also invented a reflecting telescope, built an astronomical clock and set up the first observatory in Scotland. David was esteemed by the English, too, and at length became Savilian Professor of Astronomy in the University of Oxford. Both, related by marriage to the first Scots portrait-painter, George Jameson, also had wide artistic interests.

The institutional writer Mackenzie displayed a similar versatility. He earned during a parallel career in politics the sobriquet of Bluidy Mackenzie for his part in persecuting Covenanters. Yet he remained just as much at home in the seclusion of his study, where he wrote on heraldry, history, philosophy and witchcraft. His political theory, set out in *Jus Regium* (1688), justified the absolutism of the Stewarts against 'madcap zealots of this bigot age, intending to mount heaven Elias-like in zeal's fiery chariot'. His own zeal could be a little relentless too, so it comes as a surprise to find the English playwright John Dryden calling him 'that noble wit of Scotland'. Mackenzie had in fact written his most interesting and ambitious works as a youngster, before a public career absorbed his energies. His *Aretina, or the serious romance* came out in 1660 and was the first Scottish novel, constructed on contemporary French and ancient classical models. His *Religio Stoici* of 1663 remained exceptional among Scottish writings of the age for treating religion from the point of view of a cultivated man, not a fanatic. For him, culture and morality went together: the Scots' qualities – 'fiery, abrupt, sprightly and bold' – fitted them to revive the public virtue of ancient Romans and Greeks. In a final underlining of the point, he had himself buried in a splendid Palladian mausoleum in the kirkyard of Greyfriars, 'the most advanced architectural work of its period in Scotland'.[35]

Sibbald proved the greatest polymath of all. His programme was pragmatic rather than rationalist: sure knowledge could not be derived from biblical or classical authority but only from research into the past and the present aimed at material or moral improvement. From his public offices he embarked on a patriotic work of analysing Scotland both historically and geographically. The results were to be published in two volumes. The first, *Scotia Illustrata*, came out in 1684 and drew on the precocious map-making expertise available in Scotland. That went back a century to Timothy Pont; scores of his hand-drawn maps are preserved on fragile sheets of paper among the greatest treasures of the National Library of Scotland. Sibbald knew of them and of later work by James Gordon of

Rothiemay, including a map of Edinburgh commissioned in 1647 (town councillors dubbed it the 'gutted haddie' because it made the city, viewed from above, look like a filleted fish). Now a grant for James Adair to carry out further surveys completed the preparation of Sibbald's first volume. Work on *Scotia Antiqua*, the second volume dealing with historical development, was done for particular counties though never for the country as a whole. Sibbald would later cooperate with an immigrant Dutch military engineer, John Slezer, to produce *Theatrum Scotiae* (1693), a lavish compilation of local scenes; Slezer did the engravings, Sibbald the commentaries. The book offers almost all we know of how Scottish towns then looked. It contains two vistas of Edinburgh, one from the Dean Village, a new industrial suburb, the second from above the West Port, showing the declivity of the Royal Mile.[36]

Another of Edinburgh's intellectual pioneers, Pitcairne, was no less of an all-rounder. To his surgical dexterity he added fluency in Latin verse, admired in Scotland ever since the work of Thomas Craig and George Buchanan a century before. While these two had mastered a range of classical genre and diction, Pitcairne focused his sharper talent on epigram. He wrote better Latin than Scots, in fact. Perhaps he composed his vernacular satires when drunk, as he often was – which is why they strain a bit too crudely for effect. And perhaps it was when he had a hangover he wrote Latin, to judge from its tart, terse quality. Of the results of the Revolution of 1688 he snapped: *Omnia vulgus erat* ('The mob was everything'). Of the period following he growled: *Jura silent, torpent classica, rostra vacant* ('The law fell silent, the classics were dulled, the rhetoric turned empty'). He composed an elegy on the first great Jacobite hero, James Graham of Claverhouse, killed in victory at the Battle of Killiecrankie. It was rendered into English ('O last and best of Scots') by Dryden, who liked the pithy elegance he could not quite capture in his own language:

> *Te moriente, novos accepit Scotia cives*
> *Accepitque novos, te moriente, deos.*

> New people fill the land now thou art gone,
> New gods the temples, and new kings the throne.

Pitcairne would never have deigned to express such solemnity in alien English; if homely Scots would not do, it had to go into sonorous Latin.[37]

Pitcairne was typical of Edinburgh's cultural leaders in looking back to the courts of that intelligent dynasty, the Stewarts. This learned literary tradition had suffered devastating blows since 1603. The Presbyterians showed no little contempt for secular scholarship, at a pinch preferring holy philistinism. And when the English military boors blundered in at mid-century, they blew open a huge hole in the capital's fruitful interplay of personal cultivation and royalist nationalism. Recovery after 1660 was imperfect, marred by further misrule and mayhem. But some continuity remained. On such a view it becomes hard to take seriously the idea, espoused by orthodox Scottish historians, that before the Union of 1707 the life of capital and country had been ineffably primitive, while afterwards it became all sweetness and light.

※

To the extent these historians have paid any attention to the intellectual ferment in the era of the Restoration, they link it with the advent in 1679 of the future King James VII and II, known then in England as Duke of York and in Scotland as Duke of Albany (he will be referred to here by the latter title). Albany was a Catholic convert, sent out of the way to Edinburgh in order to defuse mounting opposition in London to his succession to the throne. He arrived in midwinter with his family, all suffering from heavy colds after a tedious journey through snow. The town council invited him to a civic reception, which must have been a lively affair for thirty-six glass ashets, sixteen glass plates and twelve jelly glasses got smashed; perhaps it was this revelation just how much alcohol Scots could put away that made his wife, Mary of Modena, introduce tea to Edinburgh. Next came a meeting with the privy council. Albany refused to take the oath of allegiance since it contained a declaration against Catholicism. At Holyrood he heard the first mass in over a century.

Albany acted in Edinburgh as a viceroy, bringing back royal patronage after barren decades. The enlightened historian William Tytler of Woodhouselee would recall before his death in 1792 how 'our fathers of the last age used to talk with delight of the gaiety and brilliancy of the court at Holyroodhouse'.[38] Yet Albany's residence was so short (fifteen months up to the spring of 1681, and those interrupted) it can hardly have accounted for the entire cultural revival stretching back to 1660. He may have given it coherence and impetus, but that is a different matter. At heart a well-meaning man, he was also slow-witted and obtuse: an unlikely solution to Scotland's problems of culture or anything else. But by his personal and institutional patronage he reinforced some existing trends.

Perhaps Albany's most direct influence came in the drama, now a minor art in Scotland after struggling to survive ever since the Reformation. Dryden mentions a phase in the fraught political conditions of the time when English players thought they would be safer in Edinburgh:

> Discord and plots which had undone our age,
> With the same ruin have o'erwhelmed the stage . . .
>
> Our brethren are from Thames to Tweed departed,
> And of our sisters all the kinder hearted,
> To Edinburgh gone, or coached or carted,
> With bonny bluecap there they act all night
> For Scotch half-crowns, in English threepence hight.

Albany himself refers to the drama in letters to his niece, the Countess of Lichfield. He complains of 'downright winter weather' when even on fine days he has to be content with 'playing at goffe – this not being a good hunting country . . . Sometimes we go to the plays . . . I am agoing to see them this afternoon, so I have not time to say more.' Again he wrote: 'We here do not pass our time so ill as you in England think we do, for we have plays . . . and have a great deal of good company . . . My daughter acted on Thursday last for the third and last time her play.' The actress in whom he took such paternal pride probably appeared in Nathaniel Lee's *Mithridates King of Pontus* (1678). For 15 November 1680, there is record of a performance 'wherein Lady Anne, the duke's daughter, and the ladies of honour were the only actors'. Lady Anne is the later Queen Anne, who kept memories of the Scots ('strange people') not too fond.[39]

Albany left the most lasting trace of his presence in the gallery at refurbished Holyrood lined with portraits of every King of Scots since Fergus Mac Erc in 330 BC – over 100 of them, by a Dutch artist, Jacob de Witt. His commission told him 'to make them like unto the originals which are to be given to him'. James VII comes at the end of the line: he would indeed be last in the direct legitimate succession of Stewarts. This succession was the proud boast of Scots, especially as it put them one up over the English. Mackenzie looked back to Scottish antiquity and found 'we are still the same people and nation, but the English are not the old Britons, but are a mixture descending from Danes, Saxons and French'. Here was the root and stock of national independence: 'No historian can pretend that we obeyed any race, save that which now reigns; whereas we can condescend, where the English and French were conquered by strangers, and had their royal line dethroned and inverted.' De Witt provided the visual proof.[40]

※

Policy was not just cultural. Brought up in England like his father Charles I and his brother Charles II, Albany yet tried harder than they did to know, understand and even win back the Scots, as though sensing he was the Stewarts' last chance. He responded, for example, to the nation's economic hopes. He called meetings of merchants to Holyrood to approve a scheme of protectionism probably borrowed from Jean-Baptiste Colbert, the French Minister of Finance. A little too drastic for Scotland, the scheme banned all manufactured imports while lifting all taxes on domestic industry and all duties on foreign inputs. It was meant to foster new products but in the event they could not be sold abroad, as the scheme provoked only foreign retaliation.

Albany initiated a reform of the currency, too. Scots governments had been debasing the coinage for a couple of centuries in vain efforts to spend money they did not have. By now, most currency circulating in the country was so-called plack, or impure copper. An investigation showed the mint in Edinburgh had issued four times as much of it as authorized. Corrupt officials, all with connections in high places, embezzled the gold and silver supposed to back it. At least £700,000 had vanished.[41] The solution was first to shut down the mint and then in 1686, once James VII ascended the throne, to recoin the Scots currency. This was good coin, so most of it soon left the country to finance the chronic deficit on the balance of payments. The problem would scarcely be solved when the Bank of Scotland was established in 1695 with a basic purpose of creating credit for a country chronically short of it. Though sheltered by monopoly for twenty-one years, the bank still acted with extreme caution. At its head office in Edinburgh (provincial branches did not survive the early months of operation) it took no money on deposit but just lent out the capital subscribed by shareholders, strictly on security of heritable and personal bonds. When it did try something new and issued in 1704 the original Scottish pound note, there was such a run on the bank it had to stop. Edinburgh got to basic principles of banking faster than most cities, yet not so fast as to avoid a painful learning process.

But the important aspect of the period from Restoration to Union of Parliaments lies in the intellectual ferment of the Scottish capital. While Albany's court at Holyrood made a contribution, the ferment had been under way before his arrival and went on longer than can be accounted for by his presence. For reasons ranging from the rigour of the Presbyterian intellect to the generosity of the royal patronage – or indeed a clash between the two – new ideas were constantly animated. Yet the city would suffer further blows before its cultural impulses took on a more modern and durable form.

❧

On the afternoon of 9 December 1688, the House of Stewart, which for over four centuries had done more than anything else to ensure the survival of Scotland, began to fall. Edinburgh was in the hands of the mob. The people knew that 400 miles away, in the south of England, William of Orange had landed with an army and was advancing on London to save Protestantism. There, the same afternoon, James VII and II was preparing to send his family to France, as prelude to his own flight.

The king's cause in Scotland seemed just as hopeless. The capital was in uproar. Rather than try to re-establish order, the Duke of Gordon, governor of the Castle, shut himself up inside its ramparts. Down at Holyrood the Scottish government, under the Chancellor, the Earl of Perth, was running out of time. It would not have lasted the night but for the presence of mind of the lord provost, Magnus Prince, who ordered the gates of the city to be locked as the gloomy winter's day waned, then posted guards to stop troublemakers reaching the palace.

Next morning, Gordon ventured a sortie, clattering the length of the High Street with an armed escort. He wanted to urge the Chancellor to come and take refuge with him. But Perth said he was about to leave for his own Castle Drummond, miles away on the other side of Stirling, in case he had to escape abroad: he would eventually be taken prisoner as he embarked for France. All he could do now was sign an order authorizing the duke to draw on the revenue for any military needs. When Gordon tried, the officials of the Exchequer refused to pay him.

Once Perth was gone that afternoon, the mob moved in on the palace and the abbey housing the chapel royal. This James VII had made a symbol of his reign. A week before, on St Andrew's Day, he had ordered it to be sprinkled with holy water and re-consecrated. Nothing could have been more calculated to goad the capital's Calvinists. The worst trouble came from students, who had been restive throughout the reign in anti-Catholic demonstrations. After they left their classes at the university on 10 December they gathered on the Meadows so the lord provost could not again trap them inside the walls of the city. They marched round to the Canongate and down to Holyrood.

The military commander at the palace, Captain John Wallace, drew his guards up in the forecourt. Outnumbered, they could not afford to lose the initiative. Contemporary methods of keeping order were rough. At the word from Wallace his men opened fire, then for good measure lobbed a couple of hand grenades into the crowd. Twelve students were killed and many more wounded. The rest fled in panic back up the hill.

Blood had been shed, and Gordon sent word he was ready to deploy his troops, but the lord provost did not want more carnage on the streets. He had men at his own disposal, the town guard and trained bands of militia, 700 in all. He sought to defuse the situation and sent to Holyrood offering to escort Wallace and the guards to safety up in the Castle. The message arrived too late.

This was because what remained of the government of Scotland had blundered in. If the lord provost kept cool, privy councillors still in the capital were trying to calm their nerves in a pub but instead working themselves up into a panic. They resolved on action of a sort. They too gave orders to the town guard, orders to go down not to help at Holyrood but to take over security there – in other words, to signal a royalist surrender. The students followed, cheering. Wallace, yet more outnumbered than before, just told his men to run; but they were all chased and caught.

Militia and mob were now in merry mood, ready to carry on in the common cause. They decided to break into the abbey and destroy its new splendours. They tore down the throne, stalls and organ, and paraded with the debris up the High Street. Some paused at the Nethergate, to take down the skulls of covenanting martyrs stuck up there on spikes so they could be laid to rest at last. Others proceeded to the Cross, where they lit a bonfire and danced round it while they burned the idolatrous baubles from Holyrood. They made an effigy of the pope and burned him too.

Others still, finished with the abbey, turned on the palace. They aimed first at a college of Jesuits installed by the king, but these had fled. So the rioters, shoulder to shoulder with the forces of order, hammered down the doors of Perth's suite and rifled whatever he had left behind. Next they penetrated the royal apartments, smashing what they did not want, destroying what they could not bear away.

Perhaps it was this jape that brought such an act of sacrilege as would have appalled any previous generation of Scots. Under Holyrood lay the burial vault of the Stewarts, though none had been laid to rest there since James V in 1542. Hallowed as the place was, the intruders did not spare it. They burst in, hacked at the tombs and scattered the royal dust. Shady characters could be seen the next day flogging lead from the coffins. Such was the disgraceful end to the direct line of descent in Scotland's native dynasty which, except in futile rebellion, would never set foot in the country again.[42]

※

Edinburgh had made a final choice between king and Kirk. The Revolution of 1688 restored Presbyterianism as the religious establishment in Scotland, and for good. The immediate impact fell on the Episcopalian clergy: seven of eight in Edinburgh and the

Canongate were deprived, with two at Leith and another at St Cuthbert's. Rabbled from their manses, they had to shift for themselves. Some were destitute, while others kept going somehow. The Bishop of Edinburgh, the Reverend Alexander Rose, led part of his flock down from St Giles to a wool-store at the foot of Carrubber's Close by the Nor' Loch; hidden here, their successors worshipped for 200 years until the present Old St Paul's was built on the site. Episcopalians at large would be persecuted with as much zeal as Presbyterians had been. Their meeting-houses were shut up at random and punitive fines exacted from their priests. Rose appealed to the government: 'God forgive those who not satisfied with the desolation of our Church and the establishment of your own also can and do bring many poor churchmen already overwhelmed with trouble unto the last extremity of misery.' But their real hope lay in a return of the Stewarts.[43]

The university suffered a purge in its turn. Under able principals since the Restoration, saintly Robert Leighton and temperate William Colvill, it had trodden a fine line through political and religious faction: a useful consequence was its novel specialization in the uncontentious disciplines of science and mathematics. Now all staff had to sign the Confession of Faith of the Presbyterian Kirk and swear loyalty to the new monarchs, William and Mary. A parliamentary visitation went round to satisfy itself of the results. Its chairman was Gilbert Rule, a tub-thumping sexagenarian who had spent much of his life in exile, including a spell on the Bass Rock. Rule carpeted the incumbent principal, Alexander Monro, who clearly did not expect to survive the confrontation. Accused of persecuting dissidents, he threw caution to the winds and retorted with spirit: 'I thank God I have no such Presbyterian temper, for I never hated any man for his opinion, unless by it he thinks himself obliged to destroy me and mine; and such truly I consider as the tyrannical enemies of humane society.'[44]

Out Monro went, with others of his professors and regents, all on personal rather than intellectual grounds. Herbert Kennedy, regent in philosophy, was condemned as 'ane habitual swearer, ane habitual frequenter of taverns, ane contemner of the sabbath, lying in his bed when he should be at church, and is seen sometimes drunk on the same day'. Once, 'about midnight he came to the college gates, and because the janitor's servant, being asleep, did not open the gate so very soon he boxed him to the effusion of his blood and throwing him down beat him with his feet'. He disliked students from Glasgow: 'There was no more whiggish hole out of hell than the place they came from.'

As for Gregory the great mathematician, he too was 'ane habitual swearer' who chased women, 'drank to a shameless excess', picked fights and won them by kneeing the other man in the crutch. Worse still, 'he spares not to declare that he is not concerned in religion . . . Let him instruct where and from whom he ever took the sacrament of the Lord's Supper,' demanded the inquisition. But before it could pronounce sentence on this paragon of Scottish manhood he took off to Oxford, spurning frantic efforts by the town council to keep him.

The purge went down as far as the schoolmaster of the Canongate, George Burnet. It was alleged that 'commonly upon Saturdays night he did play at cairds with those that did nothing all the time of their playing but mock at the present government, and that until 12 of the clock at night'. He had taught his son Alexander 'that when any speaks of King James to clap his hands for joy, but when they speak of King William to boast [fret] and frown and not to hear his name'. Burnet retorted that as wee Alex could not even talk yet, his motives might be hard to fathom.[45]

☙

Having completed his purge of the university, Rule stepped into the principal's shoes. He would make his son, still a student, professor of Hebrew. The revolutionary government gave money for new chairs of divinity and for undergraduate bursaries to turn this into a seminary of Presbyterians. Whatever they had learned from three decades underground, it was not toleration. The General Assembly of 1694 met in Edinburgh and recited the sins it saw on every hand: 'God is dishonoured by the impiety and profaneness that aboundeth . . . in profane and idle swearing, cursing, sabbath-breaking, neglect and contempt of gospel ordinances, mocking of piety and religious exercises, fornication, adultery, drunkenness, blasphemy, and other gross and abominable sins and vices.' In the parishes ministers should 'denounce the threatened judgments of God against such evil-doers, to bring them to a conviction of their sin and danger', while kirk sessions must 'exercise church discipline against all such scandalous offenders'. Clergy and elders ought to visit each household to see domestic worship performed and children instructed. The untiring General Assembly would keep up its high moral dudgeon for a generation, reinforced by fasts to avert the 'heavy displeasure and just indignation of the Holy One'.[46]

The capital seemed especially sinful. What were its busty young ladies up to as they walked out 'under pretence of selling lemons and oranges', just like Nell Gwynne in London? The surmise had to be that they, too, 'do go through the city and become common whores and thieves'. Any female independence remained an object of suspicion on account of 'the many immoralities and abuses that are occasioned by single and unmarried women their keeping of chambers, shops and cellars'. According to the Reverend James Webster, one of the new ministers, the ubiquitous turds were a fitting symbol of the whole place: 'We may say of cities in a moral sense, what they do in a natural sense, they have an ill air. The streets of Edinburgh are not so filthy as the hearts of the citizens are, every one debauches another.'

In ethical temper the capital almost seemed to be heading back to 1560, except its kirk sessions could no longer mobilize the same popular zeal. Instead, a self-appointed Society for the Reformation of Manners, meeting monthly at John Knox's House, poked its nose into every venial sin from swearing to brawling. It wanted a team of constables to go round the taverns on the stroke of ten at night and tell landlords to stop serving; that would remain the closing time favoured by the authorities until 1976. Even then there might be tippling in 'naughty, bad and suspect houses' or in private homes; constables should stop this, too, at least on a Sunday. Yet such fanaticism tended again to dissipate itself in triviality. Among those hauled up was a farmer accused of letting his family and servants break the sabbath by 'carrying in great stoups full of milk into Edinburgh'. His wife sprang to his defence, a trifle wanly, saying: 'But it was in little stoups.'[47]

There was a heavier human cost in the case of twenty-year-old Thomas Aikenhead, a medical student hanged for blasphemy in

1697. The authorities had ordered a search in the bookshops for volumes deemed 'atheistical, erroneous or profane or vicious', such as those by René Descartes, Thomas Hobbes and Baruch Spinoza. For voicing opinions alleged to be found in them, Aikenhead was tried under two Blasphemy Acts then in force, one of 1661 prescribing capital punishment, a second of 1695 graduating penalties from prison and sackcloth for a first offence, to an additional fine for a second offence and to death only for a third offence. Though a first offender, he received a sentence of death. He sought reprieve on grounds of his 'deplorable circumstances [as an orphan] and tender years'. The privy council refused unless the Kirk interceded. The General Assembly happened to be sitting in Edinburgh. It urged 'vigorous execution' to curb 'the abounding of impiety and profanity in this land'. A pathetically friendless Aikenhead was strung up, the last person to die for blasphemy in the British Isles.[48]

※

What the Revolution did to Edinburgh's culture the Union would consummate. But whereas the Revolution had enjoyed wide support in the city, the Union enjoyed next to none: it was a deal between the ruling classes of Scotland and England, though both had sense to see it could not be a straight takeover of the one country by the other. One ultimate price of the deal had been omitted from the first draft of the treaty but was later exacted by the Presbyterians: that they should inside the Union be guaranteed their place as Scotland's established religion, with control of universities and schools to boot.

Many Presbyterians, probably most outside Edinburgh, all the same opposed the Union. The Church of Scotland had now, however, come under the leadership of a clerical clique in the capital who declared for the Union once they extracted that crucial concession. The leader was the Reverend William Carstares, minister of Greyfriars and from 1703 principal of the university, appointed there after years close to the heart of government under William of Orange, for whose Dutch secret service he had long worked. There were other influential figures: the Reverend David Cuthbertson of St Cuthbert's, once a Covenanter; the Reverend George Meldrum of the Tron, also professor of divinity at the university; the Reverend Thomas Wilkie of the

Canongate; the Reverend William Wishart of South Leith. It so happened these men held office as Moderators of the General Assembly, one after the other, from 1702 to 1707.

High politics were of no concern to the people of Edinburgh: they hated the Union. While the treaty was being passed inside Parliament House, riots became daily events outside. The leader of the nationalist opposition, the Duke of Hamilton, often sparked them off as he passed up and down the Royal Mile. A rowdy though still good-humoured throng would gather round him, 'shouting and crying out, God bless his grace for standing up against the Union, and appearing for his country and the like'. Having worked themselves up into patriotic mood they would then turn nasty when they spotted the coach of the man charged with pushing the Union through, Queen Anne's Lord High Commissioner, the Duke of Queensberry. He would gallop past with horseguards in front and panting footmen behind, these the targets for volleys of stones from onlookers and 'all the insults, reproaches and indignities offered him that they durst'. The word 'indignities' is another euphemism for the excrement lying about the wynds and closes, handy to hurl at the official party.[49]

By the time a secret agent of the English government, Daniel Defoe, arrived in Edinburgh in October 1706, big trouble was brewing – and, as he said, 'a Scots rabble is the worst of its kind'. One evening the mob as usual cheered Hamilton down the High Street. This time when they came up again they threw stones at the town guard and broke windows along the Royal Mile. 'I was warned,' Defoe went on, 'that I should take care of myself and not appear in the street.' He heard a bunch of thugs say as he went into a stair: 'There is one of the English dogs.'

That night an effort was made to break into the house of Sir Patrick Johnstone, lord provost and unionist politician. As recounted by Defoe, 'the mob came upstairs to his door and fell to work with sledges to break it open, but it seems could not'. The gallant target of the attack had left Mrs Johnstone to it: 'his lady in the fright with two candles in her hand that she might be known, opens the window and cries out for God's sake to call the guard'. A passing apothecary heeded her distress and went to the guardhouse in the middle of the street: he 'found the officers to be very indifferent in the matter, whether as to the cause or, is rather judged, through real fear of the rabble'. Defoe took the chance to slip back to his own lodgings, yet the tumult was far from over: 'I had not been there long but I heard a great noise and looking saw a terrible multitude come up the High Street with a drum at the head of them and swearing and crying out all Scotland would stand together, No Union, No Union, English dogs and the like.' By now the whole city was alarmed and everyone put their lights out for fear of provoking more vandalism. Town guards 'were insulted and stoned where they stood'. So it went on for hours: 'They are a hardened, refractory and terrible people,' Defoe concluded.[50]

They still could not stop the Union. On the day it came into force, 1 May 1707, Edinburgh was subdued and depressed. Queensberry's eldest son, James, held a little celebration of his own at their residence in the Canongate, with feasting. This heir apparent to the dukedom, to which in the end he would never be permitted to succeed, suffered from gigantism and was a homicidal maniac kept under lock and key at all times. In the absence of his father, who had gone to London for the occasion, he managed to escape. He caught and killed a kitchen-boy, then roasted him on a spit. The deed was discovered as he sat down to his horrid repast. Scots said it was judgement on the duke for his part in the Union. Otherwise there were only official gestures. In the morning the bells of St Giles rang out the tune, 'Why should I be sad on my wedding day?' Guns later fired a salute from the Castle. That was about it.[51]

☙

Edinburgh saw little to celebrate, indeed. The Union meant no more Scottish government, one engine of the city's economy. The other was trade. That had suffered ups and downs and ground to a virtual halt in the civil wars and Cromwellian occupation. While some recovery followed, it continued to be hampered by external forces. Scotland and England had formed a common market under James VI, but by the time of Charles II the English decided to push the Scots out again. In general European nations showed growing rivalry and hostility to one another. The commercial counterpart to continual war was the policy of mercantilism. This imposed protection at home and, where possible, excluded competition overseas.

The point might be made that this was just what the merchants of Edinburgh had always done. But Edinburgh, indeed Scotland, formed just a tiny portion of the international trading system. Once larger cities and countries took up the same cudgels, smaller ones stood little chance.

In part mercantilism was inspired by colonialism. Each European power sought to hog to itself the products of its distant possessions. Scotland had tried to join this game at Darien in 1698–1700 and been at once knocked out. Otherwise, her colonial traffic consisted of smuggling to English territories in America. After 1707, that traffic became legal. But this did not help Edinburgh. The shortest route across the North Atlantic Ocean goes by the 'great circle', and along its circumference the distance from Virginia or Massachusetts to Scotland is shorter than to England. For reasons not too clear, this trade went into Glasgow rather than Edinburgh – perhaps because Edinburgh never tried to win it, remaining happy with its old links to Europe, safe and sound, profitable enough, but unlikely to bring an economic breakthrough. The attitude was another product of outdated complacency among the city's merchants. It allowed the start of the shift in commercial, then industrial leadership that would drive the west of Scotland ahead of the east throughout the nineteenth century and up to the end of the twentieth.

Though trade with England was freed, it did not thrive just on that account. In a British common market which behind a wall of tariffs worked on proto-capitalist principles, the pricing and quality of Scottish products became crucial. Coal in the Lothians, the region's primary industry, was hard to work. That made it too dear for English markets. Rather, coal came to Scotland from Newcastle. Scottish textiles were inferior, and had stayed so because made solely for domestic use. They soon ran into trouble against superior English products. Manufacture of cloth at Newmills near Haddington, in which the merchants of Edinburgh had invested over half a century, was wound up by 1711.

So Edinburgh fared ill. In 1709 its treasurer ran out of money: 'The revenue of the good town being considerably fallen, [it] is not in a condition to answer these demands of debts owed to tradesmen.' The council resolved 'that all may be cautious against unnecessary spendings and that nothing be done concerning the public works but what is absolutely necessary'. In 1714 a unionist conceded 'Edinburgh indeed has suffered by the Union, and so has the countries about it in some measure, that used to furnish the town, for there is not that consumption nor employment for tradespeople that has been formerly.' The lord provost, Sir Robert Blackwood, wrote to the MP Sir Patrick Johnstone on its unquenched nationalism: 'It is no wonder that inhabitants of this place should be of that mind who have so sensibly languished ever since the Union, for it is the voice of the whole nation as everyone knows.' In 1715, when Scotland tried to break free, the Lord Advocate, Sir James Stewart, feared the capital was the place most likely to explode, because of the 'decay of business of all kinds, and the thinness of the streets with the infinite bills on the houses' [that is, for sale].[52]

Later in the century Adam Smith, the father of economics who upheld the Union in his own day, would look back to 1707 and say: 'Nothing appears to me more excusable than the disaffection of Scotland at that time. All orders of men conspired in cursing a measure so hurtful to their immediate interest.' Later still, Robert Chambers would recall the slump in his *Traditions of Edinburgh* (1824): 'From the Union up to the middle of the century, the existence of the city seems to have been a perfect blank. An air of gloom and depression pervaded the city. In short this may be called the dark age of Edinburgh.'[53]

Townsfolk demonstrated every year on 10 June, birthday of the Jacobite claimant to the throne, the son of James VII, also James, known as the Old Pretender. And every year the crowds grew bigger. In 1712 bands played rebel songs in the streets, where toasts were openly drunk to restoration of the legitimate line of Stewarts. Along the Shore at Leith ships put out flags bearing the old royal arms, while at night bonfires lit up the High Street and Arthur's Seat. In 1713 a symbolic coronation of James was staged and a spoof house of Hanover was burned down. In 1714 a ban had to be slapped on all public gatherings, and orders went out (yet again) for the taverns to shut at ten in the evening. Queen Anne was still alive, just about. In August she died and German George was proclaimed King of Great Britain.[54]

On 6 September 1715, Jacobites raised the Old Pretender's standard on the Braes of Mar in Aberdeenshire. On 8 September the Lord Justice Clerk of Scotland, the staunch unionist Adam Cockburn of Ormiston, received at home in Edinburgh an alarming message from his sister. Her disaffected husband, Dr William Arthur, had let slip there was to be a coup in the capital that night. Cockburn sent warnings to the magistracy and the military. The magistrates called out the town guard and at the Castle the watch was strengthened.

The conspirators of a Jacobite storming party meanwhile spent the evening drinking to their prospective success, in town or at country houses roundabout. Perhaps forty made it to a rendezvous in the Grassmarket. They meant to follow a plan somewhat like that which had let young William Francis recapture the castle for King Robert Bruce four centuries before: they would mount the crags and walls rising above them by means of rope ladders. The trouble was the ladders supplied by Dr Arthur looked not nearly long enough. Now the Jacobites were waiting for an engineer, Charles Forbes, to bring them longer ones. But Forbes carried on drinking and did not arrive until all was over.

At 11 o'clock John Thomson, one of four sentries in the Castle suborned by the conspirators, called down that they had better hurry because he was due to be relieved in an hour. They decided to wait no longer. They told him to lower a weighted cord already given to him, which they would attach to a grapnel tied to a rope ladder; he should haul up the grapnel, wedge it to bear the weight of the ladder – and the assault could get under way. It turned out the ladder was indeed six feet too short. John Holland, another suborned sentry, had a fit of panic and urged Thomson to make haste. Thomson decided he had pushed his luck far enough. He cried to the Jacobites: 'God damn you all! You have ruined both yourselves and me! Here comes the round I have been telling you of this hour. I can serve you no longer.' And he loosed the grapnel. Thomson and Holland then shouted 'Enemy!' and fired their muskets. The Jacobites took the hint and scrambled off the Rock to disperse. Those who came late were caught by the patrol the magistrates had sent out.

Sir George Warrender of Lochend, lord provost and MP, just about kept the city under control. He wrote to London appealing for troops on the grounds that 'had not I given detachments of our city guard on that immediate exigence and service the conspirators had been masters of the Castle and we had then been reduced to the extremest danger, and by this the government of the city taken out of our hands and lodged in the hands of our enemies'. There was no response: London gave an impression it could not care less about Scotland, even in this hour of peril.

Next month Warrender, while in Fife, witnessed another Jacobite stroke, this time successful. Rebels seized all the harbours on the northern shore of the Firth of Forth. By night they sent forces over in small boats to East Lothian, through waters supposedly patrolled by the royal navy. Their commander, William Mackintosh of Borlum, concentrated his strength at Haddington and marched on the capital. He headed for Leith and occupied the Cromwellian citadel. But in the end he meant to turn south and link up with other insurgents. When he did, he left behind only stragglers the worse for wear after looting a shipload of brandy. The Jacobites' threat to Edinburgh evaporated. It is amazing how often, and how often through drink, they were to snatch defeat from the jaws of victory. In this case they at length came to grief, along with their English allies, at the Battle of Preston in Lancashire.[55]

❧

Jacobites then had to go underground, and they took the best of Edinburgh's culture with them. It was another blow to the capital, hardly sustaining the view among orthodox historians that the culture had never existed but was awaiting the Union before it could spring to life. The actual sequence was the reverse: despite daunting difficulties the city had sustained its culture in remarkable diversity up to the turn of the eighteenth century. In 1707 it plunged back into another black hole as dark and deep as the Cromwellian occupation – and destined to last longer.

Could the culture of Edinburgh survive at all? It was touch and go. The Parliament, a source of patronage, had followed that older source, the royal court, to London. Intellectuals from the era of the Restoration were dead or decrepit. Sibbald lived yet, though with his preference for a quiet life reinforced. Now people like him found themselves borne down again by grim Calvinists. The ministers of the city ranted against heresy and vice, above all against the theatre.

These were the kind of men still, three decades later, capable of getting David Hume turned down as professor of moral philosophy at Edinburgh on account of his scepticism. After the purge of the university in 1690, there could be no guarantee its intellectual flame might be rekindled. Carstares as principal set out to reform it on the model of the Dutch system, but died in 1715 short of completing the task. His greatest innovation had been to appoint specialist professors in place of regents teaching the entire curriculum. But one pregnant consequence, establishment of a medical faculty, could not go ahead before 1726. A counterpart in the humanities was the foundation of a chair of public law in 1707. Its first occupant, unionist placeman Charles Erskine, used it as a base for more congenial activities, such as travelling round Europe. He made little attempt to teach, and Scots students of law would continue to go to Holland until the end of the century.[56]

At least Pitcairne, before he died in 1713, passed on his torch to a protégé, Thomas Ruddiman, destined in turn to be the leading Latinist of his day, as well as keeper of the Advocates' Library. He revered the humanism of the Renaissance enough to edit the *Opera Omnia* of George Buchanan, even though that old Presbyterian radical stood for everything he detested; this was in part a labour of hate, blackening Buchanan's reputation even while extolling his Latinity. Ruddiman harked still further back to the makars with an edition of Gavin Douglas's translation of Virgil's *Aeneid*. He appended to it a long glossary amounting to a dictionary of the older Scottish tongue. He was the sort of scholar who put his real arguments in the footnotes: these contended that in Scots a classic corpus of works existed on a par with the Middle English literature of Geoffrey Chaucer or John Gower. In fact that corpus displayed linguistic riches unmatched except by Greek or Latin – superior in any case to the weak, dilute quality of English. Yet now, as the genteel started to ape a southern accent, the old speech was becoming a dialect of the vulgar. Still, Ruddiman added his stone to the cairn of literary prestige Scots was again to erect by the late eighteenth century.

It was significant that a publishing industry survived in Edinburgh. The best printers, Robert Freebairn and James Watson, also belonged to the Jacobite underground. Freebairn was the son of a deprived Episcopalian cleric now obliged to earn his living as a bookseller (though he ended up as Bishop of Edinburgh). The young Robert had been one of the daredevils who managed not to storm the Castle in 1715. He fled the country but by 1722 was back to resume his trade. He brought out Ruddiman's redaction of Buchanan, then himself edited and published a *History of Scotland* by Robert Lindsay, humanist of the sixteenth century, with a didactic preface picking out from it 'those great and good qualities' which 'ought to be employed in the public service' as a guide along 'rugged paths of virtue'. Here was a bridge between Renaissance and Enlightenment.

As for Watson, his first production had been a book by Harry Maule, *History of the Picts* (1706). Of little value according to modern conceptions, it did offer one idea novel then yet accepted today: that ancient Caledonians, Britons and Picts had come of a single race, so Scotland could pride herself on an indigenous stock dating far back into the mists of time, before any written record. It also reinforced the Jacobite claim that a single line of kings had always ruled the country. The royalist tradition, beaten in a political sense in 1688, continued to flourish on a cultural level, indeed to be the main bearer of Scottish culture into the eighteenth century. Philistine Presbyterians, in their mistrust of secular learning, could not compete and did not want to. Watson went on to republish William Drummond of Hawthornden and Sir George Mackenzie of Rosehaugh. He used Edinburgh's newspapers to advertise for Scots poetry still in manuscript or unknown otherwise. Three volumes of it followed, in his *Choice Collection of Comic and Serious Scots Poems* (1706–11). This, the first printed anthology of poems 'in our own native *Scots* dialect', set forth what was known at the time of the older literature. Watson took up a pen himself to record his respect for the standards of early Scottish printing: its decline, he said, had gone hand in hand with disloyalty to the Stewarts.[57]

※

For the rest, the culture of Edinburgh withdrew behind closed doors, to private clubs and convivial dinners where the state of the nation could be bemoaned all the more gloomily and patriotism fired all the more brightly with each glass downed. Serious drinking might also go along with serious thinking, however, and the clubs would become vehicles of Enlightenment. They have remained part of the city's social and intellectual scene ever since.

Among them was the Easy Club, so called 'because none of ane empty conceited quarrelling temper can have the privilege of being a member'. It was run for young men of literary leanings to read aloud and discuss their work. In subsidizing publication by one of its members, Allan Ramsay, the club produced one of Edinburgh's leading men of letters. For that role Ramsay's background was unusual: he had been born at the bleak, isolated mining village of Leadhills in Lanarkshire. He was left an orphan and his stepfather sent him as apprentice to a wigmaker, a trade he would practise in the Grassmarket. He felt self-conscious about this humble background; it may have prompted him to write his indifferent versions of Horace, just to show he could, even though he had no Latin.[58]

But at length Ramsay could give up his time-served trade for bookselling. He ran a shop in the Luckenbooths which served also as a literary venue. He had there a circulating library too, the first in Britain. And in 1720 he helped to found a school of drawing and painting, the Academy of St Luke, modelled on the Accademia di San Luca in Rome. He did so not least because his son, also Allan, was at the age of sixteen showing great artistic promise; he would go on to found the school of enlightened Scottish portraiture. A final, and expensive, venture by the elder Ramsay came with his opening a theatre in Carrubber's Close in 1736, though it had only a short life before being forced to close under pressure from the presbytery of Edinburgh. Ramsay protested at 'the impoverishing and stupefying the good town by getting everything that tends towards politeness and good humour banished'. He suspected the dirty work was being orchestrated from the 'sad shadow of a university'. About 1740 he retired, and on Castlehill built himself an octagonal house, still standing, known as the Goose-Pie: not the only pie, evidently, in which he had put a finger.[59]

It is less the quality of his poetry than his versatility that endows Ramsay with cultural consequence. He builds a bridge between the classic corpus of the makars and the romantic revival of Scots verse, though his work is not as good as the best of either. His linguistic persona remains uncertain. His range of themes or moods is limited, at their best when comic. One popular poem was the elegy for Maggy Johnston, who had run a tavern at Bruntsfield:

> *Auld Reeky! Mourn in sable hue,*
> *Let fouth of tears dreep like May dew.*
> *To braw Tippony* [beer] *bid adieu,*
> *Which we with greed*
> *Bended as fast as she could brew,*
> *But ah! she's dead.*

Even in mock-elegiac mode, Ramsay shows the frankness about physical function that gave and gives the city's muse a distinct savour:

> *Fou closs we used to drink and rant,*
> *Until we did baith glowre and gaunt,*
> *And pish and spew, and yesk and maunt*
> *Right swash I true;*
> *Then of auld stories we did cant*
> *Whan we were fou.*

> Tanked up we used to drink and rant,
> Until we did both stare and yawn,
> And piss and spew, and belch and burble
> Well oiled indeed;
> Then we would tell merry old tales
> When we were drunk.[60]

Ramsay's achievement was to renew Scots literary language out of the mouths of the people, now that intellectuals had abandoned the practice of enriching it in learned ways. The nation's huge fund of folk-song would for the future inspire not only natives, Robert Fergusson or Robert Burns, but also foreigners, Haydn and Beethoven. Ramsay was the first to set out in conscious effort to preserve that fund. He began to record or imitate it, if not always as faithfully as his successors did. But he deserves credit for showing how its language, its genres and its metres could still bear fruit.

❦

Edinburgh's culture might have carried on into such cosy provinciality except for a last great political upheaval: in the autumn of 1745 Prince Charles Edward Stewart and his Jacobite army occupied the city. After a hazardous voyage from France the prince had landed almost alone in the Highlands, but loyal clans flocked to his standard. He marched on Edinburgh and, as he approached, sent the town councillors a demand for surrender. He couched it with care. He commanded them to fling wide their gates to him, promising to preserve their rights and liberties. If, on the other hand, there was any opposition he would not be answerable for the consequences; the unspoken alternative to surrender was storm and sack.

Sir John Cope, the British government's commander in Scotland, was with most of his troops in the north trying to contain the rebellion there. Prince Charles had just evaded him. Now, as Cope shipped his force back from Aberdeen, a single regiment remained in the capital. It was deployed at Coltbridge (today Roseburn), the hamlet where the main road from the west crossed the Water of Leith. Officers were discussing tactics when they heard savage yells in the open country beyond – from Jacobites, they assumed. People had come down from the city to look. They stared amazed as the soldiers abandoned their position and moved off to encamp for the night on Leith Links. The 'Canter of Coltbrigg' showed that the British army was not going to make a stand before Edinburgh.

The capital could then be taken by a ruse on 16 September. While the main body of Jacobites waited at the western approach, Prince Charles sent a Highland chief, Donald Cameron of Lochiel, with 800 men round to the east after dark. Occupying a position outside the Netherbow Port, they had only to await their chance. Somebody was fool enough to open the gate and let out a coach. The clansmen rushed in. With bloodcurdling cries they ran up the High Street to the guardhouse. Edinburgh fell.

The clansmen's behaviour was afterwards restrained and disciplined. Prince Charles meant to impress on the people that he had arrived not as conqueror but as regent for their rightful sovereign: 'I am come to save and not to destroy,' he avowed. At noon on the first full day of occupation, Lochiel formally took possession of the city for him. He mustered his men on the High Street while the bells of St Giles tolled. From the Cross the Ross Herald, with others of the Lyon Court in their splendid uniforms, proclaimed King James VIII, then read out the prince's commission of regency and a manifesto of his aims.

In the crowd Lady Murray of Broughton, wife of the prince's secretary, sat on horseback, drawn sword in hand, wearing a white dress and handing out white cockades. A salute was fired and pipers struck up a pibroch. Gaelic was being heard on the tail of the Rock for the first time in 700 years. The clans numbered in their ranks a renowned bard, Alasdair mac Mhaighstir Alasdair, who had left his day job as schoolmaster in Ardnamurchan to join his prince (and teach him his language). Now he wrote a poem on the theme:

> 'S iomadh àrmunn, làsdail, treubhach
> An Dùn Eideann, ann am bharail.
>
> There's many a valiant, daring hero
> In Edinburgh, well I know it.[61]

Jubilation greeted the entry of Prince Charles later. In Highland dress he stood in the King's Park to show himself to the people, then mounted a horse to ride to Holyrood. It turned into a triumphal procession, cheered by a huge crowd pressing close to touch him. At the gates he dismounted and was led into the house of his fathers by James Hepburn of Keith, veteran of 1715, holding a sword aloft. Celebrations continued into the night. Crowds surged about the streets and gathered before the palace, to applaud whenever the prince appeared at a window.

That evening Prince Charles heard Cope had landed at Dunbar. He prepared for a trial of strength. On the morning of 20 September he reviewed his army to the sound of bagpipes in its camp at Duddingston. He gave a confident, uplifting speech, drew his sword and told his soldiers he had flung away the scabbard. He promised to make Scots with God's help a free and happy people.

Cope was believed to be heading for Tranent to take up a position on low hills between that village and the capital. The Highlanders raced to intercept him and reached Tranent before nightfall. They bivouacked in the stubble of surrounding fields, protected only by their plaids from a chill, misty night. Their leaders wrangled over tactics, yet Prince Charles felt elated as he dined on soup and meat at the local inn. The landlady had hidden her pewter from the clansmen, so he and his staff had to make do with two wooden spoons between them.

The prince now learned Cope was advancing to the north, over low ground between Seton and Prestonpans. The British soldiers bivouacked along the road joining the two and lit fires round their camp, protected on one side by the sea and on the other by a bog. Their well-chosen position posed a problem. It was to be solved by the son of a local farmer who offered to show the Highlanders an unguarded path through the bog. In the night 1,200 of them crept in single file down this path, until they formed up just 200 yards from the enemy without being opposed or even observed.

By the time Cope's soldiers awoke to their peril, it was too late. He could hardly form them up in line of battle before a Highland charge crashed down on them with a 'hideous shout'. He had his infantry in the centre, cavalry on the flanks. The clansmen struck at the noses of the horses, which bolted round and threw the deployment into chaos. On one flank the 13th Light Dragoons were unable to fire a single shot. On the other the 14th Light Dragoons stood for thirty seconds under the onslaught before turning and riding down the guards round the artillery; the gunners had already run away. Infantrymen in the centre were then left unsupported as the Highlanders slaughtered them. The Jacobite victory at the Battle of Prestonpans suddenly threatened the existence of the United Kingdom.

Flushed with that, Prince Charles settled back in at Holyrood and began to act as ruler of Scotland, appointing governors to captured burghs and ordering taxes to be collected. Most of his days followed a set pattern. At nine o'clock in the morning he would convene his council of Jacobite noblemen, Highland chiefs and aides brought from France. Business done, they lunched in public to the sound of bagpipes. Lifeguards then escorted the prince to his army's encampment on the far side of Arthur's Seat. He inspected it before returning to Holyrood to receive ladies in his drawing room. Supper was taken in public too, again to music. A ball followed.

These were the legendary nights destined to live on in popular memory for the Jacobite beauties that lent enchantment to them. Prince Charles 'was very cheerful and took his share in several dances, such as minuets, Highland reels and a Strathspey minuet'. From the exile that awaited them all again in future a companion would look back and recall:

The prince went to see the ladies dance, made them compliments on their dance and good grace and retired. Some gents followed him and told him that they knew he loved dancing, and that the ball was designed for him to amuse him. 'It's very true,' says the prince, 'I like dancing and am very glad to see the ladies and you divert yourselves, but I have now another air to dance, until that be finished, I'll dance no other.'[62]

CHAPTER FIVE

'CITY OF EVERYWHERE'

(Norman MacCaig)

ON 23 FEBRUARY 1827, a Theatrical Fund Dinner took place in Edinburgh to raise money for old or sick actors. It was organized by William Murray, manager of the capital's Theatre Royal, who secured the services as chairman for the evening of Sir Walter Scott, a celebrity much in demand at every occasion calling for a witty speech. Probably it was above all the Great Unknown that sold 300 tickets. One guest recorded of his appearance: 'He stands very erect, and without gesture, presenting, as an ingenious friend remarked to me, almost the appearance of a statue. His style of speaking is conversational and not fluent, but full of that frankness and indescribable charm which impart ease and spirit to a company.' Scott felt glad to be helping Murray, for he loved the theatre and went whenever he could. Its current popularity in Edinburgh, after a long period of being frowned on by Presbyterians was arguably owed to him as a native son of the city, not to say the cultural leader of the nation.

Yet the dinner would be remembered for something quite different from its charitable purpose. It was here Sir Walter at last ceased to be the Great Unknown and for the first time publicly confessed he was the author of the Waverley novels. These had made him the most famous writer of the age, in Scotland, Britain, Europe and America. Strange, then, how none of them, starting with *Waverley* itself in 1814, carried his name on the title-page; each was published anonymously. As poet, scholar, lawyer, above all gentleman, he evidently felt he might otherwise have had something to lose. To be precise, his reputation could have been sullied if he had stooped to flaunting his name over a type of literature, the novel, which for much of its history had proffered pap to the public and was regarded still in some quarters as less than respectable: liable, for example, to excite passions in young ladies yet to acquire a proper degree of self-control. Sales of his works waxed enormous, but every successive volume bore not his name, just the legend 'By the Author of Waverley'.

Still, the authorship had become an open secret after Scott admitted to it in private, though not because he wanted to. This followed the financial collapse in 1825 of his publisher, Archibald Constable; since Sir Walter owned a large share in the business he faced ruin himself. His lawyer, John Gibson, went to a fraught meeting at the Bank of Scotland to disclose to the directors, with Scott's permission, who the author of the Waverley novels truly was – a man therefore able to meet his obligations or at least, as the bank agreed, to set up a trust to pay them off from the proceeds of works already published or still to be published. Sir Walter averted bankruptcy yet was obliged to spend the rest of his days in the hard labour of writing himself out of debt: the effort killed him. But by the time of his death in 1832 he had more or less done it.

Even after the deal with the bank, nothing was revealed to the public about the authorship of the Waverley novels. But Scott's own desire to keep up the facade of anonymity flagged: 'The joke had lasted long enough and I was tired of it.' It would just be a matter of time before he gave way, then, though he insists in his journal he had no particular plan to do so at the Theatrical Fund Dinner. Another guest sitting at the top table that night was the judge Alexander Maconochie, Lord Meadowbank. In the past, while an MP and law officer, he had been prone to rash, impulsive behaviour. Yet Sir Walter liked the 'kind and clever little fellow', even though he was 'somewhat bustling and forward'. Before they went in to dine Meadowbank asked, 'Do you care anything about the mystery of the Waverley novels now?'

'Not I,' Scott replied, 'the secret is too generally known.' He thought Meadowbank was rehearsing a joke, but when 'instead of skirmish of that kind he made a speech in which he seriously identified me with the Author of Waverley I had no opportunity of evasion and was bound either to confess or deny it and it struck me while he was speaking it was as good and natural occasion as I could find for making my avowal'.

Meadowbank favoured yet the florid rhetoric he had deployed earlier in his career. He ended his disclosure with a eulogy of Sir Walter: 'He it is who has conferred a new reputation on our national character, and bestowed on Scotland an imperishable name.' The man of the hour waggishly replied: 'I am now at the bar of my country, and may be understood to be on trial before Lord Meadowbank as an offender ... Every impartial jury would bring in a verdict of Not Proven. I am willing, however, to plead Guilty.'[1]

❧

World-famous as Sir Walter was, his compatriots admired him most for saying things about them nobody else had ever put into words. This counted for much in a country with a nationhood now so fragile, so precarious and so provisional. As the ancient Scotland faded away and a modern one struggled to be born, his achievement looked all the more formidable.

There is hardly one of the Scottish novels that does not open with a formula echoing the subtitle of *Waverley* itself, '*Tis sixty years since*'. In his introduction Sir Walter goes on to explain: 'Some favourable opportunities of contrast have been afforded me, by the state of society in the northern part of the island at the period of my history, and may serve at once to vary and illustrate the moral lesson.'[2] So this is a work of multiple significance, like the real events of 1745 it deals with. They meant a lot to Scott, and he sought in the novel to explore or define their meanings. Steeped in Jacobite lore as he was, nobody could have been better equipped to write a story following the whole drama from Prince Charles Edward Stewart's raising of his standard at Glenfinnan to his escape through the heather after catastrophe at the Battle of Culloden. Yet this is not what Sir Walter does.

The novel actually starts off in England. Its hero or anti-hero, Edward Waverley, is a young military officer from an old royalist family, who is posted to Scotland. With a letter of introduction he visits a stubborn loyalist to the House of Stewart, Baron Bradwardine, at the castle of Tully-Veolan, a dismal pile, an image of decay. Jacobite futility comes across yet more clearly in the character of Bradwardine.

His undying devotion to the cause is matched by his own punctilious, not to say pedantic, sense of honour. It renders him useless for any practical purpose. So the first we learn of Jacobitism is that it has lost all connection with reality.

A second figure Waverley then meets, Fergus McIvor, is both like and unlike Bradwardine. McIvor represents more of what we expect from a Highland chief: he is brave, dauntless and ready to die for what he believes in (as he finally will). But we also learn he is a calculating man who might never have chosen this course unless urged on by a sly sister. It occurs to Waverley, and to us following his adventures, that people can become Jacobites as they might become Whigs – for their own gain. In making the point Scott divests his Jacobites not just of their romance but also of their strangeness, perhaps especially to English readers. While Jacobites support a lost cause they may also cherish the same ambitions as those on the winning side. This means, in more basic human terms than is provided by a long history of enmity, that the Union of England and Scotland can be successful – and in Scott's view it was, by his own time, successful. It had been right for both nations.

☙

Nobody felt more aware than Sir Walter of Scotland's dark past, of the loss she suffered when her sovereigns moved south or the pain she felt in the sacrifice of her freedom and in her subordination to England. She had sustained internal wounds which he wanted to heal too. *Waverley* dealt with one: the cleft between Highlands and Lowlands, which in Scott's time was being left behind by history. Yet the cost, in destruction of a traditional society, had been huge. Sir Walter thought to compensate by reuniting Scotland on Highland rather than Lowland terms.

Here was a task Scott need not leave in literature but could render into reality – as he did with the visit by King George IV to Edinburgh in 1822, the first from a reigning monarch in 171 years. Sir Walter, who stage-managed the junketing, had a sixth sense its tartan pageantry was bound to be splendid while the alternative of Presbyterian sobriety would have looked drab. Indeed, the occasion set off a tartan frenzy far into the future. Sir John Graham Dalyell would write in 1849: 'Thirty or forty years ago no reputable gentleman would have appeared in a kilt on the streets of Edinburgh.' He recalled 'some expressions denoting surprise, not unmixed with disapprobation from ladies, that a young Highlander, though a person of family distinction, should appear in one at an evening party where I was present'. Dalyell put it in a nutshell: the kilt was for lithe, handsome, devil-may-care youths, not for aged curmudgeons with paunch and arthritis. The pageantry would pass but, performed to perfection, it could win in popular memory a long afterlife: indeed, while the tartan frenzy has risen or fallen according to fashion, it is not over yet. The Edinburgh of 1822 forever fixed a certain image of the Scotsman, to himself and to the world.[3]

The recent past of the city itself formed the subject of another novel, also one of Scott's best, *The Heart of Midlothian* (1818). This, too, starts out from a standard historicist formula: 'The times have changed in nothing more than the rapid conveyance of intelligence and communication betwixt one part of Scotland and another. It is not above twenty or thirty years . . .'[4] Behind the action of the novel there again lies an acute sense of greater social movement in the country and in the capital. And once more it runs a risk of going off the rails, of crashing, of issuing in fatality and dissolution – something Scotland might well have suffered if Sir Walter had not hastened to her rescue. His title offers a symbolic backdrop to that schema: it refers to the Tolbooth of Edinburgh where common criminals were held before being marched down to their doom in the Grassmarket.

The action takes place, amid some fine evocations of local landscapes,[5] at a crucial juncture in the history of Edinburgh. Three decades after the Union of 1707, English power over the place is palpable yet native defiance still flares up. It even seethes beneath the surface of domestic life among the characters Scott presents as central, a family dwelling on the outskirts at Dumbiedikes. There is a father, Davie Deans, long ago a Covenanter, and two daughters, Jeanie the good girl, Effie the bad girl. Both Davie and Jeanie are religious, but while Davie likes to blow on the embers of old theological disputations, Jeanie turns away to seek serenity in a gentler fashion. His instinct is to reject Effie as a whore; Jeanie, no less shocked by her sister's sins, sees a need for mercy and finally saves her life.

But the novel's greatest scene is played out, right at the start, on a public rather than private level. At that level the Heart of Midlothian stands for injustice done to individuals which others must challenge and requite. In the plot Sir Walter deploys true history, the history of Captain John Porteous condemned in 1736 for having ordered his soldiers to fire on unruly onlookers, killing several, at an execution in the Grassmarket. Later, just as in punishment Porteous is about to be led to the same scaffold, a reprieve arrives for him post-haste from London. Scott creates an uneasy sense of foreboding as he describes the crowd of spectators breaking up, disappointed of a hanging. They ask: 'Is this to be borne – would our fathers have borne it? Are we not, like them, Scotsmen and burghers of Edinburgh?'[6]

Sir Walter is preparing us here for one of the greatest scenes in literature, when that night Porteous will be dragged from the Tolbooth and hanged high in revenge. The pause in the action is reinforced as the narrative zooms in on people climbing back up the West Bow into the city. We walk along with them. We hear their voices. Of course they speak Scots. One utters a sentence often quoted as summarizing the political predicament of Scotland after the Union: 'I ken, when we had a king, and a chancellor, and parliament-men o' our ain, we could aye peeble them wi' stanes when they were na gude bairns – but naebody's nails can reach the length o' Lunnon.' Being ordinary folk, however, they waste little thought on the great issues of the time before returning to concerns of their own. Two are bores: Saddletree, a shopkeeper learned in the law, and Butler, a schoolmaster who keeps correcting his companion's Latin. They wrangle without listening to each other over obscure points of syntax and statute. Eavesdropping, the reader observes how Scott captures, for now softened into comedy, his countrymen's wilfulness.[7]

Scots show another visage when after dark an enormous mob erupts with ugly fury into the streets of Edinburgh. Sir Walter hated mobs of his own time, yet his depiction of this one is sympathetic. Porteous's end appals us, as he is strung up and hacked at while he dangles, but he gets his just deserts. The people's rage cannot be condoned, though it can be understood. The cardinal virtue of justice is finally enjoined on all, whatever their station in life. Justice triumphs, first in a brutal and arbitrary way, later because rulers of men see their way to temperance. One lesson Scott drew for his own time was that the Porteous Riot had been an episode 'unmingled with politics of Whig and Tory [which] must simply be regarded as a strong and powerful display of the cool, stern and resolved manner in which the Scottish, even of the lower classes, can concert and execute a vindictive purpose'.[8] A century later Edinburgh had moved on – or had it?

※

Change certainly arrived in a rush after 1745. Historians have argued that the last Jacobite rebellion, a spoiled boy's madcap adventure, remained much less serious and important than the one of 1715, which never won any big victories but sprang from stronger roots in the hearts and minds of Scots. There is truth in this – yet still little doubt that for Edinburgh itself 1745 held the deeper significance. It was as if the city then made a resolution to put the past behind it and enter on a fresh phase of its history, not now in the guise of anything so banal as a national capital. Instead it set out to reinvent itself as a republic of letters, a universal realm of progress free from the constraints of mere borders.

This entailed both physical and mental change. Physical change came with the construction of the New Town. It was mooted within a decade of Culloden. By it the city would breach bounds that had since the start confined it to the tail of the Castle Rock. The New Town would first cover the terrain, a mile by half a mile in extent, on the further shore of the Nor' Loch, along a shallow ridge falling on one side gently into its waters and on the other more steeply down towards the Firth of Forth. This was still farmland which six centuries of the burgh's existence had barely touched – open fields corrugated by runrig, the Scottish system of communal cultivation. Now it was to yield to an experiment in living by the light of reason, a triumph of the will over nature and history.

The will was first to regularity and symmetry. Formal townscape would sweep over the whole site, ironing out valleys, filling lochs and spanning rivers. It outdid by far any scheme of improvement contemplated in Scotland before. The North Bridge to be thrown across the cleft between Old Town and New Town was erected in a country with just a few miles of good roads and most waterways still passable only by ford or ferry. A backward economy with a peasant population would here find fresh focus in an ideal urban community with hundreds of houses on dozens of streets. After half a century of slump since the Union, a vast building project started up with no guarantee it could pay off.

There had been lesser schemes of improvement in Edinburgh, of course – the previous chapter showed some being carried through a century before. Now the main sites lay outside rather than inside the Old Town. To the south, James Brown had already designed George Square, which when built from 1766 was the biggest programme of unified architecture yet attempted in the city (though its ambitions did not otherwise go far). To the north, but further east than the future New Town proper, the uniform terraced tenements of St James's Square would in their 'bleak nobility' arise by 1773 (and be demolished only in 1965). Even inside the Old Town something similar was begun in 1774 at Merchant Street, today on a subterranean level of its own underneath George IV Bridge.[9]

※

Improvers would henceforth make a much more concerted effort to recreate this squeezed, swarming, stinking city. Their leader was George Drummond, six times lord provost between 1725 and 1764. He rose by obsequious service to those in higher stations of life, something necessary for anyone in his time who arrived from nowhere (Drummond arrived from Perthshire). It was true he had always been anti-Jacobite: he himself fought on the Hanoverian side in 1715 and he raised men to repel Prince Charles Edward Stewart in 1745. Still, the real point was that he linked Whiggery not with a dynasty or religion but with social and economic progress. An unheroic figure, he got things done.

If Drummond had achieved nothing else, he would deserve well of the capital for his part in founding the Royal Infirmary in 1729, soon housed in the Palladian pomp of purpose-built premises by William Adam (a fragment survives in Drummond Street). It was financed by public subscription as a charitable institution for the sick poor. It would show how medicine might benefit the people, not just the privileged. A frugal cure at this local hospital proved quite as effective as any contemporary therapy for the rich, the consumption of outlandish delicacies or departure on a grand tour. Its treatment of common folk also turned out visibly better than what was on offer otherwise from quacks and speywives, charms and spells, elixirs and healing wells; popular acceptance of a scientific approach itself made a huge contribution to public health. For anybody else than Drummond this might have been fulfilment enough: for him it was just a beginning.[10]

In 1751 a tenement collapsed and opened up a gap-site in the middle of the Royal Mile, almost opposite St Giles. A further civic initiative beckoned, now in commerce: 'So lucky an opportunity for a well situate exchange ought not to be lost,' the town council resolved. On the gap-site arose the Royal Exchange, meant as a meeting place for the merchants still wont to hang round the Cross on the other side of the street. In fact they would spurn this new abode, which was at length turned into, and today remains, the City Chambers, seat of the council. The surge of municipal enterprise found a clearer channel in the draining of the Nor' Loch in 1759, without which a healthier Edinburgh was impossible. That left a chasm to be crossed by the North Bridge: Drummond laid its foundation stone in 1763, during his final term as lord provost. He would not live to see the New Town, but the way to it then stood open.[11]

※

The New Town was conceived on a scale never seen in the burgh before. Its amplitude can be traced back to a pamphlet, 'Proposals for Carrying on certain Public Works in the City of Edinburgh', which had appeared in 1752 from the hand of a rising political star, Gilbert Elliot of Minto – though Drummond doubtless urged him on. Elliot argued that all Scotland would benefit by his bright ideas:

The national advantages which a populous capital must necessarily produce are obvious. A great concourse of people brought within a small compass occasions a much greater consumption than the same number would do dispersed over a wider country. As the consumption is greater so it is quicker and more discernible. Hence follows a more rapid circulation of money and other commodities, the great spring which gives motion to general industry and improvement. The example set by the capital, the nation will soon follow. The certain consequence is general wealth and prosperity, the number of useful people will increase, the rents of the land rise, the public revenue improve and in the room of sloth and poverty will succeed industry and opulence.

It was odd to claim cities caused riches, rather than the other way round. But Elliot filled the holes in his argument with explicit proposals 'to enlarge and beautify the town, by opening new streets to the north and south', while the Nor' Loch would become a canal with promenades along each bank. He assured readers there were previous examples of provincial capitals – Berlin or Turin – that had been transformed into centres 'of trade and commerce, of learning and the arts, of ... refinement of every kind'. Edinburgh, in other words, need not mourn its old status as grim citadel of an embattled kingdom.[12]

An architectural contest was at length chosen as the way forward. Announced in 1766, it called for 'plans of a New Town marking out streets of a proper breadth, and by-lanes, and the best situation for a reservoir, and any other public buildings, which may be thought necessary'. A year later the adjudicators named the winner: James Craig, a young man already working on St James's Square. He was awarded a gold medal and freedom of the city. His entry was 'entirely sensible, and almost painfully orthodox', says A. J. Youngson, historian of classical Edinburgh. The proposal seems to have followed the example of a project at Nancy in Lorraine. It envisaged a strict, regular layout with nothing fancy, just landscaped parks, shady walks, a Register House, a Theatre Royal, Elliot's canal (never completed). At the head of his plan Craig quoted a poem by his uncle, James Thomson, which avowed this unifying vision:

> August, around, what public works I see!
> Lo! stately streets, lo! squares that court the breeze!
> See long canals and deepened rivers join
> Each part with each, and with the circling main,
> The whole enlivened isle.

Here is also a hint of wider purpose. One proposal had been to lay out over the shallow ridge a pattern of streets in the shape of a

Union Jack, though finally an oblong was preferred. Names of streets still recalled that first unionist inspiration. George Street ran along the crown of the ridge, dignified by a square at each end. Running in parallel to the north, Queen Street contained houses on only one side and on the other ornamental gardens looking out at the Forth. Running in parallel to the south, Princes Street had to make do with plainer, often quite modest buildings gazing across to the jumble of the Old Town.

The houses were, with rare exceptions, uniform. They had three storeys, three windows on each and a basement beneath. Some offered scope for symbols of status in the style of doorways and rustication of ground floors, later in giant pilasters and bow windows. But there was rather a risk of monotony, relieved otherwise only by a little vernacular eccentricity at the gables of cross-streets, or by the layout on the eastern side of St Andrew's Square where the first idea for a church was set aside in favour of a grouping of mansion and forecourt. Monotony would not be sublimated in higher unity until Robert Adam's Charlotte Square of 1791. Here it was a refined classical vocabulary that held together a more varied composition. Adam gave the four terraces unified frontages reaching a climax at the central pediments of the northern and southern sides. All the parts fitted into a greater whole, which came to more than the sum of its parts.[13]

Charlotte Square still conformed to Craig's basic plan, which was succeeding because it suited the site yet set a pattern that could transcend it. Building had started at the eastern end in 1767 and went on westwards to form what is now often known as the first New Town; it contained about 2,000 houses. Afterwards it would spill over from the shallow ridge covered by the original oblong. The second New Town was completed in the 1820s, mainly on lands descending to the Water of Leith owned by the Earl of Moray, and increased the number of houses to about 5,000. Nor was this an end of it, for building continued to the north and west (less satisfactorily to the east) with the original chastity of style yielding over time to Victorian fancy. The ensemble was the stately city we know today.

❧

The New Town was revolutionary; and revolution took shape not just in stone but also in flesh and blood, because it changed lives. A prime feature of the Old Town had been how different social classes lived cheek by jowl. There was room for everybody, only on different levels: the lower class at the bottom or top, the middle class in the middle (together with such of the upper class as kept a *pied à terre* in the capital). Before long anybody who could afford it moved to the New Town. The atheist philosopher David Hume was one who led the pack: not quite a wealthy man, though of independent means, he flitted in 1769 from James's Court to a house in what became St David's Street – facetiously so named after him. The rich did not rush: it took half a century for them all to go. But the last gentleman in the Royal Mile, James Ferguson of Pitfour, left for good in 1817.

Those then occupying the New Town embraced the idea of an ordered society because they would sit at its summit. Their sentiment found one expression in the grid's symmetry, the long, broad thoroughfares and commodious squares, later varied by handsome circuses and elegant crescents. The interiors of houses showed a corresponding spaciousness, even splendour. One in Princes Street was advertised as offering a dining room, drawing room, seven bedrooms, kitchen, scullery, servants' apartments, cellars, laundry, stable, coach-house and pigeon-house, together with a wonderful new amenity, 'a lead cistern with a pipe within the house' (which still did not stop the old sanitary problem seeping on to the new roadway). Doubtless the owners entertained, but the design of the house was above all meant to assure them a private life away from the intrusion or even gaze of neighbours and employees. Nobody in scruffy and penniless yet intimate and demonstrative Scotland had ever lived like this. It was the cool, clean, coherent statement of a class with the will to break from a chaotic past and impose its own values inside this machine for a rational existence.[14]

❧

Where did the will come from? More to the point, where did the money come from? While Edinburgh enjoyed greater stability after 1707, it was not as if the city got rich quick. In Glasgow, by contrast, the Union set in motion a commercial then industrial revolution

through the opening of colonial traffic to America. Ports of the Firth
of Forth fell far behind those of the Firth of Clyde, seeking at best to
restore older trading links damaged by the Union. Leith did in the
end succeed to a reasonable extent. By 1791, 130,000 tons of shipping
were registered there.[15] This tonnage represented hundreds of smal-
lish vessels, most sailing to northern and eastern Europe: they took
out the natural resources from the Lothians and Borders to bring
back timber, iron or tallow. It was trade humdrum, though profitable
enough, compared with the exotic merchandise by then entering the
Clyde.

To create wealth, the east of Scotland had had to look rather to
an agricultural revolution. John Cockburn of Ormiston, 'father of
Scottish husbandry', showed the way on his estate eight miles east of
Edinburgh. He aimed to make it and its people at least self-sufficient,
then capable of generating a surplus. He swept away runrig and
divided the land into farms for single tenants, each with its own
steading, field and pasture. Members of his active peasantry came
together every month in a local agricultural society to assess experiences and propose further improvements. Craftsmen and cottage
industries in a model village (most of it still there) met other basic
needs. Like many pioneers Cockburn finally went bust, yet he had
set an excellent example. Following it, luckier landowners prospered so far that they could commemorate themselves in mansions
on their estates yielding nothing in magnificence to the capital's.
Some – Hopetoun, Penicuik, Yester – were among the most palatial
in Europe.[16]

But all this took time, and meanwhile the east of Scotland
stagnated or declined. Even the government in London grew worried.
In 1727 it set up in Edinburgh a Board of Trustees for Fisheries
and Manufactures. The task was to stimulate new activities, if out
of a paltry budget. The board had to concentrate its resources,
then, and one thing it favoured was manufacture of linen. Scots did
have experience here, even if their output before the Union had been
cheap and cheerful. Now a fresh experiment was essayed of bringing
over French weavers of fine linen and setting them up in a little
colony of their own at Picardy Place in the capital, whence they could
transfer their technology. Results were mixed but, under such heavy-
handed official intervention the industry flourished enough to allow

in 1746 the launch of a chartered British Linen Company, again based in Edinburgh. Its aim was by various incentives to rob foreign producers of markets in Britain and capture for domestic producers such new outlets as those in America. Since it was supposed in the end to pay for itself, the incentives were temporary. As soon as they started to be withdrawn, however, underlying economic reality asserted itself. The company survived, though by turning itself into a bank (which it long remained). This evolution in Edinburgh from manufacture into finance proved prophetic.[17]

Otherwise, development in the east of Scotland would remain rural rather than urban. This held true even for its main industry and second obvious creator of wealth, coalmining. The carboniferous basin of Midlothian reached within hailing distance of Edinburgh, right up to Duddingston at the back of Arthur's Seat. The basin comprised a bloc of parishes to the east and south: Borthwick, Cockpen, Dalkeith, Inveresk, Liberton, Newbattle and Newton. Most land here belonged to great nobles, the Duke of Buccleuch, Marquis of Lothian, Earl of Dalhousie or Earl of Wemyss, and other opulent proprietors, the Dundases of Arniston, Hopes of Craighall or Wauchopes of Niddrie. Their estates also covered the finest farming soil in Scotland, so they had no wish to see coal generate urban settlement; their workers, though freed from serfdom in 1799, remained penned inside villages of squalid miners' rows. Beyond the pits, no heavy industry grew. The nearest lay at the Carron ironworks near Falkirk, twenty miles away, while Edinburgh rested content with brewing or publishing enterprises that did not abuse the environment. Though the mines were vital to the region's economy, Midlothian still bore with its resident county set more resemblance to, say, feudal Perthshire than to industrial Lanarkshire or Renfrewshire, where merchants and millowners from Glasgow married into or bought out the effete gentry. All this affected the society of Midlothian's metropolis, Edinburgh.

After 1707 some landowners had headed south, Cockburn (as MP for East Lothian) being typical. But London did not offer a warm welcome to these sharp-set Scots. Luckily, most kept one foot in their homeland, a foot its improved agriculture planted the more firmly. In time sentiment, too, called them back. People read much into the return in 1767 of the third Duke of Buccleuch, after an English upbringing in high Whig circles and a grand tour with Adam Smith – qualifications, surely, for moving straight into politics at Westminster. Yet when the young duke had to choose a future he came home to Dalkeith, to fit out his house there with a new library where he could cultivate himself in silence and solitude, while serving as lord lieutenant of three counties, colonel of fencible regiments, patron of the Royal Society of Edinburgh, Royal Bank of Scotland and Royal Company of Archers. With all that he won the devotion of his kinsman Sir Walter Scott, who liked to spend Christmas with him. Another admirer wrote in 1782:

> At a period when many of the British nobility are wasting their patrimonial estates in profligate dissipation, men trained to arms in defence of their rights and liberties, villages beautified and rendered salubrious, and their inhabitants rendered happy, have been the monuments of expense of the Duke of Buccleuch.[18]

Buccleuch and his peers might spend the social season in Edinburgh too. For such cultivated people St Cecilia's Hall had been built in 1761–3; it has hosted concerts in the Cowgate ever since. The Theatre Royal opened on Princes Street in 1769, soon to be graced by the greatest actress of the age, Mrs Sarah Siddons. In 1781 the town council donated a site in George Street for the Assembly Rooms. A public subscription was raised to erect this work of advanced continental classicism (in the end too severe for local taste) as a venue for every sort of do. The first Edinburgh Festival took place not in 1946 but in 1814, inspired by Miss Angelica Catalani, a diva who had often visited the city. More than 9,000 tickets were sold for seven concerts over a week, with works by Handel, Haydn, Mozart and Beethoven. A second festival followed in 1819. And with dinners and dances throughout the winter, Edinburgh sustained or even enhanced its role as an aristocratic resort, for its own region and for Scotland as a whole. According to its habitués, it was a city more virtuous than London – and much cheaper.[19]

※

While some people abandoned Edinburgh for good in 1707 and some who left later came back, others never got away in the first place. One level down from the nobility were those who had to stay on to man national institutions guaranteed by the Union – the Church, university and law. They also at length found means to prosper.

With a line drawn under faction and feud, Scots now had to settle their differences in court. At the same time, aristocrats trying their luck in London needed managers of their estates at home. Edinburgh's clever, diligent solicitors stood ready. The other branch of the legal profession proved still more useful to a peerage with too many sons. Younger ones might be put to the law as advocates, ready to plead for their kin in the Court of Session. By the mid-eighteenth century the Faculty of Advocates doubled in size to about 200 members. Of these, one in three came from titled families, far in excess of their proportion in the population as a whole.[20]

Influx of talent and extension of business raised the quality of the judiciary. The fifteen judges in the Court of Session were usually landowners themselves, as implicit in their usage of taking the title 'Lord' followed by a territorial designation. One of the most celebrated, Robert MacQueen, was Lord Braxfield after his home near Lanark – celebrated above all for throwaway lines from the bench, as to a sharp but guilty defendant who had put up a good fight, 'Ye're a vera clever chiel, man, but ye wad be nane the waur of a hangin.' Another, David Rae, was Lord Eskgrove from his actually quite modest house at Inveresk; also cherished for his *obiter dicta*, as when recalling, to prisoners about to be condemned, their brutal treatment of victims during a break-in, 'All this you did; and God preserve us! joost as they were sitten doon to their denner!' A third, George Fergusson, Lord Hermand from his estate in Midlothian, directed a jury over one of those incidents in the everyday life of Scotland, still familiar today, when two pals got so mindless on booze that one stabbed and killed the other, 'Good God, if he will do this when he's drunk, what will he not do when he's sober?' Judges spoke Scots and felt proud of it: Henry Home, Lord Kames from his home in the Borders, said, 'I ken very weel that I am the coarsest and most black-avised bitch in a' the Court of Session.' They had their own way with the nation's social habits. A successor, Henry, Lord Cockburn, would recall how in the old days 'black bottles of strong port were set down beside the bench with glasses, carafes of water, tumblers and biscuits, and this without the slightest attempt at concealment'.[21]

There emerged in Edinburgh a landed and legal class for which practice at the bar and interest in a country estate were normal. We have met examples in James Boswell and Henry Dundas, each also able to win renown in yet a third field, respectively literature and politics. This became normal, too. A youngster of family waiting to make his mark in life could sign up to the Faculty of Advocates and mix with his fellows while earning money if he needed to. Having interests in common, they pursued them from the professional into the private sphere. In their free time they followed the city's custom of joining clubs. Notable now was the Select Society founded in 1754 by Allan Ramsay the painter, son of Allan Ramsay the poet. Ramsay the younger recruited David Hume and Adam Smith along with advocates and a sprinkling of noblemen. Good claret and good talk lubricated reflections by these public-spirited chaps on the role of rank and property in a developing country. They saw themselves as its leaders, of course – a virtuous elite intent on preserving its historic liberties while exploiting its opportunities in the Union.[22]

Beside law courts and landed estates, such people had a third haunt, the New Town. To this day, most judges and senior advocates live in grand houses in Heriot Row or Moray Place. Their forerunners gave a practical demonstration of how civic spirit might blend with professional skill to yield, in the townscape, a general public good. One result visible yet is the preservation of the original plan for Princes Street and its picturesque outlook to the Castle Rock. In any other city, over the two subsequent centuries of commercialism, that outlook might have vanished behind or beneath bricks and mortar. In Edinburgh it is still there because Scots lawyers homed in on the nation's ancient feudal system and adapted it by their expertise to modern urban needs.

The system had once been common in Europe, but was now dead or dying in most countries. In Scotland it survived until legislated away by the new Scottish Parliament in 2001. Under that system, all land belonged in theory to the crown. But the crown had over time granted it to tenants who in turn might grant it to subtenants in a pyramid of occupancy. During this process of subinfeudation – or simply feuing – the superior could impose binding conditions on his vassal, the purchaser of the property. The conditions, known to Scots law as feudal burdens, typically regulated the use of the land or the nature and appearance of buildings on it. There was no such thing as freehold, in other words: the Scottish system meant in general that absolute, unfettered ownership did not exist.

This became important as private housing expanded faster than ever before. Feudalism would turn out to be of enormous value for preserving the character of Edinburgh. Builders in the eighteenth century worked on a smaller scale than is normal now, when a single firm buys a piece of land and constructs all houses on it, subject to planning controls. Before such controls existed it was for the land's original owner, the feudal superior, to produce a feuing plan and set out the lines of the streets and mark plots for each house. He sold the plots usually by auction to different people, who then had their houses erected on them. As each might employ a different builder, means were needed of preserving some uniformity and standards of workmanship. The feu-charter, drafted by the owner and subscribed by the purchasers, did the business. It imposed the real burdens on the houses and the neighbourhood.

In the New Town, experience of feuing on such a scale and over such a long period had a deep, durable effect on the evolution of the law and practice of real burdens. The town council held the superiority of the land where the early feus were made. At this stage the council relied on the plans drawn up by Craig for the first New Town, then by Adam for Charlotte Square. The council itself as yet imposed few real burdens but in its feudal grants it often referred to the plans, which would therefore assume decisive legal importance.[23]

Such was the result of a test case in 1772, when the feuars on the northern side of Princes Street, organized by the philosopher Hume, applied for an interdict against the town council's decision to authorize development on the southern side. In their view their feu-charters guaranteed them an outlook to Edinburgh Castle, and Craig's plan confirmed as much by showing buildings only on the northern side of Princes Street. The council claimed that other decisions taken meanwhile had overridden the plan. The case went eventually to the House of Lords, where the council's claim failed. The Scots-born Lord Chief Justice, Lord Mansfield, had fun at its expense:

> After some time, the plaintiffs were surprised by the appearance of buildings upon the ground, which they always supposed destined to the health and beauty of the place. And in place of terraces and walks upon the North Loch they find a new street a-making in its way, as a peculiar favourite of the corporation, under the name of Canal Street. These gentlemen immediately bring the complaint before the corporation. They appeal to the plan and pray to be informed how such an infringement could ever be imagined, far less carried into execution – or how the town could allow themselves to act against the good faith of the public and express terms of their sale. Now, my lords, what answer did the corporation make to all this?
>
> 'Plan!' they say. 'Why, gentlemen, you have egregiously deceived yourselves, that is not the plan at all.'
>
> 'No!' say the plaintiffs. 'Where is it then?'
>
> Here,' replied the corporation, 'in an act of council of such a date. Did you ever see that before?'
>
> 'No indeed,' rejoined the feuars, 'we never did.'
>
> 'Impossible,' continue the magistrates. 'You are men of business, your receipts for the money bear the date of this act; and it is in vain to say you so far neglect, or impose upon yourselves. Why, you are to have no canal, no walk, no terrace, no pleasure ground. Here is Canal Street! there is a coach-house! there a butcher's shop! there a tallow-chandler! Can your lordships approve the conduct of this corporation on the contemptible idea upon which this conduct has been endeavoured to be justified?'[24]

Their lordships did not approve and banned all building on the southern side of Princes Street – a ban still in force, maintaining one of the city's finest features in that open outlook to the Castle. The ruling gave a basis for gradual extension of feudal law to more general needs of modern urban life. As greater numbers of private landowners took part in development, building conditions grew more elaborate and the law controlling them more watertight. Soon it was normal to write a range of details into feu-charters: conditions on height, roofs, areas, railings, pavement, windows and stonework of houses. The practice spread from Edinburgh to the rest of Scotland. Real burdens could then be used to set out elaborate programmes for the development and use of land. Lawyers employed them in conveyances. Courts upheld them.

So, where Scottish cities and towns have preserved a historic character, this is often due to feudalism. Evolution of the system was shaped by modern requirements for civic amenity, which it met better than other branches of the law. Alas, one of the first things the Scottish Parliament did on being restored after 1999 was to abolish feudalism, under a delusion that this medieval relic oppressed the lieges. Now Edinburgh and the rest of Scotland depend for amenity on the decrees of public planning authorities – which cannot fill anyone with confidence given some of the appalling mistakes made in the past, not least in the capital.[25]

❧

As the New Town arose, the Old Town sank into decline. That destroyed the medley of rich and poor living on one stair, saluting noble neighbours as they stepped over beggars at the close-mouth. Social differences there had always been, but now they yawned. The publisher William Creech noted how 'in 1763 people of quality and fashion lived in houses which, in 1793, were inhabited by tradesmen or by people in humble or ordinary life. The Lord Justice Tinwald's house was possessed by a French teacher – Lord President Craigie's by a rouping wife or saleswoman of old furniture.'[26]

Yet, poised for this plunge, the Old Town found its poet in Robert Fergusson. Born there in 1750, in a close soon swept away for construction of the North Bridge, he was educated at the High School and went on to university at St Andrews. In travelling backwards and forwards he must often have surveyed one of the great prospects of Edinburgh, where the road out of the Howe of Fife comes over a saddle down to the northern shore of the Forth; the traveller can never be sure if he will be soothed by the serenity of the scene, be scowled at under a storm or will sense his mood turn as sunny as the light dancing on the waters before him. Fergusson could have captured any of these sights but, in addressing his native city, preferred the last:

> Aft frae the Fifan coast I've seen
> Thee tow'ring on thy summit green;
> So glowr the saints when first is given,
> A fav'rite keek o' glore and heaven;
> On earth nae mair they bend their ein,
> But quick assume angelic mein;
> So I on Fife wad glower no more,
> But gallop'd to Edina's shore.[27]

Fergusson had not yet finished his studies when his father died and left the family destitute. He had to return to Edinburgh and take any job he could get. He found one in the Commissary Office dealing with wills and matrimonial cases. It was ill-paid drudgery, unworthy of him but not too onerous on a young fellow eager to write. What he did write shows he spent his free time in taverns, or else at the club he joined, the Knights of the Cape, towards the bohemian end of the range available.

Any visitor to Edinburgh's best pubs today will recognize what Fergusson found irresistible in them:

> *Auld Reekie! thou'rt the canty hole,*
> *A bield for mony caldrife soul,*
> *Wha snugly at thine ingle loll,*
> *Baith warm and couth'*
> *While round they gar the bicker roll*
> *To weet their mouth.*

> Edinburgh! you are the cheerful hole,
> A shelter for many a spiritless soul,
> Who snugly at your fireside loll,
> Both warm and cosy;
> While round they make the glasses roll
> To wet their mouth.[28]

Fergusson is often the poet of such humdrum scenes – also, for example, of girls cleaning the stairs in the Old Town:

> *On stair wi' tub, or pat in hand*
> *The barefoot housemaids looe to stand,*
> *That antrin fock may ken how snell*
> *Auld Reekie will at morning smell:*

Then, with an inundation big as
The burn that 'neath the Nore Loch Brig is,
They kindly shower Edina's roses,
To quicken and regale our noses.

On stair with tub, or pot in hand
The barefoot housemaids love to stand,
That strangers may know how keen
Edinburgh will smell in the morning:
Then, with an inundation big as
The stream that runs beneath North Bridge,
They kindly shower excrement,
To quicken and regale our noses.[29]

Fergusson could also be outrageous at the expense of people towards the upper end of the social scale. When Boswell brought Dr Samuel Johnson to Edinburgh in 1773 Fergusson asked, in merciless derision of his sesquipedalian Latinity, what might ensue if the 'Great Pedagogue' tried porridge or whisky, perhaps while wearing a kilt:

Have you as yet the way explorified
To let lignarian chalice, swelled with oats,
Thy orifice approach? . . .
. . . Or can you swill
The usquebalian flames of whisky blue,
In fermentation strong? Have you applied
The kilt aërian to your Anglian thighs,
And with renunciation assignized
Your breeches in Londona to be worn?[30]

Still, it was low life Fergusson preferred to write about – because he knew it well. Syphilis would kill him in 1774. His last months were wretched and terminated by an accident. He fell down a stair, banged his head and was carried home delirious to his mother. She could not look after him so he had to be removed as a 'pauper lunatic' to Edinburgh's bedlam, where conditions were frightful. And there he died.

❧

Yet in his short span Fergusson made an impression on brother Scots as one that gave the vernacular muse a further lease of life after her revival by the elder Ramsay. Robert Burns would remember him, for some reason in English, at his grave in the kirkyard of the Canongate:

> O thou my elder brother in misfortune,
> By far my elder brother in the muse,
> With tears I pity thy unhappy fate.
> Why is the bard unfitted for the world,
> Yet has so keen a relish for its pleasures?[31]

This is doubly circumspect: both Burns and Fergusson knew well enough they belonged to the Devil's party. But Burns, unlike Fergusson, was a country bumpkin, awestruck at coming to the capital. That, in any case, is the impression conveyed by the lifeless Augustan style he often felt obliged to adopt for his poetry while in Edinburgh, on and off, from 1786 to 1788 – as in a contrived paean to the capital, 'Edina! Scotia's darling seat!', or an elegy on the death of the second Lord President Arniston, 'O heavy loss, thy country ill could bear!', which the Dundases understandably did not bother to acknowledge. Burns, feted in the city's salons as the 'heaven-taught ploughman', was doubtless giving a genteel audience what he thought it wanted: a style 'correct' in the sense of being written in English and conforming to classical canons (similar to the correctness of the New Town's architecture). We may wonder if this classicism was not beginning to turn into a facade for sterility.[32]

Burns sensed as much himself. The best thing he wrote in Edinburgh was the 'Address to a Haggis', still popular today for its innocent irony couched in earthy Scots, and most familiar in the ritual of the Burns Supper. In real life, too, he felt a need now and again to burst out, get drunk and seduce servant girls, his May Cameron or his Jenny Clow. His hosts knew all about this: it gave them, or especially their wives and daughters, a frisson. When Burns met Mrs Agnes McLehose, niece of the judge Lord Craig and deserted wife of an erring husband, the pair entered into an intense relationship. But they conducted it largely by letter, he signing himself Sylvander and she Clarinda. We do not know if this stylized courtly romance led them to bed: Burns, however dapper in the drawing room, probably remained barred from the boudoir. Clarinda broke off the affair, such as it was, once she came to see how devouring Sylvander's sex-drive could be. All that remained was one of his greatest songs, 'Ae Fond Kiss'.[33]

The salons took notice of Burns as they had never taken notice of Fergusson, nor yet of another poet then living in the city, Duncan Bàn Macintyre. Macintyre composed in Gaelic, however – and orally, for he was illiterate. He had been born on the borders of Argyll and Perthshire, whence Gaels could easily move to central Scotland as their old way of life died out; no need of clearance here. There is scant record of this internal Scottish migration after Culloden, but several observers remarked how more and more menial tasks in the capital seemed to be carried out by humble Highlanders. They added a further tongue to Edinburgh's tally and the city provided a Gaelic chapel in 1767, about the time Macintyre arrived. He had been published already with the help of his Jacobite brother bard, Alasdair mac Mhaighstir Alasdair. That made no difference now. In the capital Macintyre was just another peasant with a dead-end job in the town guard (he no doubt still felt grateful, since he had a criminal record for illegal distillation of whisky). In 'Oran Dhùn Eideann' ('Song of Edinburgh') he could in his happy-go-lucky fashion cast from his obscurity a cool eye on the gentlemen he was supposed to be protecting:

> 'S iomadh fleasgach uasal ann e,
> A bha gu suairce grinn,
> Fùdar air an gruagan
> A suas gu bàrr an cinn.

> Many noble beaux are there,
> Urbane and elegant,
> Having powder on their wigs
> Right up to their crowns.

Or indeed on their ladies:

> 'S mòr a tha de bhaintighearnan
> A null 's a nall an t-sràid

Gùntaichean de 'n t-sìoda orr,
'Gan sliogadh ris a'bhlàr.

Many patrician ladies
Go up and down the street
All wearing gowns of silk
That brush against the ground.

Only in two lines of over 300 in this poem does Macintyre allow
himself a hint, here in the high temple of Hanoverianism, of an older
allegiance. He says there are in town

Na taighean mòra rìomhach
Am bu chòir an rìgh bhith stad.

Large and splendid houses
Wherein the king should stay.[34]

๕

That completes the count of authentic popular voices from the
era of the first New Town. There are hardly more from the era of
the second New Town, now expressing themselves in prose. When
Alexander Somerville left Berwickshire for Edinburgh in 1825 the
economy was falling into recession (the one that bankrupted Scott).
Somerville had a job to go to in a sawmill, but the other sawyers gave
his strange face no warm welcome – quite the reverse, 'on several
occasions they told me I might probably get my head broken, and
would probably be found by somebody dead in the Cowgate Burn'.
If they could have been sure of alternative work, he thought, they
would have downed tools, 'but as it was otherwise, and so many
being out of employment and suffering dreadful privations, they
were powerless'. They did at last relent and admit him into their
'brotherhood', on condition he got them all drunk on whisky. Later
he swapped to being a nurseryman at Inverleith: 'We lived meagrely
in the bothy, oatmeal porridge of small measure and strength in the
mornings, with sour dook, a kind of rank buttermilk peculiar to
Edinburgh, potatoes and salt, and occasionally a herring for dinner,
and sour dook and oatmeal for supper. We never had butcher's meat,
and seldom any bread.' He earned six shillings a week but spent no

more than four on necessities. The rest he devoted to educating himself, 'frequently sitting up half the night, or rising at daybreak in the summer mornings, to reading, writing, arithmetic and other studies; and an expenditure for books and stationery could not be dispensed with. Nor could newspapers be omitted at that time. The Reform Bill had been laid before Parliament.' Such was the urge to self-help in a Scots working man.[35]

About the same time and in the same conditions Hugh Miller came to Edinburgh from Cromarty. He was a stonemason who out of observations in the rocks he worked on would publish a best-selling book, *The Old Red Sandstone* (1841), which made some contribution to the development of geology and to Victorian controversy over the creation of the world as recounted in Genesis. Landing at Leith in 1825, Miller found a job at Niddrie and in his turn had a surly reception from other workers: 'As the hewing shed was fully occupied at the time I arrived, I was set to hew in front of it exposed to the sun and wind, and what annoyed me more to the contemptuous observations of the workmen it sheltered.' They latched on to his being a Highlander: 'With a few exceptions they all appeared decidedly hostile to me, and seemed to consider me as a legitimate butt for their ridicule.' As a devout Calvinist he felt amazed at their urban habits. When three of his mates got a fortnight's wages, amounting to £6, they blew the whole lot on drink and women over a single weekend. Another lad from the country who had arrived with him yielded to the mockery of the rest and fell in with their debauchery. When he boasted about his sexual exploits and even about catching a dose of venereal disease, Miller would not believe him. He exposed himself. Miller believed him.[36]

※

Except for such rare personal testimony from the working class, we have to rely on bourgeois observations. These grew obsessive amid the strains Scotland suffered as her modern economy emerged. In almost every country, down to the present, the Industrial Revolution has been a necessary but painful experience. People are wrenched out of age-old ways of life and cast adrift in a new world atomized and, at its lowest levels, degraded. Potential for unrest, indeed for revolution, is clear. In Britain it was avoided by philanthropic and political efforts to identify problems and solve them. For this reason, documentation of the condition of labour became rich.

But we have seen how for Edinburgh and its hinterland there are problems with assumptions often made in academic literature, notably of an older, Marxist kind, about the Industrial Revolution. The main work here was mining, which as yet had undergone next to no technological advance. In Midlothian's pits men wrought as their fathers had wrought since the Middle Ages. As the geology was difficult, with seams narrow and wet, miners often had to stand or even lie in water while they dug at the coalface with pickaxes. Another archaic aspect lay in the way the labour got shared among all the family. If father was off with an injury, or just with a hangover, wife and children carried on in his stead. As usual, once the coal was mined, they dragged it from the face to the shaft, then bore it up a stair to the pithead: equivalent, it was calculated in one case, to climbing Arthur's Seat with a burden of two hundredweight four times a day. Youthful frames became deformed, and many miners contracted silicosis, or 'black spit'. The average age at death was thirty-four, compared to fifty for hands in factories. To fulfil their productive potential, children had to start work as early as possible, even at five or six years of age. In 1840 a royal commission inquired into the mines. Its report led to an Act of Parliament banning employment underground of women and girls, and of boys below the age of ten; up to the age of thirteen, they were no longer to work more than twelve hours a day.

One place where the commission took evidence was Liberton, today a leafy suburb of Edinburgh, then a mining village. It found children toiling as hard as adults. Janet Cumming, aged eleven, told how she 'works with father, has done for two years. Father gangs at two in the morning. I gang with the women at five, and come up at five at night, work all night on Fridays and come away at five in the day.' For Agnes Reid, aged fourteen, things seemed still worse: 'I bear coal on my back. I do not know the exact weight, but it is something more than a hundredweight. It is very sore work and makes us often cry. Few lassies like it. I would much prefer to work out by or in service but suppose father needs me.'

Boys picking coal (digging it with a pickaxe) laboured as hard as men. George Reid, aged sixteen, said: 'I pick the coal at the wallface, have done so for six years. The seam is twenty-six inches high and when I pick I am obliged to twist myself up. The men who work in this seam lie on their broadsides. Father took me down early to prevent me from going owre wild about the town. It is horrible sore work.' John King, aged twelve, did not even eat properly: 'I work all the time that I am below and get kale or porridge afterwards. The work takes away the desire for food, as it is owre sair. I go down at three in the morning, but leave home at two, and come up about four or six in the day.' Alexander Reid, aged twelve, had still less time off: 'I go below at two or three in the morning and hew until six at night. After that I fill and put the carts on the rails to pit bottom . . . When first below I used to fall asleep, am kept awake now. It is most terrible work. I am wrought in a 30-inch seam and am obliged to twist myself up or work on my side.' Nor for John Jamieson, aged twelve, was the day over even when such backbreaking toil came to an end: 'I have picked coal for two years with my father, have got used to the work, don't mind it now only too long at it. I work never less than from four in the morning until six at night, sometimes all night. I go to Mr Robertson's night-school at Clayburns to learn the reading and am doing a little at the write, no muckle.' We have to wonder at the artless articulacy of these children, even more at how they strove after hours of punishing physical exertion to school themselves – though this was too much for David Naysmith, aged twelve: 'I have worked in coal-pits five years, been obliged to do so because father is off work with bad breath, that is, short of breath occasioned by his working in bad air . . . The work is very sore, and am frequently too much fatigued to recollect school lessons.' William Woods, at fourteen, was probably already falling victim to silicosis: 'I have been three years below. I hew the coal and draw it to the pit bottom. I gang at three in the morning and return about six. It is no very good work, and the sore labour makes me feel very ill and fatigued. It injures my breath.'[37]

❦

Hardship outside the city formed a continuum with hardship inside. Families from the country seeking something better would not find it if they ended up in the Old Town of Edinburgh, which by now had been emptied of all but an underclass, those with no choice where to live. The Reverend John Lee, minister of St Giles in the 1830s, was himself the son of a weaver in Midlothian and painted a picture of the urban conditions so harrowing as to catch the attention of Friedrich Engels, who in 1844 quoted him in *The Condition of the Working Classes in England (sic)*: 'I have seen much wretchedness in my time, but never such a scene of misery as in this parish.' Many of the poor had nothing by way of personal possessions, even though some got the maximum support the Church could offer. Lee could name '78 houses where there was no bed, in some of them not even straw'. He recalled a case 'of two Scotch families living in a miserable kind of cellar, who had come from the country within a few months, in search of work'; some of their children were already dead. They lived the whole time in darkness, and 'there was a little bundle of dirty straw in one corner, for one family, and in another for the other. An ass stood in one corner, which was as well accommodated as these human creatures. It would almost make a heart of adamant bleed to see such an accumulation of misery in a country like this.'[38]

The Scots Poor Law gave Lee a responsibility for parishioners in this condition. But the law had not grown less mean since first passed in 1579. Even now it forbade help for the able-bodied if they just happened to have lost their jobs, lest their will to find a new one be sapped. Benefits paid out to the deserving poor came from rates or charitable donations, but the burgesses of Edinburgh still did not like putting hands in pockets for paupers. Lee stressed that relief could hardly be effective even if the law made greater resources available. The world had simply changed since 1579: then there had been the steady rhythm of traditional agriculture, now there was the volatility of modern commerce. Both might lurch into crisis, but at least rural society had been sustained by resilient structures, while in the city the poor led lives too unstable to form anything that might be called a community.

In the early nineteenth century about 1,000 people usually claimed outdoor relief in Edinburgh. This still marked them out as citizens in some sense: to get it, they needed to show they were native to the burgh. But already in 1743 its parishes had pooled resources to run one big workhouse, erected near the Bristo Port (a wing of the building survives in a cul-de-sac). This became a dump for undesirables. Even by local standards of filth it was 'extremely nauseous'. It held 700 inmates, still with strict criteria for admission: first 'the begging poor entitled to the town's charity', as of old; then those who could bring their own blankets or furniture, always in short supply; then orphans; then burgesses and their families who had fallen on hard times; then anybody else that room could be found for. The welcome was not warm. Inmates had to wear a drab blue uniform. They were fed only on porridge, broth and bread. Yet the managers of such a spartan regime still felt overwhelmed. Paupers were bad enough but patients discharged as incurable from the Royal Infirmary tended to end up here too, having nowhere else to go. A large ward was allocated for people baldly labelled as 'depraved'. And the bedlam for the insane lay in the cellars, out of sight, out of mind – it was where the poet Fergusson died. Nothing here fostered charity.[39] Scott in *The Heart of Midlothian* hints at routine brutality. His character Madge Wildfire often tells the truth in her madness, and she sings of her time in the workhouse:

> I had hempen bracelets strong
> And merry whips ding-dong
> And prayer and fasting plenty.[40]

❧

Even this did not plumb the bottom of the social heap. Still out on the streets were prostitutes. Fergusson had, of course, known them:

> Near some lamp-post, wi' dowy [gloomy] face,
> Wi' heavy een [eyes], and sour grimace,
> Stands she that beauty lang had kend,
> Whoredom her trade, and vice her end.[41]

In 1793 Creech the publisher reported there were now hundreds like her, in unfavourable contrast to 1763 when, he claimed, only five or six brothels had existed in the whole town: 'A person might have gone from the Castle to Holyroodhouse . . . at any hour of the night, without being accosted by a single street-walker.' He is hard to believe. In these pages we have seen prostitution rife in Edinburgh since at least the sixteenth century, on account of the limited urban opportunities for poor girls and of the numbers of men having to spend time alone in the capital for one reason and another. But public acknowledgment of the situation came only in 1797, when the Edinburgh Magdalene Institute was founded to take the whores off the streets and make honest women of them, as laundresses. Most ran away from employers they found unbearably condescending; there were easier ways to make a living.[42]

Meanwhile, in 1776, halfway through Creech's period of comparison, Boswell had had no trouble stilling his lust whenever he felt like it. He would get drunk, wander the wynds and closes and take his pick. From 25 November that year he did so, or meant to, three nights running. The first time, 'as I was coming home at five, I met a young slender slut with a red cloak in the street and went with her to Barefoots Parks [next to the building site of the New Town] and madly ventured coition. It was a short and almost insensible gratification of lewdness.' In the High Street, the second time, he met 'a plump hussy who called herself Peggy Grant. It was one of the coldest nights I ever remember. I went with her to a field behind the Register Office, and boldly lay with her. This was desperate risking.' The third time, 'the girl with whom I was last night had told me she lodged in Stevenlaw's Close, and at my desire engaged to be at the head of it generally at eight in the evening, in case I should be coming past. I thought I could not be in more danger of disease by one more enjoyment the very next evening, so went tonight; but she was not there.' The names do not quite tally but she might have been a girl in the *Impartial List of the Ladies of Pleasure in Edinburgh* circulated in 1775: 'This lady is little, black hair, round-faced, tolerable good teeth, and about twenty-four years of age. She is extremely shy and artful in her devotions at the shrine of love.' Be that as it may, Boswell had to go home crestfallen to his wife and baby son. The New Town would prove a boon to him because he no longer needed to copulate in the open during Edinburgh's winters. The gardens had room for sheds and the houses fewer windows than in the Old Town whence he might be spotted. The risk, as he says, came from venereal disease in an age when all remedies were painful and useless. It was probably of renal failure secondary to gonorrhea that he would die in 1796.[43]

🌿

The story of Edinburgh's working class in this era was not simply one of segregation and degradation, however. The town had also had since at least the end of the Middle Ages a tradition of communal artisan self-assertion, often in alliance with other social elements. The mob assumed here, too, a role common in European capitals. Popular riot could amount to more than mere anarchy. When the trades of Edinburgh raised the blue blanket, the banner granted them by King James III, they proclaimed themselves set on serious business with the state.

Behind the blue blanket people of different stations in life could unite in troubled times: at the Reformation, for the Covenants, at the Revolution, at the Union and later. For example, many taking part in the Porteous Riot of 1736 wore disguise – it was suspected the anonymity hid respectable citizens as well as wild young men. Later on in the century Joseph Smith, a cobbler in the Cowgate, acted as leader of the mob: 'His person was low, almost without legs, and with the sole good property of great muscular strength in the arms,' says the Victorian chronicler Robert Chambers. Beyond the normal discontents at material shortage and high prices, Smith articulated deeper social or political grievances. 'With all his absolute power over the affections of the mob,' Chambers notes, 'he never employed it in a bad cause, or could be said . . . to outrage the principles of what we may call natural justice'. When a poor man was evicted and hanged himself, Smith had the landlord's house ransacked. Deformed and disreputable as he was, the magistrates needed to deal with him: 'They frequently sent for him in emergencies, in order to consult with him regarding the best means of appeasing and dispersing the mob.' A hogshead of beer was the going rate. Smith died after a fall from a stagecoach while returning drunk from the races at Leith Sands.[44]

Though not exclusively proletarian, nor was the mob always progressive by modern conceptions. In 1778 a group calling itself the Committee for the Protestant Interest organized protests against a proposal from the liberal Lord Advocate, Henry Dundas, to lift the penal laws against Scots Catholics. The members of the committee were a solicitor, a solicitor's apprentice, a schoolmaster, three clerks, a goldsmith, a merchant, a grocer, a hosier, an ironmonger, a dyer and 'an intaker for several bleachfields': a fair cross-section of the urban mass. Behind the blue blanket they demonstrated on the High Street, and got out of hand. They sacked a discreet Catholic chapel in Blackfriars Wynd. They assaulted peaceable papists living nearby. They wanted to press on to the principal's house at the university, for they did not like intellectuals either. Dundas had to deploy troops from the Castle round the town. So violent did the trouble become that he abandoned his proposal of Catholic emancipation. The fiasco almost brought his political career to a premature end when he had to explain himself to Parliament in London. It would be pleasant to record the men on Edinburgh's streets had been the sturdy, freedom-loving radicals beloved of national mythology. So some of them may have been – but they were bigots too.[45]

If sequestered in the Old Town, popular prejudice festered on and sometimes could not be stopped from bursting out. Edinburgh's next big riot in 1792 found a focus at one of its best addresses, 5 George Square, townhouse of the Dundases of Arniston. On 4 June Henry Dundas, now MP for the city, was in London while his family held a party to celebrate the birthday of King George III. They were joining after their genteel fashion in a general Scottish tradition that had grown up, of taking this opportunity to toast the monarch. Whether for the people at large it implied actual loyalty, as opposed to a chance to get drunk, was a different matter. A crowd gathered in the square in front of the Dundases' house, and two nephews went out to confront the unwelcome visitors, brandishing a golf-club and their granny's crutch. Forced by threats to retreat, they offered their backsides for kissing before they vanished indoors. This put the mob in more menacing mood. The municipal authorities had no means of keeping order except the arthritic town guard, which stayed well away. So troops had again to be called down from the Castle; they happened to be English troops. The rioters dispersed to find more drink. Later they came back and goaded the sentries with shouts of 'Johnnie Cope!' The sentries kept so admirably cool that they provoked the rioters to hurl cobblestones and chant an ever more frenetic chorus of 'Buggars, fire!' At length the soldiers obliged: they killed one man and wounded six. Cockburn, another nephew of the Dundases, recalled 'no windows could be smashed at that time without the inmates thinking of the bloody streets of Paris'.[46]

In Paris revolution was raging, and even faraway Edinburgh found conclaves of radicals gathering to think how the aspirations of a new age might be awakened here. The town council struck a pose of vigilance, though its officers usually busied themselves on tasks hardly political. One, John Hutton, was employed to make minute inspection of the markets, enforcing day after day the burgh's still medieval regulations; he seems to have shown the same dour and officious manner as its modern traffic-wardens. He reported for 21 July 1793: 'This morning seized a quantity of unripe gooseberries – summoned the owners before Bailie Carfrae, acquitted on a promise to be cautious in the disposal.' In fact it was Hutton who got called aside by the bailie, to be told 'at this critical time, when so many eyes are upon the magistrates, rather to pass over some things, viz. summoning shopkeepers'.[47] Carfrae evidently feared, now Britain and France had gone to war, any provocations of the people. But over his head Dundas would stand for no nonsense, and saw to the suppression of all trouble in Edinburgh. To make sure, even so, he had legislation passed in 1805 to give the city a regular police force. This would be run by its own board and not by a council that had let the town guard decay into impotence: the guard would be disbanded in 1817.

Yet at its first big test the police force hardly covered itself in glory either. The French wars continued for two decades, causing privations on the home front. The years 1811–12 proved especially hard, with inflation and shortages. Still, most life went on as normal. At Hogmanay 1811 citizens of Edinburgh gathered at the Tron in the High Street to bring in the New Year in the way they long had done, and still do. But with midnight drawing near, a mob mounted from the Cowgate by way of nearby Niddry Wynd, as if from a blocked sewer spewing its foulness upwards. Young thugs wielding bludgeons attacked and knocked down the revellers, stealing their money and valuables, killing a man who resisted them. They even beat off the police, and killed one of them too. Three youths were later arrested as ringleaders: shoemaker Hugh MacDonald, an illiterate orphan not sure how old he was, apprentice painter Neil Sutherland, aged eighteen, and another shoemaker, Hugh MacIntosh, aged just sixteen. Tender years did not save them. They were hanged at the mouth of the close where they had booted the policeman to death.[48]

The New Town had yet to see anything like this. But trouble at last arrived on its monumental doorsteps in the agitation for the Reform Act of 1832. When a crucial stage of the legislation passed at Westminster by a single vote, 10,000 people went out on to the High Street to make merry. Supporters preferring to stay at home 'illuminated', that is, displayed candles in their windows. The demonstrators decided the New Town ought to illuminate too. But down the hill they found Heriot Row and Abercromby Place in darkness. They gathered before the unilluminated windows of the lord provost and threw stones. The sound of breaking glass whetted appetites for more. Somerville, the nurseryman from Inverleith, was present and reported: 'This human sea, storm risen, rounded the Royal Circus, Moray Place, Queen Street, Charlotte and St Andrew's Squares ... as dash went the stones, smash fell the glass, and crash came the window frames – dash, smash, crash, from nine o' clock to near midnight.' Wherever the people went they cried, 'Up with reform light, down with Tory darkness!' The interests of Old Town and New Town now seemed wholly at odds.[49]

❧

But aspiration was also a mark of Edinburgh's working class. Tradesmen followed toffs in exodus from the Old Town, though the most thriving could afford only to live in the backstreets of the New Town where their best business was now found. Many would flit instead into an industrial belt which, especially after arrival of the railway, was to run on a horizontal line along the midriff of the expanding city. Others crowded into the new suburbs of Greenside to the north or St Leonards to the south, sometimes in tenements no better than those of the High Street. Further off into the future a cooperative building association would be founded, to form the Victorian model colonies for working families still to be seen at Stockbridge, Dalry Road and London Road.

Mobility arose also out of the desire of Edinburgh's workers for their children to be educated. The prestige of the medieval High School had risen along with the tone of the modern city. By many this was reckoned the best school in Scotland, and landed families arriving for the social season routinely sent their sons here; on the roster of former pupils appear scions of the noble houses of Buchan,

Dalhousie, Hopetoun, Lauderdale and Melville along with the off-spring of burgesses. In 1825 the school would in its turn shift up from the Old Town into a thrilling new building, modelled after the Temple of Theseus at Athens, on the airy southern slope of Calton Hill. But educational aspiration cost money, and the town council had long before felt a need to deal with the problem of children whose parents could no longer afford the High School. As early as 1699, it asked George Clerk, precentor in the Tolbooth kirk, to teach as many other pupils as he could take, forty in the first instance. The council founded in 1733 a hospital for orphans where they, too, received an education. The same arrangement aided children forced with their pauper parents into the workhouse. There were besides schools run by the charitable foundations of George Heriot and George Watson.[50]

So an education was not too hard to get in Edinburgh, and with it the respectable working class might start climbing the social ladder. Some bore witness to this. George Combe was born amid 'unwhole-some surroundings', one of a brewster's seventeen brats. He traversed the nether regions of Scottish schooling, set to learn by rote under a cruel master terrorizing the pupils with his leathern tawse. Combe's parents, 'from a consciousness of their educational defects', never discussed anything with their brood but drilled them through the catechism and made them sit long hours in church. The young Combe took articles with a solicitor and qualified in 1812, after eight laborious years. He pursued a quiet interest in radical politics and bore the marks of the autodidact: pleasant enough in a vapid kind of way, he would drone on and on until he bored listeners rigid. Nor did he have any money before he married a daughter of the actress Mrs Sarah Siddons; from her they got a modest legacy. Then Combe's life took shape as the apostle of phrenology, on which he wrote the key work, *The Constitution of Mind* (1828). It met with contempt from the academic establishment. But Scots at large were among the first to follow phrenology in the huge numbers it would attract during Victorian times, fated though it was to be banished finally to the far fringes of pseudo-science and recalled as a mere study of bumps for the ignorant and credulous.[51]

Most citizens still formed what views they held of the world through membership of the Church of Scotland. Not only that, but in a nation without a formal political system after 1707 the Kirk took its place. The General Assembly might discuss last things but also present things, how to run the schools or look after the poor. It did so at its annual meeting every May in Edinburgh.

Presbyterian zeal had done much to win and safeguard this established status. The zeal showed little sign of flagging. The people were instructed in Calvinist theology and equipped to argue about it in line with that democratic intellectualism espoused by the nation ever since the Reformation. 'Even the Scotch peasantry and working classes possess the habit of making observations and reasoning thereon with great acuteness,' the Welsh social reformer Robert Owen would find on crossing the border in 1801.[52]

One shape the instruction took was in campaigns against little vices vexing the Kirk. In 1719 it singled out swimming on Sunday, though the smelly citizens of the capital might find neither time nor water for a good wash otherwise. For the presbytery of Edinburgh dirtiness was preferable to desecration of the sabbath. It called on the lord provost for 'a competent number of soldiers in the city guard to attend upon the elders and deacons every Lord's day that they go to Bonnington Water for suppressing effectually these horrid outrages on the Lord's day' – that is, people splashing about in the Water of Leith. But the presbytery was biting off more than it could chew when it also sought to stop people 'standing in companies in the streets, misspending the time in idle discourse, vain and useless communication', or 'withdrawing from the city to take their recreations in walking through fields, parks, links and meadows', even 'entering into taverns, ale houses, mills, houses, gardens or other places to drink, tipple or otherwise misspend any part thereof', or just 'idly gazing out of windows, beholding vanities abroad'. It succeeded in suppressing none of these sins.[53]

𝕩

Still, while there were those like Fergusson and Burns committed to the opposite camp, decades of pious exhortation do seem to have made the people of Edinburgh more godly. In return they influenced the character of the Church of Scotland, which remained plebeian in its ambitions, fervent in its devotions and homely in its preaching compared to, say, the Church of England.

Edinburgh housed the clique running the Kirk, but others of its ministers better reflected the popular character of Presbyterianism. The Reverends James Hart at Greyfriars and James Webster at the Tolbooth had denounced the Union and preached that its clerical supporters were traitors. Diehards felt unabashed when the Union went through regardless. The Reverend John McLaren at the Tolbooth, giving not a fig for the sovereignty of Westminster, raged against its interventions in Scotland. Most of the capital's ministers ignored its command that they should publicly condemn the Porteous Riot. But time showed the Presbyterian nationalism of old had to change. The Jacobites' approach in 1745 concentrated minds. While they wanted to restore Scottish independence, it was unlikely to be on terms Presbyterians could accept. At St Cuthbert's, the Reverend Neil McVicar found his own way of praying for Prince Charles Edward Stewart: 'In regard to the great man who has recently come among us in search of an earthly crown, may he soon obtain what is far better, a heavenly one.' By now the most popular preacher in Edinburgh was the Reverend Alexander Webster of the Tron, unusual in Evangelical circles in his capacity for drink: 'a five-bottle man, he could lay them all under the table'. Yet he never grew so befuddled as to be incapable of carrying out the unofficial Scottish census in 1755, by questionnaires he circulated to every minister in the country. The Kirk did sidle towards the modern world, then. Today's academics have with their best efforts been unable to find much wrong in Webster's results: he computed the population of Scotland at 1,265,000 and of Edinburgh at 55,000.[54]

The clique running the Kirk from Edinburgh tended in the long run to get its way, above all by keeping the British government sweet. The most devout Presbyterians then felt overborne by the less devout. There had since the Killing Time been a ready answer to such tension – schism. No less than four dissenting sects seceded from the Church of Scotland in the half-century after the Union: Auld Licht Burghers and New Licht Burghers, Auld Licht Anti-burghers and New Licht Anti-burghers. They once would have brought savage persecution down on themselves, but since 1707 there could be no question of that. Scott, on the contrary, was to find their sectarianism charming in the way it transformed the nation's intellectual vices, of hair-splitting and obtuseness, into virtues of honesty and constancy.

The difference between Auld Licht and New Licht was that the one regarded the Covenants as forever binding on Scots, while the other thought they might be adapted to changing needs. Meanwhile, those faithful to the Covenants had to live in an uncovenanted state, and the difference between Burghers and Anti-burghers lay in willingness, or not, to swear oaths it exacted – for example, of holders of public office. The four sects' names suggest their permutations of dogma on these matters. An unrelated secession in 1752 produced yet another, the Relief Church, more liberal in outlook. To balance it there were still the Cameronians or Reformed Presbyterians, even now refusing to accept the settlement of 1690, some indeed advocating armed resistance to the British state. A group of these suffered expulsion from a congregation in Lauriston Place as late as 1792, but then split among themselves into Lifters and Anti-Lifters (of the bread being blessed for communion). Dissent remained vigorous, then, and by the early nineteenth century accounted for 40 per cent of churchgoers in Edinburgh, mostly artisans.[55]

❧

One reason the sects flourished was the difficulty under the Union for the Kirk to maintain its vaunted apostolic purity. Corruptions crept in through legislation inspired by the perfidious English, but more through the native politics run by the ducal House of Argyll. Heads of that house had once been martyrs for the Covenant. Now they were deists, believing the universe to be guided by some divine force, maybe, but not by anything explicable in terms of Christian revelation. The second Duke of Argyll was also the one who set up the unionist regime of keeping Scotland quiet by distribution of patronage; it would survive for a quarter of a millennium. Among his many clients was the architect William Adam, who rebuilt both the duke's residence in Edinburgh at Caroline Park and his splendid feudal castle in the midst of Clan Campbell's territory at Inveraray in Argyll.

Adam, at his own townhouse in the Cowgate, ran a little intellectual salon where he liked to invite bright young candidates for the ministry of the Church of Scotland. One was his nephew

William Robertson, whom we have already met in future guise as principal of the University of Edinburgh. Among the others was Hugh Blair, who at the height of his career would be minister of the Canongate, then of St Giles, a charge he held concurrently with the chair at the university of rhetoric and belles-lettres (that is, as the first professor of English literature in the British Isles). Then there was Adam Ferguson, born in a Highland manse, who came south to qualify as a minister but then had problems finding a parish and would get a better bargain as professor of moral philosophy at the university. Another was John Home, son of the town clerk of Leith and minister of Athelstaneford, who would shock strict Calvinists by writing and staging a play, *Douglas*; later he left for London to become private secretary to the Prime Minister, Lord Bute. John Jardine, minister of the Tron, would forge a local political link as son-in-law to Drummond, the lord provost. Finally, Alexander 'Jupiter' Carlyle, minister of Inveresk, renowned for his good looks, verve and wit, would leave us his reminiscences of the rest. They were a good-humoured bunch and long recalled these student years as the best of their lives. Among the excitements was the approach in 1745 of the Jacobite army led by a Prince Charles the same age as themselves. They joined volunteers raised to defend the capital. As the clans occupied it, this force was disbanded without a fight. The friends might otherwise have been ordered out to the Battle of Prestonpans, to die alongside the redcoats; the history of Edinburgh would than have been different.[56]

Instead this younger generation could set out to take over the Kirk. It had to confront an older generation still championing orthodoxy and intransigence as the best defences of Presbyterianism. But the spirit of the age grew more secular, inclusive and elegant, while the new British state turned more venal, cynical and imperious. So the ground for battles in the cause of innovation sometimes looked rough.

For example, the rising ministerial stars rallied round the philosopher Hume and the judge Kames as they came under attacks threatening to ruin their careers. Hume's atheism had already ruled him out for the chair of moral philosophy at the University of Edinburgh on a vacancy in 1745 – though that did not sate his vengeful clerical enemies. Kames had said or done nothing so offensive, only expounded in his writings a standard theory of the Scottish Enlightenment that mankind had gone through successive stages of development, from hunting and gathering to commercial society, each marked by improved manners and advancing morality. It was an account leaving out the appearance, once and for all in human history, of a saviour. It could therefore be deemed heretical and deserving of censure.[57]

Militant Presbyterians determined to do for Hume and Kames in 1755. The Reverend John Bonar of Cockpen in Midlothian published a pamphlet attacking them for heresies which he called on the forthcoming General Assembly to condemn. If he had got his way, it would have stopped Hume ever finding any public preferment in Scotland, while Kames's position on the bench would have been compromised too. This was an extreme and provocative move. But by now most of the young ministers had parishes and so sat in the assembly. They did not like Hume's atheism or Kames's history with God left out. But they did recognize that fanatical attacks on Scots thinkers would show up the Church as an enemy of free enquiry and hold the whole country back. An older ally, the Reverend Robert Wallace of Greyfriars, asked if the assembly proposed to persecute 'calm contemplative wrongheaded writers' because it had got nowhere with 'drunkards, revellers, whore-mongers, adulterers': a good question.[58]

At that General Assembly, thanks to the youngsters' taking a hand, the charges of heresy were watered down almost to nothing. A hostile resolution, as at length amended and passed, did no more than point out the risks of impiety and immorality. 'My damnation is postponed for a twelvemonth,' Hume told Ramsay, 'but next Assembly will surely be upon me.' Yet the renewed attack in 1756 was repelled still more easily. It did not even get to the floor of the assembly, being instead sidelined in committee: this had all over it the fingerprints of Robertson, already a manipulator of genius. As for Kames, he had consulted his lawyers, who combined offence with defence. They set out his claims to 'freedom of enquiry and reasoning'. Then they published a pamphlet showing that, while he might never have mentioned any divine revelation, the judge and Jesus did not disagree. The move against Kames equally failed to get on the agenda of the assembly. He was found, despite questionable ideas and 'unguarded expressions', to have meant no harm to religion.[59]

Such was the bland, bureaucratic way presbytery had learned to go about its business while securing its hold on Scotland, with anything sensitive kept behind closed doors. But there were times when these tactics did not work. One came in 1756 after Home undertook to give his drama *Douglas* a public performance. The Kirk continued to denounce the theatre for promoting vice, onstage and off. Confrontation looked inevitable.

There seems little reason to doubt Home's claim of a moral purpose for his play, to show noble virtue triumphing over base treachery. In that it was no worse and no better than other productions of its time, equating the pathos onstage with the sympathy supposed to be excited in the audience. Most are forgotten, and a revival of *Douglas* at the Edinburgh Festival of 1986 showed it merited the same fate, at least as an aesthetic phenomenon. Perhaps Home had an uneasy sense he might have done better, to judge from a hammy patriotic appeal in the prologue:

> Often has this audience soft compassion shown
> To woes of heroes, heroes not their own.
> This night our scenes no common tear demand
> He comes, the hero of your native land.[60]

For the first night he need not have worried: there arose in the pit 'an uproar of exultation that a Scotchman had written a tragedy of the first rate'. Out of it came the cry, 'Whaur's yer Wullie Shakespeare noo?' Perhaps audiences of the eighteenth century just had a different taste.

The Kirk fumbled its response. Even clergymen had to admit Shakespeare might not be wholly bad. It was then awkward to explain why a playwright more decorous (to put it mildly) ought to be denied all tolerance, one of their own brethren though he might be. The presbytery of Edinburgh pressed on regardless and ordered an 'admonition and exhortation' to be read from every pulpit in the city, condemning plays as illegal and 'prejudicial to the interests of religion and morality'. Once again, an attempt to win the backing of the General Assembly was foiled. Home still thought it as well to resign his charge at Athelstaneford. He soon had bigger fish to fry in London.[61]

※

A pattern emerged from these disparate episodes and lesser ones. The Kirk was conceding secular autonomy in areas of life over which it had since 1690 – indeed since 1560 – claimed jurisdiction. This happened not only with the acquiescence but even with the connivance of a faction of the ministry in Edinburgh. Such men thought the world would improve not through ranting sermons and righteous wrath, rather through general social and intellectual advance to which they could and should be parties. In their outlook Christianity and Enlightenment converged.

The moving spirit of this enlightened Kirk was Robertson, especially after he took over at the University of Edinburgh in 1762. He made a fine principal. To be sure, he was a crafty autocrat. His vindication came in the results: out of an era of mediocrity he led the town's college to greatness. Edinburgh was still a poor institution (compared, say, with Oxford or Cambridge), and his genius lay in getting the best out of what he had. When he could he saw to the endowment of new chairs and filled them with brilliant professors (not usually drawing much pay, but living on fees they collected for lectures). He revised the curriculum – for example, so as to make moral philosophy compulsory for all taking arts, something that marked the Scottish intellect almost down to the present. His pot of gold was the medical school. It burgeoned until it accounted for 400 of the university's 1,000 students, drawing bright young men from as far away as America or Russia; here, given a successful professoriate, he was inclined to leave well alone and confine himself to financing new facilities. He did otherwise all he could for any project enhancing the intellectual life of college and town, from the Speculative Society for undergraduate debate (1764) to the Royal Society of Edinburgh for formal scholarly enquiry (1783).[62]

And Robertson left us the superb physical memorial of a new home for his university. Today perversely known as Old College, it was the greatest public architectural achievement of Robert Adam. Begun in 1789 though not finished until 1820, the composition is of elegant symmetry, a little ponderous in a Roman sort of way. But its monumental facade makes it the most magnificent building in the city. It might have looked yet more splendid if Adam had been able to realize his entire plan for the South Bridge, carrying a road from the High Street over the chasm of the Cowgate to the college. He wanted towering colonnaded buildings all along – but they proved too expensive, and in the end only ordinary tenements and shops could be afforded. Still, from the opposite end of this roadway, down the North Bridge, a fine view opens up of Adam's earlier Register House (1774), a design of less force but greater suavity – so along a single thoroughfare we may appreciate the range of his genius. Or at least that view would still be fine if the hideous St James's Centre (1970) had not been built behind it.[63]

The alliance Robertson personified at Edinburgh between Church and university was a prime feature of the Scottish Enlightenment. It made this Enlightenment different from others in Europe. Those in Paris and Berlin were in religion sceptical and in politics progressive (if in a despotic fashion). The enlightened men of Edinburgh espoused polite religion but still orthodox religion, and in politics remained conservative – the French Revolution, itself a product of Enlightenment, would horrify them. In a small nation with no power over its own fate, public aims had to be modestly confined to the general virtue and happiness expected from a society intent on rational progress. Scottish thinkers were reasonable without falling for elaborate constructions of rationality, unlike the Jacobins in France or idealists in Prussia. The Scots put humane values first. They took a rounded view of the past and present. They may have been almost too cosmopolitan when they wanted to emulate the example of England even while, as patriots, they strove for the equality of Scotland. But, whatever its incidental faults, the Scottish Enlightenment was much the nicest of them all – at its most agreeable in its social life, with good drink and good talk.

※

The main caveat to be entered about the role of Robertson and his Presbyterian circle is that they were not themselves thinkers of the first rank – except Ferguson, originator of the science of sociology by his authorship in 1767 of the *Essay on the History of Civil Society* (another work where God never appears). The two greatest figures of the Scottish Enlightenment, David Hume and Adam Smith, did not belong to Robertson's entourage. They had imbibed the Enlightenment in France, from French *philosophes*, French *physiocrates* – and French sceptics.

Hume was an atheist, intent on destroying the notion that morality proceeded out of the word of God. He discredited conventional morality by an analysis tearing apart the mental processes meant to make it plausible and by pointing up what absurdities it implied. He was the philosopher of perception and causation, then, in particular of necessity – or rather of the dangers of expecting too much from familiar conjunctions of cause and effect (the basis of one old argument for the existence of God). Hume often feared he was being too obscure yet he took care to lead his philosophy back to ordinary experience. When his opponents (not Robertson himself especially, but other enlightened Presbyterians) set out to answer Hume, they too relied on propositions of common sense, claiming God guaranteed proof of them where it seemed difficult. To their own satisfaction they succeeded in their task. Yet while Hume is still alive as a philosopher they, and the so-called philosophy of Common Sense they constructed, are dead. This philosophy all the same dominated Scottish universities until the mid-nineteenth century; it is now no more than a historical curiosity.

As for Smith, he too set out to posit, in his *Theory of Moral Sentiments* (1759), canons for conduct based not on theological but on material or rational assumptions, notably a natural sympathy among human beings. His *Wealth of Nations* (1776) was a similar exercise for the special case of what Scots called political economy, if with a slightly confusing emphasis on self-interest as motor. It let him argue that 'perfect liberty', not protectionist privilege, offered the best basis for progress. This bible of economics made him immortal, yet he meant it only as part of a greater project, never completed, of creating in several volumes an all-embracing explanation of human conduct, implicitly without reference to any divine revelation. Smith avoided polemics and never had to face Christian critique of his work. But he revealed one underlying impulse in a remark he made on Hume's death in 1776. Smith said his friend had approached in life 'as nearly to the idea of a perfectly wise and virtuous man, as perhaps the nature of human frailty will permit'.

In other words Smith, too, denied a necessary connection between Christianity and morality. In private he had been blunter, writing how Hume on his deathbed was departing 'with great cheerfulness and good humour and with more real resignation to the necessary course of things than any whining Christian ever died with pretended resignation to the will of God'.[64]

※

The Scottish Enlightenment otherwise focused on science. We met James Hutton earlier, chipping away at Salisbury Crags. His impact on geology compared with Hume's on philosophy or Smith's on economics, even if his fame never equalled theirs. He put forward his theory of the Earth in 1788 after decades of tireless observation. He reasoned the surface of the planet was at once being destroyed by erosion and remade from sediments first laid down in the sea then consolidated and elevated by heat. This cycle had been repeated, and would be repeated, endless times over an infinitely long period, so that no vestige of the original Earth remained and nothing could be known of it. With this bold thesis Hutton freed geology from theology and laid the foundation of the modern discipline – which still agrees with him on basics.[65]

Edinburgh pioneered chemistry as well. Joseph Black, another of the city's polymaths, pushed this science forward in fundamental ways. His own education had been medical, and it was while searching after a cure for kidney-stones that he investigated the nature of alkalis, first in practical applications such as bleaching cloth, boiling soap and making glass. Later he poured vitriol on chalk, limestone or magnesia, and gave the name of 'fixed air' to the gas released; we call it carbon dioxide. This discovery was a key to understanding a further range of empirical phenomena, from animal respiration to safety in mines to fertility in soil to making soda-water. On a conceptual level, Black probed the nature of heat in relation to different states of matter, hit on the theory of latent heat – and so came back to the everyday world in helping James Watt to understand how a steam engine might function. Then, suddenly, Black's studies in philosophical chemistry ended and his interests changed. This break in his career coincided with his appointment to a chair of medicine and chemistry at Edinburgh.[66]

The university was now, after decades of endeavour, becoming a centre of medical research, practice and teaching – in fulfilment at last of the hopes of Robert Sibbald and his fellows one hundred years before. By the first quarter of the nineteenth century Edinburgh would be producing more surgeons and doctors than anywhere else in Britain, with 2,000 degrees awarded during the period.[67] The real step forward from uncertain beginnings had come with the founding of a chair of anatomy in 1720. The inaugural holder was Alexander Monro *primus*, so called because he sired a dynasty. He stayed in harness up to his death in 1767, when his son Alexander Monro *secundus* succeeded him in the chair, he being followed on his own death in 1817 by his son Alexander Monro *tertius*, who expired only in 1859. More medical chairs were meanwhile created: half a dozen by the end of the eighteenth century. The professors could then cooperate on a diversity of courses leading to a comprehensive medical degree. For students this opened up a range of careers from scientific research to general practice. Patients, too, might now do more than submit to the inscrutable decrees of the Almighty, indeed were better off following the profane advice of professors. No wonder these came themselves to wield a godlike authority, over public health, the operating theatre, the student classroom. They all seemed to live a long time, which must have said something for their talents. And they were usually eager to cling to their chairs until the Grim Reaper prised them loose, as Robertson's frugal academic regime did not provide pensions. They also often wanted in clannish Scotland to make sure who would take over from them, preferably one of their own kin. The Monros were merely the best example of this veritably Sicilian nepotism.

No less Sicilian was the taste for vendetta. Enlightened Scots lost none of the national love of disputation, for which an advancing medical discipline offered plenty of scope. James Gregory, descendant of the mathematical adepts of the seventeenth century and now professor of the practice of physic at Edinburgh, vaunted polemics as part of the country's heritage. This was most obvious in religion, but 'even with the aid of the Holy Scriptures to enlighten their under-standing, determine their faith and soften their hardness of heart, theologians have differed rancorously on a thousand points. What better, then, could be expected of physicians and surgeons when left entirely to the faint light of their reason?' Or indeed when left to the darkness of their suspicions. Gregory first gained something more than medical renown in 1792, after supposing an anonymous pamphlet that defamed him to have been written by two professorial colleagues, a father and son, Alexander and James Hamilton. So, meeting James in the street, he beat him with his walking stick. Hamilton sued and won £100 damages. Gregory paid gladly, saying he would give £100 over again for a second go. He wrote in all seven volumes of attacks on and ripostes to his colleagues, covering 3,000 pages, collected in his *Historical Memoirs of the Medical War in Edinburgh*.[68]

Versatility was another attribute of the medical men. Charles Bell became a professor on the back of his service as chief surgeon at the Battle of Waterloo in 1815. To a later generation he was more renowned as the 'father of neurology'. He looked not only forwards but also backwards to an era when anatomy had been conceived as part of the divine plan; he wrote a study of the hand, demonstrating its design by God. A sensitive soul, half-scientist and half-artist, he taught the painter David Wilkie how to represent the blush on canvas. A more modern figure was William Pulteney Alison, who from his chair of physiology argued disease had more to do with poverty than with sin, the usual contemporary explanation. If he was right, there could be no argument against better public relief: he foreshadowed a system of collective, universal welfare. James Syme gained most renown as an innovator in operative technique, especially for the amputation of joints. But he too marked up achievement in a distant field, as inventor of the mackintosh: he found a solvent for india-rubber and the means of impregnating cloth with it, though it was Charles Mackintosh who took out the patent. Syme cut an awesome figure. A colleague said he 'never wastes a word, a drop of ink or a drop of blood'. He played on others' expectations of his aloof and imperious nature. Once he received a patient he had treated for an anal fistula, but gave no sign of recognition. Only when the man bared his bottom for examination did Syme exclaim: 'Ah, now I know who you are.'

Not just the professors' temper but also the futility as yet of much treatment, especially of infectious diseases, fuelled the polemics. The major advances in knowledge occurred for the time being in anatomy. Understanding here could often be extended only by trial and error. The cost might fall on patients who never got up from the operating table or, better, on the dead coming into the surgeons' hands not for surgery but for dissection. The university could by law lay claim to the cadavers of hanged criminals, though they were too few to meet the needs of tuition. A student of Monro *tertius* recalled: 'In Dr Monro's class, unless there be a fortunate succession of bloody murders, not three subjects are dissected in the year. On the remains of a subject fished up from the bottom of a tub of spirits are demonstrated those delicate nerves, which are to be avoided or divided in our operations; and these are demonstrated once at the distance of one hundred feet.'[69]

An alternative source existed to the gallows: the cemeteries. There the 'resurrection men' saw to a supply of bodies by digging them up from their fresh graves after dark. Older churchyards in Edinburgh still have the watch-houses built to deter this ghoulish enterprise. But it was hard to suppress while there existed a demand for dead bodies in a market for medical instruction. The market was created by men worthy of a chair at the university but lacking the connections to get one. They could all the same, because of the great influx of students to Edinburgh, earn their bread by setting up as private tutors in the streets round the Old College. From the fees they collected, they paid for bodies to dissect in front of their classes.

The best of these freelances was Robert Knox. He attracted hundreds to his lectures and left the classes of Monro *tertius* empty. With a blasted eye and satanic smile, Knox made an unlikely ladies' man or object of devotion to pupils. Yet he was both: women fell for him still faster than the male students, who found him, unlike Monro, considerate of them, eloquent at the rostrum and eager to impart his mastery of medicine worldwide. He bought his cadavers from two Irish labourers, William Burke and William Hare, who dispensed with the bother of digging up bodies and smothered victims in the slums of the West Port where they were unlikely to be missed. When their crimes came to light in 1829, Burke was hanged after Hare turned king's evidence, while Knox had to flee Edinburgh, pursued by the mob.

Medical advance, the whole project of scientific Enlightenment, perhaps the very progress of Edinburgh, seemed to have turned sour, at least in the court of public opinion. Scott could not suppress a macabre fascination. But when he went back – in a carriage – to streets he had walked as a student he was filled with horror and shame at the thought that, if people like him had stayed in the Old Town, it might never have sunk so low. And he wrote: 'I am no great believer in the extreme degree of improvement to be derived from the advancement of science; for every pursuit of that nature tends, when pushed to a certain extent, to harden the heart, and render the philosopher reckless of everything save the objects of his own pursuit; all equilibrium in the character is destroyed.'[70]

⁂

If in equivocal fashion, progress had taken place all the same. Enlightened Edinburgh might no longer have been a royal residence or political capital or much of a commercial centre, but it succeeded as a republic of letters. Its great men were intellectuals, in old disciplines or new; amazing was the number of them adept in several. Tobias Smollett in his novel *Humphrey Clinker* (1771) had the misanthropic hero, Matthew Bramble, declare in awe while writing home: 'Edinburgh is a hotbed of genius'. And the printer William Smellie quoted a real-life visitor saying, 'Here I stand at what is called the Cross of Edinburgh and can, in a few minutes, take fifty men of genius and learning by the hand.' Still, there were costs too, in a loss of human intimacy and human sympathy: not quite what the Enlightenment intended.[71]

Though more than one group had risen in the city, the liberal professions especially prospered. Their rule has hardly been challenged since – it made and makes Edinburgh unique. Surely there had to be matching falls, though. One came for the merchant elite, dominant since the burgh began. The merchants had lost the business of the royal court in 1603, then of the Scots Parliament in 1707. The long economic slump that followed did them more damage. Despite an effective majority in the town council guaranteed by the burgh's sett, they could no longer casually wield their privilege. Indeed in 1729 the council announced an end to its rigid controls on commercial activity by people not members of the merchants' guild, always provided they 'occupied some low and inconsiderable branches of trade such as the retail of ale, beer, milk, horsehiring, cowfeeding and the like'. The strings did not stay long attached. In an economy opening up, the merchants' monopoly just crumbled away.

The terms of the Union made no alteration to the sett, but did transform that wider context which had sometimes allowed the council a degree of independence, either with the support of the crown against the nobility or later against the crown itself, once the Stewarts began to oppress Scotland. After 1707 the priority of the councillors, along with all other Scots, had to be finding a place on the chains of dependence by which the governors of Hanoverian Britain controlled it. The city's MP, Sir George Warrender, summed the task up when he told the council in 1715 'to shun extremes and to consider the need we have of favour'.[72]

The town council took Warrender's advice and pursued a course of studied sycophancy, especially towards the House of Argyll soon ruling the roost in Scottish politics. In fact this won no favour. Twice in the first half-century of the Union the city was humiliated on purpose for failings just as well to be laid at the door of the Hanoverian state. The first time came after the Porteous Riot of 1736. In London's view, this could never have happened without local connivance. Harsh penalties were proposed: burning the burgh's charter, dissolving the town guard and knocking down the Netherbow Port (so troops might enter the High Street more easily). The second Duke of Argyll managed to soften the spite. Still the lord provost, Alexander Wilson, was deposed and disqualified for life, while the city had to pay a heavy fine. Another burst of English displeasure came after 1745. The effortless Jacobite seizure of the capital was in turn blamed on the lord provost, Archibald Stewart (rather than, say, on the British regiment which had run away from Coltbridge). Stewart was shut up in the Tower of London and tried for neglect of duty, though acquitted.

The Argylls' regime did not survive the death of the third duke in 1761. Gilbert Laurie, failed lawyer turned apothecary, ran the council for a while. But he had sense to see he could not keep control without more powerful backing. So Edinburgh set out in quest of another patron. Muscling his way in came the Nabob of the North (parvenus were called nabobs after those who got rich quick in India). This was Sir Lawrence Dundas, high-handed and ruthless but local lad made good, son of a draper who had begun his career selling stockings in the Luckenbooths. He later earned a fortune, first as commissary to the Duke of Cumberland during his march to Culloden, then in the Seven Years' War. Dundas returned to Edinburgh its richest man. In 1764 he had himself appointed governor of the Royal Bank of Scotland (founded in 1727 as a unionist rival to the Bank of Scotland). In 1767 he persuaded Parliament to pass the Edinburgh Improvement Act, the enabling legislation for the New Town. In 1768 he was elected MP, after lavish donations to the Merchant Company and its charities. The merchants observed with notable disingenuity: 'It is more agreeable to our happy constitution that a member be chosen by the free voice of the electors than in consequence of solicitations or other more unwarrantable means.'[73]

Boswell called Dundas a 'comely, jovial Scotch gentleman of good address but not bright parts'. While at his best a benefactor, he always made sure to look after number one. For example, he appropriated in secret the plot of land at the far eastern end of the New Town, disfiguring the symmetry of Craig's original plan. The church designated for that site was instead set awkwardly to one side of George Street, while Dundas built himself the palatial house still standing there, later the seat of the Royal Bank. Through a council led by Laurie, Sir Lawrence could be as insolent as he liked. The city soon felt itself a mere prop for his ambitions. Poisonous pamphlets appeared mocking 'the stout Earl of the German plains' on account of his humble origins, flashiness and yen for a peerage.[74]

A challenge came at length from a distant kinsman, Henry Dundas. As Lord Advocate of Scotland from 1775, Henry set out to seize the patronage of Edinburgh for himself. The older, declining mercantile interest round Sir Lawrence was forced into a losing battle against Henry's cohorts among the new and rising forces in the city, the incoming landed gentry or the legal establishment servicing them.

One key to the struggle lay in control of the Royal Bank. Henry seized it from Sir Lawrence by some notably dirty work in 1777, and made Buccleuch its governor in his stead.

The struggle would only come to an end with Sir Lawrence's death in 1781. Henry reflected: 'The party left by Sir Lawrence must be broke, and the town of Edinburgh brought under some respectable patron on which government can rely, for they must not be permitted to govern the town by a knot of themselves without the imposition of some such patron.' The patron might be Buccleuch, for example (Dundas actually meant himself as the duke's political mentor). In that case 'the whole council of Edinburgh will be completely and permanently placed, as they used to be, in the hands of government.' History was then rewritten. The council, by this time set in its sycophantic ways, bowed down all the lower to Henry Dundas.[75]

⚜

A generation later the subservience still seemed entire to Henry Cockburn, Dundas's nephew (though political opponent). Wanting to paint a picture of municipal affairs, Cockburn started with the council's premises:

> a low, dark, blackguard-looking room, entering from a covered passage which connected the south-west corner of the Parliament Square with the Lawnmarket. At its Lawnmarket end this covered passage opened out on the south side of the 'Heart of Midlothian' ... The Council Chamber entered directly from this passage, and, if it had remained, would have been in the east end of the Writers'[Signet] Library. The chamber was a low-roofed room, very dark, and very dirty, with some small dens off it for clerks.
>
> Within this Pandemonium sat the town council, omnipotent, corrupt, impenetrable. Nothing was beyond its grasp; no variety of opinion disturbed its unanimity, for the pleasure of Dundas was the sole rule for every one of them. Reporters, the fruit of free discussion, did not exist; and though they had existed, would not have dared to disclose the proceedings. Silent, powerful, submissive, mysterious and irresponsible, they might have been sitting in Venice.

For effect Cockburn overdid the omnipotence; in fact the council had lost power. It was an object of disdain to those now treating Edinburgh as an aristocratic resort. Lady Elizabeth Grant of Rothiemurchus came of a landed family in the north of Scotland, one owning a townhouse in Charlotte Square. Earlier the Grants had been a gutless clan, swithering between Stewarts and Hanoverians, above all keeping their heads down. Who was she to scorn the lord provost's political coyness? Yet she dismissed him as 'a tradesman of repute among his equals, and in their society he was content to abide'.[76]

On his death in 1811 Dundas, now Viscount Melville, left control of capital and country to his son, the second viscount. He felt appalled at the state of the town council and 'the public inconvenience, to say nothing of the personal and constant plague arising from an inefficient and unsafe magistracy'. He was right to worry: bankruptcy threatened after Edinburgh spent £300,000 on improvements to the harbour at Leith.

For any hope Leith might catch up again with Glasgow it had to have a better harbour. The Shore, with its quays at the mouth of the Water of Leith, could not take many ships and no big ships at all. The approaches were shallow and encroached on from the east by a shifting sand-bar. When in 1821 George IV arrived in his royal yacht, not a huge vessel, he had to anchor two miles out and clamber into a lighter to come ashore – with difficulty, given how fat he was.

There had been a plan to deal with all this since 1799. Its author, John Rennie, proposed to block the progress of the sand-bar by a pier to the east and to form a fresh approach through three connected wet docks to the west, stretching over a mile to the greater depth of water at Newhaven. Some work was carried out – though at staggering cost, largely borrowed from the British government on the security of Edinburgh's rates. Still the plan remained incomplete. In 1824 William Chapman updated and extended it. He had the pier on the east lengthened by 500 yards and an outer harbour formed on the west. The only trouble with this definitive scheme was that it led to the bankruptcy of the city of Edinburgh in 1833.

Town councillors had seen it coming. This was why they piled duties on ships and cargoes at Leith. Captains entering the port had to pay anchorage, beaconage, berthage, flaggage, pilotage and dock dues, even before officers of HM Customs arrived to charge them on the contents of the hold. Such practice hardly encouraged use of the harbour, the point of the whole exercise. Trade stagnated and in some years fell, to the profit of Grangemouth and Dundee. The council had little choice but to go back to the government, which for a final loan in 1826 took security of all the town's property, including the docks. The last resort was a scheme for a joint-stock company to own and run the port from dues charged at a rate enabling its debts to be serviced. This rate, local merchants could see, would ruin them. And who would be shareholders of the company? Why, the councillors of Edinburgh, after flogging its property to themselves.

Melville sought compromise. He vested control of the harbour in commissioners drawn in equal numbers from capital and port. But the result was deadlock broken only when Edinburgh did go bankrupt, overwhelmed by its deficit and unable to borrow more. Some debt was cancelled and some rescheduled. The government made the commission for the harbour tripartite, with its own delegates to hold the balance between the two sides. And it liberated Leith from long thraldom by turning it into a separate burgh.[77]

This was crushing defeat for Edinburgh. Its independence of five centuries under royal charter would shortly come to an end. The Municipal Corporations (Scotland) Act of 1833 put the capital on a par with any other burgh – every one now a creature of the absolute sovereignty of the British Parliament. But all the people rejoiced.

CHAPTER SIX

'CITY OF REFUGE'

(Henry Cockburn)

ON AN EVENING early in March 1828, Thomas Carlyle set out from his home in Comely Bank, at the north-western extremity of Edinburgh, walked east to Stockbridge and crossed the Water of Leith, then climbed the steep hill to Great King Street, to the home of the philosopher Sir William Hamilton. Carlyle was on his way to one of Hamilton's literary salons. He would join James Browne, editor of the *Caledonian Mercury*, who for all his usual ebullience sat blushing because in print he had sneered at Carlyle's 'murky cloud of German Transcendentalism'; Thomas de Quincey, still spaced out 'in the low stage of his opium-regimen'; Thomas Hamilton, younger brother of Sir William, hero of the Peninsular War and author of a now neglected novel, *Cyril Thornton*; George Moir, already the translator of Schiller and afterwards the professor of rhetoric at the University of Edinburgh; James Russell, its professor of clinical surgery; and a Captain Skinner of Kirkcaldy, hotfoot from Weimar, who sang to the company a setting of Goethe's poem 'Kennst du das Land, wo die Zitronen blühen?'. The air of the soirée was Teutonic, evidently. It appeared to make Carlyle feel even gloomier than usual, though he was no stranger to the national conviviality. He later groused: 'Cyril Thornton and I drank half a glass of claret, and supped on one potato each. One "mealy root"; and this without comment from anyone, which I reckoned polite.'[1]

A single slightly grim evening did not affect the friendship of Hamilton and Carlyle, which they cultivated on long walks together in the scenic surroundings of the capital – if very much in the guise of master and pupil. Hamilton was a man of distinguished antecedents, though of the mind rather than of the blood implied in the dormant baronetcy he had reclaimed from a covenanting ancestor. In fact he came of a kind of academic dynasty typical in Scotland, and had been born not in a stately home but actually inside the old college of Glasgow. His father was professor of anatomy there, like before him his father, who had helped to set up its school of medicine. When young William began his studies in the same hallowed halls, he also meant to follow a medical career. Transfer to the University of Oxford widened his horizons even if, like many Scots, he thought little of the place. He did find himself, by its lights, well-read. For his degree, in which he took a brilliant first, he offered four times as many Latin classics as stood on the syllabus and knew more Aristotle than anybody else in the university. Yet he was offered no fellowship: Tory Oxford still disliked Scots Whigs. So, it would turn out, did Tory Edinburgh.

Hamilton returned as would-be continuator of the philosophy of Common Sense. This had flagged after finishing its self-appointed task of finding answers to the scepticism of David Hume, and thinkers elsewhere in Europe were losing interest in what Scots found to say. In his project of renewing the national school, Hamilton did not beat about the bush. At the first chance in 1819 he went straight for the most eminent academic chair in Scotland, if not in Britain, the chair of moral philosophy at Edinburgh, a focal point whence the Enlightenment had diffused its glow. As with most chairs at the town's college, the council elected to it. First refusal had been offered to Sir James Mackintosh, lawyer, social theorist and now MP following imperial service in India, but he was another Scot preferring to spend more time with his opium-pipe. Two younger candidates then appeared, John Wilson, the dark horse, and Hamilton, the abler man. Wilson won for being the Tory candidate; Hamilton lost for being the Whig.

But Whigs had been building their own networks, notably in the Faculty of Advocates. Hamilton joined it even though he nursed no legal ambitions, a common ploy among rising stars in Edinburgh – the faculty retained a cultural, not just professional role in the life of the city. Within months his move paid off in the shape of an academic consolation prize. The university boasted a chair of universal history (no less) for which, exceptionally, the faculty held the patronage. The chair had been erected a century earlier to give students of Scots law some background to their subject's Roman sources. It was in effect a sinecure, but men of merit had occupied it and gone on to greater things. So would Hamilton, after his colleagues at the bar chose him for it. He wasted no time on universal history but pursued his mission of rescuing the philosophy of Common Sense. He set out to do so by linking it with the revolutionary developments in German philosophy, above all the teachings of Immanuel Kant.

❧

In metaphysical Scotland this mission did not necessarily lead up an ivory tower. To Hamilton and others like him, the *Edinburgh Review*, the most famous periodical in the world, stood ever ready to open its pages. It had been launched in 1802 under the editorship of Francis Jeffrey, working with a group of friends who, like him, were failing to make it at the Scots bar. Most of these bright young Whigs had been pupils at Edinburgh of a pioneer of Common Sense, Dugald Stewart, who himself had been a pupil of Adam Smith. But the Scots bar, like the nation's political establishment in general, remained at that point conservative, not to say reactionary, in the face of the threat posed to Britain by revolutionary France. The *Edinburgh Review* first appeared during an interval of peace between the two powers. After a decade of war they had just signed the Treaty of Amiens, but they would before long break it and embark on an even longer phase of struggle destined to go on until the Battle of Waterloo in 1815. In Edinburgh meanwhile, those advocates who were anything less than true-blue got no briefs. They had to live off something else.

The *Edinburgh Review* filled the bill. With its lengthy, weighty articles on great issues of the day, and its shorter, sharper critiques of books just out, it represented a revolution of its own, a journalistic one. Before it appeared, no British newspaper or magazine wrote in any candid fashion about politics, let alone culture; the press was shackled by regulation or bought by subsidies from the government or full of puffs for people the editors knew. By contrast, the *Edinburgh Review* set out to mould opinion by force of argument. It was in effect the ancestor of modern serious journalism – clever, probing, irreverent. It succeeded because it identified a gap in the market among a rising bourgeoisie wanting to learn about and judge of events for itself. According to Henry Cockburn, Jeffrey's sidekick and biographer, it was 'an entire and instant change of everything that the public had been accustomed to in that sort of composition ... The learning of the new journal, its writing, its independence, were all new; and the surprise was increased by a work so full of public life springing up, suddenly, in a remote part of the kingdom' (meaning Edinburgh). That did not stop some locals taking a dim view of it. Sir Walter Scott observed in scorn how the authors 'have a great belief in the influence of fine writing and think that a nation can be governed by pamphlets and reviews'.[2]

Strictures on Jeffrey have not stopped there. Acknowledged though he was on every hand as the leading literary critic of his time, it is hard from the distance of two centuries to see why. In fact he failed to appreciate some of the best and most enduring works of his contemporaries. In England, he found no virtue in the Lake Poets, Samuel Taylor Coleridge, Robert Southey or William Wordsworth. He dismissed Wordsworth's 'The Excursion' with the terse comment, 'This will never do.' His attack on Lord Byron provoked the latter's satire *English Bards and Scotch Reviewers*, in an altercation from which Jeffrey came off worse. In Scotland, he criticized Scott's *Marmion* for its 'faults' – a choice of word showing a lack of sympathy with, if not plain failure to understand, the romantic sensibility. Jeffrey remained in his aesthetics a man of the eighteenth century, holding to standards of literary correctness he identified with artificial diction and deliberate design. Carlyle, one of his own contributors, called him 'a potential Voltaire' who had yet turned out 'not deep enough, pious or reverent enough to have been great in Literature', and instead had rendered criticism banal. Quite so: he urged his readers to 'adopt a style of literary and political principles, which was rooted, not in eternal principles, but in the ordinary experience of ordinary literate and responsible men living in the modern age'.[3]

Jeffrey's complacency might not have been so bad if it had stopped at his criticism. But his cultural mousiness and conceited modishness made him represent at large a conventional middle-class respectability. He and his circle had an obsession with correct English and a horror of the old Scots tongue. The fact a man used it, as anyone from the common people to the judges in the Court of Session still did, was enough to mark him down as barbarous.

Probably Jeffrey himself already spoke in the strangled tones adopted since his time by the bourgeoisie of Edinburgh – one judge whose accent he reproved said, on his return from finishing his education at Oxford, that 'he has tint [lost] his Scots and found nae English'.[4]

Jeffrey's outlook never got him far in literature, yet in politics it stood him in good stead. Because of the war with France, he had pulled his partisan punches in the early numbers of the *Edinburgh Review*. Given his immediate success there, the Scots bar felt embarrassed to keep him without work, and so he began to pick up briefs. Not all earned him money, for he was often asked to defend radical scapegoats of the Tory government's internal repression. He did that for free, but his prowess in the courtroom made him in effect a leader of the Scottish political opposition, which was mostly extra-parliamentary. He struck out in favour of reform, above all constitutional reform, the case for which strengthened amid economic and social crises after the war. The landed and legal class long in charge of Scotland found its grip loosening, though it could still stop its foes getting to Westminster. Not until the unreformed system started to break down did Jeffrey manage that. He then became Lord Advocate, chief officer of Scottish government.

The local Whigs whom Jeffrey led were unashamed admirers of England, in their eyes the home of liberty ever since the Glorious Revolution of 1688. Cockburn seemed seriously to believe Englishmen ought to run Scotland. He now rejoiced at a prospective end of 'the horrid system of being ruled by a native jobbing Scot' and told Jeffrey that 'the nearer we can propose to make ourselves to England the better'. So the Lord Advocate took the opportunity of the Reform Act of 1832, which he piloted through in its Scottish version, to start getting rid of uncouth relics of the old Scotland and imposing the model of modernity England offered. Then, having created a popular Scots electorate for the first time, he decided he had done enough. Running out of steam, he did not linger in office. He promoted himself to the judicial bench, where he sat, full of years and honour, until his death in 1850.[5]

By then Jeffrey and his fellow reviewers could feel well pleased with themselves. Imitation is the sincerest form of flattery, and they created a product so successful that dozens of other reviews sprang to life, in Scotland, England, Europe and America, each with its own opinions and qualities. During the Victorian era, reviews became forums for society at large to work out its problems, not just cultural but also political and economic. Hamilton's series of philosophical articles for the *Edinburgh Review* over four years from 1829 marked a step towards that higher function. As his definitive restatement of Scottish thought and its relation to German thought emerged, it needed only the death of Scott for Hamilton to step forward as a new leader of enlightened Scotland.

☙

Scott died in 1832 as reform was handing power from Tories to Whigs. But the Tories had fought all the way, and one of their stratagems was a review of their own – *Blackwood's Edinburgh Magazine*, founded in 1817 by a publishing entrepreneur, William Blackwood. As editors he chose John Wilson and John Gibson Lockhart, who called it the *Maga* for short.

Wilson was a large, lusty fellow, intellectual yet clubbable, generous yet capricious, a mass of contradictions. Born at Paisley, son of a rich manufacturer, he too had finished his education at Oxford. Next he went to Westmorland to hobnob with the Lake School and write some poetry himself. Forced to return by the bankruptcy of his father, in Edinburgh he hoped to recoup his fortunes at the bar – but never did. So he had time for a wide circle of friends and scope for his prolific journalism under the pen-name of Christopher North. More than any of his contributors, he turned away from the Whigs' obsession with correct English. He composed his pieces in vivid Scots, wrote them in haste and dipped his pen in vitriol: all of which made them better. That was also the sum of his qualifications for the chair of moral philosophy at Edinburgh.

Lockhart brought the *Maga* a connection it treasured. He married Scott's daughter Sophia and would become his biographer. Altogether he grew almost too devoted to the great man; it has struck some as fitting that, in death, he lies in Dryburgh Abbey at Sir Walter's feet. It was the quirky old Scotland rather than the bright new Scotland that *Blackwood's* sought to reflect. Lockhart hated Whigs. He thought their offensive habits of mind grew out of the 'diet of levity and sarcastic indifference' they had swallowed in the high Enlightenment. He picked on Hume as one so stunted that his lack of feeling had 'acted with all the force of a terrible lever in pulling him down from the height of authority to which the spring of his originality had elevated him'. An intellectual movement led by him could not have produced and never did produce imaginative literature of any worth. Lockhart concluded of its luminaries: 'Their disquisitions on morals were meant to be the vehicles of ingenious theories – not of connections of sentiment. They employed, therefore, even in them, only the national intellect, and not the national modes of feeling.' So they had turned out unpatriotic too. And the heir of Hume was Jeffrey (a judgement vastly overrating Jeffrey).[6]

The *Maga* carried as its foremost feature the 'Noctes Ambrosianae', satirical pieces written anonymously by Wilson and Lockhart, who levelled a brilliant, cutting wit at complacent Whigs and other Aunt Sallies. Each took the form of an imaginary conversation (no doubt drawing on real ones) among contributors to *Blackwood's* at their drinking den, Ambrose's Tavern in Picardy Place. Funny, racy and pungent, the talk ranged over people, events and books, shrinking from no raillery, libel or slander.

※

The biggest character in the 'Noctes' wore a thin disguise as the Ettrick Shepherd: in real life, this was James Hogg. A Borderer, he had grown up poor and illiterate but in adulthood carved out for himself a versatile literary career. By the time he got to *Blackwood's*, to help with the editing, he was a celebrity. He had mixed feelings about this. Soon he would be overcome not just by pleasure at inclusion in a charmed circle but also by unease at the mischief it made. Taking a rise out of Whigs was fair enough, yet the portrayal of himself in the 'Noctes' seemed none too flattering either. Indeed Lockhart and Wilson acted towards him with a patronizing snobbery which today would be outrageous, though then it appeared normal to young chaps of their class. Hogg protested to Scott: 'I am neither a drunkard nor an idiot nor a monster of nature.' The gibes never got him down yet they did let him be taken less seriously than he ought to have been, then and long afterwards.[7]

Scott had written a great novel of Edinburgh; Hogg wrote a yet greater one, *The Private Memoirs and Confessions of a Justified Sinner* (1824). It remains little known outside its city or country. Yet many think it the finest of all Scottish novels in its miraculous subtlety of construction.

The *Private Memoirs* was already underrated in its own time. On the one hand, its vernacular vigour struck the genteel as an insult to refined modern taste. And its relentless interrogation of Presbyterianism made it, on the other hand, in the eyes of the devout no better than an infidel polemic. The blend proved enough to consign it to obscurity for over a century. Then in 1947 a new edition was published with a glowing introduction by the French novelist André Gide. Knowing almost nothing of Hogg, or of Scottish history and literature, Gide came to the work with an open mind. And he read it 'with a stupefaction and admiration that increased at every page ... It is long since I can remember being so taken hold of, so voluptuously tormented by any book.' Later critics have followed him. Now everybody appreciates its Gothic horror, its unsparing satire of religious hypocrisy and bigotry, its dissection of the totalitarian mentality, its honest realism about criminals and prostitutes, its acute analysis of mental breakdown and schizophrenia. It is rich not only in content but also in form, in its echoes of Romantic poetry, its exploitation of the Doppelgänger as literary device, its mixture of tragedy with comedy through ironies, symbols and puns.[8]

Hogg is indeed concerned with religion here, but at the service of art rather than of theology. The motor of the action is a Calvinist heresy, antinomianism, which asserts the elect of God cannot be damned even in committing the foulest crimes, because they are predestined to salvation. The arid logic comes to life against a vivid interplay of character and incident, much of it set in Edinburgh just before the Union of 1707. The tension in the air is such that a walk up Salisbury Crags can produce hallucinations, while the Old Town forms a perfect backdrop to still deeper confusions of mind and sense. At one point, mutually hostile mobs of Whigs and Jacobites rush back and forth through closes and wynds, disappearing and reappearing, until two groups on the same side attack each other. They realize what they have done only when, bloody, battered and bruised, they come to be treated by the same surgeons. Such is the vanity of human perceptions and of human affairs in general.

20} Modern flats replaced medieval jumble, as at Milne's Court (1690). In this photograph of 1910 it has degenerated into a slum for the barefoot, but today it has been restored.

21} By the end of the seventeenth century the city had an industrial suburb in Dean Village, where the mills were powered by the Water of Leith, shown in this engraving by John Slezer.

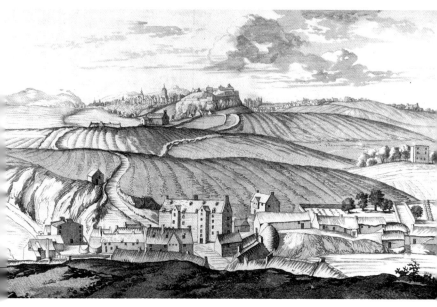

22} The people of Edinburgh remained recalcitrant and defied authority in the Porteous Riot of 1736, painting by Drummond.

23} Romantic past and rational present came together in the works of Sir Walter Scott (1771–1832), portrayed with family at his country house of Abbotsford by Wilkie.

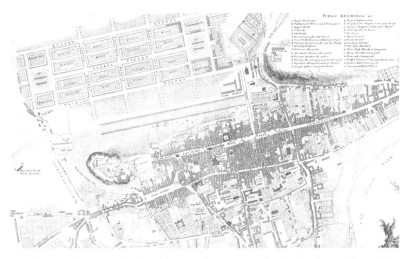

24} Romantic past and rational present also came together in the physical shape of the city with Old Town and New Town juxtaposed, shown in this map of 1773 by William Faden and Thomas Jefferys.

25} The opulence of the interiors matched the grandeur of the exteriors as in the dining room at 7 Charlotte Square, today headquarters of the National Trust for Scotland.

26} The view down the High Street from the Cross of Edinburgh where, an English visitor said, he could 'in a few minutes take fifty men of genius and learning by the hand', painting by Allan.

27} These were also troubled, revolutionary times and patriotic citizens enlisted in the Royal Edinburgh Volunteers, sketch by Jenkins.

28} The prophet of doom for the modern era was Thomas Carlyle (1795–1881), portrait by Millais.

29} Yet the domestic life of Edinburgh went on, perturbed by nothing more than the sort of social awkwardness portrayed in *The Letter of Introduction* by Wilkie.

30} The greatest lord provost of the nineteenth century was William Chambers (1800–83) who cleared slums from the quarter of the city now dominated by the National Museum of Scotland, which his statue surveys.

31} Edinburgh's Victorian paradoxes found their great literary metaphor in *The Strange Case of Dr Jekyll and Mr Hyde* by Robert Louis Stevenson (1850–94), portrait by Nerli.

32} Respectability was due in large part to the lawyers of the city: here the Lord Advocate, Francis Jeffrey (1773–1850), statue by Steell.

33} Victorian certainties were shattered by the First World War, commemorated at Edinburgh Castle by Robert Lorimer's solemn and beautiful shrine to the collective sacrifice of the Scots people.

34} Government returned to Edinburgh when the Scottish Office was transferred from London in 1939 to a purpose-built home at St Andrew's House, by Thomas Tait.

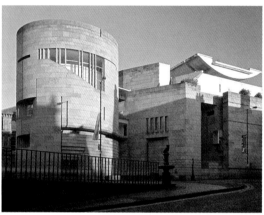

35} Distinguished modernist architecture found a belated continuation in the extension of the National Museum of Scotland (1998) by Gordon Benson and Alan Forsyth . . .

36} . . . and reaches fulfilment in the restored Scottish Parliament (2003), by architect Enric Moralles, where in the think-pods the future of the nation is pondered.

While Wilson could never have plumbed such profundity, he was the one who in his time acquired at least the outward trappings of serious intellectual status. Yet he hardly tried to teach his students any moral philosophy, and got his lectures written by a complaisant friend. If he had a pedagogic role it came out rather in his own salon, held at home in Ann Street. While no doubt his boozing buddies turned up too, these soirées took on their bohemian air rather from the presence of artists, of painters or sculptors. The rollicking 'Noctes' do sometimes reveal a more sensitive side to Wilson, showing among other things how he was a connoisseur of the Scottish school of art. He befriended the painters Alexander Nasmyth, Henry Raeburn and David Wilkie, as well as the sculptor John Steell.

Nasmyth upheld a tradition dating from the start of the Scottish school a century before, that its artists should go to refine their technique in Italy. There he copied works by old masters in the various cities where they were housed. For light relief he would paint his own pictures of the surrounding *campagna*. His mature landscapes of Scotland, most of the Highlands but some of the Lothians too, displayed according to *Blackwood's* 'a prodigious power of perspective'. If, however, they bathe in more sunshine than seems quite realistic, and if that sunshine points up greens dark enough for cypress (which yet cannot be cypress here in his chilly homeland), then the Italian influence is probably the reason. Later study of French and Dutch landscapes brought Nasmyth closer to a northern style of realism. The overall effect was to imbue him with a classical restraint to which he gave a romantic twist – a refreshing blend of his own. He saw himself as reproducing nature: 'The nearer you can get to it the better,' he said. When Nasmyth died in 1840, Wilkie wrote: 'He was the founder of the landscape painting school in Scotland, and by his taste and talent has for many years taken the lead in the patriotic aim of enriching his native land with the representations of her romantic scenery.'[9]

Raeburn had also spent time in Italy. He made himself a master of portrait, ready once he got home again to put Edinburgh's great and good on canvas. If today we feel we know them better than Scots of any other age, we owe that to his vivid and revealing art. In a grey city, his instinct is to let the light tell him how his subjects actually look, rather than rely on any preconception of how they ought to look. Yet he manages to show them in a moral, not just physical sense; he paints their characters, not just their features. Among his best subjects are people who have lived long enough for experience to mark them, such as mature women. His Highland chiefs come across splendidly as well, for the ruder virtues to be glimpsed through the polite veneer they put on for the capital – a blend equivalent in paint to what Scott committed to print in *Waverley* or *The Lady of the Lake*. Of Sir Walter himself Raeburn produced two portraits, the first of a youngster, a restless poetic genius tensed to burst on the world, the second of an older and wiser man, his humanity deepened by tribulation. Robert Louis Stevenson would write that Raeburn could 'plunge at once through all the constraint and embarrassment of the sitter and present the face, clear, open and intelligent as at the most disengaged moments'.[10] If he is romantic, he is not sentimental. Nor does he reproach or satirize his subjects. Painter and sitter share standards and values. A classical Scottish culture is there for all to see.

In chapter 21 of *The Antiquary* (1816), Scott paid homage to the third painter frequenting the salon in Ann Street: 'In the inside of the cottage was a scene which our Wilkie could have painted, with that exquisite feeling of nature that characterizes his enchanting productions.' He responded that these words had placed him under 'a debt of obligation' as 'with an unseen hand in The Antiquary, you took me up, and claimed me, the humble painter of domestic sorrow, as your countryman'. It was a typically modest sentiment. Born in the Howe of Fife, son of the minister of Cults, young Wilkie had moved to London to learn the art of portraiture – in which he turned out good, if not as great as Raeburn. Yet his own study of Scott and family at Abbotsford was a masterpiece of homely restraint, under-stood in Scotland for its sympathetic insight into a private sphere but offensive in England for depicting a 'vulgar group' unworthy of an 'elegant poet'. It pointed the way for Wilkie to develop his true genius in genre painting, the depiction of domestic scenes among anonymous characters. In this he revived a style largely absent from European art since the Dutch golden age. It satisfies as composition yet makes a social statement, comic or moving. It might lend itself to sentimental excess, but Wilkie avoids this. While his images are faithful they apply a light touch to human nature. Scott felt close in his writing to what Wilkie did in his painting.[11]

Finally, Wilson's salon benefited from the fact that, as the 'Noctes' noted, 'Scotland is making great strides even in sculpture.' Steell was one young sculptor the host held in high regard. It had come to be shared among many others by the time he was chosen to fashion the statue of Scott inside his enormous monument in Princes Street of 1840-6. Compared to the soaring, rocket-ship shape of the Gothic housing, the actual effigy of Sir Walter, seated with his deerhound Maida at his side, strikes a homely note true to his character. Later works by Steell in Edinburgh are either far bolder, such as his Queen Victoria atop the Royal Scottish Academy and his Duke of Wellington on a horse outside Register House, or more reverent, such as his Jeffrey in Parliament House and his Prince Albert in the middle of Charlotte Square (for which the queen gave him a knighthood). Finally, in Princes Street Gardens, Steell made the memorial to Wilson on his death in 1854 and managed to convey, even in stone, something of his wildness. Wilson had many faults, but one small thing to his credit is how well he chose the artists to come to his salon in Ann Street. They all live on because they give us an authentic picture of pre-industrial Scotland, without distortion or sentimentality: Nasmyth her landscapes, Raeburn her people, Wilkie her domestic scenes, Steell her monumental achievements.[12]

❧

Enlightened Edinburgh remained an agreeable place, then, even if it had now entered on a silver rather than golden age. Only for Carlyle was that not good enough. Within a year of his sober night at the salon in Great King Street he abandoned the capital and returned to his roots at Craigenputtoch in Dumfriesshire. Necessity forced the move, for he was finding it hard to make money out of his writing, but he and his wife Jane kept in touch with friends in Edinburgh. Craigenputtoch did not solve their problems either. In 1834 they took a more drastic step. Carlyle then became the first man of genius to decide that Scotland was too small, and that as a bright spirit of the next age only the larger life of London would do for him. Scots of any social or intellectual standing over the previous couple of centuries had all been to London, just as they had been to Paris or Rome, yet with the intention of coming back. Carlyle set a new trend: excepting brief visits, he was gone for good.

But then Carlyle had never been happy in Edinburgh. Born in 1795 to poor, toiling peasants, Auld Licht Burghers believing most of humanity doomed to hellfire, he left home aged fourteen. He walked the 100 miles to the capital to begin his higher studies with the aim of becoming a minister in their sect. They fretted that urban life might break his religious devotion. His mother wrote: 'Have you got through the Bible yet? If you have, read it again.' When he replied that he was delving into books, 'Italian, German and others', of which she had never heard, he upset her: 'I pray for a blessing on your learning ... Do make religion your great study, Tom.' She sensed the doubts that at length caused him to abandon any idea that salvation might come through a particular Church.[13]

Yet, while Carlyle could not remain a Burgher, he would always revere Calvinist Scotland: 'A country where the entire people is, or even once has been, laid hold of, filled to the heart with an infinite religious idea, "has made a step from which it cannot retrograde". Thought, conscience, the sense that man is denizen of a Universe, creator of an Eternity, has penetrated to the simplest heart.' Scots had come to worship God through the intellect and not, like lesser breeds, through the senses or feelings: 'Thought, in such a country, may change its form, but cannot go out; the country has attained *majority*; thought, and a certain spiritual manhood, ready for all the work that man can do, endures there.' No wonder Carlyle even as a student mutinied against the form thought took in the infidel aspect of the Enlightenment. In the classes at the university 'the young vacant mind was furnished with much talk about the Progress of the Species, Dark Ages, Prejudice and the like'. But this learning Carlyle found too self-satisfied in its liberal consensus and facile teleology. It could not nourish his spirit. On the contrary, it made the Enlightenment, the late Scottish Enlightenment at least, insufferable to him for shallowness and complacency. But London never solved his problem either.[14]

Carlyle was a huge loss, yet Edinburgh managed to rub along without him. In one way this city ought to have gratified the great cultural critic of his time. Unlike others in Scotland or Britain it never suffered the ravages of the Industrial Revolution. Yet it grew fast. During the nineteenth century the population rose fourfold, to pass 400,000 by the census of 1911 (then the pattern changed, the growth slowed and the figure has never quite reached half a million). Meanwhile seven extensions of the boundaries had trebled the municipal area. This was not just a matter of the annexation of inner suburbs spilling over from the crowded centre. Large open spaces got swallowed up too: the Braid Hills, Blackford Hlll, Corstorphine Hill, the Craiglockhart Hills, even part of the Pentland Hills. Once the railways came, development sometimes jumped over the open spaces to create a ring of outer suburbs at Barnton, Colinton or Corstorphine. Edinburgh's territorial demands foresaw future urbanization far beyond the Old Town and New Town. Yet a lot of the greenery within the extensions remains unspoiled, or at worst turned into golf-courses.[15]

Economic and social change continued, but up to the end of the century the capital preserved many features it had shown at the beginning of the century. Edinburgh remained a city of the intellect, of the liberal professions generally, and one where the landed gentry came to do business or spend money. The rest of the population earned its bread by meeting the needs of these elites. There were craftsmen to supply every material want, shopkeepers to sell the goods, legions of diligent clerks, armies of faithful servants, labourers hewing wood or drawing water and finally an underclass eking out its existence from the leavings of all the rest.

Apart from the dominance of classes distinguished by trained minds there was little to explain why printing and publishing became a keystone of the economy. Lockhart remarked that in his time English authors sent their works to Edinburgh, whereas in the past Scots authors had needed to send theirs to London. In the Scottish capital Adam and Charles Black, William Blackwood, William and Robert Chambers, Archibald Constable and Thomas Nelson were all big British publishers of the nineteenth century; some of their houses survived the twentieth century, too, until gobbled up by today's multinationals. While economic growth and social advance were raising demand for books all over the United Kingdom, this could not in itself promote one place of publication rather than another.

Telling in Edinburgh's favour was its large educated population. One in forty men practised as a lawyer (compared to one in 240 in Glasgow), one in sixty worked in the arts and entertainment (compared to one in 135), one in 100 was a teacher (compared to one in 200), one in 100 a clergyman (compared to one in 300) and one in 300 a scientist (compared to one in 500).[16] On a wider scale, too, the critic Robert Mudie found that the 'accumulation of intellect among the lower and labouring classes is a delightful thing'. He was most struck by the experience that 'when I visited the public libraries, the men whom I found borrowing the classical or philosophical books wore aprons' – in other words, were workers. Though startled by all the boozing at this social level, he still felt entranced that 'you find one man laying aside his apron to consult Adam Smith, dispute with Malthus or rejudge the judges of the *Edinburgh Review*; another will be found solving mathematical problems, or constructing architectural plans'.[17] Here was the democratic intellect in action. And then as now, Edinburgh also housed a floating population of indigent literary men who could find no lucrative or congenial employment, and perhaps did not want to. They had at least nothing to lose from trying to get themselves into print, in anything from poetry to legal texts. Besides, all citizens of Edinburgh belonged to a nation believing knowledge was a passport to progress.

Yet nothing here accounts for growth in the city's other big business, brewing. Households once brewed their own beer, but now industrial production supplied it. Apart from the citizens' hard drinking, the abundant crops and good water in the hinterland might have been reason enough for this development. Brewers kept in touch with the countryside, since many of their tasks were akin to a farmer's. Their output remained seasonal, affected by the harvest and the price of grain – and for transport they used wagons and drayhorses until after the Second World War. At the height more than forty breweries existed in Edinburgh, standing out from the townscape with a brewhouse on three storeys and yard containing cellars, cooperage, counting house, maltings and stables. The model was the Holyrood Brewery founded by William Younger in 1749, and closed only in 1986. Younger's business had grown until, halfway through its history, it dominated the Scottish trade (together with Tennent's in Glasgow).[18]

Scots prefer to drink their own beer, though it is today harder to tell from others than it used to be. There was a technical reason for the difference, in the national method of fermentation at low temperatures. This gave rise to two main styles of beer. One was dark and heavy, earlier known as 'nappy'. Robert Burns's poem 'Tam o' Shanter' has the line: 'While we sit bousin at the nappy, an gettin fou an unco happy'. The other was small ale made by brewing up the grains a second time, to make it much lighter and about half the strength; anybody could drink this, not just men meaning to get drunk. What made the outside world aware of Edinburgh's beers was India Pale Ale or IPA, created for export and robust enough to withstand long voyages. Nostalgic for home, thirsty Scots took it to far-flung outposts of the empire, so creating an international market. With good beer, Edinburgh has good pubs to match. The oldest date in their present state, not much altered, from the 1890s: the Abbotsford, Barony, Bennet's Bar, Cafe Royal, Canny Man's, Diggers, Doric Tavern, Ensign Ewart, Guildford Arms, Kenilworth, Leslie's Bar. They no longer have spit and sawdust on the floor, but bear little resemblance to the chintzy kind of hostelry that seems most favoured in England. As Stevenson said, 'A Scot of poetic temperament, and without religious exaltation, drops as if by nature into the public house. The picture may not be pleasing, but what else is a man to do in this dog's weather?'[19]

Publishing and brewing were the sum of the Industrial Revolution here. Cockburn thought it 'merciful' that the city lacked manufactures, 'that is, tall brick chimneys, black smoke, a population precariously fed, pauperism, disease and crime, all in excess. Some strong efforts have occasionally been made to coax these things to us; but a thanks-deserving providence has hitherto been always pleased to defeat them. For though manufactures be indispensable, they need not be everywhere ... There should be Cities of Refuge.'[20]

In social terms, apart from *nouveaux riches* publishers and brewers, the professions still ruled the roost. But they faced crises.

❧

Edinburgh's medical profession underwent its crisis after the scandal of Burke and Hare exposed it as callous and grasping. The surgeons' pitiless procedures certainly terrified the suffering and their relations, while as yet offering relatively little prospect of success. It seems bizarre that the surgeons almost compounded their problems by performing their operations in public, weltering in blood while the patients screamed in pain, even after seeking to stupefy themselves on whisky. And this took place in theatres packed with ghoulish spectators or with young students – though they, of course, had no other way of gaining a first experience of surgery. If those under the knife were not to bleed to death, those wielding it needed steady nerve and fantastic dexterity to complete the operation as quickly as possible. Any mistake and they had a corpse on their hands. Students might first stare in horror but once hardened to the sight they looked on in excitement, thrilled at the speed and skill of their mentors. When in mere minutes or even moments the operation succeeded, the students cheered and went off to celebrate. When it failed, they jeered. No wonder we read how the surgeons, their hands plunged in the wound, broke out in sweat, from time to time glancing at the patient's face in case the sudden pallor of death should sweep over it. The almost greater peril of sepsis, of post-operative infection, as yet occurred to none of them: they wiped their scalpels on the tails of their coats, already filthy and stiff with congealed gore from previous operations. Survivors of the surgery and shock still ran a high risk of perishing.

The medical professors of Edinburgh wielded godlike authority over theatre, classroom and public health in general; like older gods they often proved capricious. The medieval plagues had disappeared but a putrid city continued to offer fertile breeding ground for new epidemics of cholera and typhus. In the 1820s and 1830s the death-rate was actually rising.

When cholera appeared in 1832 at Leith a local doctor, Thomas Latta, found a remedy for its worst symptoms. Injecting the sufferer with a saline solution was later adopted universally as the first line of defence against this virulent disease. But at the time the professors of Edinburgh refused to credit Latta's success in saving lives. Leading the pack was James Gregory, of the chair of practice of physic, scion of an academic dynasty dating back two centuries. Faced with the horrible symptoms of cholera, Gregory drew a conclusion that owed more to ancient Aristotelian logic than to modern medical science: if the infected body expelled salt and water in ceaseless diarrhoea, it must have an excess of these substances. Injection of more would only make things worse: 'Gregory, who is a tolerably acute man, but disagreeably dogmatic, seemed at once to settle the matter in his own mind – that the practice referred to was inconsistent with physiological principles – that it was dangerous.' Instead he urged the physician to 'seize nature by the throat' by 'free blood-letting, the cool affusion, brisk purging, frequent blisters and vomits of tartar emetic': vigorous methods indeed, but against cholera worse than useless, unless to put the patient out of his misery all the sooner. Nobody else followed Latta's procedures, and thousands died a squalid death.[21]

※

Probably not just Latta's novel method but also his lack of social or academic standing led to his being pooh-poohed. The impression is underlined by the reception in Edinburgh of a greater figure who gave the whole world reason to be thankful to him, James Young Simpson. He was a man of the people, born in 1811 at Bathgate in West Lothian, then just a stage on the turnpike between Glasgow and Edinburgh, a younger child of the humble hamlet's baker. All his life he looked like a peasant, but a Scots education was his birthright, too. He went aged fourteen to the University of Edinburgh, first learning Greek and Latin while also reading modern authors, Byron and Scott. Two years later he started his medical training. That at once took him into the operating theatre. He felt appalled at what he saw there, thought of giving up medicine for law but persevered.

Once Simpson qualified, he became a house-surgeon at the Lying-In Hospital of Leith. His duties often took him out into the stinking tenements of the port where poor, sick or abandoned women had to bear their brats. He balked at nothing. Even at this outset of his career he was asking: 'Cannot something be done to render the patient unconscious while under acute pain, without interfering with the free and healthy play of the natural functions?'

For now he had to rely on his own kindness and care. He soon won enough of a reputation to set up in private practice. Genteel ladies flocked to him for their accouchements.

By 1839 Simpson felt ready for a step up in his career. When the professor of midwifery at Edinburgh resigned, Simpson applied for the job. By the gerontocratic standards of the existing professoriate Simpson was a novice, and by their nepotistic standards a nobody. The occupant of the chair of midwifery did not have to hold a doctorate of medicine, but from classrooms of the Old College down to drawing rooms of the New Town the professors whispered that Simpson could scarcely be considered an enlightened man of letters like themselves. He might know his business, yet so did any number of common midwives, those old crones still called on by most women to help them in childbirth in Scotland and everywhere else. For a chair it was not enough to be an able practitioner; this university needed somebody learned in science and its literature.

In the event Simpson overcame all professional hostility to him. As a man of the people he found his support in other quarters, crucially in the political arena where the contest had to be settled. The session of the town council that elected him was still a close-run thing. He won by a single vote. He would be Edinburgh's professor of midwifery until his death more than thirty years later. The whole time, while making many scientific contributions to medicine, he remained a working doctor ready to go out and treat the people of Edinburgh in every station of life, not only a great man but also a good one.[22]

Simpson heralded a new era because he relied on experiment, not on the pseudo-philosophical dogmas of previous professorial generations. From his chair he stepped up the search for an effective anaesthetic. He did this at home in Queen Street, using himself and colleagues as guinea pigs. The stuff they sampled often produced unpleasant side-effects, until the great day of 19 January 1847 when they tried ether. They sat around a table and drank tumblers of it: 'Immediately an unwonted hilarity seized the party; they became bright-eyed, very happy and very loquacious – expatiating on the delicious aroma of the new fluid. The conversation was of unusual intelligence, and quite charmed the listeners.' The babble grew louder and louder until 'a moment more, then all was quiet, and then – a crash'. The guinea pigs had dropped off into deep sleep, then fallen under the table. Soon Simpson discovered that chloroform made an even better anaesthetic.

Yet, despite these achievements, the haughtiest of the old guard, James Syme, continued to regard this upstart as an enemy. He would rend apart Simpson's writings in front of a class as he denounced the author's vulgarity. Syme even dismissed chloroform, arguing that efforts to reduce the frequency of operations or simplify their performance would achieve as much as laughing gas. It took Queen Victoria to resolve the dispute in Simpson's favour. She had herself anaesthetized for the birth of a son in 1853. At this point, it can well be said, the tarnished reputation of Edinburgh's medicine was restored.[23]

※

Meanwhile the clergy of the Church of Scotland had faced a yet greater crisis. This arose from the Disruption (or schism of the Kirk) on 18 May 1843. That day the General Assembly was due to open in Edinburgh, at St Andrew's Church on George Street. As a huge crowd waited outside, the retiring moderator, the Reverend Dr David Welsh, professor of ecclesiastical history at the university, led a prayer to open proceedings. A roll-call ought to have followed. Instead Welsh remained on his feet and, to a breathless hush, said: 'There has been an infringement on the constitution of the Church, an infringement so great that we cannot constitute its General Assembly.' He went on to read out a long protest against attacks on the Kirk mounted over ten years by the Parliament at Westminster. Redress had been sought in vain, so he and all who held to the spiritual independence of the established Church now had no choice but to leave it. What he meant was, among other matters, its right to determine how to appoint ministers to its parishes. The Kirk took the view that, as a spiritual corporation under the headship of Jesus Christ, it should decide this and other religious questions for itself. Parliament took the view that within the United Kingdom the Church of Scotland, not to say Jesus Christ, must be subject to its own absolute sovereignty. So at will it could overrule the General Assembly – and had done.

Welsh laid his protest on the table, turned and bowed to the royal commissioner, the Earl of Bute, then stepped down from the chair and walked to the door. As he went, other ministers and elders got up to walk behind him, row after row of them. Outside, when they emerged, the crowd first cheered but then fell into solemn silence. Many more who had pledged to leave the Kirk were waiting in the street. Though no plan for a procession had been made, the crush grew so great they were all forced to walk in column, three or four abreast. They marched to a meeting place prepared for them at Canonmills, a couple of miles away down the hill. There they constituted themselves as the Free Church of Scotland. About 450 ministers, 40 per cent of the clergy, signed a deed of demission giving up their charges, manses and incomes. Perhaps half the laity all over Scotland followed in seceding from the Kirk. In Edinburgh the defection proved still greater: two-thirds of members walked out into the Free Church, making it by some way the largest denomination in the capital.[24]

'Well, what do you think of it?' a friend asked Jeffrey, spending the day at home in Moray Place. He replied, 'I'm proud of my country. There is not another country on earth where such a deed could have been done.'[25]

❧

The issues behind this caesura in national life are so remote from today's concerns as to be scarcely explicable to modern Scots, let alone to anybody else. They turned on much more than technicalities of law or relations of Church and State. Ever since the Reformation of 1560 a continuum had in most respects been maintained in Scottish life, to which even the Union of 1707 made little difference. The state looked after temporal concerns and the Church looked after spiritual concerns, widely defined to include education, care of the poor and curbs on Scots' sins of drunkenness and fornication. There had been collisions when the state interfered in the government of the Church, but gradually the two came to terms and in the late eighteenth century reached an equilibrium. This was embodied in the circle around Principal William Robertson of Edinburgh: the established Kirk behaved itself as a polite member of civil society and in return got its constitutional privilege respected.

The Free Church was in part a popular revolt against Robertson's kind of Kirk. There was steady dissent and secession from it, and the drops of its life's blood drained away into each new independent congregation: slow death beckoned. The danger appeared dire to the Reverend Thomas Chalmers by the time that, after ministering in Fife and Glasgow, he arrived in 1828 as professor of divinity at the University of Edinburgh. For him, saving the Kirk meant saving its role in society, as guardian of its morals, teacher of its children and protector of its poor. The religious establishment had to extend its presence in the burgeoning cities and build many more places of worship to reach the submerged proletariat. Where would the money come from? Chalmers's first answer was the British state, which turned him down. One reason was that, while demanding the money, he refused to submit to any kind of official supervision: the Kirk required freedom of action to meet its challenges. The conflict inherent in his analysis led to the great crisis. The state would not concede control, and the Disruption followed as an act of defiance.

Chalmers claimed victory, yet he deluded himself. His vision for Scotland depended on the maintenance of established religion. In fact he had caused it to collapse. For the four years of life left to him, he strove rather to prove the Church was better off without the state. And so it might have been in worship or discipline, yet the key lay in the social role he had always stressed. In the slums of Edinburgh, at the West Port, he sought to run an experiment in welfare on the voluntary principle. In other words it was to be financed not by taxation but by the free contributions of the rich; it would give the poor not hand-outs but means to help themselves. The experiment failed.[26]

Chalmers's actual achievement had been to smash the equilibrium of Church and State constructed by Robertson. On one side of the scales established religion dropped away, no longer able to perform its appointed tasks in society. The balance then fell down on the opposite side, the side of the British state, the only other entity that seemed equal to those tasks in the modern era. And its influence proved to be an anglicizing one. Scotland, with a vital element of her identity gone, had to adjust to a much less autonomous position in the United Kingdom. She began to feel more like a province than a nation. We might read into the Disruption a presage of later Scottish nationalism, in its political rejection of the absolute sovereignty of Parliament. But the ancestry was indirect, and the Disruption's leaders took care to play down its patriotic aspect. Rather, it was the social development of a more British Scotland, which few Scots wanted but all found inevitable, that sowed the seeds of later discord.[27]

The upheaval marked the physical face of Edinburgh too. The Free Church set out to match the Kirk with a place of worship and, if possible, a school in every parish in Scotland. At the same time, the schism prompted most of the older dissenting sects to form a united front. So Presbyterianism regrouped into three well-organized factions. Doctrinal rivalry was matched by architectural rivalry, each trying to erect bigger and better churches than the others. The standard work on Edinburgh in the series *The Buildings of Scotland* (1984) lists eighty-two places of worship still standing in the central city – a minimum tally, for a good number have in recent times been secularized or demolished. Holy Corner, at the foot of Morningside Road, has three of them glaring at one another across the junction. They range otherwise from the Episcopalian cathedral of St Mary's, a massive synthesis of early Gothic by Giles Gilbert Scott, its three spires looming over the western skyline of the city, to the anonymous chapel of the United Associate Synod in Lothian Road, which to any non-Scottish eye can have nothing in the least sacred about it; in fact it now serves perfectly well as the city's Filmhouse. An acute problem of redundancy has arisen from the decline and merger of congregations right across Scotland but most of all in Edinburgh, where perhaps half the churches remain no more than artistic assets and luxuries of the townscape. Secularization can be the best option, as elsewhere at Hope Park Chapel, now Queen's Hall for chamber concerts, and at St George's in Charlotte Square, now West Register House for holdings of the national archives.

※

The Free Church's educational efforts also gave the city a landmark – New College with its twin towers at the head of the Mound, set up to train ministers for this latest Scottish sect. The initiative marked how the religious fissures might spread deep into the social fabric preserved by the Treaty of Union. All of a piece, the national institutions had allowed a kind of semi-independent Scotland to flourish for over a century. Now disruption of one meant disruption of others. It proved impossible, for example, to avert collateral damage in the system of education run by the Kirk.

In the University of Edinburgh, to be sure, the Church of Scotland represented only one of the lines of force. The law said professors had to be members of the Kirk, but the electorate for most chairs was the town council, which in the early nineteenth century chose several Episcopalians, so could not have been taking the religious test too seriously. By and large it performed its duty well except for a little nepotism – and in clannish Scotland this was no great matter. Unwelcome novelty came when something other than merit or nepotism, namely politics, decided the contest of Hamilton and Wilson in 1819. Worse, the wrong man won.

Otherwise the town council had not been in the habit of interfering in details of academic life. Apart from compulsory moral philosophy the university set no formal curriculum and professors taught what they liked. Nor was there even any obligation on students to meet a set standard. They could drop in and out of classes according to need or taste, at the end of the session collecting a ticket to say they had joined in the bouts of question-and-answer that gave trained Scots minds of this era their verve. Most studied for no more than a year or two, and perhaps just one in five or six took a degree. The only real pressure on their professor was to attract enough of them, since in this frugal nation an academic salary remained meagre and professors had to make a living from the fees they charged.

Professors might succeed in different ways, as the history of the chair of chemistry showed. Joseph Black made fundamental discoveries and students flocked to learn at his feet. His successor, the handsome and debonair Tommy Hope, went off on a different tack with, according to Cockburn, 'amusing and brilliant experiments'. He hit the jackpot when he let his students bring their girlfriends, and then he was lecturing to 300 at a time: 'the ladies declare there was never anything so delightful as these chemical flirtations. The Doctor is in absolute ecstasy with his audience of veils and feathers . . . I wish some of his experiments would blow him up. Each female student would get a bit of him.'[28]

The town councillors' role did not remain passive, though. As the nineteenth century proceeded they grew anxious their college should move with the times. Universities in Germany were mounting a formidable challenge to the earlier ascendancy of universities in Scotland. In England, Oxford and Cambridge remained sunk in torpor, but London founded a college that managed to poach John Ramsay McCulloch, latest leader of the Scottish school of political economy. Yet councillors often had different ideas from academics of what the university ought to be doing. They wanted to see a chair of conveyancing, for example, something of obvious use to a booming city; this idea did not go down well with the professors, though at length it was accepted. The councillors also wanted to see a chair of midwifery (the one Simpson would hold), against which the medical faculty rose up in arms. A huge row followed. The councillors exercised their right of visitation, allowing them to summon, question and pressurize the professors. Still getting nowhere, they called for and secured a royal commission on the Scottish universities in 1828. Academics from Edinburgh who appeared as witnesses expressed nothing but contempt for the merchants and tradesmen they had to deal with on the council. But these had set off a process of reform that at length remodelled the university.[29]

※

Growing political partisanship further complicated relations of town and gown. The municipal reform of 1833 brought in a different kind of councillor. It was no longer the old closed clique that held the academic patronage but a body of men chosen democratically, though on a suffrage extremely restricted by today's standards. The qualification, for male occupiers and owners of buildings worth £10 a year, enfranchised 5,000 of Edinburgh's 137,000 citizens, of whom prosperous tradesman made up a large proportion. The council needed to respect their views, which were not always comfortable ones. They tended in politics to radicalism, and in religion to the dissenting sects. One consequence became clear as the new council carried out its duty of providing for the city's established churches. In fact, it rather sought to limit the number of ministers and hold down their stipends. This did not bode well for the university.

The dissenters' political leader was Duncan McLaren, a draper in the High Street. He got on the new town council at the first election and served for three decades; he rose to be lord provost and finally

MP for Edinburgh. A rigid sectarian, he saw the Kirk as one among many enemies, not even the worst. When some property of the Episcopal Church suffered damage by collapse of a wall for which the council was responsible, McLaren refused on its behalf to receive a request for compensation from anybody styling himself a bishop: 'I object to the thrusting upon a Presbyterian community of sets of men who are to assume titles of superiority over other ministers in Scotland. Such an assumption of superiority in a Presbyterian country where Presbyterianism is enacted by law is altogether out of the question.' Nor did McLaren like being reminded of his city's popish past, however remote. Part of the deal for the railway to be built through the centre in 1844 was that the medieval Trinity kirk standing in the way should be shifted, that is, dismantled stone by stone and rebuilt on a different site. McLaren objected on the grounds it had never been adapted for Protestant worship (with a pulpit in the middle); such a relic of superstition should just be razed. And of course he joined the long succession of preachers against the sins of the Scots people: 'it was a matter of public notoriety that drunkenness prevailed to an enormous extent in Edinburgh, and on Sundays it was particularly marked and offensive, by reason of the fact that well-behaved citizens on their way through the streets saw drunken people reeling about in large numbers, using bad language and otherwise rendering themselves great nuisances'.[30] By his blinkered doggedness McLaren also got into a position of influence over the council's academic patronage.

All was further complicated by the Disruption. A league of Free Churchmen and dissenters could then command a majority on the town council, though they did not act always in concert, having bones to pick with each other. The rump of the continuing Kirk was foolish enough to provoke them by trying to revive the obsolete religious test for chairs at the university, seeking absurdly to hog them for itself. This led to the test being legislated away, but meanwhile the dispute did yet more damage.

McLaren was lord provost when in 1850 Wilson at last resigned the chair of moral philosophy he had held with some style but no distinction for three decades. Since he had diminished its standing, the succession was crucial. An obvious candidate stood ready – James Ferrier, professor of moral philosophy at the University of St Andrews but scion of a leading legal and literary family in Edinburgh, Wilson's nephew and son-in-law to boot: in the old days he would have followed on without question. In this case he would have done so on merit, too. He was the great white hope of the Scottish intellect, ready to carry its work forward into the second half of the century, initially by once again coming to terms with what the Germans were doing (on which the aged and ailing Hamilton had given up). But Ferrier was a member of the Kirk and had weighed into the public polemics over the Disruption – which was enough to set the Free Churchmen and dissenters against him. And there may already have been a question mark over his moral conduct as well as over his moral philosophy. He would not long afterwards catch syphilis from a prostitute, so putting an end to any serious intellectual activity on his part.[31]

Whatever the reason, McLaren and friends decided Ferrier had to be stopped, yet faced the problem of finding a plausible alternative. The best they could do was Patrick MacDougall, professor of moral philosophy at New College. He was a nonentity, however – a philosophical, or rather theological, hack and bootlicker to his backers with nothing to say for himself. Candidates for a chair often brought out a quick publication to impress the electors; all he could manage was a slim volume of book reviews, most written for house organs of the Free Church. Yet in the town council, with McLaren presiding, MacDougall beat Ferrier. After this catastrophic break in its apostolic succession, Scottish philosophy lay helpless before the coming renegade onslaught of John Stuart Mill, son of the émigré John Mill who had gone to London and teamed up with the utilitarians around Jeremy Bentham. In 1863 the younger Mill would publish an *Examination of Hamilton*, tearing its subject to pieces; his reputation was destroyed forever. With Ferrier too brain-dead to do anything, Scottish philosophy had run its course. So how could it continue to underpin higher education at the University of Edinburgh or anywhere else?

❧

Only Edinburgh could have generated cultural crisis on such a scale, in this stupendous broil of religion, philosophy, education and politics. It seethed on even after intervention from Westminster, in the shape of a second royal commission and then legislation, the Universities (Scotland) Act of 1858. Here the basic answer to the horrible mess was the Whig one of anglicization. Scots students should no longer learn what they liked but follow a curriculum on English lines. Many in Scotland had doubts about this policy, though it did foster a fine system of scientific and technological training. Otherwise the Act gave each of the Scottish universities a new form of government under a Court, where professors, graduates and students would all be represented, as befitted these public and indeed popular institutions. For Edinburgh, previously a municipal college, there was special provision deferring to its history, that the lord provost and an assessor from the town council should also be members of the Court. Otherwise the intimate relationship of council and university dating back almost 300 years came to an end. Edinburgh would join a national system of higher education and in future respond to forces at work there, rather than to local ones.[32]

Yet on a different plane the university's ties to the city were to be preserved, even strengthened in the decades ahead. In 1870, 34 per cent of its students came from Edinburgh itself and 42 per cent from the rest of Scotland, while 20 per cent came from outside Scotland. By 1910 the figure for Edinburgh had risen to 42 per cent, with 26 per cent from the rest of Scotland and 29 per cent from elsewhere. Once women gained admission in 1896 about half of them were from Edinburgh. A system evolved by which, without ever leaving home, pupils from the city's schools could proceed to its university and then into well-paid careers in its professions. The more ambitious might, of course, still get away to do something else, and plenty did. But a secure and prosperous existence in familiar surroundings was enough for many. Without doubt this has helped to shape and sustain coherence in the character of the city.[33]

※

But the cultural crisis reached down into Edinburgh's schools as well. The High School, with its by any standards distinguished record, had been on the point of celebrating its 700th anniversary in 1824 when doubts surfaced, in certain quarters, about the quality of the education there. Cockburn claimed this had been 'lowered, perhaps necessarily, so as to suit the wants of a class of boys to more than two-thirds of whom classical accomplishment is foreseen to be useless'.[34] Scottish Latinity had been formidable. Even at this time, Edinburgh's lawyers and doctors used Latin, and established ministers at least learned it. The reason was practical. Scots had never expected foreign nations to understand their own tongue so needed another language to communicate – up to the eighteenth century, and to some extent still in the nineteenth century, this could be Latin. The fetish of the classical ideal that would emerge in Victorian England, as means of ruling an empire, was a different kettle of fish. All the same, Whigs like Cockburn thought England a paragon in education as in everything else: if the best English schools were turning out people with the same mental equipment as a well-read ancient Roman, that was what the best Scottish schools ought to be doing as well. His odd view now had a result in the foundation of Edinburgh Academy. This set out to attain higher classical standards by recruiting teachers from England, who could also prepare boys for entrance to Oxford and Cambridge.

There was a more general and reasonable recognition in a thriving city that it needed to exert itself to keep up the relatively high standards of schooling it had always attained. Edinburgh's rich history of educational philanthropy was an asset here too. Older schools of the Merchant Company and Heriot's Trust, usually known as hospitals, showed how deep this impulse ran. Now the benefactions of the wealthy flowed faster.

A single spot on the sheer western bank of the Water of Leith, in the garden suburb beyond Dean Bridge, commands a view over nearby buildings, sober or swaggering, of four institutions so endowed in the mid-nineteenth century; in winter, when the trees are bare, a fifth may be glimpsed by a little craning of the neck. They are Donaldson's Hospital (1841–51), John Watson's School (now the National Gallery of Modern Art; 1825), the Dean Orphanage (now the Dean Gallery; 1831–3), Stewart's and Melville College (1848) and, just out of sight, Fettes College (1864–70). There were more in different parts of the city, so many that some came spontaneously to concentrate on special needs (like Donaldson's on the deaf). They date from a time before any national system of schools existed in Scotland, when all had to be financed at local level – and this in a culture holding frugality to be one of the highest virtues.

Yet the city had charities if anything in excess. Most of their income arose from urban property, and so was soaring. Since frugality here blended with philanthropy, the question followed whether the available resources were really being put to the best use. For example, many pupils in the hospitals boarded, yet nearly all were sons or daughters of Edinburgh – as they had to be under the terms of the relevant bequests. Was this the most effective way to spend money on them?[35]

The Merchant Company decided not. In 1879 it resolved to change the nature of its hospitals. It formed five big day schools, fee-paying on a modest scale and with charitable free places still. They flourished. Within a couple of years they had 4,000 pupils and 213 teachers, compared to the previous 400 and 26 respectively in all the hospitals combined before 1879; the expansion benefited girls especially. Heriot's Trust had to decide whether to follow suit. This was a matter of hot dispute because, among the educational institutions of Edinburgh, Heriot's School most clearly prepared its boys for entry to the trades, where nearly every one ended up. The trust was by now so wealthy it had also built thirteen free, elementary 'outdoor schools' in the city. Altogether, upwardly mobile members of the working class felt the trust was there for them and did a great job in meeting their needs. As Edinburgh trades council put it, the successful aim had been 'to raise up a respectable, thinking, able class of artisans or citizens'. So there was fierce resistance to any idea Heriot's Trust might ape the Merchant Company and make its main school fee-paying. Yet that was what happened, after a long struggle, in 1885. It has struck historians as inexcusable: a glaring example of Victorian predation by the privileged on the unprivileged.[36]

❧

The affair raises pointed questions about class in Edinburgh. Yet the city's paradoxes have not in all cases resolved themselves in victories of toffs over proles: in fact, after two revolutions in the seventeenth century, two rebellions in the eighteenth century and the Disruption in the nineteenth century the honours had come out just about even. Edinburgh did not lack social tensions yet still showed an egalitarian spirit probably owed in the final analysis to its religion but also fostered by a civic spirit strong and rare (for instance, absent from London).

The one avowedly Marxist historian of Victorian Edinburgh, R. Q. Gray, though ever on the lookout for symptoms of coming class war, conceded the difficulty of finding them here.[37] On the contrary, social distinctions seemed to be growing more fluid rather than more rigid. At the turn of the nineteenth century the predominant form of proletarian organization had been the incorporated crafts, dating from the late Middle Ages, still with limited entry and similar restraints on trade: bakers, bonnetmakets, caulkers, cordiners, fleshers, furriers, goldsmiths, hammermen, masons, skinners, tailors, websters and wrights. They lost their guaranteed places in the town council with the municipal reform of 1833, but since many of the new voters were craftsmen the real difference this made to them might not have been great. Their economic privilege was something else. In 1846 a Tory government in London, without so much as a by-your-leave, passed a measure opening all Scots royal burghs to unrestricted commerce. But even this might not have made much real difference. Though it came in the middle of the Hungry Forties, the standard of living would soon rise again and carry on rising into the future. Edinburgh's craftsmen could either have identified themselves as proletarians and gone on to the sort of militancy that would later characterize (let us not say ruin) Glasgow, or else they might have reinvented their middling position in a modern city, now about to enter on its era of high Victorian prosperity.

Edinburgh did not go free of industrial dispute, but the second of those paths was clearly what its workers chose. If they had no more privileges, they did have indispensable functions in this city with its peculiar economic structure. Again, its lack of heavy industry proved to be an advantage. For one thing it meant a relative absence of the Victorian cycles of boom and bust that caused huge instability in other local economies, especially if reliant on some staple product. Edinburgh's prime demand out of its comfortable professional incomes was for food or drink, clothing or housing: demand fairly stable, not least on those who supplied it with regular manual labour. Beyond basic needs, incomes went on conspicuous consumption. This meant handmade goods produced by skilled craftsmanship of high quality. It also meant obliging craftsmen.

Workers could still organize. The old incorporations survived because in a fragmented local market for labour they could mediate between consumers and producers by proposing general agreements on wages and conditions for journeymen or regulations for apprentices. This saved everybody trouble. So the peculiar economic structure of the city, regardless of the state of the law, was what gave the crafts their resilience. It meant the so-called labour aristocracy, that intriguing backbone of Victorian Britain, was salient and secure in Edinburgh. Compared with other cities it enjoyed more stable employment, earned more money, even managed to save a little.

All this found reflection in the records of the workers' only common organization above the level of incorporated crafts. In Russia it would have been called a soviet; in Edinburgh it was the trades council (founded in 1853). We have seen it arguing for preservation of wide access to good schools. That was consistent with its other efforts in favour of free public libraries or lower prices of admission to art galleries. The final aim, expressed by James Hart, general secretary of the masons' union, lay in raising 'the moral tone of trade unions in the opinions of those whose good opinions and co-operations [sic] are really worth having'. One of these was reckoned to be a Lord Advocate, James Moncreiff, whom the council elected as honorary president. He would come along to give the lads lectures under such titles as 'Some Thoughts for Artisans'.

In the city a few young converts to the exotic creed of socialism found their efforts accordingly confined to the 'propagandist and educative'. One socialist would remember in exasperation how, during a dispute of rare acrimony, 'the slowly moving mind of the average member of our trades council was at last aroused to think that this subject of socialism was one which might possibly concern *them*; and naturally perhaps for Scotchmen, they went to a clergyman for enlightenment'.[38]

The situation in Edinburgh can be contrasted with that in the mining hinterland. There the working conditions continued to horrify even contemporaries. In efforts to remedy them, the miners of Midlothian had since the turn of the century sought to make collective bargains with the coalmasters. On the whole they failed. Sometimes strikes followed, though the men could seldom summon up the economic or political strength to win them. In Scotland at large, miners were just starting to move towards some kind of national organization under Alexander MacDonald (who came from Lanarkshire). But he advised them to avoid confrontation, just because they were so vulnerable. He would tell a parliamentary committee that workers 'should endeavour to meet their employers as far as they can'. He saw no way around capitalism, and so thought winning friends at Westminster the best means of getting laws passed in his members' interests; nothing else had worked in any case. In both city and county, then, we witness the weakness of workers in the Victorian economy. But in the city they were not crushed, and could even modestly prosper. This aside, it is hard to see how legislation could have helped a class of independent craftsmen. The people of Edinburgh chose the right course for them.[39]

Did economic structure determine social superstructure, in the classic Marxist sense? Glasgow's heavy industries generated social discord, with conflicts of class persisting down to the present. It may be going too far to say Edinburgh's peculiar economy produced social harmony. But Gray sees his dialectic working itself out in some interesting features of everyday life in the Victorian city. There was a growing number of marriages between members of different classes, that is, examples of barriers falling rather than rising. In 1865–9 more than half of men and women in semi-skilled and unskilled households intermarried. By the end of the century, the proportion of building labourers marrying into skilled and white-collar occupations doubled. According to Gray, this 'confirms the impression of a weakening of social segregations and cultural distinctions within the working class'.[40] A crucial further question is whether social segregations and cultural distinctions between working class and middle class were also weakening rather than strengthening.

❧

The query may prompt a second look at the educational controversies in Edinburgh. If the bourgeoisie was out to despoil the proletariat, we might expect it to have kept its stolen privileges to itself. In the city's system this does not seem to have been true. The percentages quoted above of male students from Edinburgh's schools entering the university, compared with the entire intake, break down into actual figures as follows: 601 out of 1,768 in 1870, and 1,151 out of

2,740 in 1910. That means access to higher education for the young men of Edinburgh, beside doubling in absolute terms, rose relatively too, faster than the city's population and faster than the size of its university. In other words, the proportion from Edinburgh inside the student body increased and at the same time formed a larger fraction of the relevant age cohort in the city. Access was widening, not narrowing, unless Edinburgh's schools simply became more efficient at winning places for bourgeois boys. Still, to get more than a thousand native sons graduating every year, in a city far from huge, cannot have added up in its cumulative effect to a system of exclusion.[41]

An alternative explanation comes from the lawyer J. H. A. Macdonald, who went on the bench as Lord Kingsburgh. Looking back over his long life in Edinburgh, he said in 1916 there was 'no city anywhere in which parents of the middle class can more easily obtain good school education for their children at a very moderate outlay. This tends greatly to the prosperity of the city. Very many persons possessed of a fixed but not high income migrate to Edinburgh, because of teaching facilities which the schools of the city provide.' Benefits were not confined to a single class, because incomers 'form the best customers for another section of the community – the retail traders – and are regular in meeting their engagements. Thus Edinburgh prospers.' Such people indeed 'are the best citizens a town can have. They give stability to a community.'[42]

MacDonald's view is plausible of an era before any universal welfare; evidence also exists that the city's superior medical facilities had the same effect of pulling in population.[43] Most doctors lived in the New Town, where the big houses might suit as lodgings for invalids with means to pay for private care. Yet nobody needed to spend a lot of money, because Edinburgh also had many medical charities. The Royal Infirmary itself, with 900 beds, was still financed by private donations and treated patients free. There were two other general hospitals, a hospital for sick children and eight special hospitals. Several had out-patient departments. In addition seven general and two special dispensaries handled 45,000 patients a year. Altogether one-third of the population got free medical treatment, according to Helen Kerr who in 1912 wrote a survey of welfare in the city. She added that it housed thirty charities providing old-age pensions for 2,000 people. It had 150 other general or special charities giving away £250,000 a year. Together with what the churches gathered in their weekly collections, and what arose from miscellaneous sources, 'we have a grand total of £365,000 available each year for the help of the poor and afflicted in Edinburgh' – equivalent to £42 million in today's money. On the whole, the same sorts of people (councillors, clergymen, experts, ladies bountiful) ran the charities, whether educational or medical or anything else. The ensemble of evidence about the policies they pursued does not point to hard and fast conclusions, yet it is difficult to believe they were class warriors in education but ministering angels in health.[44]

❧

The welter of institutional change in Edinburgh still scarcely shook the hold on it of one elite – the lawyers. The fashion continued for talented, ambitious men to join the Faculty of Advocates even if they had no professional interest in the law, to find congenial company or mark up status. We saw Sir William Hamilton doing that. Late on in the century he was followed by figures as disparate as James Clerk Maxwell, the great physicist best known for Maxwell's Demon (explaining why warmth disperses and time passes) or the writer Robert Louis Stevenson.

Yet the Faculty of Advocates changed too, not always for the better. It became less cosmopolitan. The custom for students of law to study in Holland or France had ended. If they now went elsewhere it was to Oxford or Cambridge, so that England became the chief foreign influence on Scots law. Whigs such as Jeffrey and Cockburn took the view English law was superior anyway and reform at home should follow English lines. The days when Adam Smith could be quoted in the Court of Session to influence judicial decisions on economic matters were long gone.

Again, advocates had often come from landed families. The nineteenth century saw many rise from other backgrounds, but over time most turned out to be just sons of lawyers, members of a caste now reproducing itself. The faculty ceased to play any role as an institution of Enlightenment and turned into a professional cartel. It started to look rather too inbred. Businessmen appeared to decide advocates were useless to them, as amateurs in all but the Scots law they made so convoluted and expensive. Commercial regulation had been common to the whole United Kingdom since 1707, so when renewed was framed in London on English principles. In Scotland, arbitration then offered better deals than adversarial litigation. A deeper threat arose from the fact that final appeals from civil causes in the Court of Session might go to the House of Lords, to be settled by people knowing nothing of Scots law and caring less. In 1858 the Lord Chancellor of England, Lord Cranworth, applied an English doctrine to a Scottish case before him and observed: 'I consider . . . that in England the doctrine must be regarded as well settled; but if such be the law of England, on what ground can it be argued not to be the law of Scotland? The law, as established in England, is founded on principles of universal application, not on any peculiarities of English jurisprudence.'[45]

As the Faculty of Advocates also supplied the personnel of such government as Scotland had (chiefly the Lord Advocate), anglicizers wielded political influence too. George Young became Lord Advocate in 1869. Even in the subordinate post of Solicitor General he had alarmed the country with his centralizing enthusiasms. His ultimate aim was to assimilate Scots to English law and do away with the Court of Session. Meanwhile, from 1872 it fell to him to introduce legislation setting up a national system of schools. This accepted the Church, or Churches, could no longer cope with Scottish education, being too obsessed with their own squabbles. There would have instead to be a secular system, one indeed excluding religious instruction, run by the state. But Young's measure offered no money for any schools above the elementary level. So in Edinburgh, already well provided for at the secondary level too, the new regime fell short of anything revolutionary except in one respect. Young insisted his law should be administered by a committee of the privy council sitting in London. Once at work it pursued a policy of anglicization unhindered until the creation of a special department for distinct functions of government in Scotland, the Scottish Office, in 1885. Even then, the civil servants in charge of education would not be based in Edinburgh until 1939.[46]

A patriotic faction also existed in the Faculty of Advocates, led by James Lorimer, professor of public law at the University of Edinburgh from 1862. He hoped for a second golden age of Enlightenment.

From his chair he sought to help in restoring his city to its former cultural and intellectual pre-eminence. To him this first meant halting the relative decline of the university, as of others in Scotland, no longer the best in the world compared with those in Germany. In 1852 Lorimer set up a pressure group to seek a way forward along the established lines of broad education based on moral philosophy (as opposed to the specialization of Oxford and Cambridge, now also striving to meet the Teutonic challenge). Lorimer accepted there would need to be some specialization in the end, because learning had to be fostered and advanced as well as communicated. But this should not happen at the undergraduate level, only in graduate schools of research: in effect he prefigured the German-American ideal of a university dominating the western world today. Yet his final purpose for his nation was more European, to foster an intelligentsia. All these concepts appeared at any rate alien to the cheerful philistinism of England, berated now even by a native cultural critic, Matthew Arnold.[47]

In his own discipline Lorimer was, with his *Institutes of Law, a treatise of the principles of jurisprudence as determined by nature* (1872), the last great institutional writer in the Scots tradition. Here again he saw a threat from England, which was now acquiring what it had never had, a philosophy of law – even if that amounted to little by the standards of other jurisdictions. At the hands of Jeremy Bentham and John Austin it extended the curious English political doctrine of absolute parliamentary sovereignty. This meant law was just what the state said it was. The function of jurisprudence lay in classifying principles, clarifying concepts, creating a logic – and not in telling the law what it ought to be. Scots, by contrast, had always looked for sources of the law outside itself. Lorimer did so too, defining the source as nature. His was an effort 'to vindicate the necessary character of jurisprudence by exhibiting it as a branch of the science of nature'. The preface of his book says he gives the name of natural law to the rule of life being recognized gradually as faith becomes more reasonable and reason more faithful: 'Before another decade elapses, the preference for the older and grander traditions which Grotius inherited from Socrates through the Stoics and the Roman jurists, over those which Bentham transmitted to Austin, will, I hope, be as universal and unequivocal as that for classical and medieval architecture over the architecture of the Georgian era has already become.'[48]

⁂

Lorimer was not in the event a prophet for Scots or any other law. But his analogy with architecture proved perfect for Edinburgh. In his lifetime the capital's architecture returned to its sources to enrich the recent Georgian austerity. A result was the second New Town, covering the lower slopes of the shallow ridge where the first New Town stood. Just as the first New Town had brought flight from the Old Town, so the second New Town caused drift from the first, if without issuing in the same social disaster. Inside James Craig's oblong the classical buildings' impersonal amplitude, their air of superior anonymity, their lack of functional precision, prolonged their life. They could serve just as well when subdivided into flats or knocked together into hotels or transformed into offices. By the end of the nineteenth century few of these houses still fulfilled their original purpose of residence for a single family. But the new, mostly commercial owners had just as much interest in preserving their fabric.

The English aesthete John Ruskin disapproved. His parents had come from Edinburgh and moved south before his birth in 1819. He grew up in London without developing any affection for his ancestral home, as became clear when the Philosophical Society of Edinburgh invited him to give a series of architectural lectures in 1853. He went for the jugular: 'You are all proud of your city; surely you must feel it a duty in some sort to justify your pride; that is to say, to give yourselves a *right* to be proud of it. That you were born under the shadow of its two fantastic mountains, that you live where from your room windows you can trace the shores of the glittering Firth, are no rightful subjects of pride.' In fact, the scenery ought to count for nothing: it was the architecture, especially the architecture of houses, rather than of palaces or churches, that made a great city. In this respect Edinburgh was dull. See the windows: they all looked the same. Each featured what Ruskin called a bold square-cut jamb (in the Lothians' language it is a lugged architrave). 'How many windows precisely of this form do you suppose there are in the New Town?' demanded Ruskin. 'I have not counted them all through the town, but I counted them this morning along this very Queen Street in which your hall is; and on the one side of that street, there are of those windows, absolutely similar to this sample, and altogether devoid of any relief by decoration, 678.' The citizens ought to rebuild their city in tune with the Victorian times: 'Introduce your Gothic line by line and stone by stone; never mind mixing it with your present architecture; your existing houses will be none the worse for having little bits of better work fitted to them; build a porch, or point a window, if you can do nothing else; and remember that it is the glory of Gothic architecture that it can do anything.' Then, he added, Edinburgh might become as fine as Verona. *Verona?* Well, it is indeed a fine city but by any standards its role in western culture has been minor compared to Edinburgh's. This was not the last English advice the capital of Scotland got to rebuild itself, nor the last it spurned.[49]

❧

In fact, even as Ruskin spoke, modern Edinburgh was changing from a classical into a romantic city as well. It was not just a matter of building up the buildings but also of seizing on the setting. Perhaps only a Londoner like Ruskin could have regarded flat terrain as the norm and deployment of townscape in landscape as a matter of no interest. If he had gone beyond George Street, he might have arrived at a different view. The expansion of the New Town had already reached right down to the foot of its original shallow ridge, to Stockbridge and Canonmills, in other words to the Water of Leith – but had already crossed it too. The city then became romantic not in the sense of Scott's 'mine own romantic town', an incarnation of history, but in a novel blend of urbanity with nature. Here houses could look out from among overhanging trees into sheer gorges – or else, where landscape itself did not do the work, a surprise might lie in wait in the built environment as streets turned on to unexpected vistas. Who, seeing the initial regularity of the New Town, would ever suspect the roadfork-cum-precipice that terminates Queensferry Street, or the undulating Royal Circus that lurks around the corner from Howe Street?

Released from its original strict classicism Edinburgh's style could wax sumptuous without the help of any phoney Gothic. What might be called a third New Town arose in the West End. Its still Georgian formality was mixed with rich Victorian detail, the ensemble giving a strong sense of the prosperous security of the city at this period. Housing here could outdo even the finest in the first New Town – for example, in the mansion on six storeys at Rothesay Terrace built in 1883 by the Findlays of Aberlour, proprietors of *The Scotsman*, together with the rear outlook they paid for, too, across a picturesque refurbishment of Dean Village. From their back windows they could also view Thomas Telford's spectacular Dean Bridge (1829–31) by which the New Town crossed to the garden suburb beyond.[50]

At the opposite eastern end the New Town descended by degrees into something still solid but less extraordinary, ending in the lines of tenements that by the 1890s ran the length of Leith Walk. This then had something about it of a Parisian boulevard, at least one in the *faubourgs* – though in quality of housing it went fast downhill from stately at the top to scruffy at the bottom. Tenements became the most distinctive type of Edinburgh's Victorian housing, invading or pressing on all but the most opulent suburbs, yet Leith was not the largest zone of them. That had to be sought rather on the opposite, southern side of the city beyond the open Meadows in Marchmont, Bruntsfield or Merchiston. Here the tone rather rose than fell with distance from the centre. The tenements, while respectable, gave way at length to a more usual sort of suburbia in the Grange. Its villas were often still classical in inspiration, if seldom so severe as in the first New Town, but could be tempted into variety. Bay windows grew popular here, to be imitated in other cities. They invited admiration of lilac and laburnum in the garden, but more especially suited Edinburgh's brief days of midwinter when more light was needed in the sitting room than a plain Georgian window flush with the facade could offer. Finally, workers' tenements teemed down Dalry and Gorgie and Slateford Roads, in a close-built quarter criss-crossed by canals and railways. That squared the circle of the ancient urban core.

Edinburgh's tenements were of stone, so they still stand and even today house about a third of the population. They are above all what make this a Scottish city (or indeed a European city, for Paris and Vienna have the same). The development was different from that in England where workers came to be housed in terraces erected in brick. The tenement created common interests and shared responsibilities; the terrace brought neither because it conveyed separate territorial rights. Scotland knows no such thing as leasehold, any more than freehold, and when work is needed on a tenement the several proprietors have to get together to agree. In their Victorian form flats could be cramped. But the workers liked things that way. An association was formed in 1860 to encourage them to build and buy their own homes. The steering committee embarked on a consultation whether to construct in Scottish or English style. The responses took a patriotic line: 'the question was whether they should recommend the English system of houses or the Scottish system of flats; and it is remarkable how much the committee, and, indeed, every working man they had occasion to consult were impressed with the idea of preserving the ancient and national character of their domiciles'. Englishmen might assume that Scots would prefer to live in houses but 'your committee believes that after all Edinburgh architecture – also substantially that of Paris – is based on a far higher principle of social philosophy. The proverb, *An Englishman's home is his castle*, contains a very selfish, if not an impractical idea.'[51]

Yet amid growing diversity of style the city preserved a vital degree of harmony. Again, the best analogy was with Paris, where even after the contemporary reconstruction by Baron Haussmann the architectures of three centuries promenaded side by side. In Edinburgh it became equally possible against an antique backdrop to follow later gradations from the severest classical buildings to the liveliest of their eclectic successors. Harmony is hardly what we expect of Victorian cities, and here it may not yet be safe from a crasser evolution of the future (perhaps indeed already under way). But the Victorian city is far from gone. This was no accident.

※

Varied as the architecture became its variation stayed under strict control, thanks again to the Scottish feudal system, which had already allowed transition from medieval burgh to modern city. This may seem paradoxical: most European countries had by now cast off feudalism. Yet in Edinburgh and in Scotland the system was rationalized and elaborated for application to new needs far beyond anything known in the Middle Ages.

The hierarchy of feudalism stayed in place but superiors embroidered it in ingenious ways. They imposed on the feuars comprehensive conditions, or real burdens, governing how land should be used and built up. This distribution of rights and responsibilities seems unequal, yet it brought inclusion and partnership. The system after all recognized no absolute ownership, no control vested in individuals free of legal constraint. Rather, as urban development gathered pace, it devolved an interest in land and buildings to more and more stakeholders. Benefits were even-handed too. Feudalism in modern guise offered the security needed for investment, while setting standards that ensured long-term quality would not be sacrificed to short-term profits. It became in effect a spontaneous system of self-regulation offering something to all concerned.[52]

Feuing plans evolved into elaborate documents specifying a wide range of real burdens. They might now not just, as before, define the layout of streets and building lines but also insist in great detail on particular features – for example, the use of certain materials, even sandstone from named quarries. For example, in Home Street the feuars were not to put up in their backyards any structure over seven foot high, and especially not steam engines. Along at Tollcross it was the builder who had to 'uphold and maintain the street, causeways and common sewers'. At Merchiston the superior made so bold as to specify he wanted only 'villas or self-contained dwelling houses with gardens or pleasure grounds which are occupied by the upper and middle classes of the city'; social prejudice was seldom expressed so unsubtly. Out at Craigleith houses would be self-contained but not have 'high doors' or 'low doors', that is, come divided into flats with their own entrances. Down at Trinity the rules were still more discreetly expressed, but made sure this would turn into a suburb of villas with large gardens. So it went on.[53]

Things sometimes worked out less than ideally. A major scheme for the land between Leith Walk and Easter Road never took off until an over-elaborate feuing plan was toned down. The original one, drawn up by the architect William Playfair, envisaged the crescents and squares of a fourth New Town. Feuars got an assurance that, in defence of the area's cachet, minimum prices would be set for the plots. They proved too high and put everyone off. The Court of Session had to step in to revoke this condition of

the feu in 1880, after which the area was covered in humble tenements.

But in general Edinburgh's housing was not cheap. Under feudalism successive interests acquiring a stake in development all wanted
a pay-off in the end. This raised the price of property. Less space was
affordable for a given rental than in English cities. Land had to be
more built up to cover the charges on it. That required construction
of tenements spreading the cost, while the densities in turn added
value to the plots. So the appearance of Edinburgh in olden times
did not change in the Victorian suburbs as much as it might have
done. Not until the emergence of bungalow-land in the twentieth
century did the city take on an entirely new look.[54]

In other ways, in security of tenure, relatively risk-free improvement and release of the intrinsic value of land, feudalism had much
to commend it. In fact it liberated the development of Edinburgh.
The classical legacy gave way to a quantity and quality of Victorian
tenements and villas that transformed the townscape. Yet within
these liberal limits it still conveyed its impression of harmony, and
does so to this day.

୬

Such was the New Town or Towns. But they left out of account the
Old Town, which seemed to have got no better since the bourgeoisie
fled it at the turn of the nineteenth century. It did trail along in the
wake of Edinburgh's general economic expansion to the extent of
somehow finding room for more and more people to crowd in,
packed into subdivided flats where the better off had once lived. This
population totalled 30,000 by its peak at the census of 1861. Among
other things the returns showed the Old Town contained 1,530 flats
of one room occupied by six to fifteen people; they had to sleep in
shifts. Middle Mealmarket Stair in the Cowgate had fifty-nine flats
with 248 occupants and no toilet. On such a stair, access to each
floor was gained by a dark, narrow flight of stone steps with passages
leading off to the flats. Tenants needed to grope about in what
natural light there was, and since the tenements had been built so
near one another the sun could not reach every window. There were
120 flats in the Old Town with no window, while another 900 lay
in cellars, dark and damp. Ill-paved closes outside remained mired in

muck. There was no main drainage. All water for domestic use still had to be lugged up the stairs and thrown out of the windows when no longer needed; then it gathered in cesspools. The only channels for carrying the ooze right out of town were 'foul burns', open sewers leading to some natural watercourse and so at last to the Firth of Forth – though the burns would also be tapped along the way to irrigate market gardens and meadows. Their stench around Holyrood grew so vile that Queen Victoria refused to stay there when she visited her Scottish capital, and descended on the Duke of Buccleuch at Dalkeith.[55]

The Old Town had once been the colourful backdrop to bourgeois life. Even now, advocates had to mount from the New Town to the law courts in the High Street, while professors could peer down at the Cowgate as they crossed the South Bridge to the university. They would not want to get closer. Observers penetrated the Old Town like explorers of an unknown land, unless some business took them there. A gynaecologist, Dr Alexander Miller, found the dwellings 'generally very filthy'. The worst were those consisting of a single room, 'always ill-ventilated, both from the nature of its construction and from the densely peopled and confined locality in which it is situated'. Remarkable was the absence of material possessions: 'A few of the lowest poor have a bedstead, but by far the larger portion have none; these make up a kind of bed on the floor with straw, on which a whole family are huddled together, some naked and the others in the same clothes they have worn during the day.' Miller at least faced all this with a stronger stomach than his colleague Frederick Hill: 'Several apartments are so close that it is difficult for a person when he first enters them to breathe. In several instances I had to retreat to the door to write down my notes, as I found the stench and close atmosphere produce a sickening sensation which, on one occasion, terminated in vomiting.'[56]

To Victorians it came as no surprise that the moral squalor of the people found its match in the physical squalor of the buildings; on the contrary, they reckoned the first caused the second. For George Bell, author of *Day and Night in the Wynds of Edinburgh* (1849), a walk up the High Street on a Sunday evening was an approach to hell. If anything, the women were the worst: 'To see the mouth of a close choked up by a few of the corrupt female inhabitants thereof, all half drunk, and making the walls of the dismal access to their infernal homes shake with their hyena-like laughter and oath-impregnated voices of rage – to see this, I say, gives origin to a flood of gloomy reflections.' The rot started early. At the Lawn-market, 'I was again arrested in my progress ... by four grown lads, who were wrestling with each other by way of amusement, and the while roaring out the most shocking obscenities and most fearful blasphemies ... My eye caught the light shed by the light of a low spirit-shop and the whole host of these unhappy youths flashed across my mind.'

So Bell blamed it all on booze: 'From the toothless infant to the toothless old man, the population of the wynds drinks whisky. The drunken drama that is enacted on Saturday night and Sabbath morning beggars description ... It is impossible to say how much is expended on the chronic drinking, or everyday consumption of whisky, and how much on the weekly exacerbation, or grand infernal orgy.' In a second tract, *Blackfriars Wynd Analysed* (1850), he tried to work out the cost of the alcohol they consumed to the 1,000 or so people living in this one thoroughfare from the High Street to the Cowgate. If each drank four gallons of whisky a year (that works out at two modern drams a day, which seems a modest estimate), it would cost the wynd over £2,000 in all. Yet the average income of each person there was £5, so £5,000 for the whole lot. Out of that, £3,000 would have to go on food and £650 on rent, not to speak of coal and clothing. So how did the wynd subsist? The answer was begging or crime, that is, theft and prostitution. 'If we learned that they yield £2,000 per annum to the wynd, it would in no degree surprise us.' A black economy indeed.[57]

William Tait, another young doctor, made a study of *Magdalenism*, as he called it, published in 1842. He reckoned 800 prostitutes worked the city. Among those treated for venereal disease, 4 per cent were under fifteen (including children aged nine or ten), 66 per cent in their late teens and only 3 per cent over thirty. A quarter of them lived 'privately' and the rest were to be sought in 200 brothels, mainly in the Old Town, fifty in the High Street alone, but some in the New Town too. There were another 1,000 'sly prostitutes', part-timers selling themselves when they needed money or felt like it. These would hire rooms in 'houses of assignation' where no questions were asked. Why did they veer between virtue and vice? 'A very great number of the prostitutes confess that the desecration of the Sabbath ... was one of the principal causes of inducing them to go astray.' And how could you tell one who otherwise might just blend into the urban scene? 'All do not drink to excess – all do not lie – all do not steal – but almost all swear. It is one of the initiatory accomplishments of their profession, which the prostitutes early acquire; and they make use of it on all occasions.' There was demand as well as supply. It often arose among 'lads who come from the country to learn businesses in town or to receive a college education'. Pornography was available, yet some still frequented brothels after embarking on their careers: 'The young lawyer, physician and general student view this kind of relaxation as indispensable for their health,' it being impossible before marriage to have sex with women of their own class. Heavens above, 'the pulpit is not even exempted from the inroads and consequences of these habits'.[58]

Isabella Bird, an intrepid lady who had been led by Sherpas across the Himalayan Mountains and had rubbed noses with man-eating Hawaiians, decided in 1869 on an expedition just as plucky through the closes of her native city. She reached a room occupied by whores, twelve foot square with ashes all over the floor and a bedstead, table and stool: 'A girl of about 18, very poorly dressed, was sitting on the stool; two others, older and very much undressed, were sitting on the floor, and the three were eating, in a most swinish fashion, out of a black pot containing fish.' It came back to Mrs Bird she had 'shared a similar meal in similar primitive fashion in an Indian wigwam in Hudson's Bay Territory but the women who worshipped the Great Spirit were modest in their dress and manner and looked *human*, which these "Christian" young women did not'.[59]

❧

What on earth could be done about this sink of iniquity? National legislation proved to be no help. The old and inadequate Scots Poor Law finally underwent reform in 1845, but while the new one may have been more efficient it was no less mean. In fact average numbers getting relief in Edinburgh declined from over 3,000 beforehand to little more than 1,000 afterwards, possibly because the capital was growing richer or because administrators of the law turned yet more tight-fisted.

A town council like Edinburgh's could get the private legislation it wanted through at Westminster but faced the same dilemmas. It hesitated between Police Acts and Improvement Acts, that is, between retribution and incentive. The first Police Act had come in 1805, when the term police connoted in Scotland more than it does now: not only catching crooks but also enforcing civil regulations, including environmental ones. The force in Edinburgh did not seem much good at whatever it did. The plods had floundered when faced with the Tron Riot of 1812 and even a quarter-century later in 1838, when a snowball fight in front of the university turned into a tumult of town and gown, troops had to be called down from the castle to disperse it. One problem may have been that the policemen were often no better, in particular no more sober, than the suspects they sought to arrest. It is hard to tell in such a boozy city, but possibly the early nineteenth century was the booziest age of all. In 1841–3, arrests for drunkenness totalled 13,858, one-sixteenth of the population, and many other offences were aggravated by drink. But then a quarter of the police suffered dismissal every year for misconduct of some kind; over time two in three were reported for being drunk on duty. A further Police Act followed in 1848, though its point was to give the council the in essence sanitary powers it needed to deal with the Old Town.[60]

The first of the Improvement Acts had come in 1827. It provided for the opening up of new streets to let light and air into the most fetid quarters, even to bypass them overhead, as George IV Bridge did. The architecture was supposed to be Old Flemish, whatever that might mean; today it looks in no way out of place. A second Improvement Act in 1867 created ten more new streets lined with model tenements. They were built in Scottish Baronial style, distantly imitating the medieval castles of Glamis and Craigievar with quaint round turrets and steep conical roofs. This became truly a national style, one for high and low: Queen Victoria used it at Balmoral in the shadow of the Grampian Mountains just as a local architect, James Lessels, did when he put up tenements surveying the tracks into Waverley Station. Such was the city's mix that Scottish Baronial could fit in with ease, in fact extremely well, yet it made a pastiche of much of the Royal Mile. One aim was to have buildings appear more venerable than they are – which seems to take in the tourists.

Under the Act of 1867 a wide zone of clearance ran south from the Cowgate to the Flodden Wall, or what remained of it, land long ago covered by monasteries and their gardens, which had come to contain some of the worst slums. One building replacing them was Heriot-Watt College, so named because it involved the opulent Heriot's Trust taking over the Watt Institution, founded in 1821. This 'mechanics' institution', a typical product of Edinburgh's democratic ethos, provided for artisans to raise their practical expertise to an academic level, say, in mathematics or engineering. Nothing like it existed in Britain or anywhere else, the nearest equivalent being the German *technische Hochschulen*. Heriot-Watt College would turn a century later into the city's second university, but then migrated to a campus on the outskirts. Opposite its Victorian home arose what is now the National Museum of Scotland with its great hall, 'a huge elegant birdcage of glass and iron'. And in between runs Chambers Street. In the middle stands a statue of the man it is named after, author of the Act of 1867 and greatest lord provost of the century, William Chambers. His goal, common among city fathers of his time, was to foster civic pride. Unique was his wish to do so in and from the Old Town.[61]

❧

William made up one half of the publishing house of W. & R. Chambers. The other half, Robert, if not so masterful, was just as interesting. The brothers had been born to a merchant in Peebles who went bankrupt. They were then put as apprentices to a bookseller in Edinburgh. Though Robert suffered from deformed feet, with a Scot's heroic resolution he walked every day the five miles from his new home at Joppa into the city and back. If William supplied commercial acumen to the firm they at length set up, Robert brought intellectual aspiration. His idol was Scott and he wrote antiquarian history himself, such as the still useful *Traditions of Edinburgh* (1824). His big bestseller was *Vestiges of the Natural History of Creation* (1844), which he preferred to bring out anonymously. This was because it removed God from history, except perhaps in some initial act of creation; the universe had since run on under its own laws. Chambers portrayed it as an epic of progress – clouds of gas condensing into stars and planets, primeval soup giving rise to life, finally man ascending from apes. That might seem to presage Charles Darwin's *Origin of Species* (1859), but it offered nothing as scientific as the principle of natural selection or the theory of evolution. Darwin, after finishing the education he had begun with medicine at Edinburgh, spent five years sailing around the world on the *Beagle* and dropped off at the Galapagos Islands to test his hypotheses by observations nobody else had made. Chambers just cobbled together others' ideas to show to his own satisfaction how nature followed some force impelling it ever onwards and upwards. It was all book-learning, but he had a gift of simple exposition. He passed on to his readers knowledge that would otherwise have remained confined in learned tomes. This was what made him a risk to religious orthodoxy: philosophers of the Enlightenment might have agreed with him in substance, but their books had not been read by the masses.

W. & R. Chambers boomed because the masses were its market, with titles such as *Chambers's Atlas for the People, Chambers's Cyclopaedia of English Literature, Chambers's Graduated Arithmetic, Chambers's Miscellany of Instructive and Entertaining Tracts, Chambers's Scottish National Histories* and so on. It was a sign how, with political reform and economic expansion, popular forces could no longer be kept in their place. Like Carlyle and Simpson, the Chambers brothers did not think the olympian detachment of the enlightened a good enough outlook on life. For them too, one offshoot of Scottish philosophy – political economy – denied human creativity and improvement. They looked rather to environmental and educational reform. If the message of the *Vestiges* was true, the value of their initiatives would increase generation by generation. Urchins were now heard bawling to their pals across the streets of Edinburgh, 'Hey, Jimmy, son o' a cabbage, whaur are ye progressin'?'[62]

The Chambers brothers rose into the capital's elite. Being public-spirited fellows, they served on the town council. Robert would have become lord provost in 1848 had he not attracted suspicion of being the author of *Vestiges*. William did become lord provost in 1865, to serve six years. He was not one to let his opinions compromise his prospects.

Chambers took over at a crux. The town council had sweeping sanitary powers under the Act of 1848 but was not using them. Demolition of slums would be fine, but where were the people to go? Cockburn twittered on about the capital's prettiness being spoiled by all these proles, but a fiery fundamentalist, the Reverend James Begg, minister of the Free Church at Newington, roared a retort: 'It is a cruel mockery to speak to the torpid and festering masses of Taste and the beauties of Edinburgh.' Begg was rare in his time in arguing bad buildings caused bad people, rather than the other way about: 'You will never get the unclean heart of Edinburgh gutted out until you plant it all around with new houses.'[63] His aim was for the workers to own their own homes, and he quoted a popular song:

> I hae a hoose o' my ain
> I'll tak dunts frae naebody.

There was a response from the people Begg wanted to reach. As already recounted, craftsmen formed a cooperative building company on patriotic principles in 1860. At Stockbridge the stonemasons laid out a 'colony', with houses 'two stories high and containing three to six moderately sized rooms, with every convenience, the best sanitary arrangements and a plot of ground 20 foot square' – they are there still, a few occupied by the descendants of the original owners. The same followed at Fountainbridge and Merchiston. The labour aristocracy of Edinburgh showed itself well capable of self-help: different trades proudly left their armorial bearings at the gable-ends.

But what of those lower down the scale? Chambers saw the difficulty of creating a new class of owner-occupiers when most workers lived at best on a slim margin. His idea was rather that the wealthy should sponsor the building of homes for rent. In 1849 he had helped to launch the Pilrig Model Dwellings Company; its prime development of an H-block, even graced by a bit of classical detail, still stands in Pilrig Street down Leith Walk. But, by contemporary conceptions, that was as far as intervention in the market could go. When in 1885 a royal commission on housing sat, Andy Telfer, joiner and president of the Edinburgh trades council, 'speaking on behalf of the working classes, strongly opposed the town council in any sense becoming responsible for the housing of the people'.[64] Public construction of homes remained inconceivable as yet.

The housing controversy in Edinburgh had meanwhile been brought up short in 1861. On 24 November a tenement in the High Street collapsed; thirty-five people were killed and many more injured. A boy trapped in the rubble won the heart of the city by urging on his rescuers with 'Heave awa, lads, I'm no deid yet!' Now, though, the talking had to stop. Horrified public reaction led within a year to the appointment of the country's first Medical Officer of Health, Dr Henry Littlejohn, with broad responsibilities for the urban environment. He at once embarked on a statistical survey exposing its huge contrasts. He showed the death-rate in the worst parishes ran twice as high as in the best.

So when Chambers came into office in 1865, he had the ammunition he needed to make himself a great reforming lord provost. As the basis of policy he drew a contrast not between bourgeoisie and proletariat but between respectable and unrespectable working class. While artisans could nowadays live well enough and so move on and up in the world, 'the dwellings from which the honestly industrious have fled are occupied for the most part by classes utterly abject – something at which the upper world would shudder to approach ... The vacating of dwellings has only rendered our Old Town closes a convenient receptacle for those who in due time furnish occupation to the inspectors of the poor, the police and the criminal tribunals.' Yet Chambers's central project, of cutting streets through the Old Town, was not meant to turn it into yet another New Town: 'I think the tenements should be mainly designed for the trading and working classes, with shops or places of business on the ground storeys.' Enlightened improvement was at last to spread its blessings right down the social scale, yet in respect for the individualism of people and places rather than in pursuit of some bloodless universal ideal. Chalmers felt sure of giving 'a new character to the Old Town without injuring its picturesque appearance'. Industry and decency were to be rewarded within the milieu that generated them – something as unlike the public housing policies of the twentieth century as could be imagined. Following his predecessor as lord provost a century before, George Drummond, Chambers remained content to start something he would not live to see finished. The new build was in one sense the easy bit: it took, for example, thirty years to make sure every home in the city had a toilet carrying away its waste into a sewer.[65]

૨૨

By the end of the century Edinburgh had solved not all its problems but at least the worst of them, and could take stock. While much of the Old Town was now sanitized, or indeed swept away, nobody wanted the better buildings to follow – and there were fine ones from earlier ages still sound enough for a further lease of life. What should be done?

Proposals general and particular came from Patrick Geddes, botanist, planner, social reformer, economic theorist. He sought to be profound as well as practical. He saw here a community once whole but now divided between Old Town and New Town. He was ready to start repairing it himself. He took up residence in James Court off the High Street, hoping to lead a movement of the middle class back. He converted the observatory on Castle Hill into the Outlook Tower. There he installed a *camera obscura* to survey the whole city and show the relations between its landscape, economy and people. The tracts he wrote read like transcripts of commentaries he might have given to visitors as they peered through his reflecting glass:

> Seldom is so full and dramatic a set of contrasts crowded into one narrow region. Hence one type of native mind, one type of visitor also, sees only the historical, the romantic aspect of Scotland; another type, another visitor, the utilitarian and the economic, and this no less truly. Here in Lothian or there in Fife, as similarly in the West, we have economic regions long self-centred and still largely self-contained, fertile enough to yield adequate subsistence, yet stern enough also not to yield this without exceptional effort, exceptional economy. The high reputation of the Scots gardener, the high standing of the Scottish insurance companies, are they not thus akin? – both going back to the same struggle of man with nature, the same peasant economy and foresight, shrewdness, calculation.[66]

Here was a vision of wholeness, of everything connected to everything else. Geddes thought the modern world had made an awful mistake dividing experience into compartments and causing minds to work the same way. By definition each compartment was contained in something bigger and could not be evaluated only from within: the result was dislocation. The same with a city – yet here the successive stages of the built environment could be viewed as facets of its wholeness. So dislocation had first to be tackled in the Old Town, where urban society had flowered before it fissured.

When Geddes turned theory into practice, however, outcomes were mixed. Refurbishment worked well in James Court and on the other side of the Lawnmarket in Riddle's Close. It worked less well nearby at Lady Stair's house. This was done up at the expense of the former Prime Minister, Lord Rosebery, a lover of Edinburgh whose own stately home at Dalmeny lay just outside the city. But the good intentions were submerged in frankly soppy notions of what a medieval building had been like: it just looks twee inside and out. An even more precious result came right at the other end of the Royal Mile, in the reconstruction of Whitehorse Close, 'so blatantly fake that it can be acquitted of any intention to deceive . . . a Hollywood dream'.

※

Geddes got Edinburgh wrong. Its architectural harmony could not conceal that behind the facades this was even yet a city of paradox, of opposites uneasily reconciled. Robert Louis Stevenson became the first to put into words how the cleft of Old Town and New Town exposed an inner truth about the place. In sublimated fashion it emerges in his *Strange Case of Dr Jekyll and Mr Hyde* (1886). The fiction is based on fact: the story from a century before of the double life of Deacon Brodie, by day a respectable tradesman and civic dignitary, by night a burglar so devilishly clever as to put the wind up the whole city. Stevenson transforms his material into something much more general and existential, a myth of modern man. Maddening, though, is that he sets the story in London – the one unconvincing thing about it. Edinburgh still intrudes.

'There is a square of ancient, handsome houses, now for the most part decayed from their high estate and let in flats and chambers to all sorts and conditions of men: map-engravers, architects, shady lawyers and the agents of obscure enterprises': obviously the rundown eastern end of the first New Town. At the time London's fogs were 'pea-soupers', descending and staying put for days on end, whereas Edinburgh had and still has fogs found nowhere else in the world, fogs which defy high winds and blow about rather than being dispersed. And what is the fog like in *Jekyll and Hyde*? 'The wind was continually charging and routing these embattled vapours ... here it would be dark like the backend of evening; and there would be a glow of a rich, lurid brown, like the light of some strange conflagration; and here, for a moment, the fog would be quite broken up, and a haggard shaft of daylight would glance in between the swirling wreaths.' Is that London or Edinburgh? Or again, 'it was a wild, cold, seasonable night of March, with a pale moon, lying on her back as though the wind had tilted her, and flying wrack of the most diaphanous and lawny texture. The wind made talking difficult, and flecked the blood into the face.' This does not sound like an English moon or an English wind.[67]

Still, Stevenson's achievement has not endeared him to all in his native city. He continues to arouse strong emotions there. Some admire him as foreigners admire him, while others detest him for his weakness in copping out to seek refuge in California and then Samoa. Edinburgh, with what he called 'the foulest climate under heaven', could have killed this invalid if he had not left – but how long was he going to live anyway, the wimp? He should have stayed and fought back, just as he shows young Archie Weir fighting back in *Weir of Hermiston* (1896), a novel of Edinburgh and potentially a great one, though in the event just a fragment. The book features a classic conflict of father and son, like that in the Stevenson family between the father who built lighthouses and the son who scribbled stories. Written in the tropics, even this distant echo of Edinburgh was too much for Stevenson. He died before he could finish it.

At least Stevenson is not to be faulted in knowledge of his hometown, or insight into it. Better even than Sir Walter Scott or James Hogg he could celebrate both the vices and the virtues lying at the heart of its paradox. He had lived its low life:

> I love night in the city,
> The lighted streets and the swinging gait of harlots.

They would call to him as he came along in his poseur's velvet coat: 'I have been all my days a dead hand at a harridan. I never saw one yet that could resist me.' Capable of being louche, even coarse, while still in Edinburgh, he would recall it from exile with almost unbearable poignancy. The single most moving poem of the city is his. He wrote it on Samoa for his wife, Fanny. After he died, she found it in the manuscript of *Weir of Hermiston*. It was published as the dedication of the work:

> I saw rain falling and the rainbow drawn
> On Lammermuir. Hearkening I heard again
> In my precipitous city beaten bells
> Winnow the keen sea wind. And here afar
> Intent on my own race and place I wrote . . .

CHAPTER SEVEN

'A VERY OLD-FASHIONED CITY'

(Dora Noyce)

ON 12 DECEMBER 1842, Francis, Lord Jeffrey, judge in the Court of Session, sat down at his home in Moray Place, Edinburgh, to write to a friend of long standing, John Ramsay McCulloch, professor of political economy at University College, London. They had been corresponding for years, most recently on the state of the United Kingdom. This they discussed in a manner that might strike a familiar note today. They saw a mature economy challenged by rivalry from developing countries which had set out to follow along the road to industrialization. McCulloch, an orthodox not to say rigid advocate of free trade, denied the principle or practice of it ought in any way to be sacrificed to threats from abroad. Jeffrey was less certain: 'I wish I could feel the same assurance you seem to do, as to our being in no danger from foreign competition, assisted and aggravated in its effects ... by national jealousies and erroneous notions of self-interest.' But he consoled himself that, without this problem, everything in the British garden would be rosy: 'I do not see how the increase of our manufacturing population should be a subject of regret or alarm, or on what grounds any serious or permanent distress need be apprehended, among these classes in particular.' Only time could tell whether the first globalization they were living through might menace the industrial leadership of the United Kingdom. In pondering an unanswerable question, Jeffrey fell back on the platitudes of one who during his life had seen most of his hopes fulfilled. He signed off saying to McCulloch he would be 'satisfied to have a closer vision of the condition of the country some time about the year 1900, before which, I feel persuaded, the problems we are puzzled about will be substantially resolved.'[1]

Jeffrey had in the first half of his career won renown at home and abroad as editor of the *Edinburgh Review*. McCulloch was a valued contributor to the magazine, even while himself editing *The Scotsman*, the city's main newspaper, founded in 1817. But his most congenial life's work lay in elaborating the political economy of Adam Smith. McCulloch added to this work as author of the classical theory of public finance. No firebrand, he was all the same a man of distinguished mind, by any standards worthy of a professorship. The post he held in the University of London had not been his first choice, however. It was a strange fact that until relatively late Scotland boasted no academic chair in the economic science she had invented. In 1827 a plan emerged to endow one at the University of Edinburgh. McCulloch appeared the obvious candidate: for that reason he was also behind the plan. But the Tory boss of Scotland, Lord Melville, preferred not to sanction the chair if a Whig was going to get it. 'The only real obstacle is Melville,' McCulloch noted, 'but I believe that will be found insurmountable, and that consequently the project will for the present fall to the ground.' The endowment went instead to London, and McCulloch with it. There he continued to teach that no government should spend a penny more than it raised in taxes. In line with this dogma he was almost a parody of the earnest, humourless side of the national character. The wags at *Blackwood's Edinburgh Magazine* pilloried him as that 'sour, surly, dogged animal', the Stot (in Scots, a castrated steer).[2]

The free trade McCulloch espoused would come in 1846 at the hands not of the Whigs but of a Conservative Prime Minister, Sir Robert Peel. His conversion to the cause got a warm welcome in Glasgow, which conducted a global commerce, but not so much in Edinburgh. It remained dominated by lawyers – and lawyers ran cartels, so showed no love of competition for its own sake, here or anywhere else. In fact local Tory intellectuals, represented in *Blackwood's*, had always denounced political economy as insane, on the grounds that unfettered markets sundered the bonds of mutual protection and loyalty holding society together. Instead the benevolent gentry and downtrodden workers should join forces against utilitarian reformers and their capitalist friends. It was a romantic notion, sometimes given romantic expression. A patriotic stalwart of *Blackwood's*, William Aytoun, professor of rhetoric at the University of Edinburgh, chose satiric verse as the vehicle for his forecast that free trade would bring violent protest (and quite right too) from the farm-workers it was bound to beggar:

> Barley from Mecklenburg, grain from Polonia,
> Butter from Holland, American cheese,
> Bacon gratuitous,
> Cargos fortuitous,
> Float to our shores with each prosperous breeze.
> What need we care though a desperate peasantry
> Prowl round the stockyards with tinder and match?
> Blandly we'll smile at such practical pleasantry:
> Downing Street's not surmounted by thatch.[3]

❦

Aytoun might have been describing the trade of Leith. The port had never greatly succeeded in intercontinental commerce, and still trafficked mainly with northern Europe. In the second half of the nineteenth century it yet recovered from its all but ruinous problems in the first half. Though now a separate municipality, it could mobilize capital from Edinburgh. That made heavy investments possible – in railways, in larger steamships and in mechanized loading and unloading. Not far short of a million tons of shipping were soon being entered and cleared from Leith in most years. Further extensions to the docks followed: the Albert Dock on the east, the Victoria Dock on the west and then in 1881 the still larger Edinburgh Dock (named after the Duke of Edinburgh, who opened it).[4]

What happened at Leith reflected what happened in statelier mode up the road in Edinburgh. Right until 1914, the city's building boom showed no sign of flagging. Brewing dynasties were lavish patrons of novel landmarks: the McEwan Hall (1888–97) at the university, 'a magnificent petrified blancmange', and the Usher Hall (1910–14), the main venue for concerts, 'executed with the utmost suavity and precision'. Edinburgh acquired modern theatres, including the Royal Lyceum in 1883 and the King's in 1905–6, huge hotels at the extremities of Princes Street, the North British in 1895 and the Caledonian in 1899–1903, and along its length big department stores, Jenner's in 1893–5 and R. W. Forsyth in 1906. The

North Bridge was reconstructed in 1894–7 with, at the southern end of the span, prominent new buildings on either side, Patrick Thomson's, yet another department store, and the offices of *The Scotsman*.

In fact the richest man in Edinburgh at the turn of the century was a builder, James Steel. He had arrived in 1862 after going bankrupt in his native Lanarkshire. As a Victorian Scot, he felt ashamed. The city offered him both the anonymity he sought while he got back on his feet and the opportunities he needed to make a fresh start. He spent the rest of his career making up for past errors, in business and in bountiful gifts to his dissenting Church. By 1903 things had turned right round for him: as lord provost he welcomed King Edward VII, who gave him a knighthood. Asked at a public inquiry what his income was, he said £80,000. When the questioner reiterated that he had asked about his income not his wealth, Steel gave the same answer; £80,000 was not what he had saved during his life but what he earned every year, in modern money equivalent to £5 million. Starting at Tollcross, he had constructed whole quarters of the city: an extension of the West End beyond Palmerston Place, the working-class district of Dalry and all sorts of intermediate areas, Comely Bank, Merchiston, Sciennes and more. In the execution he was a feudal despot. A typical charter drawn up at his behest required that 'the whole of the fronts, as well as the ornamented parts, shall be of a style and quality of work to be approved of by the superiors', while the actual walls were to be 'in stone from a quarry which in their opinion is suitable in colour and quality'.[5] He not only served but also commanded – and sustained for a further term the architectural harmony of Edinburgh.

※

On a smaller scale the material culture of the city grew more opulent as well, if still inspired by the traditions of its own crafts. The best bearer of those traditions was Robert Lorimer, son of the James Lorimer who had been a patriotic professor of public law at the university. James's devotion to the national legal legacy found a counterpart in Robert's commitment to Scottish domestic architecture and the allied arts. He too had first been set to learn the law, but could not take to it. The family numbered among its friends one of Edinburgh's leading architects, William Burn, and under his wing young Lorimer set out to practise the same profession. His interests ranged wider, however, to embrace craftsmanship in everything that can go into a building – stone, wood, iron, plaster, glass – or indeed its plenishing – furniture, bedspreads, curtains and so on.

Lorimer's interiors survive in the New Town and the West End, at Belgrave Crescent, Drummond Place, Heriot Row and Rothesay Terrace. He himself lived in Melville Street, where he varied a typical uniform terraced house with his own additions, a balcony and small-paned windows. He found ampler scope in spreading suburbs, especially at Colinton. Here he designed modern homes with a Scots accent in their crowstep gables, stair-towers, harling and pantiles. Out in the Lothians, he helped to develop what are now resorts or commuter towns, Gullane and North Berwick. He restored castles: Bavelaw at Balerno is an example. He designed churches, such as the Church of the Good Shepherd at Murrayfield, a small building on a suburban hillock constructed of rich Hailes stone with red dressings, Victorian Gothic again in Scottish guise. His greatest Gothic work was the Thistle Chapel at St Giles, a lavish composition both inside with its furnishing, carving or glazing and outside with its graceful buttresses.

Wherever possible, Lorimer employed local artists and materials. He discovered the woman painter Phoebe Traquair: 'I don't know anyone who is as sympathetic to me artistically. She's so sane, such a lover of simplicity, and the things that give real pleasure are the simplest things of nature.' She produced the enamelled armorial plates in the Thistle Chapel, but most memorably the mural decoration of Bellevue Chapel in the New Town with its heavenly hosts of trumpeting angels. Lorimer had his furniture made by the firm of Whytock & Reid, which traced its origins back to the eighteenth century and went out of business only in 2004. He collaborated best of all with two wood-carvers, Messrs W. and A. Clow. He was himself in his element in a carpenter's workshop: he loved the noise of plane and chisel, and drew inspiration from the slow emergence of form out of a shapeless block of wood. The Clow brothers had never met an architect so eager to exploit their skills, and for their part they set themselves to study and develop his ideas. Their stalls in the Thistle

Chapel show how perfectly they came to understand his mind. Lorimer's first biographer, Christopher Hussey, went to interview them after his death in 1929:

> I wish I could draw a lifelike portrait of the brothers Clow to whose genius in carving Lorimer owed so much. On the upper floors of a gaunt Edinburgh mansion one comes upon them out of a dark passage, surrounded by a garden of wooden flowers: two identical middle-aged men looking, in their long grey overalls, like Tweedledum and Tweedledee grown spare and kindly. To this day I do not know which is W and which is A for they have long since become a single personality and tend to speak antiphonally. To hear their memories of 25 years' work with Lorimer was like hearing the psalms read by a small congregation:
>
> W: No architect has given us such scope.
> A: We worked for him exclusively.
> Both: Aye, for 30 years we worked for nobody else.
>
> A: We met Sir Robert in 1892.
> W: He had been in practice a year.
> Both: He wanted someone to take an interest, ye see.
>
> W: At the same time he wanted to cultivate the crafts in
>   Edinburgh.
> A: And give work to Edinburgh craftsmen for preference.
> Both: We took trouble.[6]

Here was how, at its most winning, the character of city and people had evolved amid the massive Victorian securities of property and class. Yet did this, as Jeffrey surmised, solve all the problems?

❧

There was always a darker underside. Some of it could be sublimated in the Scottish martial tradition. The roughest and toughest lads might go for a soldier. If unlucky they would turn into the glorious dead of the wars commemorated on monuments that rose around the centre of the city. Edinburgh Castle, no longer needing to be garrisoned by any great number of troops, became a monument as well. The First World War would reinforce the role. It demanded huge sacrifices of the country and the city, and not just of the roughest and toughest. It got them.

Like the rest of Scotland, Edinburgh showed astounding levels of recruitment in the autumn of 1914. Most went into territorial battalions, raised in one locality with men from every walk of life. This could bring terrible consequences, and not only on the battle-field. In 1915 the burgh of Leith was devastated when a transport of troops crashed near Gretna. Two trains collided killing 227 and injuring 247. All but nine of the dead were from the 7th battalion of the Royal Scots, recruited in Leith.

Edinburgh and the Lothians felt proud of the Royal Scots, their own regiment and the oldest in the British army. First mustered in 1633, it had been originally a mercenary outfit and was taken on to the English establishment in 1688, as the decrepit Scottish state could not pay for it on its return from overseas. It had since won a long list of battle honours around the world. When war now broke out again, it comprised two regular battalions. By the end of the year it swelled to three regular and fourteen territorial battalions, with seven of the New Army.

The British commander-in-chief, General Douglas Haig, himself came from Edinburgh and had the highest admiration for his Scots soldiers. In fact he believed that, with their bravado and tenacity, they would win the war for him. This was why, in his relentless attempts to break through on the Western Front, he often sent Scots over the top first. And this again was one main reason why 128,000 of them died in the conflict, in proportion the highest death-toll of any Allied nation. Of these, 583 officers and 10,630 other ranks were Royal Scots.

The greatest action the Scottish regiments fought, under Haig's personal command, was the Battle of Arras in the spring of 1917. In fact it was the greatest action Scotland ever fought. Her troops numbered one-third of the Allied force on the field: more than the whole British army at the Battle of Waterloo and seven times the size of King Robert Bruce's army at the Battle of Bannockburn. Among those regiments were the 15th Royal Scots, recruited in central Edinburgh. Their commander, Colonel Gavin Pagan, died in fer-ocious hand-to-hand combat; many of his men would have known him from before the war as minister of St George's church at the

West End. Scotland won the first day of this battle. Her regiments advanced four miles, by the standards of the war a stupendous gain. On the second day, the attack petered out. Within a month the whole offensive was called off. It had turned into defeat.

Worse was to follow at Passchendaele, or the third battle of Ypres, fought in Flanders the following autumn. The offensive opened on 31 July amid heavy downpours of rain that had not stopped by the time the 15th and 16th Royal Scots went into the attack on 20 October. What happened to them had become all too familiar on the Western Front: men toiling to advance through bottomless mud were mown down by German machine guns. Then the enemy struck back. The 15th Royal Scots retreated to their original position and just held on until relief came. At that point they numbered, out of an original complement of over 500, 120 men and four officers. Lieutenant Robert Johnston had no doubt about the futility of it all:

We lost 20 officers and 400 men in this shambles in conditions almost indescribable for their sheer misery and despair. The staff work was both inadequate and inept. We never saw a staff officer in the forward area. When the attack commenced we were all tired, dispirited and exhausted men without thought of victory. Our morale was very low, no jokes or singing in the ranks, a feeling of dumb despair, strangely enough accepting our position without thought or questions, dumbly obedient but certainly lacking the inward fire required to enthuse the spirit for success in the attack.

When Johnston came to reflect on these events after the war, his view hardened:

The generals who ordered us forward for this attack ... ought to have been sacked. I look back in anger at those responsible. For once – and once only – we were unable to bury our dead and that in itself is proof of the impossible task we were ordered to carry out. The battalion never recovered from the Battle of Ypres. It lost its heart.

It took the Allies most of a further year to make their breakthrough on the Western Front. The 7th Royal Scots were the first battalion to cross the frontier from France into occupied Belgium. At a small town on the other side called Bonsecours they had, according to Major William Kermack, 'the most extraordinary reception. The place was hung with flags, and everybody was waving flags, clapping their hands, and rushing out with cups of coffee and bunches of chrysanthemums, calling *Vivent les Alliés, Vivent les Anglais.* This last did not satisfy the General, who kept correcting them and telling them we were *Ecossais.*'[7]

When the time came for Scotland to commemorate her dead, Lorimer was chosen for the task. The result is the Scottish National War Memorial in Edinburgh Castle, on the site where St Mary's Church may have stood for a thousand years before it. Around this apex of the Rock, as Lorimer wrote, 'Scottish history in all its rugged and varied picturesqueness has revolved.' His solemn and beautiful shrine mirrors the mood of its era, forsaking the individual heroics Scots had extolled in the past to stress the nation's collective sacrifice.[8]

※

Now, so far from the problems being all solved, they multiplied. Survivors of the war came home to a country bled of its Victorian vigour. In high patriotic spirit, with no disaffection from the British state, Scotland had fought this tragic and wasteful struggle to the end. The peace turned out to be tragic and wasteful in a different way. Ruin of the Victorian heavy industries rendered the nation comparable to those in Europe that suffered breakdown and chaos. In Scotland the main result was rather a huge increase in emigration, which by 1931 reduced the population for the first time in the modern era. About the only place to escape the exodus was Edinburgh; its population rose by 4 per cent over the decade. As slump struck everywhere else, it seemed once again an advantage that the city had never known an industrial revolution.

Yet Edinburgh's big companies, such as they were, suffered in their turn as the crisis fed through to curb income and demand. That was bound to affect optional spending, for example on books. The city had remained a major publishing centre. The Blackwood family used the *Maga* to bring out in serial form the novels of John Buchan, as well as those of Joseph Conrad and other non-Scottish

authors. The house did well enough to keep going for another
half-century. W. & R. Chambers remained a Scottish firm too, con-
centrating still on educational works and now on dictionaries in
particular; but today it is a subsidiary of the French giant Hachette
Livre. A. & C. Black, which in the nineteenth century had bought up
the *Encyclopaedia Britannica*, then the copyright of Sir Walter Scott's
writings, decamped with the lot to London in 1895. Archibald
Constable had bounced back from the crisis that bankrupted both
him and Scott but died before he could exploit the mass market for
literature he foresaw; his enterprising successors did do so, though
at present their house has after a complex history become an
independent in London. That was where Thomas Nelson also moved,
while its American branch underwent various commercial transfor-
mations of its own to be born again as the world's largest religious
publisher in the twenty-first century.

   Edinburgh's other main industry, brewing, had also modernized
and rationalized, not least through cutting the number of breweries.
The trend reflected the consumption of Scottish beer. Output had
peaked in 1899 at two million barrels, but sank through the first half
of the twentieth century, touching bottom in 1918, under restrictions
imposed for the war, and in 1932, at the depth of the Depression
when drinkers had no money. Amalgamation followed for two of the
biggest companies, William Younger and William McEwan. So things
carried on after the Second World War. In 1950 there were still thirty
brewers in Edinburgh, by 1960 just thirteen. McEwan Younger took
over three of them and itself entered into voluntary merger with
Newcastle Breweries. Yet production had started rising, then soaring.
It got back to two million barrels in 1951, reached three million in
1968, four million in 1971 and five million in 1974. That made
Scottish & Newcastle one of the largest enterprises in the country,
though still not large enough to survive in global markets in the
long term. It was itself taken over in 2008 by a Danish–Dutch
consortium of Carlsberg and Heineken. By then what had continued
as a staple industry of Edinburgh for centuries was almost extinct,
its last survival being the Caledonian Brewery at Slateford. Long may
it yet brew its Deuchar's IPA.[9]

   Otherwise, too, Edinburgh had followed its own economic course
between the wars. A difference that then opened up on either side of

the Anglo-Scottish border was the absence to the north of an emerging society of mass consumption wanting to own homes, cars and other luxuries. To the south this trend in sprawling London lifted the Depression by the late 1930s. Edinburgh fell in between, neither as acquisitive as England nor as destitute as the rest of Scotland. A survey in 1936 showed unemployment at 14 per cent of the city's workforce, little worse than London's 10 per cent and far better than Glasgow's 29 per cent.[10]

※

Recovery in Edinburgh may have lagged by southern standards but at least it took place. It did so, for example, in the building industry – though not in any form familiar in Metroland. Like most European peoples, Scots regarded renting their homes as the norm, and owner-occupation would remain low until the 1980s. This did not stop tracts of land east and west of Edinburgh getting covered with modest and, if truth be told, rather unprepossessing houses. The new townscape looked uniform and featureless. Scots, having seldom been interested in suburbs, just could not do them as well as the English – and hollyhock refused to grow here in any case. Yet suburbs still seemed desirable to the clerks, tradesmen and shopkeepers of Edinburgh who could aspire to a detached house. They moved from tenements in the centre to bungalows on the periphery. They got a warm welcome from landlords seeing in them respectable, deserving tenants able to afford the rents and cost of travel to work. In this way private construction began again, if at a slower pace and with less pleasing results than before the war.

The building industry got a boost also from a force other than free markets. During the war a royal commission on Scottish housing had sat and reported with horror on conditions in the west of Scotland. In the east of Scotland they were not so bad, except in mining areas, but the remedy recommended – intervention by public authorities – would be common to both regions. The brief Labour government of 1924 set afoot the construction of council houses, though it took a while for Edinburgh to respond to the inducements offered. There were still slums in the inner suburbs, in Broughton, Leith and St Leonard's, which had been built or rebuilt in the nineteenth century to standards often no higher than those then being eradicated from the Old Town. During the 1930s the town council tackled these remaining nests of squalor, with mixed success.

People from Leith were moved westwards to Granton. They occupied homes designed by the city architect, Ebenezer MacRae, and described in the relevant volume of *The Buildings of Scotland* (1984) as 'extremely boring'. Even so the layout of estates was reasonably spacious, with views over the Firth of Forth not obscured from every point by the factories and gasworks offering jobs. At Wardieburn, one such scheme, the people could recreate some semblance of the teeming life of the tenements. A survey published as late as 1975 showed 83 per cent had relations in Edinburgh, in 27 per cent of cases living no more than a mile away. So traditional roles of different ages and sexes in the working class could continue, now amid modest beginnings of consumerism: 'Ubiquitous is the cherry moquette suite, the contrasting wallpaper, the television set in one corner and the budgie in another.' Cosiness began to break down as in time the better families moved on to newer property, to be replaced here by people with problems. But meanwhile it was a section of the city probably functioning better in social terms than petty bourgeois Silverknowes, the suburb next along the firth, true bungalow-land where only 35 per cent of families had relations in Edinburgh.[11]

Things could have turned out worse for the displaced proles, and so they did for those from St Leonards who got shifted eastwards into Craigmillar. If Wardieburn was council housing about as good as it came at the time, from the start Craigmillar seems to have been the pits. It descended almost at once into a slum merely not so old as the one it supplanted, and bereft of urban amenities such as shops or pubs. Yet this lower standard was the one followed in estates built after 1945, at Pilton and Muirhouse by the Forth and out of town at Wester Hailes. West Pilton, for example, is described as a 'graveyard of good intentions in local authority housing, with indifferent planning as its congenital disease, poor design and management as undertakers'.

The point holds for the period between the wars that a moderate level of private construction and the beginnings of public construction had helped to sustain economic activity in Edinburgh when it was plunging in the rest of Scotland. But the character of the city emerged from it diminished rather than enhanced.[12]

☙

At least for the high bourgeoisie the experience of the Depression was comparatively untroubled. A survey of 1934 showed 7 per cent of the city's population in the top bracket of incomes, earning more than £10 a week, compared with 2 per cent in Glasgow and an English average of 5 per cent; at the same time 64 per cent in Edinburgh and 71 per cent in Glasgow earned less than £4 a week.[13] There is testimony that life in the grand houses of the New Town and West End carried on in an almost timeless fashion. The broadcaster Ludovic Kennedy was born in 1919 at Belgrave Crescent, home of his grandfather, Sir Ludovic Grant, professor of public law at the university, and he spent much of his childhood with the doting old man:

> Allowed to watch him dress in the mornings, I was fascinated by the things on his dressing table – a very long shoehorn, an instrument for lacing boots, two ivory hairbrushes marked L.J.G., a tortoiseshell stud-box and rows of silver-topped bottles. Hand in hand we would go down the two long staircases to a dining room decorated with targes, where the food came rumbling up on a lift from the kitchen and every day without variation my grandfather carved himself a plate of cold ham to be accompanied by a lightly boiled egg.

Teatime was even better, especially in winter as the darkness fell in mid-afternoon:

> Then my grandmother's maid Helen, in black taffeta with white cap and pinny, and feet pointing out like a ballet dancer, came in to draw the curtains and lay the tea. And what a tea! Two silver teapots, one for China and one for Indian tea, and a silver kettle resting on a flame from a spirit lamp; toast and a honeycomb of heather honey; treacle scones, drop scones, ordinary scones, oatcakes, shortbread, gingerbread and butter – long pats for the salted butter, round for the unsalted – or was it the other way about?[14]

Though things grew worse in the outside world during the 1930s, in this part of Edinburgh nothing much seemed to change. The lawyer and politician Nicholas Fairbairn, one of the children of Ronald Fairbairn, a leading psychiatrist, then spent his first years in a 'huge house' at Lansdowne Crescent: 'It had four floors, the basement being the empire of the servants and the attic being the habitat of nanny and us.' But just as the brothers Clow had felt an affinity with Lorimer across their different stations in life, so the boy Fairbairn insisted, as it were from the opposite direction, that

> what I enjoyed most were visits to nanny's friends. My early world was peopled with humble Scots folk like her mother, and Agnes Knox, and Lizzie Miller, and Katie and Effie, who were on the staff in the house. People with good hearts, good manners and goodwill. They were all natural. Their language, like their habits, was entirely Scotch which was the mark of their perfect naturalness. They dressed and spoke as they chose. Their views were forthright and unstuffy. Their manners were a pleasure to see and a delight to recall. There was nothing scruffy or third-rate in anything they did. They were the salt of the nation.[15]

Servants may have still spoken Scots, while doubtless Sir Ludovic Grant spoke English after his education at Fettes and Balliol College, Oxford. But, at a level in between, the language of the city had grown pale and wan, as in the notorious accent of Morningside with the contorted vowels speaking only of repression, alike of the local dialect and of the vital instincts. Here the word sex (as even people elsewhere in Edinburgh quipped) meant what coalmen brought coal in.

Still, contrary to a frequent assumption, this mode of speech might have been not so much a ludicrous, mangled imitation of English as a descendant of the genuine Scots of the upper class in the previous two centuries. Lord Cockburn had recalled hearing in his childhood ancient ladies who still spoke Court Scots, probably last used in public when the future James VII was at Holyrood in 1679–81 but harking back still further to before the Union of Crowns. And in 1879 there died at Rothesay Place, aged eighty-five, just such 'a genuine Scottish matron of the old school', Dame Margaret Sinclair of Dunbeath. She had been born in the Canongate in 1794 into a class even then vanishing, 'the clear-headed, stout-hearted yet reverent and gentle old Scottish ladies whom Lord Cockburn loved to portray'. Her final home was in the West End, but the accent is not so different from Morningside's, and Dame Margaret possibly offers one line of descent for it. The rest of the city and country still mocked. Even an American visitor to Edinburgh, the poet Ezra Pound, found 'most of the denizens wheeze, snoffle and exude a sort of snozzling whnoff whnoff, apparently through a hydrophile sponge'.[16]

❧

Did vapid voices bespeak baffled brains? The university remained famous but there could be no mistaking its greatest days were over. The noble edifice of Scots law had been built here, yet a standard history says of this era that 'Scotland gave nothing of any significance to legal philosophy', or that 'in dogmatic exposition of Scots law . . . the twentieth century was a period of inadequate activity, particularly during the years 1914 to 1945'. Ambition did not perish altogether. Arthur Berriedale Keith, actually professor of Sanskrit, seems to have seen himself as the James Madison of the British Empire – in other words the author, at least in potential, of a constitution for it. He wrote many weighty tomes on the form and content of such a constitution, all an utter waste of time because there was never going to be one. 'He had prodigious learning and endless energy, and his books were highly authoritative though now mainly of historical value': enough said.[17]

Custody of political economy had devolved on Shield Nicholson, professor of this discipline for forty-five years, who contrived to argue the classical doctrines left room for a system of imperial preference because free trade had in Victorian times 'assumed a dogmatic simplicity and universality not recognized by Adam Smith';[18] if Nicholson could believe that he could believe anything. The tradition of David Hume found a better guardian in Norman Kemp Smith, who broke out of the parochialism of current Scottish philosophy by bringing the insights of Freud and Nietzsche to bear on its favourite problems, especially the theory of knowledge. The national literature was well served by the professor of English, Herbert Grierson, editor in twelve volumes of the correspondence of Sir Walter Scott. Fine as these achievements proved, they could not restore the international eminence the university had once enjoyed. Only for medicine was that maintained, as in the Edinburgh Scheme by which Sir Robert Philip pioneered treatment of tuberculosis, applying a range of healing measures in the light of the discovery it was an infectious disease.

On the student level, at least, the university looked a more promising place. There was a circle centred on the budding philosopher George Davie, whose book *The Democratic Intellect* (1964) would sway thinking about Scotland for the rest of the century and beyond, on James Caird, who in later life sought as a chief inspector of schools to promote the national culture, and on Sorley MacLean, the greatest Gaelic poet of the twentieth century or, many would argue, of any other. All three felt enthralled by the lyrical debuts of Hugh MacDiarmid in *Sangschaw* (1925), *Penny Wheep* (1926) and *A Drunk Man Looks at the Thistle* (1926). Here modern consciousness came cast in an old tongue – Scots.

৺

MacDiarmid was the leader of the Scottish Renaissance, the cultural reaction to all the economic and political woes. This renaissance remained a literary movement – though parallel to it the Scottish National Party was founded in 1926, if with meagre support from Edinburgh. Fresh currents in the country's life left the city cold. The feeling was reciprocated. A literary movement remained unimpressed by a place that for now had no good writers. At best they swept in from afar, as like as not seizing the chance to berate Edinburgh for its disservices to the nation.

Edwin Muir, from Orkney via Glasgow, traced the disservices back to Scott. He dwelt on Sir Walter's defects, resulting from the fact 'he lived most of his days in a hiatus, in a country, that is to say, which was neither a nation nor a province, but had, instead of a centre, a blank, an Edinburgh in the middle of it'.[19] It can quite be believed Muir found the city of his own time a bit of a blank. But the city of the Enlightenment, even of the late Enlightenment? Muir gets too carried away by his polemic.

Eric Linklater, from Aberdeen via India, took a view less stark. His novel *Magnus Merriman* (1934) features hilarious scenes in Edinburgh. He pokes fun at the most mannered of its Scots poets, Lewis

Spence, as the character Padraig McVicar who turns up straight from the speakers' corner off Princes Street: 'He got his turn to be at the Mound tonight. He was talking about Nationalism, but he speaks in a very solemn way and the crowd thought he was a Mormon, and rushed him.' Linklater even went the perilous length of satirizing MacDiarmid, as Hugh Skene: 'I'm a Communist. And I'm a Scottish Nationalist because I believe that if Scotland were independent we could do a great deal towards establishing a central state in Western Europe.' Linklater wrote of another Edinburgh too: 'The taxi stopped in Rothesay Crescent, a semi-lune of tall houses, solemn in mien, dignified, wealthy in fact and implication. Here was respectability achieved in such perfection and most zealously preserved.' Not that he necessarily approved, to judge from a further fictional figure: 'Now I'm Miss Forsyth of Rothesay Crescent, and my life is ordered and comfortable and generally as dull as ditchwater.'[20]

MacDiarmid himself waxed more rancorous. Born at Langholm in the Borders, he would settle at various places in Scotland, but never in Edinburgh. A key concept he contributed to the Scottish Renaissance was the 'Caledonian antisyzygy': the English were welcome to their penchant for compromise, but Scots should glory in the irreconcilables coexisting in the life of their nation. Yet, as he set forth in a poem under the plain title of 'Edinburgh', the city no longer seemed capable of formulating propositions that might be irreconcilable with others:

> The capital of Scotland is called Auld Reekie,
> Signifying a monstrous acquiescence
> In the domination of the ends
> By the evidences of effort.

He urged it to

> Learn again to consume your own smoke like this,
> Edinburgh, to free your life from the monstrous pall,
> To subdue it and be no longer subdued by it.

Even so, he did not feel change could come through any internal impulse:

> But Edinburgh – Edinburgh – is too stupid yet
> To learn how not to stand in her own light.

MacDiarmid's cynicism on this score no doubt accounts for his refusal in a second poem, 'Talking with Five Thousand People in Edinburgh', to go beyond heaping more scorn on its condition of

> ... a blinded giant who has yet to learn
> What the motive spirit behind his abilities really is ...
> There is no one really alive in Edinburgh yet:
> They are all living on the tiniest fraction
> Of the life they could have ...
>
> Let a look at Edinburgh be called
> Just an educational film then
> Such as we see any day on the screen,
> 'The Abortion', say, or 'Why Does It Rain?'
> Or 'How Silk Stockings are Made', or, finally,
> 'What is the Difference between A Man and a Beaver?'
>
> It's far too late in the day
> For a fellow like this
> Trying to organize a conspiracy of feelings
> In Edinburgh of all places.[21]

❧

It would take a while for the city to fare better in the national literature. A younger generation of writers bred up here could seem more savagely hostile than the outsiders. In 1940 Ruthven Todd wrote an autobiographical poem, 'In Edinburgh':

> I was born in this city of grey stone and bitter wind
> Of tenements sooted up with lying history:
> This place where dry mounds grow crusts of hate, as rocks
> Grow lichens ...[22]

The best novel about Edinburgh in the period between the wars did not appear until 1961 when Muriel Spark came to terms with her upbringing in *The Prime of Miss Jean Brodie*. The off-putting heroine, recognizably a type of Edinburgh's womanhood, at least shows an invincible independence of mind. A rebellious spinster schoolteacher at a posh school, she has dedicated herself to making her favourite girls, *la crème de la crème*, grow up. Yet they grow up not

necessarily as she would like them to, if anything in reaction to her –
and some fail.

One freezing day Miss Brodie takes her favourites, including a
girl called Sandy, on an outing from their school beyond the
Meadows. They march towards the centre of the city through a poor
area, the Grassmarket:

> It was Sandy's first experience of a foreign country ... A man sat
> on the icy cold pavement; he just sat. A crowd of children, some
> without shoes, were playing some fight game, and some boys
> shouted after Miss Brodie's violet-clad company, with words the
> girls had not heard before, but rightly understood to be obscene.
> Children and women with shawls came in and out of the dark
> closes ... The smell was amazingly terrible ... A man and a
> woman stood in the midst of the crowd that had formed a ring
> around them. They were shouting at each other and the man hit
> the woman twice across the head.

Further along their route Miss Brodie and her girls arrive at the
labour exchange:

> A very long queue of men lined this part of the street. They were
> without collars, in shabby suits. They were talking and spitting
> and smoking little bits of cigarettes held between middle finger
> and thumb.
>
> Monica Douglas whispered, 'They are the Idle.'
>
> 'In England they are called the Unemployed,' said Miss
> Brodie.

Here is a little nationalist joke, but at the service of the general
thesis that a conventional bourgeois upbringing in Edinburgh (or
indeed an unconventional bourgeois upbringing) divorces people
from realities of life, as the girls find out. Spark herself, having got
all this off her chest, left Edinburgh, scarcely came back and did not
again write at any length about it.[23]

❧

Where could renewal come from? If MacDiarmid was an optimist
(on balance), Muir remained a pessimist. But few outside literary

circles thought culture the key. If not that, there were older answers, in religion and in politics.

Presbyterians at last sought to put schism behind them. The Churches, after splitting again and again during the eighteenth and nineteenth centuries, in the twentieth began to come together. The year 1900 had seen the merger of the Free Church and the United Presbyterian Church, itself an earlier merger of dissenting sects. Intermittent progress went on towards full Presbyterian reunion in 1929. Its leaders expected it to lead to a rebirth of the nation.

But the clergy failed the test they set themselves. Nearly all had supported the war and denounced its critics.[24] Now they blamed unemployment on spiritual and moral decay. When by the 1930s sin seemed no longer to offer the complete explanation, the church and nation committee of the General Assembly suggested it might 'in a limited measure' support the search for secular solutions. Yet the Reverend James Black of St George's West, for one, had little patience with alleged social problems such as housing, and threw in some racism to sweeten the pill of his teaching: 'I am reminded of the old story of the Irishman who so loved his pig that he believed that its usual filthy ways were entirely due to the conditions in which it was forced to live. So he built for it a kind of palace, and said, "Now you will see the change!" He was right. There was a change. But the only change was in the palace!' Too many clerical eyes came to rest with reproach on trivia. 'One is frequently amazed at the fashion in which parents nowadays allow themselves to be addressed by their children,' intoned the Reverend Charles Warr of St Giles. 'Modern slang, too, sometimes apt and clever, but frequently silly, vulgar and quite unintelligible, ought to be watched. It is degrading our noble language.'[25]

At least the odd minister could see this religion as others might see it. The Reverend Norman MacLeod of St Cuthbert's told of a family returning from Calcutta to Edinburgh and bringing their native servants with them. These, a few days after arrival, looked out and saw the street quite still except for black-clad figures striding along with doleful expressions. The servants jumped to the conclusion Victoria, Empress of India, was dead, and began to weep and wail. Their masters had to assure them it was just a normal sabbath in the city. Here is another of MacLeod's anecdotes:

> Two divinity students on the way to a Sunday morning fellowship meeting, emerging from the Lothian Road into Princes Street, saw a sight which halted their steps with the shock of amazement. It was a solitary cyclist pedalling swiftly along the broad empty street.
>
> 'If desecration like that is going to be permitted, what will become of the Church?' exclaimed Norman Macfarlane, afterwards minister of Juniper Green.
>
> 'It is a shocking spectacle indeed,' replied Alexander Martin, afterwards the principal of New College.

Given this straitjacket of respectability, it was no surprise the Kirk remained weakest in working-class areas. There Presbyterian reunion did not make places of worship more welcoming to those without Sunday best to wear or money to put in the collection.[26]

But Edinburgh remained a churchy sort of city, and Calvinism of a more popular kind continued to flourish in certain quarters. At Newington this local tradition went back to the Reverend James Begg in mid-Victorian times. The parish included Potterrow, a poor place since the sixteenth century, and Causewayside further out along the road south. The untiring minister, the Reverend James Goodfellow, still pursued the social vision of Thomas Chalmers, of a 'Christian community, self-respecting and moral, among the families and tenements of his area of work'. At his halls he met groups of parishioners on eighteen different occasions a week, for informal worship, discussions among working men, mothers' meetings, a Band of Hope, separate religious instruction for young men and women, a sewing class and a penny savings bank. Elsewhere the faithful might turn to Evangelical missions or to sects spurning rapprochement with established religion. With 1,000 worshippers every Sunday, Charlotte Chapel in Rose Street housed one of the largest Baptist congregations in Britain. Born-again Christianity appeared here long before the term came into general use, and has not faltered since. The chapel stood in the first New Town, but nobody living roundabout would have been seen dead in it: worshippers came in, by bus or on foot, from humble suburbs.[27]

Still flagging, then, the Church of Scotland bore some resemblance to another past pillar of the nation, the Liberal Party, which indeed probably supplied most of its membership. Since 1832 Edinburgh had elected Liberal MPs to Westminster with scarcely any exceptions (and even they were renegade Liberals). But the First World War caused divisions in the national party heralding its more or less terminal decline. At the Khaki Election of 1918 it all the same held its seats in Edinburgh except for a single loss to Labour when Willie Graham, a journalist, took the Central constituency. Otherwise Labour did not even contest every seat in the city until 1924. There were several elections in that decade and, while other Labour MPs sometimes got in, Graham was the only one to hold on without a break until his party's debacle at the General Election of 1931. Meanwhile he became one of Labour's financial experts, devising the orthodox economic policy that led to the debacle. His brother wrote of him: 'He had no antagonism towards the rich ... All he wanted was that everyone should have a reasonable chance to live and to work out his own destiny.' The sniffy metropolitan socialist Sidney Webb observed that Graham 'doesn't really like any radical or collectivist proposals' and was 'sceptical about any democratic reform which will always be tinged by corruption and tyrannical interference with individual liberty'. This was radical Liberalism in all but name. In Edinburgh, Labour had to wait until 1945 to establish a more distinct and permanent presence.[28]

The position stood in stark contrast to that in Glasgow, where in 1922 Labour had already captured ten of the fifteen seats. The wonder of it moved the new MPs and their following to a veritably religious fervour. Before the victors left for Westminster they held a service of dedication where their ringing speeches on the promise of socialism were mixed with the congregation's singing of covenanter hymns. Hundreds came to give them an emotional send-off at St Enoch Station, where one looked around and proclaimed: 'When we come back all this will belong to the people!' There was no such defining moment in Edinburgh, but there could have been. Apart from Central, the most proletarian constituency was Leith. Between the wars the port stagnated along with the industries, notably rubber, which had grown up around it. More than that, it suffered the greatest possible blow to its pride when in 1920, much against its will, it was reincorporated into the city of Edinburgh. Practical matters dictated this: the built-up area of the two municipalities had become continuous and they already ran joint utilities. But the people of Leith were not consulted, because everybody knew what they would say. Their council organized its own unofficial referendum, which showed 5,000 voters for amalgamation and 30,000 against.[29]

The shotgun marriage with Edinburgh has never been forgotten or forgiven in Leith, and could not suppress the port's maverick character. This came out in politics, too. The parliamentary seat – at one stage held by William Gladstone, no less – remained Liberal until 1945, even while the party collapsed elsewhere in Scotland. The MP from 1920 was William Wedgwood Benn (father of Tony Benn), leader of the most radical faction at Westminster. He decided in 1927 to cross the floor to Labour. He resigned his seat, as men of honour did in those days. A by-election followed. With a Tory government in power in London, it could have been the moment for Labour to take Leith. That might then have been claimed as Edinburgh's counterpart to the breakthrough in Glasgow. It was not to be.

The Liberals found just the right candidate in Ernest Brown, a Baptist lay preacher and an able man otherwise – he would rise to be Secretary of State for Scotland during the Second World War. His Evangelical fervour and booming voice went down well with the people in a deprived part of the city, another where that old-time religion still throve; even today there are mission halls in its backstreets. While devout, Brown managed to wear his religion lightly. Unlike most of his constituents, he did not drink or bet. But when asked by the Baptist Union of Scotland to close down the local dog-track at Powderhall, among others, he replied that 'it would be unreasonable to deprive those who wish to attend race meetings of all opportunity of doing so'. And when urged by the Scottish Temperance Alliance to do something about the amount of alcohol these and other Scots drank, he said only that 'a careful watch is being kept on the incidence of consumption'.[30]

Others did not wear their religion so lightly. A ticklish situation arose in Brown's constituency because it was also the stronghold of a fringe party, the Protestant Alliance, blaming all Scotland's ills on immigrant Irish Catholics. In 1934 the Baptist leader of this alliance,

John Cormack, won the seat on the town council of Edinburgh he
was to hold until 1962. He became respectable in time, but at the
outset he claimed to have a bodyguard and an armoured car, as if
this were Chicago, and he incited violence against Catholics. When
a eucharistic congress took place in the city in 1935, with a closing
mass in a priory at Morningside, he led thousands of supporters to
surround it, to jeer and to throw stones at worshippers as they
sought to get away. The Reverend Andrew McDonald, Archbishop
of St Andrews and Edinburgh, published a protest: 'For some time
it has hardly been possible for a priest to appear in the city without being subjected to unspeakable indignities. They have not only
been the target for vile abuse and most filthy and obscene language,
but they have repeatedly been spat upon and molested in the public
streets.'[31] Militant Protestantism was not yet dead in Edinburgh.

Cormack said he supported Brown at parliamentary elections,
though Brown seems to have had no contact with him and gave no
countenance to his sectarianism. Yet when we look for reasons
why Leith, and the rest of working-class Edinburgh, proved relatively
immune to Labour's blandishments before 1945, the strength of
Evangelical religion has to be one plausible explanation. Glasgow is
more guilty of sectarian sins, but whereas in Glasgow socialism and
Evangelical religion had to some extent come together in the 1920s,
in Edinburgh they stayed apart; Evangelical religion here if anything
acted as a check on socialism until 1945. Brown turned Leith into a
safe Liberal seat and held it until he retired that year.

Religion and politics in Edinburgh soon reached a parting of the
ways they had travelled together since 1832, with observance in one
reinforcing commitment in the other. From now on churchgoing
became more and more confined to the middle class. In a survey
written up in 1966 of the suburb of Prestonfield, which in social
terms is about average, two-thirds of people in manual occupations
did not go to church, while two-thirds of people in non-manual
occupations did.[32] That was not, of course, the sole reason why the
bourgeoisie still spurned Labour. Its MPs from 1945 tended to be
dreary trade-unionist types like those in the west of Scotland, with
little appeal to any non-industrial electorate. Nothing that might
be called liberation from their drab outlook on life appeared on the
Left for a quarter-century: not, perhaps, that Edinburgh was ready

for liberation. The city's real political quirk lay in a lack of swing, even of swing uniform with the rest of the country. After the Second World War it had seven seats in Parliament: four Tory (North, Pentlands, South, West) and three Labour (Central, East, Leith). None changed hands before 1983.

❧

Edinburgh remained a novice in modern politics, though not to the same extent in modern government. Since 1885 it had housed the Scottish Office, after a fashion. This put a stop to the Whigs' drive for the complete assimilation of Scotland to England. The trend went into reverse, if gently to begin with. But up to the First World War most staff of the Scottish Office were still based in London. In Edinburgh they numbered two, while the grand total of all civil servants in Scotland was 944. They worked for an average salary of £350 a year, so central government's Scottish payroll amounted to a magnificent £320,000. By 1999, when this system of ruling Scotland came to an end, the number of civil servants had soared to 3,677 and the annual cost of administration to £152 million.[33]

Lacking a proper civil service, Scotland had continued with the older practice of having governmental functions overseen by boards of experts and interested parties for which the Scottish Office at first amounted to just an umbrella. They were, by 1918, the Board of Agriculture, Board of Health, Prisons Board, General Board of Control for the mentally ill and handicapped, Board of Trustees for the National Galleries of Scotland. To these a regular Department of Education would soon be added. They all occupied offices in Edinburgh but not in any one place.[34] During the 1920s this unwieldy system was replaced by a single department of the civil service, divided functionally at a subordinate level, under a Secretary of State sitting in the Cabinet in London.

The trouble was the senior civil servants also still sat in London, with only lower grades in Edinburgh. As nationalism started to stir again in the country at large, here was a potential grievance. Others existed, one being that discussion of Scottish affairs hardly ever reached the floor of the House of Commons; since 1832, it had been as a rule confined to committees of Scots MPs. On the centenary of the first Reform Act came a gesture of redress. In the debate on the king's speech opening the new session of Parliament, a whole day was given over to Scotland. The best contribution came from John Buchan, MP for the Scottish Universities, remembered today rather as author of *The Thirty-Nine Steps* (1915) and other pacy thrillers. He had grown up in Glasgow but spent a year or two working from Edinburgh as editor of the *Scottish Review*. He told Lord Rosebery that under himself it would 'deal fully with all interests, literary, political and social, with something Scottish in the point of view. We want to make it the centre of a Scottish school of letters such as Edinburgh had a hundred years ago.' The city was no longer able to sustain anything like that, however. The magazine soon folded.[35]

Buchan had since made good in other fields, and the Commons listened to him with respect. Something must be done, he insisted, to save the historic character of his country: 'It seems to many that we are in danger very soon of reaching that point where Scotland will have nothing distinctive to show to the world.' The root of the malaise and source of the recent nationalist upsurge was a passionate desire among Scots that the country should not lose its character. What, though, could any government do about that? Not much, perhaps, but something: 'Agriculture, education and health are already administered in Scotland, and I think that other problems of Scottish administration should be administered from Edinburgh, and that Whitehall should be no more than a London office for the Scottish Secretary.' There was also a need in any fresh arrangement for some 'outward and visible sign of Scottish nationhood'. Buchan proposed there should be in Edinburgh a dignified and worthy home for the civil service of the country, now scattered about to the detriment of efficiency, cohesion and the convenience of the public. Even the Secretary of State on his visits had to make do with a poky room in Parliament House normally used by somebody else.[36]

The idea soon turned into the reality of St Andrew's House on the southern flank of Calton Hill. The site had been occupied by the city's prison ever since the demolition of the old Tolbooth in 1817, and the Gothick house of the governor still stands there. Next door Thomas Tait's new building, severe to the front but at the back romantically ranged across the rocky setting, was of a resolute modernism new to Edinburgh and not universally welcome. But *The*

Buildings of Scotland rates it high, comparing it to Henri-Paul Nénot's Palais des Nations in Geneva, 'strictly symmetrical in the Beaux-Arts tradition, but much less classical and, in its exploitation of the dramatic view from the south, much more rhetorical'. Its entrance, though, is 'unashamedly authoritarian' (it looks rather like Hermann Goering's Luftministerium in Berlin). Still, 'whatever is thought about the politics of this architecture ... its abstract qualities and consummate handling of detail cannot be denied ... Tait's south front is a work of real imagination and grandeur, meriting comparison with the old Royal High School to the east.' Considering what mindless mediocrity pervaded all else in Edinburgh at this period, it is indeed 'by far the most impressive building erected in Scotland between the wars'. Yet it marked a beginning rather than a consummation for Scottish government. In fact the premises were already too small by the time the civil servants moved in, and colleagues continued to be dispersed in offices across the New Town. It did not matter: St Andrew's House made Edinburgh more truly a capital city again.[37]

❧

The new headquarters of the Scottish Office opened as the Second World War broke out. On foreign fields the Royal Scots, the local regiment, again often bore the brunt. The 1st battalion was captured at Dunkirk in 1940 as part of the heroic rearguard that held off the Germans while 300,000 other Allied soldiers were evacuated; on their surrender, the infuriated SS Totenkopf murdered some of these sons of Edinburgh in cold blood before the rest were led off to German camps. Captivity also awaited the 2nd battalion forming part of the garrison of Hong Kong when in 1941 it fell to the Japanese; here again, treatment of prisoners was not gentle. At home, the Royal Scots needed to be rebuilt from scratch.[38]

All British cities had the Luftwaffe to fear. In Scotland, Clydeside suffered a blitz but Edinburgh was barely touched. The enemy concentrated on vain attempts to destroy the Forth Rail Bridge and sink ships in the firth. So innocent of the worst were the locals that at the first air-raid in October 1939 they did not even run for the shelters. On the contrary, thousands 'went out into the streets from houses, offices and shops and stood gazing upwards. Generally there was no excitement, as it was believed almost everywhere that the firing was merely gun practice on a fairly large scale.'

A year later the bombers did strike in earnest at Edinburgh, if still doing little damage. There was general confidence a city of stone could withstand anything the Germans threw at it. *The Scotsman* reported that a bomb on London might destroy four or five houses, 'whereas a bomb of similar character which fell in Edinburgh in front of a heavily built tenement in Marshall Street had no effect on the building, save the doors and windows were broken'. While waiting for the bombers to come back, citizens were invited to demonstrations where they could watch children and old-age pensioners 'showing how easy it is to control and extinguish an incendiary bomb fire by the use of the stirrup pump'. Men not on active service were recruited into the Local Defence Volunteers. They made ready to defend Edinburgh street by street and house by house: 'This form of training called for a thorough knowledge of the byways and back-courts of the city, and a certain agility in scaling backgreen walls and negotiating roofs. The older men cheerfully learned the knack and engaged in these exercises with no little zest.' In fact the only Germans to appear were prisoners-of-war being transported to remote camps: 'As the train waited by the platform, the prisoners leaned out of the windows, and while some chatted with station employees others waved to girl employees standing at office windows in the station. A railway guard and several porters gave cigarettes to some of the prisoners, many of whom were able to speak English fairly well.'[39]

❧

On a different plane, one effect of the war on Edinburgh came in the vast expansion of Scottish government, matching the vast expansion of British government; both would stay vastly expanded long after the peace. In time of national peril nobody objected, in Scotland any more than in England. Yet the Prime Minister, Winston Churchill, still took care to keep the Scots sweet. During the First World War he and other political leaders had had to watch like hawks for signs of sedition in socialist Glasgow, and he wanted no trouble anywhere north of the border this time. So the centralization necessary for the war effort should not on any account upset the Scots. Luckily there was now a Scottish Office in Edinburgh through which the centralization could be channelled.

The story of the Scottish Office in the war has been told elsewhere. Here it is enough to observe with what relish it took to a collectivist, interventionist role. This it then sought to exploit and enhance for more than three decades after peace came, spurred on by final collapse over the period of the traditional economy in the west of Scotland. The Scottish Office remained convinced it might not so much replace as renew that economy if only it could identify the heavy industries of the future. The policy waxed expensive, without obvious return, but London would pay. Finally Scotland was making motor vehicles in both east and west, supplied with steel from in between, while smelting aluminium in the north and producing paper even in the distant Highlands. After 1979 London would no longer pay. The historian of the Scottish Office, John Gibson, can scarcely maintain his official objectivity in describing the closures that followed: 'These were bitter blows, salt being rubbed into the wound by dismissive comment from some quarters about the regional development policy in Scotland of the 1960s of which Linwood and Bathgate, Invergordon and the Lochaber mill, along with the steel strip mill at Ravenscraig in Lanarkshire, had been the cornerstones.'[40]

Gibson makes no mention of Edinburgh. Alone in Scotland, it had never been subject to the tender mercies of regional policy. Their architect, Dr Gavin McCrone, wrote that the exclusion might seem 'absurd'. Edinburgh's status as capital city of Scotland was perhaps of no great importance in this context, but at the least it seemed to be 'the most natural growth point' for the region surrounding it. Yet 'its economy is prospering even without regional development assistance and there are, of course, many sites suitable for industrial development in the development area immediately outside the city. For these reasons the case for its inclusion is less strong ... but the position needs to be carefully watched.' In fact, without either heavy industry or regional aid, Edinburgh continued to prosper more than all the areas that did have them.[41]

Second thoughts began to arise about this supremacy of central government and of public authority in general. Since England remained the biggest nation in the United Kingdom, a statist system was most likely to follow English norms. Yet Scots, ever since 1707, had been left to their own devices. If they could unite in favour of doing something in their own way, the English had been content to leave them to it, intervening only in cases (admittedly not infrequent) where Scots preferred to carry on fighting among themselves.

With centralization this easy-going arrangement was no longer so straightforward. For example, after the First World War the British government had intervened in Scottish housing and would do so on a greater scale after the Second World War. There was a huge impact on building practices in Scotland, the product of centuries of separate history. Out went stone and in came brick, out went tenements and in came cottages, out went urban jungle and in came garden city. Many, perhaps most, houses now built in Scotland looked not like Scottish houses but like English houses. Local conditions sometimes forced a quick change back. Mortar crumbles in the deep frosts of a northern winter so unharled buildings soon look sorry for themselves; it became clear, to those who never knew, that an English house designed for a kindly climate needed Scottish harling to cope with a harsh one. But for the most part the industry on either side of the border was subjected to uniform regulation. Bureaucrats in London set standards for housing materials, styles and densities, with Scottish agencies just following suit. Benign bureaucrats might have been unaware of any difference in Scotland; malign ones insisted on conformity – and did their bit to make Scots feel put upon.[42]

For cities bombed by the Germans, political judgements on the future after 1945 seemed necessary and desirable. If the unplanned history of urban Britain was to be corrected, a better chance would not arise. Everything came under scrutiny: housing, roads and commercial development. By the 1960s the consequences were visible and in the twenty-first century we still have to live with them. They often spelled the ruin of cities emerging unrecognizable to any previous generation and unpalatable to the present one. The civil destruction might have been forgiven if it had produced utopia, as intended. But the antonym, dystopia, was invented for what did result. Edinburgh alone escaped this fate – though only just.

❧

Before the war there had been little by way of town planning in Edinburgh. National political parties did not always contest mere local elections and the council was run by a loose coalition, often drawn from the ranks of small business, calling themselves Progressives. Rather reactionary in fact, they had but two aims: to keep Labour out and the rates down. Sir William Darling, lord provost during the war, made it a matter of civic pride: 'Edinburgh has a long history of public economy.'⁴³ So grandiose schemes of social engineering did not figure. Still, some firmer view of the development of Edinburgh was now necessary, not because of any destruction wrought on it but because in 1939 all building had been suspended. By 1945 it was perhaps 10,000 houses short – yet heroes returning from the battlefields expected to find somewhere nice to live. There was enough land within the ample municipal boundaries. To meet its need, the capital city of Scotland would settle for no less than Britain's foremost planner, Patrick Abercrombie, who had already set about rebuilding London. From his name he could have been a Scot; in fact he came from Liverpool. This would soon be held against him.⁴⁴

From the start Abercrombie got hold of the wrong end of the stick. He was not just a town planner by trade but a social engineer by conviction. And he mistook Edinburgh for London or perhaps Glasgow, a divided city where divisions would get worse unless somebody did something (namely himself). It was true that, compared with times when everybody had jostled cheek by jowl down the Royal Mile, the people of Edinburgh were now spatially differentiated. But this is true of every modern city. Urban society can still work if held together by other things, such as a population with shared values and strong civic institutions, accustomed by a long common history to cohabitation and – best of all if possible – sustained by economic success. Edinburgh had these things in a way other places planned or re-planned by Abercrombie did not: say, Plymouth or Hull, flattened in the war, or Crawley and Harlow,

English New Towns. This did not matter to him. He felt more impressed by his statistical analyses and by what might be called his topographical determinism. He was another who, like Ruskin, would have preferred Edinburgh flat. Instead there were these hills and dells, mountains and waters, rocky bits and boggy bits. They separated people and hindered a sense of community: far better for the future to treat them as if they were not there.[45]

The first mistake Abercrombie made was not to leave well alone. There are few urban areas with so little by way of problems as the broad belt of Victorian villas stretching south of central Edinburgh from the Grange to Merchiston. These tranquil quarters of the city had no congestion or pollution and were full of professional people looking after their property and environment. But what concerned Abercrombie was that they did not show the density of population adequate for provision of services (a matter which, of course, could be mathematically calculated). The anomaly threatened his vision: 'If the Dalry and Gorgie industrial zone is to be depopulated in accordance with the zoning principle of industry and home separation, the Merchiston area at least will require to be redeveloped to house a proportion of the workers in this industrial zone.' The Grange might have to be redeveloped, too, with blocks of flats to house refugees from the new proletarian paradise of Merchiston.[46]

That was just the suburbs. When Abercrombie looked at the centre he found two main routes running through, the east–west axis of Princes Street and the north–south axis of the Bridges. Princes Street would be reconstructed on separate levels, road underneath and shopping promenade on top. In anticipation some people began to tear down the old buildings, seeking out the best Victorian ones to go first. As for their two-tier replacements, according to *The Buildings of Scotland*, 'the few isolated examples are of historical rather than architectural interest, and the scheme was abandoned about 1979'. Meanwhile the Bridges would be bypassed with a dual carriageway tunnelling through Calton Hill, emerging into the light before burrowing under the High Street and then crossing the Cowgate to head out of town. Yet it was Leithers who, as usual, would come off worst of all from what was done to Edinburgh. Abercrombie in fact wanted to liquidate Leith as a place of human habitation, much as Hitler had done with Warsaw after the rising of 1944. With just 600 years of civic history behind it, Leith was to house only industry in future. Even Abercrombie, when pressed, admitted the idea might be 'a bit on the drastic side'.[47]

The people of Edinburgh can come across as a stolid lot, recognizable descendants of the dogged Northumbrian peasantry that tamed the Lothians over a thousand years ago. This was perhaps why in the past they had been inclined to let schemes of their rulers wash over them while minding their own business, pious or prurient. But they have some Celtic blood in their veins, too, and some Celtic fire in their bellies. Abercrombie produced in them a rare explosion of fury. Of its many expressions one will have to stand for all, from Melville Clark of the Cockburn Association, named after Lord Cockburn and since 1878 a voluntary guardian of the city's beauties. In a letter to *The Scotsman* (the main medium through which the battle was waged), Clark described Abercrombie's report as an outrage embodying 'sacrilegious proposals' for a 'streamlined necropolis'. Throughout the letter he attacked Abercrombie for being a foreigner whose experience lay in planning the reconstruction of blitzed cities. But 'Edinburgh is an unblitzed city – as yet.' Against universal hostility, the plan just petered out. It did no more than blight certain areas as decisions were awaited on their future. Decisions never came. On the whole, the planners lost and the people won.[48]

✣

Even then, the people's victory was not final. In the 1960s the planners regrouped and counter-attacked. Their leader now was Professor Colin Buchanan, who in his long career (he died only in 2004) was associated most with policies to keep cars out of cities – and this remains even today the principal aim, if unrealized, of town planning in Edinburgh. Yet in the hallucinogenic 1960s, the chief means chosen was an inner ring road. If it had been built it would doubtless have had the same effect as its counterpart in Glasgow; this, while only ever half completed, still did a good job of destroying urban life in parts of the city it traversed.

When Buchanan proposed an *inner* ring road he meant it. On the southern side it would have passed over the Meadows, half a mile from the High Street, on an elevated motorway. Today we still know the Meadows for their melding of mellow sandstone buildings with green open spaces where children play on bouncy castles and students jog; it does not take much imagination to see the dereliction and the dustbowl Buchanan would have created. On the northern side his road would have ploughed through the New Town, half a mile from Princes Street. He made the same mistake as Abercrombie in underestimating Edinburgh's bourgeoisie. Houses here were owner-occupied by articulate professional people who could, and did, make sure his plan never got off the ground. They defeated not just him but also the collusive officials of the town council and Scottish Office who thought of this urban fabric as mere putty in their hands to be shaped for a new era. Other British cities were more easily suborned because the population had either long ago abandoned the centre or was even now in the process of fleeing it. Yet in Edinburgh people liked living in the centre and showed no sign of wanting to leave, not to make room for roads. The centre after all contained housing which, apart from its historical and aesthetic value, would be sound and serviceable for a long time ahead: destruction of it was wanton. The entrenched conservatism of Edinburgh saved it, said some. Actually, from the coign of vantage of the twenty-first century, it is the planners who appear backward in their thinking and the protesters who appear forward-looking. Either way, the public inquiry rejected Buchanan's plan.[49]

These were crucial episodes in the history of modern Edinburgh. They affected its politics too. The town council had shown an incapacity to reconcile the claims of history and the demands of modernity. The reactionary Progressives and the Labour dinosaurs alike merely became complicit in the prospective ruin of the city. In both parties revolt followed. The affair in fact helped to bring about the extinction of the Progressives because the official Conservative Party decided it was high time to contest local elections in Edinburgh on the startling programme of trying to reflect voters' wishes. And in the Labour Party the trade unionists were elbowed aside by younger educated professionals unlikely to be overawed by planners and closer to the conservationists articulating popular anger. In effect the council had lost basic popular consent. Wholesale change of policy followed, since there was no choice from now on but to rescue and restore rather than raze and refashion. And perhaps it is to this juncture we must date a novel political volatility which means that today no party has safe seats in Edinburgh. Still, old arguments often appear in new guises. The city continues to wrangle over transporting its citizens to and from its preserved urban core, rather than sparing them the trouble by obliterating it. But the same conflict goes on between what planners plan and what people prefer.

⚜

Before its brief heyday ended, town planning left behind a couple of catastrophes, just to show what the rest of the place might have come to look like. St James's Square (1773) had marked the eastern end of the first New Town but consisted of big houses always gloomy and latterly seedy, though standing on one of the finest urban sites in Europe. To the mind of the Progressives the site could only be rededicated to shopping. St James's Square came down and St James's Centre went up, contriving to make a spacious area look jumbled. Not only local but also central government joined in the desecration. The same complex contained New St Andrew's House, bringing together dispersed bits of the Scottish Office into a hollow hexagon six storeys high – all in concrete, too, presumably as a deliberate insult to the stone-built city. To stress the insolence, the height went up to eight storeys above the domes of Register House and of Sir Lawrence Dundas's mansion in St Andrew's Square, at the points where these were best viewed from afar. New St Andrew's House had later to be abandoned because full of asbestos. At the time of writing, there is a good chance that it and St James's Centre will be demolished.[50]

The other victim of planning was George Square (1766), south of the Old Town. Its architecture hardly counted as distinguished, but a historic city that is not a museum ought to find room for the middling as well as the monumental. The square formed a tranquil island in a bustling quarter. Its fate was sealed by proximity to the university, which bought up property roundabout then let it decay with a view to redevelopment. For that reason alone, this was a hard fight for conservationists to win.

Defenders of the city had also to do battle with the chilling bureaucrat Sir Edward Appleton, who was principal of the university – 'a philistine Englishman', according to Nicholas Fairbairn. Indeed, the large collection of papers Appleton left behind shows him to have been without interests except in his own subject of zoology and in academic administration. To graduates who wrote in protesting at his plans he was rude. He brushed aside all proposals other than his own as 'wholly unacceptable to anyone who understands the workings of a modern university' (a category evidently confined to himself). Objectors were subordinating the academic present and future to preservation of two terraces of houses. By contrast, his redevelopment would produce 'a modern university based on a series of quadrangles of varying shapes and sizes, with reasonable seclusion, and full of interest – in the very heart of Edinburgh!' His institution was not just being selfish, then: 'It adheres to its choice because it sees in it the prospect of creating, not for itself, but for Edinburgh and for Scotland, an academic precinct unique for any civic university in the world.' The destruction might be regrettable, but 'the present charm and quality of the square had been outweighed by the unparalleled opportunity of erecting something fine in our own time, and by offering to Edinburgh the future as well as the past achievements of a liberated and integrated university'. In the resulting reality, nobody hangs about here once classes end. Academics flee to the suburbs. Students go off to bars and cafés in the few older streets left nearby. What exists today is a concrete desert of dreary, shabby buildings from an era at the nadir of British architecture.[51]

It does not look like coincidence, though it probably was, that the university about the same time finally abandoned its role as the town's college drawing the larger part of its students from Edinburgh and giving them a broad education, in the great days based on moral philosophy. Of course the university could not stand still, and by now that tradition was looking threadbare. But at least Edinburgh and other Scottish universities might exploit a relationship with government leaving them some autonomy: the relationship was regulated by a committee of the privy council, so segregated from official policies pursued in English universities. In 1970 this was swept away. All higher studies of whatever kind in the United Kingdom came under a new Department of Education and Science. Again, centralization in London meant anglicization in Scotland. At Edinburgh, for example, Scottish philosophy vanished from the curriculum, displaced by the analytics of Oxbridge (despite screams of anguish from George Davie). For a while no trace of the Scottish

Enlightenment could be discerned at Edinburgh, its sometime citadel, until a few historians were appointed to resurrect its study. Only
the school of law saw a resurgence of scholarship under Professor
T. B. Smith, himself a disciple of the most patriotic judge of the
century, Lord Cooper; the resurgence has been sustained.[52] But in
general a couple of decades of physical and intellectual vandalism by
the university killed off what affection remained for it in its parent
city. Relations remain cool.

꙾

Edinburgh had yet survived in the twentieth century everything that
might have destroyed its character. But the question of revival, rather
than of mere survival, remained open. As often in the past the answer
would be unexpected, though long in gestation.

It is strange to recall now that until a quarter-century ago many
people had also been pessimistic about the future of Edinburgh's
financial industry. It lay distant from the powerhouses of western
capitalism in an era when big battalions overran everything. It was
gentlemanly but old-fashioned. It did not appear capable of rejuvenation.

A survey by economic experts in 1980 dwelt on external threats:
'Scotland has long since enjoyed a measure of financial development
and independent financial enterprise unusual among the regions
of the United Kingdom where financial markets and the direction of
financial institutions are heavily concentrated in London.' There was
in Edinburgh a mixture of native and expatriate institutions; among
native ones, banks and insurance companies figured prominently.
'In both cases, however, Scotland was their home but not their sole
or even their main market. Alongside and in many cases competing
with the native institutions were all those based elsewhere which
operated in Scotland through branches and agencies forming parts
of national, even international, networks of offices.' Competition had
grown, with English and foreign banks entering Scotland just as
Scottish banks looked outwards. Questions were posed by this
picture of a sector composed partly of local enterprises, partly of
national or international institutions contesting domestic markets.
One question could even be, for example, over 'the consequences,

beneficial or otherwise, to Scotland of this financial structure, and of the changes to which it was subjected'. So the consequences might somehow not be beneficial? It was hardly an upbeat assessment.[53]

These economic experts devoted three times as much space to manufacturing industry in Scotland (and even more to the role of government in sustaining it). It was evidence how far, even at this late stage, the Industrial Revolution defined the modern Scotland to her people and to their rulers. There are still those who find it hard to believe a man is seriously working unless he wears a boiler-suit and hard hat while toting an oil-can. But in Edinburgh the evidence of industrial revolution lay not, to quote Cockburn again, in tall black chimneys and black smoke. It lay instead in a surplus of capital arising from investment in such things. That stood in for what production and trade could not supply. It was why Edinburgh had become a financial centre.

❧

Banking was established here before the Union of 1707 and expanded up to the mid-nineteenth century. By then the city also housed an insurance industry. A stock exchange opened in 1844. New professions emerged, got organized and won recognition: the Society of Accountants in 1853 and the Actuarial Society of Edinburgh in 1859. The same pool of people took a lead in developing investment trusts. The innovations emerged in Edinburgh from solicitors' offices (in London or in Glasgow from mercantile enterprises). They grew fast, accountancy in particular. An English commentator noted in 1895: 'There can be no doubt that in Scotland accountancy has developed a degree of importance and that Scotch accountants rank higher than in any other part of the world'; today accountants appear to rule business everywhere. By 1911 one in twenty-five of Edinburgh's employees already worked in the financial industry. Now the figure is one in four.

In the eighteenth century Scotland remained a poor country, and in the nineteenth century Edinburgh produced no great capitalists making huge fortunes as Glasgow did. A financial industry sprang up because, unlike Glasgow, Edinburgh had in over a century of Union failed to build much by way of intercontinental trade. Another course stood open: to export not goods but capital. As a city of professionals rather than of manufacturers, it was better suited to that option. Outflows of money took place alongside stupendous demand for cash at home: there was evidently more than enough to go around.

The basis of the system was the banks. While the financial needs of the nation had been modest until 1707 and for some time afterwards, still Edinburgh became the headquarters of two leading banks, the Bank of Scotland founded in 1695 and the Royal Bank of Scotland founded in 1727. Small though the system was, it managed to benefit humanity by inventing the overdraft. In time other Scottish banks set up. The most important thing was that they gave Scotland a banking system separate from England's, and it remained relatively unaffected by the Union.[54]

After 1707, as the treaty specified, the official currency of Scotland was the pound sterling. The old pound Scots maintained a ghostly existence as a unit of account, at an exchange rate of 12:1 (it was, for example, the currency in which the port of Leith calculated its dues). Yet a common currency did not itself unite different banking systems, any more than it does in the European Union today. In fact the Scottish one ran on with minimal English interference until 1845. Scotland kept a sort of monetary semi-independence matching her political semi-independence. It appears the Bank of England would have been the lender of last resort in any real monetary crisis, though no statute or other document said so. But such a crisis never occurred, even in the period of greatest economic instability after the Napoleonic Wars (as Karl Marx remarked in wonder). To all intents and purposes this was a monetary system without a central bank, where various automatic mechanisms combined to control the note issue, and so the money supply, and so the rate of inflation.[55]

Sir Robert Peel changed everything by the Banking (Scotland) Act of 1845. His general economic policy was to free trade and lift regulation. But there had in his view to be a counterpart in a centralized monetary system for the United Kingdom, which could only be run by the Bank of England. Scottish banks were allowed to carry on in some ways regardless, in particular to continue issuing notes as the ordinary medium of exchange in their own country, which they still do. But in future their operations were to be limited to its territory, so far as possible; efforts to compete in England had already been stamped on, and would be again. By way of compensation no English banks could compete in Scotland because without a note issue of their own they would do so at a competitive disadvantage. The consequence was the confinement and cartelization of the Scottish banks (though many Scottish bankers worked for non-Scottish banks, especially in the empire).[56]

In 1918 Scotland still had eight note-issuing banks (cut to three by 1969). In such a small market they needed to pursue every penny of business, so service was comprehensive to a degree. Often several banks competed in, say, a well-to-do suburb of Edinburgh, saving customers the trouble of travelling into town even though six of the eight banks had head offices there. Banks might be an important source of local jobs. Because of shortages of manpower in the First World War many women were taken on, often in the charming role of 'lady typewriters'. After the war, this continuing trend must have compensated for the number of men thrown out of work in other sectors. Banking in Edinburgh and Scotland remained in a secure situation of modest but undemanding prosperity until near the end of the twentieth century.[57]

✣

Insurance formed a second big part of the financial industry. The earliest insurance company in Edinburgh, the Friendly Society, had been founded as long ago as 1719. Further development depended on two things. One was a scientific basis for assessing risk, which Scottish mathematical prowess could provide. The other was the quickening economic development of the country, creating greater wealth but more danger of fire and accident. From the turn of the nineteenth century the industry grew fast. The North British Insurance Company was founded in 1809, Scottish Widows Fund in 1815, Edinburgh Life Assurance Company in 1823 and Standard Life Assurance Company in 1825. They employed eager young agents to recruit customers and trained them to ask the right questions: 'Is he temperate or free? Is he thin? Is he middle-sized? Is he lusty? Is he bloated?'[58]

Standard Life became the biggest. It demonstrated that a financial institution seeking respectability and security did not have to be, as the banks were, tied down to Scotland. Nor did the company timidly assume that foreign business ought to be viewed as suspect, or that high rates of interest signalled unacceptable risk. In 1866 it took over a firm that had already extended operations to Canada and India, then grew still more profitable from investments there. It played the markets while taking care they should be reliable markets, as in the securities of colonial governments. After half a century, it was transacting the largest amount in Britain of new annual life business.

The First World War hit the financial industry hard, along with everything else in Scotland. Insurance had most to fear, because war takes lives and destroys property. Some companies were affected worse than others, and went through a period of stringency. But quick recovery followed, helped in Edinburgh by two special aspects of the industry. Competition was not cut-throat. Local institutions stuck together in hard times. In 1922 the Scottish Life Assurance Company came under attack from a 'group of speculators ... hard-faced businessmen out to contrive mergers in order to make profits by speculation in shares of the companies concerned'. Getting wind of the nefarious practice, Scottish Life refused to register transfers of shares to these fellows. They protested and the chairman of Edinburgh's stock exchange felt moved to point out it could not function if, 'when people bought shares, they did not know whether they would be allowed to complete the transaction'. He threatened to withdraw the quotation for Scottish Life, but the board stood firm and the speculators 'faded away'. There was another means of thwarting any threat from competitors. In 1925 Standard Life decided to mutualize itself. This was expected to foil rivals by attracting custom: in a mutual company no shareholders take dividends, and all profits can be shared by with-profits policy-holders as legal proprietors of the company. The mutual structure was abandoned only in 2006, to allow Standard Life to raise money on the stock market again. But set against that advantage was the chance it might become vulnerable to a predator.[59]

❦

In the nineteenth century the next great financial innovation was the founding of Edinburgh's stock exchange in 1844. This went hand in hand with a great economic innovation, the railways. There was already a line laid in 1836 to Leith and Newhaven, connecting by ferry with Fife. In 1842 the line from Glasgow came into Haymarket, today the oldest working station in the world. That marked the outbreak of railway mania in Scotland. Indeed in Britain as a whole the next few years saw frantic investment in this revolutionary mode of transport and rapid coverage of the country by a network which in large part is still in place. Two lines were built to Scotland from London, the North British up the eastern route via Berwick and the Caledonian up the western route, heading towards Glasgow but crossing from Carstairs to Edinburgh too. The city's main station, Waverley, dates from 1866. The opening of the Forth Rail Bridge in 1890 made this the junction of routes from north and south, and Britain's biggest station after Waterloo in London. Alongside, a revolution had taken place in finance as well as in transport: with so much going on, the market in shares of railways remained lively, not to say hectic. It was why Scottish exchanges had come into being. In Edinburgh there were engaged in broking in 1844 four individuals, three partnerships, four companies; by 1846, fifteen individuals, fourteen partnerships, six companies. So the exchange had taken off at once.

By far the biggest stock exchange lay, of course, in London. To it Edinburgh and others in Scotland were linked by telegraph early on. Scottish exchanges quoted some of the same securities and these overlaps grew in time, as did the number of exchanges they covered, so differences were eroded. Yet the exchanges kept going because so many joint-stock companies had Scottish bases and interests. Even in such major shares as the Caledonian or North British railways, held all over Britain, the main markets stayed in Scotland. By the end of the century these markets had grown mature, and were so regulated as to make them widely accessible through brokers or their agents in the country. This was not a truly independent structure; nor was any other in the precocious Victorian globalism. But in Scotland, stocks and shares became an important, distinct form of property served by its own intermediaries.[60]

※

Capital was accumulating, in other words. In mid-Victorian times all taxation was indirect, so that professional people could keep what they earned or inherited. Below them a strong urge to frugality emerged among the people, if only because no other means existed of providing for illness, old age or widowhood. Edinburgh had a savings bank – in essence for deposit rather than for current accounts – as early as 1813, and another from 1836, founded in hopes of dissuading the workers from spending their money on drink. The man behind it, John Hay Forbes, thought it might foster sexual continence too: 'The foundation of virtue is laid in the restraint of passions; while a wasteful expenditure of money, in selfish gratifications, is at once the cause and effect of most of the vices of the poor.' His scheme explicitly sought to attract small sums – once an account reached £10 it would be transferred to a commercial bank.[61]

But at that point there were better ways to lay out the money, not least in other forms of investment available in Edinburgh. Aggregations of in themselves tiny savings represented an important source of funds for urban improvement, tapped by landowners, developers and builders. A builder, for example, might put together finance for a scheme of construction by taking out bonds or loans payable over fifteen years and yielding interest at, say, 1 per cent above the current rate on gilt-edged stocks. In a world of the most marginal returns to capital, but with inflation unknown, that made for an attractive investment – especially in a local market where it was easier to sustain confidence among everybody involved. Again, feudalism offered scope to generate a small but regular income because the superiority of a property could in law be separated from the ownership. Feu-duties then payable from vassal to superior might be combined into a modest annuity.

Edinburgh seems to have had legions of frugal savers interested not in spectacular financial coups but only in regular income built up out of trifling components. The task required close attention to detail, and was usually handed to solicitors. In Edinburgh these had plenty of experience of investment in everything from stocks and shares to administration of large estates, but they also showed enough patience to deal with a range of clients, not all rich. They became skilled at drawing networks together and making up bundles of capital from diverse sources. All this served also to open Edinburgh to the world. More could be earned overseas than at home, such as from the development of the Americas and Australasia. In the close circles of Scots law, many men kept up contacts with family and friends from school or college who had gone somewhere exotic to seek a fortune. These brother Scots felt happiest dealing with one another, as they would not have felt dealing with some outsider.[62]

※

Here were the building blocks of the investment trust as a vehicle for collective deployment of capital. It managed risk by taking money from many investors and spreading it over many investments. It became a major part of the financial industry in Edinburgh, and remains so.[63]

The man who developed the concept, William Menzies, apparently borrowed it from Belgium. But Edinburgh could network as Brussels could not. Menzies himself was the son of the professor of conveyancing at the university. He first ran a firm of ecclesiastical lawyers, though by now even Scottish Churches were losing their taste for litigation. So he had time to take an interest in the outside world, and trips to the United States showed him the huge potential of a country that remained a net importer of capital until the First World War. In 1873 he set up the Scottish American Investment Trust, soon known as Saints, which financed projects in the Wild West, from railways to ranches. He wrote: 'The immense fertility of the soil and the boundless resources of the country lead to enterprise and speculation such as are quite unknown here ... The tendency to speculation in America is on a scale to which there is no parallel in this country.'[64]

A key figure in a later generation, James Ivory, also came from a legal background – his father, William, had as sheriff of Inverness to try revolting crofters, while his grandfather was a judge in the Court of Session. The young Ivory preferred accountancy and in 1895 formed a partnership with Thomas Sime. Ivory & Sime showed how investment trusts could thrive on niche markets that might put off a conventional investor. Australia had suffered financial collapse in 1890 from a downturn in global prices of the raw materials it produced. So far from steering clear of a mess, Ivory & Sime waded in to buy up assets of banks and insurance companies bound to recover as this economy indeed did. Profits were reinvested in the next undervalued market.[65]

In the generation after that, Carlyle Gifford teamed up in 1908 with Augustus Baillie, a landowner in the Borders, to form the firm of Baillie & Gifford. During the new century trusts would face volatile conditions a world away from the even tranquillity of Victorian capitalism. The First World War destroyed foreign investments, but the rising markets of the 1920s revived them. Ruin followed in the Depression, and recovery was only just gathering momentum when the Second World War broke out. Gifford had become an expert on the economy of the United States but, more to the point, a friend of John Maynard Keynes: both enjoyed risky speculation. At Keynes's prompting, the British government put Gifford in charge of all its citizens' holdings of American securities requisitioned in 1940. His task was to liquidate them and so provide finance for the immense matériel being shipped for the war across the Atlantic Ocean. It was a big job and a delicate one, as the holdings represented 2 per cent of all securities in New York and their disposal could have caused a bear market, if not worse. It hurt Gifford's brother Scots: Saints alone gave up over $7 million of income and capital. But his formidable bargaining power at least meant good prices were achieved.

Nothing daunted, the trusts rebuilt their overseas holdings after 1945, in some cases to almost half their portfolios. Now it was Scottish industry that felt starved of funds. The Labour MP for Motherwell, George Lawson, complained to Parliament in 1955 that more money flowed from Edinburgh into North America than into Scotland. Of course: the trusts were responsible to their shareholders rather than to some wider group of companies or industries. Their purpose was profit. That was what in the end would create most employment and income, at least in Edinburgh – if not in Motherwell. In 1959 Motherwell got instead a brand-new steelworks, Ravenscraig. Today the steelworks is gone but the trusts are still there.[66]

❧

By the 1980s it became clear that capitalism was going to be organised on a much greater scale in the future than in the past. There were implications for Scotland, with a financial industry big in her own terms but no more than middling by international standards. Now larger Scottish groupings would have to be formed. For the investment trusts two men led the way, Donald Marr in Dundee and Grant Cochrane in Edinburgh. In 1984 they established Dunedin

Fund Managers, based in Edinburgh: a loss to Dundee, but in a fast-moving scene there was no room for sentimentality. Economies of scale prompted continued consolidation of the trusts, and with some success. By 2009, more than £150 billion was being managed from Edinburgh. A leading figure, Robin Angus, said: 'Edinburgh is not a suburb of the City [of London]. It is a world financial centre in its own right, communicating directly with other world financial centres like New York and Tokyo.'[67]

But it also followed that Edinburgh could not be shielded from the problems of globalization. It did help that the city's asset managers remained relatively conservative in crucial respects. They steered clear, on the whole, of the huge boom in novel forms of investment, in hedge funds or in private equity, that came with the twenty-first century. And by the middle of 2008 they were screaming at clients to get out of the world's stock markets. So some Scots proved as canny as ever. Once the boom was over (with a bang) their cautious stance appeared comparatively sensible amid the general folly that brought on the credit crunch, thereby partly salvaging one of the nation's competitive advantages: its reputation for trustworthiness. This could again prove crucial now the spectacular capital gains of the early twenty-first century would be no longer available.

꙰

The credit crunch was a long-term result of what had become known in Britain as the Big Bang, the general financial deregulation of the 1980s. It destroyed cosy old networks in the City of London especially. But Edinburgh had cosy old networks of its own, albeit smaller and more vulnerable. First in the firing line stood the Scottish banks.

At breakfast on 17 March 1981, Alexander Fletcher, Minister for Industry at the Scottish Office, opened the papers to read bad news – the Royal Bank had agreed to merge with the Standard Chartered Bank. The first was his country's biggest bank. The second was one that did not really belong anywhere: though registered in the United Kingdom, it conducted little business there and had most of its interests in Asia or Africa. That did not worry Fletcher so much as the stingy deal it was offering, well below the net value of the Royal

Bank's assets. While after a takeover there were to be eight Scots directors on the board of Standard Chartered, this seemed meagre recompense for removal of control over a Scottish bank to London – if that was where the merged headquarters would go, as seemed likely.

A chummy chap, Fletcher knew everybody who mattered on the Scottish economic and political scene. He found his dismay widely shared, not least by his boss, the Secretary of State for Scotland, George Younger, as well as in London by the Secretary of State for Trade, John Biffen. He, among English unionists, was unusual in not being hostile to the Scots. In fact he thought more could be done to satisfy them within the existing constitution, and should be done if it was to survive. Here he had an example. It was as well to win him over, for Biffen would have to decide whether to let the merger go ahead or refer it to the Monopolies Commission.

It fell to the junior minister, Fletcher, to make the running because members of the cabinet could not campaign openly on one side or the other of what at length became a quasi-judicial cause. He saw the problem, that grounds for referral to the Monopolies Commission were not salient. The parties to the proposed merger had after all reached agreement. And no monopoly, or risk of monopoly, existed in British banking. Cartels did exist, but they were a different matter. A cartel existed among four English clearing banks, while the fifth, Williams & Glyn's, had a link with the Royal Bank, and so with the cartel of three Scottish clearing banks. One tacit rule of the two cartels was that neither should encroach, at least not far, on the territory of the other. A little competitive pressure was still thought desirable, in the cautious manner of those days. It had long been expected that a 'fifth force' in British banking would emerge, though nobody could quite say how. Some potential for it lay among the Scottish banks, yet none was strong enough to pull itself up by its own bootstraps. Merger with a third party appeared to be the way forward.

At least, this was how it appeared to the stolid chairman of the Royal Bank, Sir Michael Herries. He seemed to take a dim view of his own bank's prospects, though perhaps that reflected general long-term pessimism at the top of Edinburgh's financial establishment.

Anyway he had been seeking alliances. Because of considerations of monopoly, he was forced to look outside the United Kingdom – for instance, to the Orient where he had himself worked. The Royal Bank might meet the specifications of two old imperial outfits, the Standard Chartered Bank and the Hongkong and Shanghai Bank, which both needed to find a role now the Empire was over, or almost. In particular they sought access to markets from which their history had shut them out, in America and in Europe. Into this latter market one way could be the Royal Bank.

But the way bristled with obstacles. The Bank of England had long insisted on separation of banking at home and abroad, allowing no company from overseas to acquire a British clearer. While Herries hoped to change that, he had to choose his ground, find a good partner and work out the right partnership. For some reason he did not like the look of the Hongkong and Shanghai Bank, so concluded that Standard Chartered was a better fit for the Royal Bank. Each could give the other what it lacked, a network abroad in return for an established position at home. And though Standard Chartered was bigger than the Royal Bank, the link could be dressed up as merger rather than takeover. For all this Herries at length won round the Bank of England.

Yet Herries appeared unaware of one obstacle facing him not down in Threadneedle Street but in a place visible from his own desk, the Scottish Office where Fletcher sat scheming. To him the vital question was whether the merged corporation would be run from Edinburgh or London. Herries refused to commit himself, but Scots at large were unlikely to accept Britain's gain might be Scotland's loss. In other words the problem was in the last resort political, and Fletcher identified it as such. Peter de Vink and Ian Noble, cronies of his, set out to mobilize support. But lines of battle were hardly formed when they had to wheel about and face an onslaught from the Hongkong and Shanghai Bank, outbidding Standard Chartered. It came up with a package much more winsome than the limp surrender to English financial imperialism implicit in the rival bid. It promised to preserve Scottish banking autonomy and make the Royal Bank the European flagship of a novel group, more of a partner than a subsidiary. As far as it went, the ploy succeeded: if the choice lay between these two, then on the whole Scottish opinion probably did favour the Hongkong and Shanghai Bank.

Herries remained unmoved, and Standard Chartered took the cue to strike back. It raised its own offer to a level where there was little to choose between the two. Now there could be no clandestine coupling, only a battle in the open marketplace, no cosy merger, only a hard-fought takeover. Willy-nilly it then become a matter for Scots at large, not just for shareholders. Various institutions took their stand, from the Scottish Office down, with a discreet lead from Younger and hardly repressed rabble-rousing from Fletcher, who went round Edinburgh calling the directors of the Royal Bank 'traitors to Scotland'. Press, political parties and pressure groups joined in. Among the voices raised was the Bank of Scotland's, junior only to the Royal Bank and owned to the extent of 35 per cent by Barclays Bank: it feared that, if the integrity of the domestic system could not hold, predators would soon arrive at its own door. The government saw a Scottish crisis looming. Evasive action was needed, and the portals of the Monopolies Commission stood open. Biffen overruled caveats from its officials to declare there was a public interest at stake beyond the private interests of the parties involved. In reaching his conclusion, he took account of the importance of Edinburgh as a financial centre and of a strong banking system for the Scottish economy: an unmistakable echo of Fletcher's view. Biffen referred both bids to the commission.[68]

※

The Monopolies Commission took a year to make up its mind. The task resolved itself into deciding whether the advantage of a British fifth force, based in London, outweighed a different case for diversity, that is to say, preserving and developing Edinburgh as a financial centre. The commission finally turned down both bids. Despite the contrary arguments, it agreed that a change of ownership would remove control of the Royal Bank from Scotland, close off careers open to Scottish talents, damp down native enterprise and hinder the general development of the country. It also accepted the case against allowing control of a clearing bank to pass outside the United Kingdom. It ruled, in other words, for the independence of the Royal Bank.

Nobody emerged unblooded from this battle. The two bidder banks spent much time and money to no purpose. For the sake of Standard Chartered, the Bank of England abandoned its long-standing segregation of internal and external banking, only to see its designs foiled. The Royal Bank had to find a new blueprint for the future. The Scottish establishment was left with egg all over its face. The men who rallied round Herries belonged to a national system of interlocking interests where directors from big companies sat on each others' boards. Herries himself became chairman of Scottish Widows right in the middle of the rumpus. His deputy at the Royal Bank, Peter Balfour, was in addition chairman of Scottish & Newcastle; he also headed the Scottish Council, a body representative of both private and public sectors that had been complaining about a stampede of decision-makers to London. Another director of the Royal Bank, Robin Duthie, doubled as chairman of the Scottish Development Agency, which channelled public money into economic regeneration; in this capacity he had just denounced the ignorance of people in London about any place north of Watford. Yet where were these, and others, when the time came to stand up and be counted over the Royal Bank? They endorsed the deal with Standard Chartered.

The *éminences grises* of this financial establishment, wholly union-ist in politics, were here failing to make the Union do what they said it did, serve Scottish interests. They had finally to give way to the general indignation, but with an ill grace that left a bad taste. The one man of similar standing to break ranks was Lord Clydesmuir, governor of the Bank of Scotland. Otherwise, the campaign against Herries relied on outsiders such as de Vink and Noble, or indeed on Fletcher himself, a Tory politician born within sight of the shipyards of Greenock where his father had worked. Nationalism was not their prime motive, yet not absent from what they did, or of no help to them.[69]

❧

The episode proved to be a turning point, but a complex one. Younger became chairman of the Royal Bank in 1989. To many it seemed a fitting reward for his role seven years before. Behind the scenes 'Gentleman George' had thwarted Herries's plans, yet without creating ill-will: both chaps got on perfectly well as members of the Scottish landed gentry, and Herries in fact wanted Younger to follow him. Still, if he expected this to maintain his patrician regime he was wrong. During Younger's own chairmanship, which lasted right through the 1990s, he did preside over the bank with grace and charm yet smoothed the path for the ambitions of the hard man under him, George Mathewson. An engineer born at Dunfermline, Mathewson was not patrician at all. He had returned from a career in America excited at his professional prospects as the oilfields under the North Sea came onstream. Back in Edinburgh he put himself about so well that in 1981 he was appointed to run the Scottish Development Agency (now renamed Scottish Enterprise). In 1987 he became a director of the Royal Bank, which had continued to underperform. When Younger succeeded Herries, he appointed Mathewson his chief executive. Ruthless reorganisation made heads roll but created a solid platform for growth. In 1998 the Royal Bank was the first Scottish company to make profits of over £1 billion. Mathewson got a knighthood.

But now the Scottish banks were being drawn right into the maelstrom of globalization, where it appeared only the strong and the swift might keep their heads above water. In 2000 the Royal Bank's local rival, the Bank of Scotland, tried in England to take over the much larger National Westminster Bank with an offer of £20 billion. Scots like fighting each other even more than they like fighting the English, and the move nettled Mathewson. The Royal Bank did not have the money to take over National Westminster so Mathewson sourced £24 billion from the United States. Out of a tough, ill-tempered battle he emerged the victor. It soon became clear that this defeat for the Bank of Scotland sounded the death-knell of its independence. In 2001 it entered into voluntary merger with Halifax, an English building society. So from the turmoil a 'fifth force' in British banking at last emerged. It would last seven years.

Meanwhile at the Royal Bank, Mathewson succeeded Younger as chairman after the latter retired through ill-health.[70] The career of Mathewson's own replacement, Fred Goodwin, proved even more dramatic than his own. Under him assets quadrupled and profits soared to a peak of £9 billion in 2006. On paper this became the fifth largest bank in the world. But Goodwin's ambition was leading him along paths a prudent banker should never have trodden.

One path Goodwin pursued was growth by aggressive acquisition, notably by the takeover of a decrepit Dutch bank, ABN Amro, which would prove disastrous. The new, bloated, Royal Bank was then relying on an excess of so-called toxic assets, there on the books but in reality worth little or nothing; it would emerge as the world's third largest underwriter of them. Meanwhile its general liquidity deteriorated. Until 2002 it remained fully funded, that is, its deposits broadly matched its loans. The telltale sign of too rapid an expansion was its increasing reliance on an external source, the wholesale money markets. As these dried up with the onset of the credit crunch in 2008, the bank found itself in trouble. Its losses for the financial year 2008–09 would exceed £28 billion, the largest in British corporate history (£17 billion of them thanks to ABN Amro). Though in the spring it made a rights issue to existing shareholders that failed to solve the problem. By the autumn there was nothing for it but rescue by the British government, which acquired a majority of the Royal Bank's spectacularly devalued shares. In bourgeois Edinburgh outraged citizens vandalised Goodwin's big house and big car. He hardly needed to worry: he had already resigned on an ample pension.

Altogether, after three centuries Scottish banking was more or less destroyed. Any future it had would not bear much resemblance to the past. But did this herald the end of Edinburgh as a financial centre? While nothing could now be certain, a long history had at least lent its operations some depth and diversity. The effects of the credit crunch would continue to work themselves out.

※

In the modern world, in such powerhouses as New York and San Francisco, there often seems to be a link between high finance and hard drugs. No doubt it was a Celtic love of intoxicants that made Edinburgh the same. An official report of 1976 had already revealed its citizens (and not Glaswegians) to be the heaviest drinkers in Scotland. And in the first wave of abuse, Edinburgh was also the heaviest consumer of drugs.[71]

There had been drugs of the opiate type in Edinburgh for 200 years. They arrived with Scots who had served in India. Addiction was then viewed not with horror but with impatience. Sir James Mackintosh, who but for that problem might have won the chair of moral philosophy at the university in 1820, was said to be 'practically, quite useless'. Thomas de Quincey, arriving in 1821 to sample the joys of the Enlightenment, came already addicted and had no trouble feeding his habit here; he wrote up his confessions as an 'opium-eater'. Knowledge of the drug did not remain confined to select circles. John Inglis, a legal clerk, reported in his diary for 28 March 1880, that his wife's toothache was 'raging furiously. She went out to the druggists and got some heroin, a stuff composed partly of chloroform if we may judge by the smell. This had a most favourable effect upon her nerves.' Heroin remained openly on sale until the First World War, when the government banned it because Scots troops in the trenches were asking their families to send out supplies. Enough still remained available in Edinburgh for a few people to become addicts. Heroin could be obtained on prescription from a chemist at Shandwick Place in the posh West End. There junkies still journey from peripheral council estates, but not all the use is proletarian, let alone criminal; a doctoral thesis on the subject is called 'From Morningside to Muirhouse'. In other words, the drug has been consumed in respectable suburbs as well as in rough ones.[72]

In Edinburgh the number of convictions for possession of narcotics in 1969 was fifteen. The next year it went up to twenty-nine. That was the small start of an inexorable rise. Surveillance by the police had so far been simple and successful but now cases in working-class parts of the city, at Craigmillar, Leith or Muirhouse, multiplied beyond control. Hardened criminals moved in to supply and deal. The trade began to generate big money, if still from a host of small sales. By 1985 there were over 300 convictions for possession or supply of heroin. At the start of the decade less than 1 per cent of prosecutions in the High Court had involved drugs; now the proportion reached 27 per cent, undeterred by a tripling in the mean length of sentence handed down to offenders.

With all this the scourge of HIV appeared, caused by sharing needles for the injection of drugs. The worst incidence of the disease was in London, but Scotland ran close. And of infections in Scotland during the late 1980s Edinburgh had the highest rate, three out of five of all cases. So this was worse than London. The reason seems clear. The police here sought to deter use of syringes and needles by seizing them at sight. With a shortage of sterile equipment, addicts saw themselves with no choice but to share. The number of arrests for the supply and possession of heroin finally dropped because the users were dead. The problem today is one of recreational drugs, and seems no worse in Edinburgh than elsewhere. In any case, many more die from the effects of alcohol and tobacco.[73]

꙰

Infection could also be spread by sex but the history of sex in Edinburgh during the twentieth century is obscure compared to the wealth of evidence we have from earlier times. Sexual misdemeanour is no longer a matter of public scandal. And women have been emancipated. That, among other things, made resort to prostitution less common, so bringing a long chapter of social history to a virtual end. Compared with 800 prostitutes and 200 brothels estimated by William Tait in 1842, a report by the police of 1901 said there were 424 prostitutes and 45 brothels, by 1911 only 180 prostitutes and 29 brothels – but perhaps the police doctored the evidence for some purpose of their own. In the 1920s one aspect of the capital's life that Edwin Muir did not disapprove of was the prevalence of sex:

> Nowhere that I have been is one so bathed and steeped and rolled about in floating sexual desire as in certain streets of . . . Edinburgh. This desire fills the main thoroughfare and overflows into all the adjacent pockets and backwaters: the tea-rooms, restaurants and cinema lounges. The only refuges from it are the pubs, which convention forbids women to enter, but which, nevertheless, are always well attended. There, like sailors after a difficult and nerve-whipping voyage, the men put into harbour and wrap themselves in a safe cloak of alcohol.[74]

The prevalent puritanism did not banish illicit sex, as one minister, the Reverend Simpson Marr of Lady Yester's kirk, was brave enough to point out: 'The Church's record in the past has often been simply deplorable. She has supported the persecution of those who have been supplying the need, and not those who have been making the demand. She has too often forgotten the attitude of Christ to fallen women.' The Church responded by abolishing Marr's parish and so depriving him of his pulpit.[75]

After the Second World War the most notorious address in the city was in Danube Street, where Mrs Dora Noyce presided over a household of fifteen regular girls and twenty-five others on call at busy times, such as during the General Assembly of the Church of Scotland. Mrs Noyce herself, clad in furs and twin-set, bore herself with dignity on the forty-seven occasions she appeared in court for living on immoral earnings. The house closed with her death in 1976. Now there is no famous brothel in Edinburgh, but two or three dozen saunas serve the same purpose. It was the epidemic of HIV that scared the town council into authorizing them, in effect as a measure of control. Legal saunas have to meet official standards which illegal brothels do not; the police seem to prefer things this way, too. Even so, prostitutes have not left the streets. Their numbers were estimated at 100 in 2004, about half of them available on any one night. They could be seen in the centre of the city sometimes, but most worked in Leith. The trouble was that Leith had got more than a little gentrified, with restaurants and cocktail bars and fashionable flats enjoying views of the Forth. So the police have tried to make the girls go elsewhere, into what a report called 'a zone of discretionary prosecution'; it does not sound enticing.[76]

※

The city's culture does not rest at this sensual level. Since 1946 it has been host to the Edinburgh International Festival, and over that time has no doubt seen all the world's greatest artists perform. Still, the people long seemed unimpressed by the annual visitation, and sometimes irritated at it. John Drummond, its director from 1978–83, went so far as to say, 'We are not welcome here'; he ran the jamboree from London, needless to say.

As in much else, the true feelings of Edinburgh can be hard to discern. There has been some ritual fawning on the Festival. While a journalist on *The Scotsman* in 1967, the quizmaster Magnus Magnusson wrote: 'I find it hard to believe that anyone could disagree that the Edinburgh International Festival has exalted Edinburgh into a real capital city after a lapse of centuries.' Perhaps he waxed so effusive because he knew there were people who did disagree. One, Tom Nairn, now professor of globalism at the University of Melbourne, retorted at the time in the *New Statesman* with a famous article, a ferocious attack on 'The Festival of the Dead':

> People comment ceaselessly on how little effect it has had upon the real, continuing life of the city, but what do they expect? The soil Scotland offers to this fragile festive culture is mildewed religiosity a mile deep, and what could thrive in this? Edinburgh's soul is bible-black, pickled in boredom by centuries of sermons, swaddled in the shabby gentility of the Kirk – what difference could twenty-one years of Festival make to this?[77]

In fact Edinburgh's religion had by now gone into steep decline. Three centuries of grim Calvinism were being cast off to reveal a hedonism always there underneath, and soon little less frenzied than in any other city of the western world. This may also be a reason why Edinburgh gradually became reconciled to its Festival.

There had been an unspoken assumption among the Festival's successive directors that high culture was something needing to be imported from outside. It could be brought to Edinburgh, it could be displayed to Edinburgh, but Edinburgh was never expected to do more than look on and be grateful – not, for example, itself to make any contribution to high culture. After five years the Scots playwright Robert Kemp decided it was about time to show Scotland had in the past been capable of some small contribution. He revived Sir David Lindsay's *The Thrie Estaitis*. The play made a great impact, but had no permanent effect.[78] The Festival still treated Scottish culture as if it did not exist. The people of Edinburgh continued to ignore the Festival.

That has changed, though not through anything the Festival has done. Rather two other Festivals have arisen to redress the balance. One is the Fringe, which brings a greater variety of culture, indeed a market in culture geared to pleasing audiences rather than gathering subsidies. At that market the people of Edinburgh turn up to buy. The other is the Book Festival, with a special appeal in this city of long literary tradition. It, too, reminds us how varied culture is, never to be fully defined by the high culture of an international elite. In its love of books, Edinburgh can display itself without self-consciousness alongside the cultures of other places. And then it appears in its true colours, little different from those David Wilkie painted two centuries ago. It is a culture not of pomp and circumstance, of glamour and glitter – but a quiet and unassuming culture, all the deeper for that, where people are content to play the fiddle or read a novel while rain beats at the window and a fire sputters in the grate. It suits Edinburgh down to the ground.

ENVOI

ON 14 OCTOBER 2004, Unesco, the cultural organization of the United Nations, declared Edinburgh to be the world's first 'city of literature'. A Scottish delegation had gone out to Unesco's headquarters in Paris to make the case that won the award.

Speaking in the shadow of the Eiffel Tower, the Minister of Culture in the government of Scotland, Mrs Patricia Ferguson (who comes from Glasgow), said: 'I'm absolutely delighted at the news that Edinburgh has been recognized as the first Unesco city of literature. This is not only good news for Edinburgh but for Scotland as a whole. It confirms Scotland's position as a country of literary excellence.'

Also piping up from Paris was James Boyle (who comes from Glasgow), chairman of a cultural commission set up by the government of Scotland, former chairman of the Scottish Arts Council and former head of Radio Scotland. He said: 'I'm overwhelmed. As soon as we heard we jumped up in the air and toasted Edinburgh.'[1]

In the recent quest for international honours Glasgow had run some way ahead of Edinburgh, so perhaps it was only fitting that Glaswegians should have spearheaded the successful campaign for this particular accolade. Or else it might have been that nobody much could be found in Edinburgh willing to take an interest in meaningless titles.

As a matter of fact the twentieth century had been Edinburgh's least distinguished for literature since the fourteenth, something that Scots from elsewhere were wont to point out with perhaps excessive glee. At least now, at the beginning of the twenty-first century, there were unmistakable signs of revival. Edinburgh was home to writers who had not just achieved success but had made it as global megastars, earning fame and fortune beyond anything known in the whole literary history of the city. And several had done so by writing about the long neglected subjects of Edinburgh and its people.

Revival in letters went along with revival in life. Edinburgh grew rich on high finance and, almost despite itself, was enjoying the experience. It flaunted its wealth as it had never cared or dared to do in the past, in the shops and on the streets, in the bars and in the restaurants, in the clothes that were worn and in the cars that were driven. The physical fabric of the city was spruced up after an era of indifference. Shameful gap-sites were filled. Statues of famous sons rose once again. New buildings looked not shoddy but exciting: the Museum of Scotland, a *château* or rather a *donjon* inspired by Le Corbusier which had caused the Prince of Wales to resign as its patron; and the Scottish Parliament – perhaps a little too Catalan without, thanks to its architect Enric Miralles, but within recalling Tristan's Wood of Celyddon, only in stone. It was above all the Parliament that made Edinburgh not just look again like but feel again like a capital city. Yet another reinvention had taken place.

Still, much remained the same. If Sir Walter Scott had come back, he could readily have traced the route from his early home in George Square to his later ones in Castle Street and Walker Street, and in the two latter cases he would have found the surroundings little altered (about George Square enough has already been said). In the parts Sir Walter could never have known, such as the southern tract of villas from the Grange to Merchiston, comfortable bourgeois existence went on in the even tenor of its ways. More bohemian quarters, Stockbridge or Bruntsfield, renewed themselves with each rising generation. Easter Road or Dalry Road were still authentic Victorian working-class suburbs. Edinburgh has changed, of course, and in some respects has changed a lot – yet it is hard to think of another British city that has changed so little.

Perhaps it is the successful blend of old and new that gives such a relatively small place its animation. The city has yet to reach half a million inhabitants, though a couple of hundred thousand might be added for commuter suburbs beyond the boundaries, in the Lothians and across the Forth Road Bridge (1964) in Fife. Even this is nothing compared with the 28 million of Tokyo or the 18 million of Bombay,

Mexico City and São Paulo. Still, in the new century mankind may tire of megalopolis and come to see once again the blessings of a smaller scale. It will find them in Edinburgh. The central area can still be crossed on foot in half an hour; anybody who does this is almost bound to meet an acquaintance. If a capital city, it often has the feel of a village. And by reason of their intimacy villages can also foster an enviable variety of human existence. Three writers of the 'city of literature' will show us this is true here.

Alexander McCall Smith has celebrated the Edinburgh of the bourgeoisie. He is well acquainted with it despite having arrived in its midst only as a student at the university (he had been born in the empire, and in that respect is a typical Scot). After briefly flirting with Scottish nationalism, he became an academic lawyer and at length professor of forensic law in the university. Meanwhile he was writing fiction as well. While his career prepared him for the genre he has made his own, gentle detective stories, his domicile also nurtured the more penetrating irony of *44 Scotland Street* (2005). The idea of a narrative covering the lives of different residents on a single stair in a typical tenement of the New Town was not original, but previous examples had turned out far too twee. McCall Smith is in a sense twee too, though satirical enough to stop well short of the saccharine: in fact he can be acid, still in the nicest possible way.

Near the end of the novel McCall Smith sets out the case against Edinburgh during a conversation between two of his characters, Angus Lordie and Domenica Macdonald. They discuss that bitter, hostile poem by Ruthven Todd. Angus says:

> 'Haut-bourgeois Edinburgh ... used to be just like that. Brittle. Exclusive. Turned in on itself. And immensely snobbish.'
>
> 'And still is like that,' said Domenica quietly. 'In its worst moments.'
>
> 'But much better than it used to be,' Angus Lordie countered. 'You very rarely see those real, cold Edinburgh attitudes these days. The arrogance of those people is broken. They just can't get away with it. That horrid disapproval of anything that moves – that's gone.'
>
> Domenica did not appear to be completely convinced. 'I'm not sure, she said. 'What makes Edinburgh different from other

cities in these islands? It is different, you know. I think that
there is still a certain hauteur, an intellectual crustiness...'

Angus Lordie smiled. 'But Domenica rather likes all that,' he
suggested mischievously 'She's a bit of a Jean Brodie, you know.'[2]

At the opposite end of the social scale is the Edinburgh of
Irvine Welsh in *Trainspotting* (1993) – the city of junkies, of young
men addicted to heroin (among other substances). Some episodes are
sickening in this loosely structured work, but one thing that makes
the whole lot bowl along is its linguistic exuberance. Welsh is an
innovator in the range of the Scots language. The convention established by the Waverley novels, and almost universally followed since,
is that while dialogue can be couched in Scots, narrative should go
into English; the sole major exception is a story entirely in Scots by
Robert Louis Stevenson, 'Thrawn Janet'. Welsh breaks the convention. He uses Scots not the whole time but certainly most of the
time, and for dialogue or narrative alike. It is a Scots that had not
appeared in print before, the modern vernacular of working-class
Edinburgh, a demotic, argotic dialect perhaps little to the taste of the
purists in the Scots Language Society.

The action of *Trainspotting* takes place in the late 1980s, the
period of HIV, and largely in Leith, before its gentrification. Few
tourists ventured down there at the time but, if they had, they would
have done best for the sake of speed and safety to start their return
from the taxi rank at the foot of Leith Walk. There Welsh sets this
scene, as his characters start to suffer withdrawal symptoms:

At the Fit ay the Walk thir wir nae taxis. They only congregated
here when ye didnae need them. Supposed tae be August, but
ah'm fuckin freezing ma baws oaf here. Ah'm no sick yet, but
it's in the fuckin post, that's fir sure.

– Supposed tae be a rank. Supposed tae be a fuckin taxi
rank. Nivir fuckin git one in the summer. Up cruising fat, rich
festival cunts too fuckin lazy tae walk a hundred fuckin yards
fae one poxy church hall tae another fir thir fuckin show. Taxi
drivers. Money-grabbin bastards ... Sick Boy muttered deliri-
ously and breathlessly tae hissel, eyes bulging and sinews in his
neck straining as his heid craned up Leith Walk.

At last one came. There were a group ay young guys in shell-suits n bomber jaykits whae'd been standing thair longer than us. Ah doubt if Sick Boy even saw them. He charged straight oot intae the middle ay the Walk screaming: – TAXI!

Hi! Whit's the fuckin score? One guy in a black, purple and aqua shell-suit wi a flat-top asks.

Git tae fuck. We wir here first, Sick Boy sais, opening the taxi door. – Thir's another yin comin. He gestured up the Walk at an advancing black cab.

Lucky fir youse. Smart cunts.

Fuck off, ya plukey-faced wee hing oot. Git a fuckin ride! Sick Boy snarled as we piled into the taxi.

Tollcross mate, ah sais tae the driver as gob splattered against the side windae.

Square go then smart cunt! C'moan ya crapping bastards! the shell-suit shouted. The taxi driver wisnae amused. He looked a right cunt. Maist ay them do. The stamp-peyin self-employed ur truly the lowest form ay vermin oan god's earth.

The taxi did a u-turn and sped up the Walk.[3]

Covering the whole social spectrum of Edinburgh, yet still because of the subject-matter tending towards the lower end, are the novels of Ian Rankin. Their hero is Detective Inspector John Rebus, on the face of it not a terribly interesting character, even to meet in his favourite Oxford Bar. Apart from his work he has no interests but smoking, drinking and brooding – though these are vices common enough in Edinburgh. He is redeemed because he shows a basic decency that lets him in his wayward fashion get things right in the end, at least some of the time, even if meanwhile he has seemed at a loss. Many readers identify with that, not only those from his own city.

The setting in Edinburgh is vital. Nothing like these novels could have been written during the middle decades of the twentieth century because the city, like the country, was then so washed out. Now colour and movement have come back, pointing up the contrast with the cynicism and world-weariness of Rebus, a man of that earlier time often out of tune with this later one.

Welsh took us to Leith, so let us see how Rankin, in his turn, has shown the place. There is a progression. In *Let it Bleed* (1995), 'Leith still retained its old, unique charm: it was still about the only part of the city where you'd see prostitutes in daytime, freezing in short skirts and skimpy jackets. Rebus had passed some on his way down Bernard Street, readying themselves for the going-home trade: one quick leap for the homeward bound.' Once we get to *A Question of Blood* (2003), Leith is no longer timeless, but 'always on the verge of some renaissance or other. When the warehouses were turned into "loft-style apartments", or a cinema complex opened, or the Queen's superannuated yacht was berthed there for tourists to visit, there was always talk of the port's "rejuvenation". But . . . the place never really changed: same old Leith, same old Leithers.' Only a year later, in *Fleshmarket Close* (2004), change can no longer be denied. 'Leith, once a prosperous shipping port, with a personality distinct from that of the city, had seen hard times in the past few decades: industrial decline, then drugs culture, prostitution. Parts of it had been redeveloped, and others tidied up. Newcomers were moving in, and didn't want the old, sullied Leith.'[4]

Against this foreground of change undeniable, if not always welcome, there is still a background of things that do not change at all. Rankin, who roots his writing so firmly in concrete reality, can also go abstract: 'Edinburgh's architecture was best suited to winter, to sharp, cold light. You got the feeling of being a long way north of anywhere, some place reserved only for the hardiest and most foolhardy.' Or again, 'there were those who said that Edinburgh was an invisible city, hiding its true feelings and intentions, its citizens outwardly respectable, its streets appearing frozen in time. You could visit the place and come away with little sense of having understood what drove it.' Even Rebus is capable of such thinking, though in him it comes back down to earth, fitting once again into the spatial and temporal: 'Divided city, Rebus was thinking. Divided between the Old Town to the south and the New Town to the north. And divided again between the east end (Hibs FC) and west (Hearts). A city which seemed defined by its past as much as by its present, and only now, with the parliament coming, looking towards the future.'[5]

Out of the original volcanic landscape, softened by sea and stream, the historic townscape had seemed to grow almost as a work of nature. Viewed from far off, the rugged ramparts of the Castle and the ponderous dome of the Old College and the innumerable spires of the churches offer a harmonious prospect. Yet the harmony is deceptive. In dips and hollows not so visible to the naked eye the deep forces at work in the city continue to well up and take shape – today in financial palaces central or suburban and in the Scottish Parliament itself, with its internal petrified forest down in the dell at the foot of Arthur's Seat. One of the glories of Edinburgh is that the entire evolution since the hill-fort on the Rock was first thrown up 3,000 years ago can open itself to the searching gaze. One of the miseries of Edinburgh is that there are still people who think this richness and variety will be improved if stretched on the rack of a rational plan. But the history of the place is an argument against all attempts at human perfection. While there is much here that aimed at perfection and indeed achieved it, the whole never broke free from imperfection. So beauty continues to stand beside ugliness, good beside evil, love of it all beside hatred of it all – and Edinburgh would not be Edinburgh unless that were so. It is a mirror of Scotland, certainly; perhaps of our world.

NOTES

ONE: 'CITY OF FIRE ON NIGHT'

1. J. Hutton, 'Theory of the Earth', *Transactions of the Royal Society of Edinburgh*, 1, pt.1 (1788), 304.
2. J. Playfair, *Biographical Account of James Hutton* (Edinburgh, 1797), 34.
3. H. Miller, *My Schools and Schoolmasters* (Edinburgh, 1874), 256.
4. G. Y. Craig, 'Topography and Building Materials', in J. Gifford, C. McWilliam and D. Walker, *The Buildings of Scotland: Edinburgh* (London, 1974), 21.
5. A. C. Kitchener, 'Extinctions, Introductions and Colonisations of Scottish Mammals and Birds since the Last Ice Age', in R. A. Lambert (ed.), *Species History in Scotland*, (Edinburgh, 1998), 63–92.
6. V. G. Childe, *Prehistory of Scotland* (London, 1935), 97.
7. S. T. Driscoll and P. A. Yeoman, *Excavations within Edinburgh Castle in 1988–1991* (Edinburgh, 1997), theme 1.
8. Ibid., 41, 222.
9. 'Traprain Treasure', in J. Calder (ed.), *The Wealth of a Nation in the National Museums of Scotland* (Edinburgh, 1989), 180–2.
10. M. Bowra, *Heroic Poetry* (Oxford, 1952), 45.
11. K. H. Jackson (ed.), *The Gododdin* (Edinburgh, 1969), vii; J. T. Koch, *The Gododdin of Aneirin* (Cardiff, 1997), introduction. MacDiarmid's comment is at 11.48–9 of his poem 'On Reading Professor Ifor William's *Canu Aneirin* in Difficult Days'.
12. Koch, *The Gododdin*, xiii, 23, 73.
13. Ibid., ll. 729–37.
14. Bede, *History of the English Church and People*, trans. Leo Sherley-Price (London, 1990), II, 2; Ailred, *St Ninian*, ed. I. MacDonald (Edinburgh, 1993), 39.
15. W. F. C. Nicolaisen, *Scottish Placenames* (London, 1976), 152.
16. I. Williams, *Bulletin of the Board of Celtic Studies*, V (Cardiff, 1926), 116–21.
17. A. Gunnlangsdóttir, *Tristan en el Norte* (Reykjavik, 1978), 183; W. Haug, *Tristanroman im Horizont der erotischen Diskurse des Mittelalters and der frühen Neuzeit* (Freiburg (Schweiz), 2000), 1–48; P. Ménard, *De Chrétien de Troyes au*

Tristan en Prose (Geneva, 1999), 98; M. Schausten, *Erzählwelten der Tristangeschichte im hohen Mittelalter* (Munich, 1989), 147.

18. G. S. Maxwell, *The Romans in Scotland* (Edinburgh, 1989), ch. 2.

19. R. Oram, *Scottish Prehistory* (Edinburgh, 1997), ch. 4.

20. Bede, *History*, I, 34; II, 12–13; III, 6.4.

21. Nicolaisen, *Scottish Placenames*, 72–3; C. I. Macafee, 'Older Scots Lexis', in C. Jones (ed.), *Edinburgh History of the Scots Language* (Edinburgh, 1997), 195; R. Burns, *The Complete Poetical Works*, ed. J. A. Mackay (Darvel, 1993), 132.

22. Nicolaisen, *Scottish Placenames*, 115, 162.

23. Ibid., 68.

24. Ibid., 69.

25. D. Rollason, *Northumbria 500–1100* (Cambridge, 2003), *passim*.

26. The latest edition of *The Dream of the Rood* is by I. L. Gordon (Rosemarkie, 1993).

27. *Historia de Sancto Cuthberto*, ed. T. J. South (Cambridge, 2002), *passim*; G. Bonner. D. Rollason & C. Stancliffe (eds), *St Cuthbert, his cult and his community to 1200* (Woodbridge, 1989), ch.10.

28. Nicolaisen, *Scottish Placenames*, 37.

29. *The Scotichronicon of Walter Bower*, ed. D. E. R. Watt (Aberdeen, 1994), III, 51.

30. Turgot, *Vita Margaretae*, trans. W. Forbes-Leith (Edinburgh, 1884), 1–84.

31. G. W. S. Barrow, *King David I of Scotland* (Reading, 1985), 92.

32. *Aelredi Rievallensis Opera Omnia*, eds A. Hoste and C. Talbot (Turnhout, 1991), III, 29.

33. C. McWilliam, *The Buildings of Scotland: Lothian except Edinburgh* (London, 1978), 173–7, 246–7.

34. W. Chambers, *Story of St Giles' Cathedral Church Edinburgh* (Edinburgh, 1879), 20; McWilliam, *Buildings of Scotland* 168–70.

35. Gifford, McWilliam and Walker, *Buildings of Scotland*, 131–4.

36. J. Grant, *Cassell's Old and New Edinburgh* (London, Paris & New York, 1883), II, 1–46.

37. McWilliam, *Buildings of Scotland*, 35, 74, 184, 235–7, 345–8, 363, 431, 446–9.

38. Ibid., 117, 168–70, 227, 230–4, 270–4, 276, 460; Gifford, McWilliam and Walker, *Buildings of Scotland*, 554–5; J. Gifford, *The Buildings of Scotland: Fife* (London, 1988), 175–80.

39. Gifford, McWilliam and Walker, *Buildings of Scotland*, 84.

40. Barrow, *King David* I, 84–104.

41. D. D. R. Owen, *William the Lion 1143–1214, Kingship and Culture* (East Linton, 1997), 188.

42. *Le Roman des Aventures de Fergus, par Guillaume le Clerc*, ed. F. Michel (Edinburgh, 1842), 142–3, ll. 11.3927–3940.

TWO: 'PRECIPITOUS CITY'

1. *Letters of David Hume*, ed. J. Y. T. Greig (Oxford, 1969), II, 171.
2. *The Manuscripts of Adam Ferguson*, ed. V. Merolle (London, 2006), 47–71; *Boswell's Edinburgh Journals*, ed. H. Milne (Edinburgh, 2001), 257.
3. D. Hume, *History of England* (London, 1762), I, 26.
4. Ibid., I, 427.
5. Ibid., II, 69, 97.
6. G. W. S. Barrow, *Robert Bruce and the Community of the Realm of Scotland* (London, 1965), 1 *et seq.*
7. Ibid., ch.1, n.39.
8. Ibid., n.49; *Calendar of Documents relating to Scotland preserved in Her Majesty's Public Record Office, London* (hereinafter *CDS*), ed. J. Bain (London, 1881), II, 459.1.
9. *Chronicle of Lanercost 1272–1346*, trans. H. Maxwell (Glasgow, 1913), 178–9; *Chronicle of Walter of Guisborough*, ed. H. Rothwell (London, 1957), 279.
10. *CDS*, III, 27; V, 475.
11. Ibid., II, 1022.
12. Ibid., III, 218, 317.
13. Ibid., III, 47.
14. *Chronicle of Lanercost*, 190–1.
15. See the list in Barrow, *Robert Bruce*, 3rd edn (Edinburgh, 1988), 325–8.
16. *Chronicle of Lanercost*, 217.
17. Ibid., 194–5.
18. *Chronicle of Lanercost*, 195; *CDS*, III, 337.
19. *CDS*, I, 386; III, 186, 245; *Rotuli Scotiae in Turri Londinensi et in Domo Capitulari Westmonasteriensi Asservati*, eds J. Caley. W. Illingworth and D. Macpherson (London, 1814), I, 107–11.
20. *Edinburgh 1329–1929* (Edinburgh, 1929), xix; *Rotuli Scotiae*, I, 111–4; *CDS*, III, 186, 337.
21. *CDS*, III, 562.
22. *Chronicle of Lanercost*, 223.
23. Barrow, *Robert Bruce*, 300.
24. *Charters and Other Documents relating to Edinburgh*, ed. J. D. Marwick (Edinburgh, 1870), 16.
25. *Rotuli Scaccarii Regum Scotorum*, eds G. Burnett and J. Stuart (Edinburgh, 1878), I, 503.
26. *Oeuvres de Froissart*, eds Baron Kervyn de Lettenhove (Brussels 1877–87), V, 133, 181, 334–5.
27. Ibid., 336 *et seq.*
28. P. H. Brown, *Early Travellers in Scotland* (Edinburgh, 1891), 26.
29. Ibid., 43.

30. J. Gifford, C. McWilliam & D. Walker, *The Buildings of Scotland: Edinburgh* (London, 1984), 84.

31. J. Ruskin, *Lectures on Architecture and Painting* (London, 1854), 9.

32. C. Wilson, 'Medieval Towerhouses, Castles and Palaces', in Gifford, McWilliam and Walker, *Buildings of Scotland*, 49 *et seq.*

33. *Charters*, 35, 121.

34. M. D. Young (ed.), *Parliaments of Scotland* (Edinburgh, 1973), II, 747–50.

35. *Extracts from the Records of the Burgh of Edinburgh* (hereinafter *ERBE*), eds J. D. Marwick *et al.* (1869–), I, 4–6, 19–20, 59.

36. Gifford, McWilliam and Walker, *Buildings of Scotland*, 183–4.

37. Ibid., 81.

38. Ibid., 125.

39. Ibid., 81, 84.

40. M. Lynch, M. Spearman and G. Stell (eds), *The Scottish Medieval Town* (Edinburgh, 1988), 4; *ERBE*, I, 28–34, 47–58, 80–3, 97–104; *Rotuli Scaccarii*, XI, xxiii.

41. *ERBE*, I, 7.

42. R. Lindsay of Pitscottie, *The Historie and Cronicles of Scotland* (Edinburgh 1899–1912), I, 282–3.

43. Sir Walter Scott, *Tales of a Grandfather* (Edinburgh, 1828), I, 266.

44. *Charters*, 19.

45. *The Scotichronicon of Walter Bower*, ed. D. E. R. Watt (Aberdeen, 1999), VIII, 12.

46. H. Dingwall, *Physicians, Surgeons and Apothecaries* (East Linton, 1995), 38 *et seq.*

47. A. Pennecuik, *Historical Account of the Blue Blanket* (Edinburgh, 1726), *passim.*

48. *Selected Poems of Henryson and Dunbar*, eds P. Bawcutt and F. Riddy (Edinburgh, 1992), 27–38, ll.1521–3, 1566–8.

49. Ibid., 161–3, ll. 8–10, 22–7, 43–53, 64–72.

50. Sir David Lindsay of the Mount, *Ane Satyre of the Thrie Estaitis*, ed. R. Lyall (Edinburgh, 1989), ll. 909–11, 1815–8, 2965–70.

51. Ibid., ll. 2031–4.

52. M. Wood, 'The Domestic Affairs of the Burgh', *Book of the Old Edinburgh Club*, XV, 1927, 15.

53. *Registrum Secreti Sigillum Regum Scotorum*, eds D. H. Fleming *et al.* (Edinburgh, 1908–), IV, nos1344, 3268.

54. J. Knox, *History of the Reformation in Scotland*, ed. W. C. Dickinson (Edinburgh, 1949), I, 6–9.

55. Ibid., I, 25, 78, 121.

56. Ibid., I, 122–3.

57. *Livre des Anglois*, ed. J. Burns (Geneva, 1839), 15.

58. Knox, *History*, I, 158.

59. Ibid., 196–204.

60. Ibid., 260–5.

61. Ibid., 212–13.

62. Ibid., 351–2.

63. Knox, *History*, II, 7–8.

THREE: 'PERILOUS CITY'

1. Manuscript correspondence concerning the appointment is in the Robertson–Macdonald Papers, National Library of Scotland, MSS 16725-6.

2. *Anecdotes and Egotisms of Henry Mackenzie*, ed. H. W. Thompson (Oxford, 1927), 171.

3. W. Robertson, *History of Scotland* (London, 1759), preface.

4. Ibid., 34-5, 133.

5. J. Knox, *History of the Reformation in Scotland*, ed. W. C. Dickinson (Edinburgh, 1949), II, 82-4.

6. *Works of John Knox*, ed. D. Laing (Edinburgh, 1854), III, 337 *et seq.*

7. Knox, *History*, II, 21.

8. *Extracts from the Records of the Burgh of Edinburgh* (hereinafter *ERBE*), eds J. D. Marwick *et al.* (1869-), IV, 166.

9. T. Craig, *Epithalamium, quo Henrico Darnelii et Mariae Scotorum Reginae nuptias celebravit* (Edinburgh, 1565), n.p.; *George Buchanan: The Political Poetry*, eds P. J. McGinnis and A. H. Williamson (Edinburgh, 1995), 154; A. Scott, *Ballattis of luve*, ed. J. MacQueen (Edinburgh, 1970), 19.

10. H. V. Morton, *In Search of Scotland* (London, 1929), 40.

11. *Historical Memoirs of the Reign of Mary, Queen of Scots and of King James the Sixth*, ed. R. Pitcairn (Edinburgh, 1836), 79.

12. Ibid., 78-85.

13. *Bittersweet within My Heart, the collected poems of Mary Queen of Scots*, ed. R. Bell (London, 1992), 61.

14. R. Sempill, *The Sege of the Castel of Edinburgh* (Edinburgh, 1573), n.p.

15. J. Gifford, C. McWilliam and D. Walker, *The Buildings of Scotland: Edinburgh* (London, 1984), 86, 103-4, 126.

16. Ibid., 207-8.

17. Edinburgh City Archives (hereinafter ECA), Moses bundle 195, no.7029; *Records of the Convention of the Royal Burghs of Scotland 1295-1597*, ed. J. D. Marwick (Edinburgh, 1866), 47-8, 514-30.

18. Gifford, McWilliam and Walker, *Buildings of Scotland*, 54, 557, 603; C. McWilliam, *Buildings of Scotland: Lothian* (London, 1978), 205, 284, 327.

19. *ERBE*, IV, 265.

20. D. Calderwood, *History of the Kirk of Scotland* (Edinburgh, 1842-9), IV, 90; J. Spottiswoode, *History of the Church of Scotland* (Edinburgh, 1851-65), I, 372.

21. A. A. M. Duncan, 'The Central Courts before 1532', in *An Introduction to Scottish Legal History*, ed. G. C. H. Paton (Edinburgh, 1958), 321-40; R. K. Hannay, *The College of Justice* (Edinburgh, 1933), *passim*; *An Introductory Survey of the Sources and Literature of Scots Law*, ed. H. McKechnie (Edinburgh, 1936), 133-53.

22. *Register of the Privy Seal of Scotland*, eds M. Livingstone *et al.* (Edinburgh 1908-82), I. no.1546.

23. J. Grant, *Cassell's Old and New Edinburgh* (London, Paris and New York, 1883), I, 110; II, 285.

24. *Register of the Privy Council of Scotland*, eds J. H. Burton *et al.* (Edinburgh, 1877–98), II, 528–9; III, 472–4.

25. J. Kirk, 'Clement Little's Edinburgh', in *Patterns of Reform* (Edinburgh, 1989), 16–69.

26. *ERBE*, IV, 200; ECA, Edinburgh Town Council Records, MSS VI, f.126; *University of Edinburgh Charters*, ed. A. Morgan (Edinburgh, 1937), 12–16.

27. *Catalogue of the Graduates . . . of the University of Edinburgh since its Foundation* (Edinburgh, 1858), 7–8.

28. *Liber Officialis Sancte Andree* (Edinburgh, 1845), 138.

29. *Poems of Alexander Scott*, ed. J. Cranstoun (Edinburgh and London, 1896), 1, 12–15.

30. *Poems of Sir Richard Maitland of Lethingtoun* (Edinburgh, 1995), 8.

31. *Buik of the Kirk of the Canongait*, ed. A. B. Calderwood (Edinburgh, 1961), 18.

32. J. A. Fairley, 'The Old Tolbooth, with extracts from the original records', *Book of the Old Edinburgh Club*, especially IV, 1911, 116 *et seq*; V, 1912, 107 *et seq.*

33. *Buik of the Kirk*, 20.

34. Ibid., 22.

35. Ibid., 54.

36. *ERBE*, I, 111.

37. *Buik of the Kirk*, 15.

38. Ibid., 30, 67.

39. G. F. Black, *Calendar of Cases of Witchcraft in Scotland 1510–1727* (New York, 1938), 15.

40. *ERBE*, IV, 48, 67; VI, 21, 259.

41. Ibid., I, 2; V, 339.

42. Ibid., II, 262; V, 12.

43. Ibid., III, 86; IV, 154,

44. Exodus 2:18.

45. Black, *Calendar*, 30.

46. No translation is offered here because the poem depends on a pun in the Scots pronunciation of the sixteenth century (and of today) making synonyms of 'fool' and 'foul' – said then like English 'fool', now like German *'fühl'*.

47. In *His Maiesties Poeticall Exercises at Vacant Houres* (Edinburgh, 1591), 61.

48. *Poètes du XVIe Siècle*, ed. A.-M. Schmidt (Bibliothèque de la Pléiade, 1953), 604.

49. *Poems of John Stewart of Baldynneis*, ed. T. Crockett (Edinburgh, 1913), 132.

50. *Poetical Works of William Drummond of Hawthornden*, ed. L. E. Kastner (Edinburgh and London, 1913) I, 143, 153.

51. Calderwood, *History of the Kirk of Scotland*, VI, 206–16; Spottiswoode, *History of the Church of Scotland*, III, 133–9.

52. J. J. Brown, 'The Social, Political and Economic Influences of the Edinburgh Merchant Elite 1600–1638', unpublished PhD thesis, University of Edinburgh 1985, 36.

53. Ibid., 65.

54. Ibid., 231.
55. Ibid., 111.
56. A. Constable, *Memoirs of George Heriot* (Edinburgh, 1822), *passim*.
57. G. Marshall, *Presbyteries and Profits, Calvinism and the Development of Capitalism in Scotland 1560–1707* (Oxford, 1981), 284–320.
58. Calderwood, *History of the Kirk of Scotland*, VI, 293–305.
59. J. Row, *History of the Kirk of Scotland* (Edinburgh, 1842), 331.
60. Gifford, McWilliam and Walker, *Buildings of Scotland*, 121; L. A. M. Stewart, 'Politics and Religion in Edinburgh 1617–1653', unpublished PhD thesis, University of Edinburgh, 2003, 63.
61. Ibid., 92.
62. Brown, 'The Social, Political and Economic Influences', 389.
63. *Diary of Sir Archibald Johnston of Wariston*, ed. G. M. Paul (Edinburgh, 1911), II, 76, 196, 272.
64. Ibid., 297.
65. Stewart, 'Politics and Religion in Edinburgh', 137.

FOUR: 'CITY OF PALACES, OR OF TOMBS'

1. *Boswell for the Defence*, eds F. A. Pottle and W. K. Wimsatt, 240.
2. M. R. G. Fry, *The Dundas Despotism* (Edinburgh, 1992), chs 1 and 2.
3. *Boswell, the Ominous Years*, eds F.A. Pottle and C. Ryskamp (London, 1963), 160.
4. Fry, *The Dundas Despotism*, chs 8 and 10.
5. Boswell, *The Applause of the Jury*, eds I. S. Lustig and F. A. Pottle (London, 1981, 144–5.
6. Fry, *The Dundas Despotism*, 85.
7. J. Fraser, *Chronicles of the Frasers*, (Edinburgh, 1905), 372
8. 'Diary of John Nicoll', *Book of the Old Edinburgh Club* (hereinafter *BOEC*), 16 (1928), 38.
9. Edinburgh University Library (hereinafter EUL), Laing MSS, I, 298–9.
10. *Diary of Sir Archibald Johnston of Wariston*, ed. G. M. Paul (Edinburgh, 1911), III, 83; *Extracts from the Records of the Burgh of Edinburgh* (hereinafter *ERBE*), IX, 199.
11. G. Burnet, *History of his Own Time* (London, 1979), 59.
12. Ibid., 62.
13. W. Wodrow, *History of the Sufferings of the Church of Scotland* (Edinburgh, 1721), I, 257–261, 443; II, 13, 265, 493.
14. EUL, Laing MSS, I, 416; W. M. Bryce, *History of the Old Greyfriars Church, Edinburgh* (Edinburgh, 1912), 119.
15. C. Larner, C. H. Lee and H. V. McLachlan, *Source-Book of Scottish Witchcraft* (Glasgow, 1977), 261–8.
16. *Diary of Sir Archibald Johnston*, 71; EUL, Laing MSS, II, 336.
17. Wodrow, *History of the Sufferings*, I, 292.

18. Ibid., 277.
19. J. Gifford, C. McWilliam and D. Walker, *The Buildings of Scotland: Edinburgh* (London, 1984), 200.
20. *Coltness Collections*, ed. J. Dennistoun (Edinburgh, 1842), II, 48–9.
21. *ERBE*, X, xlii, 120, 181, 298; XII, 88
22. Edinburgh City Archives (hereinafter ECA), Minute Book 75, 206–7; Hugh Arnot, *History of Edinburgh* (1782), 512: M. R. G. Fry, *The Union: England, Scotland and the Treaty of 1707* (Edinburgh, 2006), 148.
23. *ERBE*, X, 161, 226–8, 282; XI, 36; J. Marshall, 'Social and Economic History of Leith in the Eighteenth Century', unpublished PhD thesis, University of Edinburgh, 1969, 444–8
24. *ERBE*, XI, 74, 180, 240–1, 272.
25. National Library of Scotland (hereinafter NLS), MS 17498, ff.70 *et seq.*
26. *ERBE*, XII, 165.
27. N. H. Nicolas, *History of the Orders of Knighthood in the British Empire* (London, 1842), 4 *et seq*; R. A. Houston, *Social Change in the Age of Enlightenment* (Oxford, 1994), 217.
28. J. St Clair and R. Craik, *The Advocates' Library* (Edinburgh, 1989), 1 *et seq.*
29. H. Dingwall, 'The Social and Economic Structure of Edinburgh in the Late Seventeenth Century', unpublished PhD thesis, University of Edinburgh, 1989, 284.
30. H. Dingwall, *Famous and Flourishing Society, a history of the Royal College of Surgeons of Edinburgh* (Edinburgh, 2005), ch. 2; W. N. B. Watson, 'Early Baths and Bagnios in Edinburgh', *BOEC*, 34 (1979), 57–60.
31. R. Sibbald, *Autobiography* (Edinburgh, 1833), 15.
32. L. J. Jolley, 'Archibald Pitcairne', *Edinburgh Medical Journal*, 60 (1953), 65–95.
33. J. Friesen, 'Archibald Pitcairne, David Gregory and the Scottish Origins of English Tory Newtonianism', *History of Science*, 41 (2003), 163–95.
34. *Testimonials in favour of David Gregory . . . as candidate for the chair of mathematics in the University of Edinburgh* (Edinburgh, 1838), 8.
35. A. Lang, *Sir George Mackenzie of Rosehaugh, His Life and Times* (Edinburgh, 1909), *passim*; Gifford, McWilliam and Walker, *Buildings of Scotland*, 162.
36. R. Emerson, 'Sir Robert Sibbald, the Royal Society of Scotland and the Origins of the Scottish Enlightenment', *Annals of Science*, 45 (1988), 55 *et seq.*
37. A. Pitcairne, *Selecta Poemata* (Edinburgh, 1726), 83; *Poems of John Dryden*, eds P. Hammond and D. Hopkins (Harlow, 2000), III, 219.
38. *Proceedings of the Society of Antiquaries of Scotland*, I, 1789, 512.
39. J. Kinsley, 'A Dryden Play at Edinburgh', *Scottish Historical Review*, 22 (1954), 129 *et seq.*
40. Sir G. Mackenzie, 'Observations upon Precedency', in *Works* (Edinburgh, 1716–22), II, 517–8; Gifford, McWilliam and Walker, *Buildings of Scotland*, 145–6.
41. J. K. R. Murray, 'The Scottish Silver Coinage of Charles II', *British Numismatic Journal*, 38 (1969), 117–18; J. K. R. Murray and B. H. I. H. Stewart, 'The Scottish Copper Coinages 1642–97', *British Numismatic Journal*, 41, 105–35.

42. Lord Balcarres, *Memoirs touching the Revolution in Scotland* (Edinburgh, 1841), 15–17; *Siege of the Castle of Edinburgh*, ed. R. Bell, 17–19, 97–8; *ERBE*, XI, 252–4; Sir John Lauder of Fountainhall, 'Historical Notices of Scottish Affairs 1661-1688', *BOEC*, 16 (1968), 149.

43. Loudoun Papers, Huntington Library, San Marino, California, LO 9347.

44. A. Monro, *Presbyterian Inquisition* (London, 1691), 36.

45. R. K. Hannay, 'The Visitation of the College of Edinburgh', *BOEC*, 8 (1916), 80 *et seq.*

46. *Acts of the General Assembly of the Church of Scotland* (Edinburgh, 1843), 241.

47. J. Webster, *Select Sermons Preached on Several Texts* (Edinburgh, 1723), 68; *ERBE*, XII, 140; Register of the Resolutions and Proceedings of a Society for the Reformation of Manners, EUL, La.III.339, especially meeting of 7 January, 1701.

48. M. F. Graham, *The Blasphemies of Thomas Aikenhead* (Edinburgh, 2008), *passim*.

49. Burnet, 802.

50. *Letters of Daniel Defoe*, ed. G. Healey, 134–40.

51. Fry, *Union*, 252.

52. National Archives of Scotland, GD220/55/383/12; GD 220/4/583; *ERBE*, XIII, 165, 181, 208.

53. R. Chambers, *Traditions of Edinburgh* (Edinburgh, 1824), I, 21.

54. *ERBE*, XIII, 266, 368.

55. D. Szechi, *1715: The Great Jacobite Rebellion* (New Haven, 2006), 59 *et seq.*

56. J. W. Cairns, 'The Origins of the Edinburgh Law School: the Union of 1707 and the Regius Chair', *Edinburgh Law Review*, 11 (2007), 300–48.

57. I. S. Ross and S. A. C. Scobie, 'Patriotic Publishing as a Response to the Union', in T. I. Rae (ed.), *The Union of 1707* (Glasgow, 1974), 96–108.

58. Allan Ramsay MSS, EUL, La.II.212, especially f.3.

59. National Library of Scotland, Advocates' MSS, 23.3.6, ff.23–5.

60. *Poems by Allan Ramsay and Robert Fergusson*, eds A. M. Kinghorn and A. Law (Edinburgh, 1985), 3–7.

61. *Orain Ghàidhealach mu Bhliadhna Theàrlaich (Highland Songs of the Forty-Five)*, ed. J. L. Campbell (Edinburgh, 1984), 'Oran Luaidh no Fucaidh (A Waulking Song)', ll.55–6.

62. Anon, *History of the Rebellion in the Years 1745 and 1746* (London, 1944), 62.

FIVE: 'CITY OF EVERYWHERE'

1. *Journal of Sir Walter Scott*, ed. W. E. K. Anderson (Oxford, 1972), 319–20; *Letters of Sir Walter Scott*, ed. H. J. C. Grierson *et al.* (1932–7), X, 173.

2. These are the concluding words of 'Chapter First, Introductory'. Because of the innumerable editions of the Waverley novels, page references will be dispensed with here.

3. Sir J. G. Dalyell, *Musical Memoirs of Scotland* (Edinburgh, 1849), 198.

4. Chapter 1, Being Introductory.

5. See especially the opening of ch. 8.

6. Ch. 4.

7. Ibid.

8. Ch. 7.

9. D. Gifford, C. McWilliam and D. Walker, *Buildings of Scotland: Edinburgh* (London, 1984), 60, 231, 328.

10. *History and Statutes of the Royal Infirmary of Edinburgh* (Edinburgh, 1778), *passim*.

11. Edinburgh City Archives (hereinafter ECA), town council minutes, 6 May, 1752, SL 1/1/70, ff.138-9.

12. A. J. Youngson, *The Making of Classical Edinburgh* (Edinburgh, 1966), 1-17.

13. Gifford, McWilliam and Walker, *Buildings of Scotland*, 293-7.

14. F. C. Mears and J. Russell, 'The New Town of Edinburgh', *Book of the Old Edinburgh Club* (hereinafter *BOEC*), 22 (1938), 106.

15. *Statistical Account of Scotland, VI: Midlothian*, eds I. R. Grant and D. J. Withrington (Wakefield, 1983), 559.

16. *Letters of John Cockburn of Ormiston to his Gardener*, ed. J. Colville (Edinburgh, 1904), *passim*.

17. *The British Linen Company 1745–1775*, ed. A. J. Durie (Edinburgh, 1996), *passim*.

18. J. Pinkerton, *Select Scottish Ballads* (Edinburgh, 1782), dedication.

19. J. L. Cranmer, 'Concert Life and the Music Trade in Edinburgh 1690-1830', unpublished PhD thesis, University of Edinburgh, 1991, 18-27, 76-8.

20. N. Phillipson, 'Lawyers, Landowners and the Civic Leadership of Post-Union Scotland', *Juridical Review*, 1976, 101-6; 'The Social Structure of the Faculty of Advocates 1661-1840', in A. Harding (ed.), *Law-making and Law-makers in British History* (London, 1980), 155-6.

21. H. Cockburn, *Memorials of his Time* (London, 1856), 114-18, 140.

22. *Autobiography of Dr Alexander Carlyle of Inveresk*, ed. J. H. Burton (Edinburgh and London, 1910), 312.

23. J. Buxton and M. R. G. Fry, *Land Reform and Liberty* (Edinburgh, 1998), 1-3.

24. Quoted in ibid., 3-4.

25. K. G. C. Reid, *Abolition of Feudal Tenure in Scotland* (Edinburgh, 2003), *passim*.

26. W. Creech, *Letters respecting the mode of living, trade, manners, literature etc. of Edinburgh, in 1763, and the present period* (Edinburgh, 1792), 36.

27. *Poems by Allan Ramsay and Robert Fergusson*, eds A. M. Kinghorn and A. Law (Edinburgh, 1985), 150-1.

28. Ibid., 121.

29. Ibid., 142.

30. Ibid., 182.

31. *Robert Burns, Complete Poetical Works 1759–1796*, ed. J. A. Mackay (Darvel, 1993), 269.

32. Ibid., 262, 300.

33. Ibid., 264, 434.

34. *The Songs of Duncan Bàn Macintyre*, ed. A. Macleod (Edinburgh, 1952), ll. 4929-33, 4937-40, 5015-16.

35. A. Somerville, *Autobiography of a Working Man* (London, 1848), 107–17, 148–51.

36. *Hugh Miller's Memoir*, ed. M. Shortland (Edinburgh, 1995), 200–19.

37. Royal Commission on Children's Employment, Parliamentary Papers (hereafter PP) (1842), pt.1, XVI, 449 *et seq.*, witnesses 1–8.

38. National Library of Scotland (hereinafter NLS) Lee Papers, NLS MS 341, f.300.

39. ECA, minutes of the Edinburgh charity workhouse, 'Categories for admission', April 1743; minutes, 14 April, 1743.

40. Ch. 29.

41. *Poems*, 144.

42. Creech, *Letters*, 18; *Report on the State of the Edinburgh Magdalene Asylum for 1806* (Edinburgh, 1806), 1–5.

43. *Boswell's Edinburgh Journals 1767–1786*, ed. H. M. Milne (Edinburgh, 2001), 275–6.

44. R. Chambers, *Traditions of Edinburgh* (Edinburgh, 1824), II, 141–55.

45. National Archives of Scotlland (hereinafter NAS), Home Office Papers; RH 2/4/87/85; Scottish Catholic Archive, Blairs Letters, 3/307/2, 3/309/11; Scottish Mission Papers, 4/16/3, 4/17/2–3, 10; 4/19/1–2; 4/40/6–9; Thomson–Macpherson Papers, sect.13, 1779.

46. NAS, GD 235/10/2/4; Home Office Papers RH 2/4/63/79.

47. Edinburgh University Library, La.III.552

48. Chambers, 144; W. Innes, *Notes on Conversations with Hugh McDonald, Neil Sutherland and Hugh McIntosh, who were executed at Edinburgh . . .* (Edinburgh, 1825), 13.

49. Somerville, 156.

50. *Extracts from the Records of the Burgh of Edinburgh*, XII, 257.

51. *Correspondence relative to Phrenoology between Sir William Hamilton, bart, Dr Spurzheim and Mr George Combe* (Edinburgh, 1828), *passim*.

52. R. Owen, *Life of Robert Owen by Himself* (London, 1857), 74.

53. NAS, Edinburgh Presbytery Register, CH2/121/9/14, 12/47.

54. *Fasti Ecclesiae Scoticanae*, ed. H. Scott (Edinburgh, 1915), I, 40, 101, 119, 123.

55. Royal Commission on Religious Instruction, PP (1837), XXX, 12–13, and (1837–8), XXXII, 13; W. McKelvie, *Annals and Statistics of the United Presbyterian Church* (Edinburgh, 1873), 187 *et seq*; R. Small, *History of the Congregations of the United Presbyterian Church* (Edinburgh, 1904), 441.

56. *Carlyle Autobiography*, ch. 7.

57. I. S. Ross, *Lord Kames and the Scotland of his Day* (London, 1972), ch. 6; E. C. Mossner, *Life of David Hume* (Oxford, 1980), ch. 25.

58. [J. Bonar], *An Analysis of the Moral and Religious Sentiments Contained in the Writings of Sopho* [Kames] *and David Hume, Esq.* (Edinburgh, 1755), especially 49; R. Wallace, *Various prospects of mankind, nature and providence* (London, 1761), 238.

59. *Letters of David Hume*, ed. J. Y. T. Greig (Oxford, 1932), I, 224; *Scots Magazine*, 19 (Feb.1757), 108–9.

60. J. Home, *Douglas*, ed. G. D. Parker (Edinburgh, 1972), ll. 9–10.

61. *Carlyle Autobiography*, ch. 8.

62. S. J. Brown, 'William Robertson (1721-1793) and the Scottish Enlightenment', in S. J. Brown (ed.), *William Robertson and the Expansion of Empire* (Cambridge, 1997), 7-35.

63. Gifford, McWilliam and Walker, *Buildings of Scotland*, 188-91.

64. *Correspondence of Adam Smith*, eds E. C. Mossner and I. S. Ross (Oxford, 1982), 203.

65. J. Hutton, 'Theory of the Earth', *Transactions of the Royal Society of Edinburgh*, I, 1785.

66. Sir W. Ramsay, *Life and Letters of Joseph Black* (London, 1918), *passim*.

67. D. Hamilton, 'The Scottish Enlightenment and Clinical Medicine', in A. Dow (ed.), *The Influence of Scottish Medicine* (Carnforth, 1986), 205 *et seq*.

68. R. Paterson, *Memorials of the Life of James Syme* (Edinburgh, 1874), 198-9.

69. Quoted in O. D. Edwards, *Burke and Hare* (Edinburgh, 1980), 119-20.

70. *Scott Letters*, XI, 108.

71. W. Smellie, *Literary and Characteristic Lives of Gregory, Kames, Hume and Smith* (Edinburgh, 1800), 161-2.

72. *Warrender Letters*, ed. W. K. Dickson (Edinburgh, 1935), 27-8.

73. H. Arnot, *History of Edinburgh* (Edinburgh, 1779), 517.

74. Youngson, *Making*, 83-4; F. A. Pottle and C. Ryskamp, *Boswell: the Ominous Years* (London, 1963), 5.

75. NAS, GD 22/1/315.

76. H. Cockburn, *Memorials of his Time* (Edinburgh, 1856), 86, 95: E. Grant, *Memoirs of a Highland Lady* (Edinburgh, 1988), II, 103.

77. NAS, GD 51/5/603/2, 612, 51/5/623, 51/5/749/2, 375.

SIX: 'CITY OF REFUGE'

1. *Collected Letters of Thomas and Jane Carlyle*, ed. C. Sanders (Durham, NC, 1970), IV, 440-1.

2. H. Cockburn, *Life of Lord Jeffrey* (Edinburgh, 1852), 131; J. G. Lockhart, *Memoirs of the Life of Sir Walter Scott* (Edinburgh, 1837), 149.

3. *Edinburgh Review*, 12 (1808), 278; 23 (1814), 3; 33(1823), 237; T. Carlyle, *Reminiscences* (London, 1881), II, 14.

4. G. W. T. Omond, *Lord Advocates of Scotland* (Ednburgh, 1883), II, 301.

5. H. Cockburn, *Letters on the Affairs of Scotland* (London, 1874), 4, 33.

6. J. G. Lockhart, *Peter's Letters to his Kinsfolk* (Edinburgh, 1819), 147.

7. M. O. W. Oliphant, *Annals of a Publishing House* (Edinburgh, 1897), 337.

8. A. Gide, 'Introduction' to Cresset Library Edition of J. Hogg, *Private Memoirs and Confessions of a Justified Sinner* (London, 1947), ix.

9. A. Cunningham, Lives of the Most Eminent British Painters (London, 1879-80), I, 459-89; II, 6.

10. R. L. Stevenson, *Virginibus Puerisque* (London, 1881), 114.

11. Ch. 2; Cunningham, *Lives*, II, 6.

12. *Blackwood's Edinburgh Magazine*, 48 (1830), 128; J. Gifford, C. McWilliam and
    D. Walker, *Buildings of Scotland: Edinburgh* (London, 1984), 123, 287, 289,
    293–4, 314–16.

13. J. A. Froude, *Thomas Carlyle, a history of the first forty years of his life* (London,
    1890), I, 65.

14. T. Carlyle, 'Sir Walter Scott', *London and Westminster Review*, 12 (1837), 42;
    Froude, *Thomas Carlyle*, I, 14–33; II, 95, 214.

15. Census of Scotland 1901, PP 1904 CVIII.

16. Census of Scotland, PP 1883 LXXXI; C. Booth, 'Occupations of the People of
    the United Kingdom 1801-1881, *Journal of the Royal Statistical Society*, 49 (1886),
    414.

17. R. Mudie, *Modern Athenians* (Edinburgh, 1825), 276–7.

18. I. Donnachie, *History of the Brewing Industry in Scotland* (Edinburgh, 1979), 148,
    237–45.

19. *Robert Burns: Complete Poetical Works*, ed. J. A. Mackay (Darvel, 1993), 410; R. L.
    Stevenson, *Edinburgh: Picturesque Notes* (London, 1881), 44.

20. H. Cockburn, *A Letter to the Lord Provost on the Best Ways of Spoiling Edinburgh*
    (Edinburgh, 1849), 5.

21. A. H. B. Masson, 'Dr Thomas Latta', *Book of the Old Edinburgh Club*, 33 (1972),
    143–9; E. D. W. Grieg, 'The treatment of cholera by intravenous saline
    injections, with particular reference to the contribution of Dr Thomas Latta of
    Leith (1832)', *Edinburgh Medical Journal*, 53 (1946), 256–63.

22. J. Duns, *Memoir of Sir James Young Simpson* (Edinburgh, 1873), *passim*.

23. R. Paterson, *Memorials of the Life of James Syme* (Edinburgh, 1874), 261–2; E. B.
    Simpson, *Sir James Young Simpson* (Edinburgh and London, 1896), 51, 63.

24. Religious Worship and Education, Scotland, PP (1854), lix.

25. Cockburn, *Life*, 431.

26. S. J. Brown, *Thomas Chalmers and the Godly Commonwealth in Scotland* (Oxford,
    1982), 363.

27. M. R. G. Fry, 'The Disruption and the Union', in S. J. Brown and M. R. G. Fry
    (eds), *Scotland in the Age of the Disruption* (Edinburgh, 1993), 31–43.

28. Cockburn, *Letters*, 137–8.

29. G. Davie, *The Democratic Intellect* (Edinburgh, 1961), 26–40; R. D. Anderson,
    Education and Opportunity in Victorian Scotland (Oxford, 1983), 38 *et seq*.

30. J. B. Mackie, *Life and Work of Duncan McLaren* (Edinburgh, 1888), I, 303–12.

31. A. Thomson, *Ferrier of St Andrews* (Edinburgh, 1985), *passim*.

32. Davie, *Democratic Intellect*, 41–75; Anderson, *Education and Opportunity*, 67–77.

33. Anderson, *Education and Opportunity*, 296–306.

34. H. Cockburn, *Memorials of his Time*, (Edinburgh, 1856), 389.

35. Endowed Schools and Hospitals (Scotland), first report of the royal
    commissioners, PP 1873 XXVII, 337 *et seq*.

36. Ibid., 36–7, 524; third report of the royal commissioners, appendix, PP 1875
    XXIX, II, 354; T. J. Boyd, *Educational Hospital Reform, the scheme of the Edinburgh
    Merchant Company* (Edinburgh, 1871), 14; *Minutes of the Edinburgh Trades
    Council*, ed. I. MacDougall (Edinburgh, 1968), 356.

37. R. Q. Gray, *Labour Aristocracy in Victorian Edinburgh* (Oxford, 1976), 11–24.

38. MacDougall, *Minutes*, 108, 284–6; J. Finlay, 'The Early Days of the Socialist Movement in Edinburgh' (1909), NLS Acc 4965, 7, 17.

39. I. MacDougall (ed.), *A Catalogue of some Labour Records in Scotland* (Edinburgh, 1978), 291; Select Committee on Coal, 1873, X, question 4624.

40. Gray, 112–20; see also, 'Thrift and Working-class Mobility in Victorian Edinburgh', in A. A. MacLaren (ed.), *Social Class in Scotland, Past and Present* (Edinburgh, 1976), 128–39.

41. Anderson, *Education and Opportunity*, 346–57.

42. Sir J. H. A. Macdonald, *Life Jottings of an Old Edinburgh Citizen* (Edinburgh, 1916), 427.

43. B. Mortimer, 'The Nurse in Edinburgh 1760–1840, the impact of commerce and professionalism', unpublished PhD thesis, University of Edinburgh, 2001, 52 and *passim*.

44. H. Kerr, 'Edinburgh', in A. Bosanquet (ed.), *Social Conditions in Provincial Towns* (London, 1912), 56–7.

45. N. Wilson, 'Sociology of a Profession, the Faculty of Advocates', unpublished PhD thesis, University of Edinburgh, 1965, 65, 77–87.

46. Omond, *Lord Advocates*, II, 260–88.

47. Davie, *Democratic Intellect*, 41–75.

48. J. Lorimer, *Institutes of Law* (Edinburgh, 1872), dedication.

49. J. Ruskin, *Lectures on Architecture and Painting* (London, 1854), 1–4.

50. Gifford, McWilliam and Walker, *Buildings of Scotland*, 378–9.

51. A. Macpherson (ed.), *Report of a Committee of the Working Classes of Edinburgh on the Present Overcrowded and Uncomfortable State of their Dwelling Houses* (Edinburgh, 1860), *passim*.

52. R. Rodger, *The Transformation of Edinburgh* (Cambridge, 2001), 504–8.

53. Ibid., 84, 156, 197, 220, 385.

54. Ibid., 26, 74–6, 84–114.

55. H. D. Littlejohn, *Report on the Sanitary Condition of the City of Edinburgh* (Edinburgh, 1865), 19; F. McManus, 'Public Health Administration in Edinburgh 1833–1879', unpublished M.Litt. thesis, University of Edinburgh, 1984, 3–6; P. J. Smith, 'The Foul Burns of Edinburgh', *Scottish Geographical Magazine*, 91 (1975), 25 *et seq*.

56. Sanitary Condition of the Labouring Population of Scotland, PP XXVIII 1842, 8–9, 156, 201.

57. G. Bell, *Day and Night in the Wynds of Edinburgh* (Edinburgh, 1849), 23–6.

58. W. Tait, *Magdalenism* (Edinburgh, 1842), 5–9, 59, 193–6, 258.

59. I. Bird, *Notes on Old Edinburgh* (Edinburgh, 1869), 22.

60. *Return by the Superintendent of Police* (Edinburgh, 1870), *passim*.

61. Gifford, McWilliam and Walker, *Buildings of Scotland*, 222–3.

62. R. Chambers, *Essays, Familiar and Humorous* (London, 1867), II, 81.

63. J. Clark, *Life of James Begg* (Edinburgh, n.d.), 7.

64. Housing of the Working Classes, PP XXXI 1885–6, QQ 18,596; 18,860; 19,188.

65. W. Chambers, *The Lord Provost's Statement to the Town Council respecting Sanitary Improvements* (Edinburgh, 1865), 5-9; *City Improvements* (Edinburgh, 1866), 12-16.
66. P. Geddes, 'Edinburgh and its Region, geographic and historical', *Scottish Georgraphical Magazine*, 18 (1902), 307.
67. R. L. Stevenson, *The Strange Case of Dr Jekyll and Mr Hyde* (London, 1888), 20, 31, 51.

SEVEN: 'A VERY OLD-FASHIONED CITY'

1. H. Cockburn, *Life of Lord Jeffrey* (Edinburgh, 1852), II, 377.
2. *Blackwood's Edinburgh Magazine*, XII, 1827, 337; *Selections from the Correspondence of the Late Macvey Napier* (London, 1877), 45.
3. *Blackwood's*, 1842, XXVII, 86.
4. B. Lenman, *From Esk to Tweed* (Glasgow & London, 1975), 119-22.
5. R. Rodgers, *The Transformation of Edinburgh* (Cambridge, 2001), 270.
6. C. Hussey, *The Work of Sir Robert Lorimer* (London, 1931), 106.
7. R. H. Paterson, *Pontius Pilate's Bodyguard: History of the First or Royal Regiment of Foot, the Royal Scots, I: 1633-1918* (Edinburgh, 2000), 336-9, 373, 389.
8. J. Gifford, C. McWilliam and D. Walker, *Buildings of Scotland: Edinburgh* (London, 1984), 99.
9. I. Donnachie, *History of the Brewing Industry in Scotland* (Edinburgh, 1979), 148, 234-41.
10. M. Abrams, *Home Market* (London, 1937), 10-20.
11. Gifford, McWilliam and Walker, *Buildings of Scotland*, 609; *Social Environment in Suburban Edinburgh*, ed. G. Hutton (York, 1975), 160.
12. Gifford, McWilliam and Walker, *Buildings of Scotland*, 627.
13. Abrams, *Home Market*, 35.
14. L. Kennedy, *On My Way to the Club* (Glasgow, 1989), 23-5.
15. N. Fairbairn, *A Life is Too Short* (Glasgow, 1987), 16.
16. J. Grant, *Cassell's Old and New Edinburgh* (London, Paris and New York, 1883), III, 62; *The Hugh MacDiarmid Anthology*, eds M. Grieve and A. Scott (London, 1972), epigraph, 233.
17. D. M. Walker, *The Scottish Jurists* (Edinburgh, 1985), 415-19.
18. S. Nicholson, *A Project of Empire* (London, 1909), 42-3.
19. E. Muir, *Scott and Scotland* (London, 1936), 110.
20. E. Linklater, *Magnus Merriman* (London, 1934), 74-5, 90-5.
21. *MacDiarmid Anthology*, 233-5, 247-50.
22. R. Todd, *Ten Poems* (London, 1940), 5.
23. M. Spark, *The Prime of Miss Jean Brodie* (London, 1961), 39, 48.
24. S. J. Brown, 'A Solemn Purification by Fire: responses to the Great War in the Scottish Presbyterian Churches', *Journal of Ecclesiastical Hstory*, 45 (1994), 82 *et seq*.

25. J. M. Black, *Days of My Autumn* (Edinburgh, 1939), 87; C. L. Warr, *Scottish Sermons and Addresses* (London, 1930), 294.

26. N. Maclean, *Set Free* (London, 1949), 97.

27. F. D. Bardgett, *Devoted Service: The Lay Missionaries of the Church of Scotland* (Edinburgh, 2002), 79–83; I. L. S. Balfour, *Revival in Rose Street, Charlotte Baptist Chapel, Edinburgh, 1808–2008* (Edinburgh, 2007), 150–200.

28. T. R. Graham, *Willie Graham* (London, 1948), 76; R. Skidelsky, *Politicians and the Slump, the Labour Government of 1929–1931* (London, 1967), 434.

29. J. S. Marshall, *Life and Times of Leith* (Edinburgh. 1985), 184–8.

30. *Hansard, House of Commons*, CCCLXV, 1940, col. 570, 15 Oct.; col. 709, 16 Oct.

31. Quoted in T. Gallagher, *Edinburgh Divided, John Cormack and No Popery in the 1930s* (Edinburgh, 1987), 192–4.

32. D. R. Robertson, 'The Relationship between Church and social class in Scotland', unpublished PhD thesis, University of Edinburgh, 1966, 48.

33. J. Gibson, *The Thistle and the Crown: A History of the Scottish Office* (Edinburgh, 1985), 45; B. Monteith, *Paying the Piper* (Edinburgh, 2007), 13.

34. Gifford, McWilliam and Walker, *Buildings of Scotland*, 61.

35. F. Gray, *Comments and Characters* (London, 1940), xvi.

36. *Hansard, House of Commons*, col. CCLXXII, 1932, cols. 235–360, 24 Nov.

37. Gibson, *Thistle and the Crown*, 90; Gifford, McWilliam and Walker, *Buildings of Scotland*, 441–2.

38. Paterson, *Pontius Pilate's Bodyguard, II: 1918–45* (Edinburgh, 2000), 66 *et seq*.

39. *The Scotsman*, 15 July 1939; *Evening News*, 17 Nov., 5 Dec. 1939, 27 Jan. 1941; *Evening Dispatch*, 29 March 1944.

40. Gibson, *Thistle and the Crown*, 175.

41. G. McCrone, *Regional Policy in Britain* (London, 1969), 212–13.

42. W. M. Ballantine, *Rebuilding a Nation* (Edinburgh, 1944), 194.

43. W. Darling, *So It Looks to Me* (London, 1953), 229.

44. C. Hague, *The Development of Planning Thought* (London, 1984), 195–204.

45. P. Abercrombie and D. Plumstead, *A Civic Survey and Plan for Edinburgh* (Edinburgh, 1949), 65.

46. Ibid., 97.

47. Ibid, 129; Gifford, McWilliam and Walker, *Buildings of Scotland*, 309–13.

48. *The Scotsman*, 30 Sept. 1949.

49. C. Buchanan *et al.*, *Edinburgh: The Recommended Plan* (Edinburgh, 1972), *passim*.

50. I will not dignify the name of the architects' firm by placing it in my main text. It was Burke & Martin. May it live in infamy!

51. Fairbairn, *A Life is Too Short*, 192; *University Development and George Square* (Edinburgh, 1960), 13, 27–8.

52. Walker, *The Scottish Jurists*, 417, 420.

53. M. Gaskin, 'The Scottish Financial Sector 1950–1980', in R. Saville (ed.), *The Economic Development of Modern Scotland 1950–1980* (Edinburgh, 1985), 114.

54. S. G. Checkland, *Scottish Banking: A History 1695–1973* (Glasgow and London, 1975), pt 1.

55. F. A. Hayek, *Denationalisation of Money* (London, 1976), 101; K. Marx, *Grundrisse der Kritik der Politischen Ökonomie* (Berlin, 1953), 125.

56. M. R. G. Fry, *Banking Deregulation, the Scottish Example* (Edinburgh, 1985), *passim*.

57. Checkland, *Scottish Banking*, pts 5 and 6.

58. A. Rae, *The Other Walter Scott: The Eighteen-twenties in Edinburgh, Law, Business, Banking, Insurance* (Edinburgh, 1971), 10.

59. J. M. Denholm, *One Hundred Years of Scottish Life: A History of the Scottish Life Assurance Company 1881-1981* (Edinburgh, 1981), 77-80.

60. R. Michie, *Money, Mania and Markets: Investment, Company Formation and the Stock Exchange in Nineteenth-century Scotland* (Edinburgh, 1981), 101-3, 197-214, 257.

61. M. Moss and A. Slaven, *From Ledger Book to Laser Beam: A History of the Trustee Savings Bank in Scotland 1810-1990* (Edinburgh, 1992), 9-11.

62. R. Rodger, *Transformation of Edinburgh* (Cambridge, 2001), 19-24, 142, 165-70.

63. J. Newlands: *Put Not Your Trust in Money* (London, 1997), 71-87.

64. W. J. Menzies, *America as a Field for Investment* (Edinburgh and London, 1892), 21.

65. Newlands, *Put Not Your Trust*, 90.

66. D. M. C. Donald, 'Scottish Investment Trusts', *Scottish Bankers' Magazine*, 47 (1956), 202-6.

67. Newlands, *Put Not Your Trust*, 71.

68. F. H. H. King, *The Hongkong Bank in the Period of Development and Nationalism 1941-1984* (Cambridge, 1991), 895-6.

69. L. Barber, 'The Scottish Economy at Mid-term: more than an invisible hand at work', in H. M. and L. N. Drucker (eds), *Scottish Government Yearbook 1982* (Edinburgh, 1982), 175-80.

70. D. Torrance, *George Younger* (Edinburgh, 2008), chs 13 and 14.

71. S. E. Dight, *Scottish Drinking Habits* (London, 1976), 23, 51.

72. V. Berridge and G. Edwards, *Opium and the People* (London, 1981), 13; L. Bulwer, *Historical Characters* (London, 1868), II, 93; J. R. Findlay, *Personal Recollections of Thomas de Quincey* (Edinburgh, 1886), 39-40; L. Foxcroft, *The Making of Addiction: The Use and Abuse of Opium in Nineteenth-century Britain* (Aldershot, 2007), 83 *et seq*; J. Inglis, *A Victorian Edinburgh Diary*, ed. E. Vaughan (Edinburgh, 1984), 106; W. Aitken, *Science and Practice of Medicine* (London, 1880), II, 115; G. S. Muir, 'The Trade in Morphine to the East', *British Medical Journal*, 1910, I, 240; N. Olley, 'From Morningside to Muirhouse; towards a local governance of the self in drug policy', unpublished PhD thesis, University of Edinburgh, 2002, especially 42.

73. Olley, 'From Morningside to Muirhouse', 81, 107-8, 121-3, 147.

74. E. Muir, *Scottish Journey* (London, 1936), 198.

75. G. S. Marr, *Sex in Religion* (Woking, 1936), 99.

76. Expert Group on Prostitution in Scotland: *Being Outside: Constructing a Response to Street Prostitution* (Edinburgh, 2004), 19.

77. *New Statesman*, 10 Nov. 1967.

78. The acting text was published: *Satire of the Three Estates*, ed. R. Kemp, introduction by T. Guthrie (London, 1951).

ENVOI

1. *The Guardian*, 14 Oct. 2004.
2. A. McCall Smith, *44 Scotland Street* (Edinburgh, 2005), 321.
3. I. Welsh, *Trainspotting* (London, 1993), 4–5: reprinted by permission of The Random House Group Ltd.
4. I. Rankin, *Let it Bleed* (London, 1995), 113; *A Question of Blood* (London, 2003), 290; *Fleshmarket Close* (London, 2004), 69.
5. I. Rankin, *Let it Bleed*, 47; *Set in Darkness* (London, 2000), 222, 260.

INDEX

Abbotsford 78, 79, 280
Abercrombie, Patrick 355–6, 357
Aberdeen and Aberdeenshire 48, 60, 71,
    123, 124, 148–9, 206, 212
Adam, Robert 226, 233, 258, 259
Adam, William 223, 254–5
Aethelfrith, King of Bernicia 17, 24
Aidan, St 25, 31
Ailred of Rievaulx 19, 42
Alasdair mac Mhaighstir Alasdair 213,
    239
Alexander I, King of Scots 38
Alexander II, King of Scots 55
Alexander III, King of Scots 55–7, 71
Alexander le Saucier 56–7
Alnwick 39, 114
Andalucia 14, 15
Aneirin (bard) 15, 16, 17–18
Angles 17, 18, 24, 25, 26, 27, 28, 29–30,
    31, 32, 33, 36
Angus (county) 124, 179
Angus, Archibald Douglas, Earl of 82–3
Anne, Queen of Scots 184, 193, 202, 205
Anne of Denmark, consort of James VI
    141, 142, 144, 150
Antonine Wall 21, 22, 23
Appleton, Sir Edward 359–60
Argyll (county) 24, 254
Argyll, Archibald Campbell, Earl of 100
Argyll, Archibald Campbell, Marquis of
    171–2
Argyll, John Campbell, Duke of 254, 266
Argyll, Archibald Campbell, Duke of
    266–7

Aristotle 272, 287
Arras, Battle of (1917) 331–2
Arthur, King 16–17, 20, 47, 50, 51
Athelstaneford 255, 258
Athens 16, 169, 251
Augustine, St 29, 31, 45, 100
Augustinians (monastic order) 44, 81
Auld Alliance (of France and Scotland)
    58, 61, 82, 98
Auld Licht Burghers and Anti-Burghers
    253–4, 282
Australia 166, 368

Balmoral 76, 316
Bamburgh 17, 26
Bank of England 363–4, 371, 373, 374
Bank of Scotland 195, 217, 267, 363, 372,
    374, 375, 376
Bannockburn, Battle of (1314) 65, 66, 68,
    331
Baptists 345, 347–8
Bartas, Guillaume de 143–4
Bass Rock 4, 178, 198
Bathgate 287, 353
Beaton, David 99, 129
Beaton, James 82, 83
Bede, Venerable 19, 24
Beethoven, Ludwig van 211, 230
Begg, James 319, 344
Belgium 333, 368
Bell, George 313–4
Bentham, Jeremy 296, 306
Berlin 225, 259, 351
Bernicia 17, 25, 36

Berwick and Berwickshire 2, 48, 50 59, 61, 62, 63, 64, 65, 67, 68, 71, 72, 74, 81, 100, 104, 146, 160–1, 240, 366
Biffen, John 370, 373
Black Rood 39, 59
Black, A. & C. 283, 334
Black, Joseph 261, 293
Blackwood, Robert 205
Blackwood, William 276, 283
Blackwood's Edinburgh Magazine 276–7, 279, 326
Borders region 8, 81, 89, 98, 119, 148, 228, 277, 341
Borthwick 37, 108, 229
Boswell, James 54, 163–5, 166, 167, 168–9, 232, 237, 246, 267
Bothwell, James Hepburn, Earl of 118, 119–20, 137
Brecht, Bertolt 96–7
Britannia (Roman province) 13, 21, 23, 24
Brown, Ernest 347, 348
Bruce, William 179, 181
Buccleuch, Henry Scott, third Duke of 220, 268
Buchan, John 333, 350
Buchanan, Colin 357. 358
Buchanan, George 32, 117, 142, 191, 208, 209
Burke, William 264–5, 286
Burns, Robert 27, 31, 211, 238–9, 252, 285
Bute, John Stuart, third Earl of 107, 108, 166, 255
Byron, George Gordon, Lord 274, 287

Cairnpapple Hill 10, 11, 14
Calderwood, David 152, 153, 154
Calvin, John 100, 114, 141, 252, 244
Cambridge 188, 258, 294, 298, 306
Campbell, Bessie 139–40
Canada 6, 167, 365
Candida Casa see Whithorn
Canute, King of England 35, 37
Carey, Sir Robert 145–6
Carlisle 15, 43, 146, 168
Carlyle, Thomas 271, 274, 281, 182, 183, 318
Carrington 26, 131

Carham, Battle of (1018) 35, 36
Carstares, William 201, 208
Castalian Band 143–4
Catterick, Battle of (598) 16, 17, 18, 24
Cecil, Sir William 104–5
Celtic languages and peoples 10, 12, 14, 15, 16, 17, 19, 20, 21, 26, 27, 29–30, 31, 32, 33, 34, 38, 39, 40, 47, 50, 357, 377
Chalmers, Thomas 291, 345
Chambers, Robert and William 78, 205, 247, 283, 317–9, 320, 334
Charles I, King of Scots 154–5, 156, 158, 159, 160, 161, 169, 172, 173, 194
Charles II, King of Scots 161, 160, 170, 171, 172, 176, 179, 187, 194, 203
Charles Edward Stewart, Prince 108, 211, 213–5, 218, 223, 255
Châtelherault, James Hamilton, Earl of Arran, duc de 98, 104
Church of Scotland 32, 105, 107, 108, 112, 114, 126, 130, 134, 135, 141, 152, 155, 156, 158, 161, 171, 176, 177, 178, 179, 187, 197, 198, 201, 231, 244, 252–3, 254, 257, 258, 289, 290, 291, 292, 293, 295, 296, 345, 346, 379, 380
Cistercians (monastic order) 46, 47
Clow, W. & A. 329–30, 338
Clyde, River 20, 21, 70, 228
Cockburn, Henry, Lord 231–2, 248, 268–9, 271, 274, 275, 285, 293, 296, 297–8, 304, 319, 338, 339, 357, 362
Cockburn of Ormiston, John 228, 229
Cockpen 229, 256
Collège Royal 98–9
Committee for the Protestant Interest 247–8
Common Sense, philosophy of 260, 272, 273, 360
Commonwealth (Cromwellian) 170, 171, 172
Conservative party 326, 358
see also Tories
Constable, Archibald 217, 283, 334
Cope, Sir John 212, 213, 214, 248
Court of Session 126, 127, 128, 129, 162, 163, 231, 274, 304, 305, 311, 368

Covenant, National (1638) 158, 159–60, 161
Covenanters 170, 171, 172, 173, 174–5, 177, 178, 190, 201, 220, 247, 254
Craig, James 225, 226, 233, 267, 307
Craig of Riccarton, Thomas 117, 185–6, 191
Craigievar 76, 124, 316
Creech, William 235, 245, 246
Cromwell, Oliver 169, 170, 171, 203, 207
Culdees (religious order) 29, 32
Culloden, Battle of (1746) 109, 218, 222, 239, 267
Cuthbert, St 31, 32, 33, 45

Dalkeith 27, 132, 170, 176, 229, 230, 313
Dalriada 24, 25, 33
Dalyell, Sir John Graham 219–20
Dalyell of the Binns, Tam 173–4
Darnley, Henry Stewart, Lord 116–8, 119, 120, 130, 137
David I, King of Scots 38, 40, 41–4, 45, 46–8, 49, 50, 51, 55, 58, 87, 96
David II, King of Scots 70, 72, 75, 76, 77
Davie, George 340, 360
Defoe, Daniel 202–3
Denmark 121, 155, 194
De Quincey, Thomas 271, 377
Dere Street (Roman road) 17, 23
De Vink, Peter 372, 374
Dirleton 43, 62
Disruption of the Church of Scotland (1843) 33, 289, 290, 291, 295, 296
Donald II, King of Scots 34
Donald Bàn, King of Scots 36, 38
Douglas, Gavin 80, 83, 93, 94–5, 144, 208
Douglas, James, the Black Douglas 68–9
Douglas Cause 164, 165
Dream of the Rood 29–30
Drummond, George 223, 255, 320
Drummond of Hawthornden, William 144, 209
Dryburgh 98, 276
Dryden, John 190, 191, 193
Dumfries and Dumfriesshire 43, 281
Dunbar 46, 59, 62, 102, 103, 118, 120, 161, 169, 213
Dunbar, Patrick, Earl of 65–6

Dunbar, William 91–3, 95, 144
Duncan, King of Scots 36
Dundas, Henry *see* Melville
Dundas, Sir Lawrence 267, 268, 359
Dundas, Robert *see* Melville
Dundee 123, 270
Dunfermline 39, 46, 47, 48, 91, 154, 375
Durham 17, 35, 72

East Lothian 9, 24, 64, 99, 108, 124, 207, 229
Edgar, King of Scots 38

EDINBURGH (within present boundaries)
[entries in square brackets are no longer extant]
1. physical features:
Almond, River 21, 22
Arthur's Seat 12, 17, 25, 101, 205, 214, 229, 388
[Barefoots Park] 246
Blackford Hill 283
Braid Hills 4, 283
Calton Hill 95, 251, 350, 356
Castle Rock 4, 6, 12, 16, 23, 25–6, 27, 31, 32, 35, 40, 43, 48, 49, 69, 75, 76, 87, 121, 122, 123, 171, 180, 206, 210, 222, 232, 321, 333, 386
Craiglockhart Hills 12, 283
Galachlaw 9
Leith Links 103, 212
Meadows 6, 23, 81, 196, 343, 357–8
[Nor' Loch] 6, 32, 83, 101, 148, 177, 181, 192, 222, 223, 225, 233
Pentland Hills 4, 25, 173, 181, 283
Salisbury Crags 1, 2, 3, 4, 45, 261, 278
Water of Leith 9, 23, 71, 87, 103, 150, 212, 226, 252, 269, 271, 298, 309
2. areas:
Balerno 329
Barnton 283
Bonnington 150, 252
Braehead 84
Braid 160
Broughton 148, 335
Bruntsfield 7, 211, 309, 383
Brunstane 124

EDINBURGH (*cont.*)
  Canonmills 308
  Colinton 283, 329
  Coltbridge *see* Roseburn
  Comely Bank 271, 321, 328
  Comiston 36, 181
  Corstorphine 4, 6, 7, 27, 96, 283
  Craigleith 311
  Craigmillar 76, 336, 377
  Cramond 21, 22, 27, 84
  Dalmeny 44, 47, 322
  Dalry 150, 309, 328, 356, 383
  Dean Village 9, 23, 191, 309
  Duddingston 8, 12, 47, 213
  Dumbiedykes 220
  Fairmilehead 9
  Fountainbridge 319
  Gilmerton 36
  Gorgie 356
  Grange 160, 309, 356, 383
  Granton 336
  Greenside 95, 250
  Hailes 5
  Inverleith 240, 250
  Joppa 317
  Juniper Green 345
  Leith 6–7, 49, 78, 81–2, 83, 102–3,
      104, 105, 121, 137, 148, 150–1,
      170, 182, 198, 202, 205, 207,
      228, 241, 247, 255, 269–70, 286,
      287, 328, 331, 335, 336, 346–7,
      348, 356–7, 363, 366, 377, 379,
      385, 387–8
  Liberton 23, 239, 242
  Marchmont 309
  Merchiston 309, 311, 319, 328, 356,
      383
  Morningside 338, 339, 348, 377
  Mortonhall 12
  Muirhouse 336, 377
  Newbridge 9
  Newhaven 269, 366
  Newington 345
  New Town 75, 222, 223, 224–7, 232,
      233, 235, 238, 240, 246, 250,
      267, 283, 287, 303, 307, 308,
      309, 311, 312, 313, 320, 321,
      322, 329, 345, 358, 383, 387

  Niddrie 241
  Old Town 44, 79, 80, 222, 223, 226,
      227, 235, 236, 243–4, 248, 250,
      251, 265, 278, 283, 307, 312–5,
      316, 320, 321, 322, 336, 359, 387
  Pilrig 319
  Pilton 336
  Portsburgh 148
  Potterrow 133, 148, 345
  Powderhall 347
  Prestonfield 348
  Queensferry 39, 46, 52
  Restalrig 102
  Roseburn 212, 266
  St Leonards 250
  Sciennes 328
  Silverknowes 336
  Slateford 334
  Stockbridge 9, 271, 308, 319, 383
  Tollcross 311, 328
  Trinity 295, 311
  Wardieburn 336
  West End 5, 309, 328, 329, 332, 339,
      377
  Wester Hailes 336
3. closes, streets and wynds:
  Abercromby Place 250
  Advocates' Close 160
  Ann Street 279, 280, 281
  Belgrave Crescent 329, 332
  Bernard Street, Leith 105, 387
  [Blackfriars Wynd] 83, 129, 248, 314
  Brodie's Close 179–80
  Burgess Street, Leith 82
  [Canal Street] 234
  Canongate 48, 80, 81, 101, 123, 135,
      136, 137, 138, 148, 171, 179,
      180, 181, 196, 197–8, 202, 203,
      255, 338
  Carrubber's Close 198, 210
  Castle Street 383
  Causewayside 345
  Chambers Street 317
  Charlotte Square 226, 233, 250, 269,
      281, 292
  Coal Hill, Leith 103
  Constitution Street, Leith 105
  Cowgate 80, 81, 99, 102, 129, 155,

180, 199, 230, 247, 249, 254, 259, 312, 313, 317, 356
Danube Street 379
Dean Bridge 298, 309
Drummond Place 329
Drummond Street 223, 224
Easter Road 82, 311, 383
Fishmarket Close 182
Fleshmarket Close 182
George IV Bridge 223, 316
George Square 223, 248, 359, 383
George Street 226, 230, 267, 289, 308
Gorgie Road 309
Grassmarket 6, 178, 206, 210, 220, 221, 343
Great Junction Street, Leith 105
Great King Street 271, 281
Heriot Row 232, 250, 329
High Street 44, 48, 75, 77, 79, 80, 81, 82, 83, 87, 101, 103, 115–6, 118, 122, 123, 131, 139, 156, 157, 162, 166, 170, 172, 177, 179, 180, 181, 182, 183, 191, 196, 202, 205, 212, 246, 248, 249, 250, 259, 266, 294, 313–4, 320, 356, 357
Holy Corner 295
Home Street 311
Howe Street 308
James Court 162, 227, 322
Lansdowne Crescent 338
Lauriston Place 182, 254
Lawnmarket 123, 179, 180, 268, 314, 322
Leith Walk 169, 182, 309, 311, 319, 385–6
Lothian Road 292, 345
Marshall Street 351
Melville Crescent 5
Melville Street 6
Merchant Street 223
Milne's Court 180
Moray Place 232, 250, 290, 325
Morningside Road 292
Mound 292, 341
[Niddry Wynd] 249
North Bridge 222, 224, 235, 236, 259, 356, 327–8
Palmerston Place 328

Parliament Square 179, 268
Parliament Street, Leith 103
Picardy Place 228, 277
Princes Street 6, 32, 226, 227, 230, 232, 233, 234, 281, 327, 341, 345, 356, 358
Queen Street 226, 250, 288, 308
Queensferry Street 308
Riddell's Court 123, 322
Rose Street 345
Rothesay Place 338
Rothesay Terrace 309, 329
Royal Circus 250, 308
Royal Mile *see* Canongate and High Street
St Andrew's Square 166, 226, 250, 359
St David's street 227
[St James's Square] 223, 225, 359
Scotland Street 383
Shandwick Place 377
Shore, Leith 81, 82, 83, 103, 205, 269
Slateford Road 309
South Bridge 259, 313, 356
Stevenlaw's Close 246
Walker Street 383
Water Street, Leith 102–3
West Bow 175, 176, 181, 221
West Port 291
Whitehorse Close 322
4. buildings and monuments:
Academy 298
Assembly Rooms 230
[Babylon] 180
Bavelaw Castle 329
[Blackfriars monastery] 81, 129
[Bristo Port] 244
Caiystane 9
Caledonian Brewery 334
Caledonian Hotel 327
Caroline Park 124, 254
Castle 39, 40, 45, 51, 55, 61–2, 68, 69, 71, 75–6, 80, 89, 101, 103, 104, 119, 121, 143, 169, 195, 196, 203, 206, 207, 209, 233, 245, 248, 329, 330, 333, 387
Constable's Tower 75
Crown Square 75
[David's Tower] 76, 122

EDINBURGH (cont.)
Half Moon Battery 75-6, 122
[St Mary's church] 40, 75, 333
St Margaret's chapel 40
Scottish National War Memorial
333
Wellhouse Tower 75
churches and chapels (outside Castle)
Bellevue 329
Charlotte 345
Good Shepherd 329
Greyfriars 81, 107, 130, 159, 179,
181, 190, 201, 253, 256
Hope Park Chapel see Queen's Hall
[Kirk o'Field] 81, 119, 120, 130
Lady Yester's 155, 175, 379
Old St Paul's 198
St Andrew's 289
St Cuthbert's 31, 32, 33, 45, 198,
201, 253, 344
St George's 331-2, 344
St Giles 8, 44, 77, 78, 79, 93, 102,
103, 104, 111, 114, 117, 122,
147, 152-3, 154, 155, 156,
157, 179, 185, 198, 212, 224,
255, 292, 329, 344
St Mary Magdalen 99, 102, 175
St Mary's 292
Thistle Chapel 185, 329-30
Tolbooth 251, 263
Trinity 159
City Chambers 224
Craigmillar Castle 119
Dean Gallery 75, 298
Donaldson's Hospital 298
Drum, The 132
Filmhouse 292
Flodden Wall 74, 81, 119, 317
Gladstone's Land 180
Haymarket Station 366
Heart of Midlothian 78, 221, 268
Holyrood (Abbey of Holyroodhouse)
44-5, 48, 70, 71, 80-1, 84, 91,
103, 105, 111, 115, 118, 119,
122-3, 129, 143, 152, 157,
178-9, 187, 192, 193, 194, 195,
196, 197, 198, 213, 214, 245,
313, 338

[Holyrood Brewery] 284-5
Huntly House 123
John Knox's House 123, 200
[Krames] 79
[Luckenbooths] 79, 88, 210, 267
Lady Stair's House 322
Mercat Cross 78-9, 84, 85, 93, 116,
171, 172, 197, 212, 224, 265
[Netherbow Port] 75, 197, 212, 266
New College 292, 296, 345
New St Andrew's House 359
North British Hotel 327
[North Gate] 48
Old College 258-9, 264, 287, 387
Outlook Tower 321
Panmure House 179
Parliament House 155, 166, 172, 179,
202, 281, 350
Patrick Thomson's (department store)
328
[Paul's Work] 150
Prestonfield House 179
Queensberry House 179
Queen's Hall 292
Register House 225, 259, 246, 281,
292, 359
Roman Eagle Hall 180
Royal Infirmary 223-4, 227, 303
Royal Lyceum Theatre 327
R.W. Forsyth (department store) 327
St Andrew's House 350-1
St Cecilia's Hall 230
St James Centre 259, 359
Signet Library 268
Surgeons' Hall 186, 187
[Theatre Royal] 216, 217, 225, 230
[Tolbooth] 77, 78, 102, 122, 125, 127,
128, 155, 220, 221, 350
Tron 79, 155, 201, 249, 253, 255,
316
Usher Hall 327
Tweeddale House 179
Waverley Station 187, 316, 366
[West Gate] 48, 191
5. municipal government:
charter (1329) 71
decreet arbitral (1583) 124, 183
Golden Charter (1482) 89

Improvement Acts (1827 and 1867) 316-7, 319
merchants' guild, Merchant Company (1681) 49, 86, 124, 148, 149-50, 151, 159, 183, 184, 204, 267, 298, 299
Police Acts (1805 and 1848) 316
town council 85-6, 116, 133, 179, 180, 181, 191, 192, 204-5, 233, 251, 265-6, 268, 269-70, 272, 288, 293-4, 295, 358, 359, 379
trades or craftsmen's incorporations 86-9, 124-5, 299, 300, 301
trades council 299, 300, 301, 316, 319
6. *other institutions:*
Academy 298
Advocates' Library *see* National Library of Scotland 109
Cockburn Association 357
[Commissary Office] 236
Festivals 97, 230, 257, 379-81, 385
Fettes College 298, 338
Heart of Midlothian FC 387
Heriot's Hospital, School and Trust 150, 298, 299, 317
Heriot-Watt College 317
Hibernian FC 387
High School 2, 129, 235, 250-1, 297-8, 351
Jenner's (department store) 327
King's Theatre 327
Lyon Court 212
[Magdalene Institution] 246
National Gallery of Modern Art 298
National Library of Scotland 109, 117, 185, 190, 208
National Museum of Scotland 13, 317, 383
Royal Botanic Garden 187
Royal College of Physicians 187-8
Royal College of Surgeons 88, 186
Royal Scottish Academy 281
[Society for the Reformation of Manners] 200
Stewart's Melville College 298
Trades Maiden Hospital 89
University 3, 10, 16, 108, 130, 144, 187, 202, 203, 208, 210, 255, 258, 259, 262, 264, 271, 272, 273, 276, 286, 287, 288, 290, 291, 293-4, 296, 297, 302-3, 305, 306, 313, 316, 326-7, 337, 339-40, 359, 360-1, 377, 383
7. *popular pastimes:*
drinking 17, 132, 134, 139-40, 149, 162, 166, 168, 183, 192, 198-9, 200, 206, 207, 209, 211, 236, 277, 285, 295, 314, 315, 316, 347, 367, 377, 378, 379, 386
drugs 183, 271, 272, 376-8, 385, 387
fighting 17, 82-3, 132, 199, 200, 249, 314, 316, 343
sex 96, 97, 133, 134, 135-7, 138, 140, 142, 158, 199, 200, 245-6, 314-5, 323-4, 338, 367, 378-9, 387
smoking 151, 183, 343, 378, 386
swearing 97, 177, 200, 295, 314, 315

Edinburgh, Treaty of
(1328) 70
(1560) 105
Edinburgh Review 273-4, 275, 284, 326
Edward I, King of England 58-9, 60, 61, 65
Edward II, King of England 58, 60, 61, 62-3, 64, 65, 66, 67, 69-70
Edward III, King of England 69, 70, 72
Edward VI, King of England 98, 100
Edwin, King of Northumbria 24, 25, 27
Egypt 2, 11
Elizabeth I, Queen of England 104-5, 109, 121, 146
Elliot of Minto, Gilbert 224-5
Enlightenment, Scottish 14, 54, 107, 127, 209, 210, 256, 258, 259-60, 261, 265, 272, 276, 282, 294, 296, 306, 312, 340, 360 1, 377
Episcopalians 171, 173, 176, 177, 197-8, 208, 292, 293, 295
Erasmus, Desiderius 83-4, 97
Erskine of Dun, John 100, 111, 112, 113
Eyemouth 103, 105

Faculty of Advocates 185, 231, 232, 272, 304–5

Fairbairn, Nicholas 338, 359

Falkirk 59, 229

Ferguson, Adam 53, 107, 255, 259

Fergusson, Robert 211, 235–8, 239, 245, 252

Ferrier, James 295–6

Feudal system, Scottish 42–3, 64, 71, 186–7, 232–5, 310–2, 328, 367

Fife 34, 121, 176, 207, 235, 280, 291, 321, 366, 383

First World War 18, 330–3, 344, 346, 349, 352, 354, 355, 364, 365, 368, 369, 371, 377

Flanders and the Flemings 47, 49, 73, 332

Fletcher, Alexander 370–1, 373, 374

Flodden, Battle of (1513) 74, 82

Forth, Firth of and River 6, 7, 8, 9, 19, 20, 21, 28, 35, 39, 50, 59, 72, 103, 124, 144, 178, 207, 222, 228, 235, 313, 336, 379

Forth, bridges over 351, 366, 383

Four Tables 147–8

France and the French 18, 19, 38, 42, 49, 51, 53, 56, 58, 64, 72, 74, 80, 82, 83, 90, 98, 100, 101, 103, 104, 105, 111, 115, 118, 127, 128, 142, 149, 166, 173, 190, 194, 196, 212, 214, 228, 249, 259, 260, 273, 275, 278, 279, 304, 333

Francis II, King of France 103, 105

Francis, William 69, 206

Freebairn, Robert 208–9

Free Church of Scotland 290–1, 292, 295, 296, 344

Froissart, Jean 73, 75

Gaels, Gaelic and Gàidhealtachd 8, 15, 24, 25, 33, 34, 35–6, 55, 70, 94, 213, 239

Galloway 18, 28, 34, 51, 52

Galloway, Patrick 153–4

Gauls and Gallic Wars 18, 22

Geddes, Jenny 156–7

Geddes, Patrick 321–2

General Assembly of the Church of Scotland 126, 137, 138, 157, 161, 199–200, 202, 252, 256–7, 289, 344, 379

Geneva 100, 101, 123, 551

George I, King 205

George III, King 108, 119, 248

George IV, King 219, 269

George VI, King 84

Germany and the Germans 17, 49, 51, 107, 160, 271, 273, 276, 282, 294, 296, 306, 317, 332, 351, 352, 376

Gibbons, Grinling 184–5

Gifford, Carlyle 368–9

Glamis 70, 124, 316

Glasgow 114, 199, 204, 229, 269, 284, 287, 300, 326, 337, 340, 347, 350, 357, 366, 377

Gododdin 16–18, 20, 24, 27, 51

Goodwin, Fred 375–6

Gordon, George, first Duke of 195, 196

Gordon of Gordon, Adam 66, 67

Gordon of Rothiemay, James 190–1

Govan, William 172–3

Graham of Claverhouse, John 191–2

Grampian Mountains 53, 316

Grant, Sir Ludovic 337, 338

Gray, R.Q. 300, 301

Greece and Greek language 15, 90–1, 99, 153, 189, 190, 208, 287

Gregory, David 189–90, 199

Gregory, James (professor of mathematics) 188, 189

Gregory, James (professor of medicine) 262–3, 286–7

Gullane 9, 47, 329

Guthrie, James 172, 173

Haddington 26, 47, 48, 62, 99, 151, 204, 207

Hadrian's Wall 21, 23

Hamilton, Sir William 189, 271–2, 273, 276, 293, 296, 304

Hare, William 264–5, 286

Haydn, Josef 211, 230

Henry VIII, King of England 98, 114

Henryson, Robert 91, 93, 95, 144

Heriot, George 150, 160, 251

Herries, Sir Michael 371, 372, 374, 375

Highlands and Highlanders, Scottish 6, 53, 55, 148, 182, 212, 213, 214, 219, 220, 239, 241, 279, 280, 353
Hogg, James 277–8, 323
Home, John 255, 257–8
Homer 15, 18
Hongkong and Shanghai Bank 371, 372, 373
Horace 160, 210
Huguenots 182–3
Hume, David 53, 54–5, 109, 208, 227, 232, 233, 255, 256, 260–1, 272, 276–7, 339
Hundred Years' War 72, 74
Huns and Hungary 15, 37, 39, 42
Hunter, John 153–4
Hutton, James 2, 3, 4, 261

Inchkeith 9, 46, 103, 137
India 166–7, 272, 344, 365, 377
Industrial Revolution 241–2, 283, 285, 333, 362
Inveresk 21, 22, 27, 229, 231, 255
Iona 25, 28, 32
Ireland 15, 20, 24, 25, 33, 155, 167, 182, 344, 347, 376
Italy 51, 74, 279, 282

Jacobites 191, 206, 207, 208, 209, 211–2, 214, 218–9, 222, 223, 239, 253, 255, 266, 278
James I, King of Scots 46, 77, 90, 127
James II, King of Scots 74, 77, 80
James III, King of Scots 81, 89, 91, 127, 247
James IV, King of Scots 74, 80–1, 83–4, 128
James V, King of Scots 81, 83, 84, 95, 98, 122, 126, 178, 197
James VI, King of Scots (James I of England) 32, 119, 121, 122, 141–3, 146, 150, 152, 154, 203
James VII, King of Scots (James II of England) 184, 192, 193–4, 195, 196, 199, 205, 210, 358
James, Old Pretender 205, 206, 212
Jedburgh 23, 60, 98
Jeffrey, Francis 273, 274, 275, 276, 281, 290, 304, 325–6, 329

Jesuits (religious order) 99, 197
John Balliol, King of Scots 58, 59, 72
John of Fordun 37–8
Johnson, Dr Samuel 167, 168–9, 232
Johnston of Warriston, Archibald 158, 159, 171, 173

Kames, Henry Home, Lord 231, 255–7
Kennedy, Herbert 198–9
Kenneth MacAlpine, King of Scots 33, 34, 35–6, 41
Kenneth II, King of Scots 35
Kirkliston 27, 47
Knox, John 99, 100–1, 102, 105, 106, 110–1, 112–5, 117–8, 126, 128, 131, 138, 140, 158
Knox, Robert 264, 265

Labour party 335 346, 347, 348, 355, 358, 375
Lanark and Lanarkshire 210, 229, 231, 302, 328, 353
Lanercost Chronicle 64–5
Latinity, Scottish 15, 25, 90, 94, 97, 100, 116, 117, 170, 191, 192, 208, 272, 287, 298
Liberal party 346, 347, 348
  see also Whigs
Lindisfarne 25, 28, 32
Lindsay, Sir David 95–6, 97, 98, 380
Lindsay, David 156, 157
Linklater, Eric 340–1
Linlithgow 46, 62, 63, 104, 136, 157
Little, Clement 129–30
Lockhart, John Gibson 276–7, 283
Lords of the Congregation 102, 103, 104
Lorimer, James 305–7, 328
Lorimer, Robert 185, 328, 329, 333, 338
Lothian region 8–9, 11, 12, 14, 16, 17, 23, 25, 26, 30, 33, 34, 35, 36, 39, 42, 49, 52, 59, 63, 66, 67, 74, 80, 94, 121, 123–4, 150, 151, 166, 181, 204, 278, 279, 307, 321, 329, 331, 357, 383
Luffness 46, 62, 64
Luther, Martin 113, 114

Macbeth, King of Scots 36, 37
McCulloch, John Ramsay 294, 325, 326

MacDiarmid, Hugh 16, 340, 341–2, 343
Mackenzie of Rosehaugh, Sir George 185, 186, 190, 204
Mackintosh, Sir James 272, 377
McLaren, Duncan 294–5, 297
Maclehose, Agnes 238–9
MacMorran, John 123, 129, 160
Maconochie, Alexander 217, 218
Macqueen, Robert 162, 231
Maitland, Sir Richard 133–4
Malcolm II, King of Scots 35, 36
Malcolm III, King of Scots 36–8, 39, 40
Malthus, Thomas 284, 287
Mansfield, William Murray, Lord 164, 234
Margaret, Maid of Norway, Queen of Scots 56, 57–8
Margaret, St 37, 38, 39–40, 41, 59
Marx, Karl and Marxist history 99, 242, 300, 301, 363
Mary Queen of Scots 98, 103, 105–6, 108, 109–10, 111, 112, 114–7, 118–21, 126, 130, 133, 140, 141, 185
Mary II, Queen of Scots 198
Mary of Guise 98, 101, 102–3, 104, 116, 118, 129
Mathewson, George 375
Matter of Britain 20, 50
Maxwell, James Clerk 1, 304
Mein, John 153, 154
Melrose 23, 31, 32, 47, 98
Melville, Henry Dundas, first Viscount 163–4, 165–7, 169, 232, 247, 248, 267, 268, 269
Meivlille, Robert Dundas, second Viscount 269, 270, 326
Midlothian 2, 19, 26, 27, 47, 49, 76, 168, 229, 231, 242, 244, 256, 301
Miller, Hugh 3–4, 241
Mitchell, James 177–8
Monck, George 170, 171, 172, 176
Monopolies Commission 371, 373–4
Monro, Alexander (principal) 198
Monro, Alexander, *primus, secundus, tertius* (professors) 262, 264
Moray, county 34, 36, 180

Moray, Lord James Stewart, Earl of 100, 122
Muir, Edwin 340, 343, 378–9
Municipal Corporations Act (1833) 294, 300
Musselburgh 49, 120, 185
Mylne, Robert 179, 181
Mynyddog, chief of Votadini 16, 17

Nationalism, Scottish 291–2, 340, 343, 349, 374, 375, 376, 384
Netherlands 83, 121, 127, 149, 150, 151, 169, 174, 188, 208, 279, 280, 304, 327, 376
Newbattle 46, 229
Newcastle-on-Tyne 50, 105, 204
New Licht Burghers and Anti-Burghers 253–4
Newmills 151, 204
Newton, Sir Isaac 188, 189
New York 369, 370, 377
Ninian, St 18–19
Noble, Ian 372, 374
Normandy and the Normans 34, 37, 41, 62, 43, 50, 51
North Berwick 4, 9, 46, 141, 329
North Sea 3, 6, 17, 24, 57, 72, 103, 141, 148, 375, 380
Northumbria 17, 24, 25, 26, 27–30, 31–2, 34, 35, 36, 37, 41, 44, 45, 52, 54, 55, 64, 65, 357
Noyce, Dora 325, 379

Ochiltree, Andrew Stewart, Lord 112–3
Old English language 26, 27
Orkney 58, 179, 340
Oswald, King of Northumbria 25, 28, 29, 45
Oswy, King of Northnumbria 28, 31–2
Owain, King of Strathclyde 35, 36
Oxford 58, 190, 199, 258, 272, 275, 276, 294, 298, 306, 340

Pagan, Gavin 331–2
Paris 2, 51, 53, 82, 99, 100, 179, 180, 248–9, 259, 282, 309, 310, 382
Parliament, Scottish 70, 77–8, 85–6, 97, 115, 121, 125, 126, 127, 128, 134,

136, 137, 141, 148, 150, 155, 157,
159–60, 161, 171, 179, 183, 184,
207, 232, 235, 265, 375, 383, 387,
388
Penicuik 1, 27, 228
Perth and Perthshire 48, 50, 51, 77–8,
102, 123, 223, 229, 239
Perth, James Drummond, Earl of 195,
196, 197
Peyrat, Guillaume du 143–4
Piccolomini, Enea Silvio 73–4
Picts 18, 19, 20, 22, 23, 28, 30, 33, 34, 45,
55, 209
Pitcairne, Archibald 188, 191–2, 208
Poland 42, 327
Poor Laws, Scots (1579 and 1845) 138,
244, 315–6
Porteous, John 221, 222, 247, 253, 266
Presbyterians and Presbyterianism 30, 32,
47, 109, 110, 117–8, 142, 156, 158,
159, 161, 170, 171, 172, 175, 176,
177, 188, 192, 197, 198, 199, 201,
209, 216, 252, 253, 256, 259, 260,
278, 292, 295, 344, 345
Prestonpans, Battle of (1745) 214, 255
Prince, Magnus 196, 197
Progressive party 355, 358, 359
Protestant Alliance 347–8

Queensberry, James Douglas, Duke of
179, 202, 203

Raeburn, Henry 279–80
Ramsay, Allan, the elder 210–1, 238
Ramsay, Allan, the younger 232, 256
Rankin, Ian 386–7
Ravenscraig steelworks 353, 369
Reform Act (1832) 241, 250, 275, 349
Reformation, Scottish (1560) 32, 97, 98,
99, 100, 102, 105, 109, 110, 114,
115, 126, 127, 130, 134–5, 139, 142,
159, 185, 193, 247, 290
Reid, George 242–3
Renaissance, Scottish 340, 341
Renfrew and Renfrewshire 63, 96, 229
Restoration (1660) 170, 189, 192, 19, 198,
207

Revolution (1688) 191, 197, 201, 247,
275
Rheged 15, 28
Richardson, Gordon 372, 373
Ripon 31, 32
Robert Bruce, King of Scots 41, 58,
59–61, 62, 63–4, 65, 66, 67, 68, 69,
70–1, 73, 75, 77, 206, 331
Robert II, King of Scots 77
Robert III, King of Scots 77
Robertson, William (schoolmaster) 129
Robertson, William (principal) 107,
108–10, 130, 254–5, 256, 258, 259,
260, 262, 290–1
Roman de Fergus 51–2
Rome and the Romans 11, 13, 18, 19,
20–2, 23–4, 26, 29, 31, 32, 36, 66,
94, 96, 99, 110, 118, 126, 127, 273,
282, 298, 306
Rosebery, Archibald Primrose, Lord 323,
350
Rough Wooing (1542) 98, 114
Roxburgh 48, 50, 59, 60, 61, 65, 67, 68–9,
74
Royal Scots regiment 331–3, 351
Ruskin, John 75, 356
Rome 180, 186, 190
Royal Bank of Scotland 240, 267, 268,
363, 379, 371, 372, 373, 374, 375,
376
Royal Society of Edinburgh 230, 258
Ruddiman, Thomas 208, 209
Rule, Gilbert 198, 199
Rullion Green, Battle of (1666) 173, 174
Ruskin, John 307–8, 356
Russia 173, 174, 258, 301
Ruthwell Cross 30–1

St Andrews 45, 61, 82, 99, 100, 125, 129,
130, 176, 178, 295, 348
Saxons 17, 23, 25, 29, 54
Scone 33, 37, 42, 57, 59, 169
Scots language and literature 27, 73, 87,
90–1, 93, 131, 191, 192, 208, 209,
211, 274, 275, 276, 338, 340, 385
Scotsman, The (newspaper) 309, 326, 328,
351, 357
Scott, Alexander 117, 132–3

Scott, Sir Walter 52, 78, 79, 185, 216–9, 220–2, 230, 245, 253, 265, 274, 276, 277, 289, 281, 287, 308, 317, 323, 334, 339, 340, 383
Scottish American Investment Trust 368, 369
Scottish Development Agency 374, 375
Scottish & Newcastle Brewers 334, 374
Scottish Office 305, 349, 351, 370, 372
Second World War 284, 334, 347, 349, 351, 354, 369, 379
Sharp, James 176–8
Sibbald, Robert 187, 188, 190–1, 207, 262
Siddons, Sarah 230, 251
Simpson, James Young 287–8, 289, 294, 318
Sinclair of Dunbeath, Margaret 338–9
Siward, Earl of Northumberland 36, 37
Smith, Adam 53, 166, 205, 239, 230, 232, 260–1, 273, 284, 304, 326, 339, 353, 358, 359
Solway Firth 21, 28, 121
Somerville, Alexander 240–1
Spain 74, 121
Spark, Muriel 342–3
Spence, Lewis 340–1
Stair, James Dalrymple, Viscount 185, 186
Standard Chartered Bank 370, 371, 372, 373, 374
Standard Life Assurance Company 364–5
Steell, James 279, 281
Stevenson, Robert Louis 52, 53, 280, 285, 304, 322–4, 385
Stirling 19, 48, 50, 59–60, 61, 68, 84, 102, 121, 196
Strathclyde 34, 35, 36
Struthers, William 152, 153
Strozzi, Leone and Piero 100, 103
Syme, James (merchant) 100
Syme, James (surgeon) 263, 289

Tait, Thomas 350, 351
Tait, William 314–5, 378
Taliesin (bard) 15–16
Tartessians 14, 15
Tay, River 21, 33, 38, 81
Tees, River 17, 42

Todd, Ruthven 342, 384
Tokyo 370, 384
Tore or Torrie, Adam 84–5
Tories 109, 222, 250, 271, 275, 276, 300, 326, 347
  see also Conservative party
Tranent 96, 213
Traprain Law 12–13, 14, 16, 29, 22, 43, 49
Tristan and Isolde 20, 50–1, 383
Tweed, River 25, 35, 41, 42, 67, 72, 81
Tyne, River (England) 21
Tyne, River (Scotland) 43
Tyningham 26, 47
Tytler of Woodhouselee , William 192–3

Union of Crowns (1603) 32, 109, 147, 148, 154, 166, 167, 170, 338
Union of Parliaments (1707) 1, 34, 54, 108, 109, 131, 140, 147, 165, 167, 169, 182, 192, 195, 201, 205, 207, 219, 220, 221, 223, 227–8, 231, 232, 247, 253, 254, 278, 290, 292–3, 362, 363

Victoria, Queen 281, 289, 313, 316, 344
Vikings 15, 28, 33, 34, 36
Virgil 94, 208
Voltaire (Francois-Marie Arouet) 165, 274
Votadini 11, 12, 13, 15, 16, 18, 19, 20, 22–3, 24, 25, 36

Wales and the Welsh 14, 25, 34
Wallace, John 196, 197
Wallace, William (hero) 59, 73
Wallace, William (minister) 256
Warrender of Lochend, Sir George 206–7, 266
Warsaw 356–7
Waterloo, Battle of (1815) 263, 273, 331
Watson, James 208, 209
Webster, James 200, 253
Weir, Thomas 175–6
Welsh, David 289–90
Welsh, Irvine 385–6
Wessex 33, 35, 37, 41
West Lothian 10, 46, 124, 287
Whigs 109, 219, 222, 223, 230, 271, 275, 276, 277, 278, 297, 298, 304, 326, 349

Whitby 32, 45
Whithorn 19, 28
Wilkie, David 263, 279, 280–1, 381
William the Lion, King of Scots 51, 55
William I the Conqueror, King of England 37, 38, 41
William of Orange, King of Scots 195, 198, 199, 201

Wilson, John 272, 276, 277, 279, 281, 293, 295, 296
Worcester, Battle of (1651) 161, 169

Yester 43, 62, 228
York and Yorkshire 24, 45
Younger, George 370, 372, 375
Younger, William 284–5, 344

www.panmacmillan.com